Putin's Propaganda Machine

Putin's Propaganda Machine

Soft Power and Russian Foreign Policy

Marcel H. Van Herpen

ROWMAN & LITTLEFIELD
Lanham • Boulder • New York • London

Published by Rowman & Littlefield
A wholly owned subsidiary of
The Rowman & Littlefield Publishing Group, Inc.
4501 Forbes Boulevard, Suite 200, Lanham, Maryland 20706
www.rowman.com

Unit A, Whitacre Mews, 26-34 Stannary Street, London SE11 4AB,
United Kingdom

British Library Cataloguing in Publication Information Available

Library of Congress Cataloging-in-Publication Data
Herpen, Marcel van.
Putin's propaganda machine : soft power and Russian foreign policy / Marcel H. Van Herpen.
pages cm
Includes bibliographical references and index.
ISBN 978-1-4422-5360-5 (cloth : alkaline paper) — ISBN 978-1-4422-5361-2 (paperback : alkaline
paper) — ISBN 978-1-4422-5362-9 (electronic)
1. Russia (Federation)—Foreign relations—Western countries. 2. Western countries—Foreign rela-
tions—Russia (Federation) 3. Ukraine Conflict, 2014– 4. Putin, Vladimir Vladimirovich, 1952– —
Political and social views. 5. Propaganda—Russia (Federation) 6. Information warfare—Russia (Federation) 7. Mass media—Political aspects—Russia (Federation) 8. Public relations and politics—
Russia (Federation) 9. Russkaia pravoslavnaia tserkov?—Political aspects—Russia (Federation) 10.
Russia (Federation)—Politics and government—1991– I. Title.
D2025.5.R8H47 2015
327.470182'1—dc23
2015026484

∞ ™ The paper used in this publication meets the minimum requirements of American
National Standard for Information Sciences Permanence of Paper for Printed Library
Materials, ANSI/NISO Z39.48-1992.

Printed in the United States of America

To Boris Nemtsov (1959–2015)

Contents

Author Note and Acknowledgments

In writing this book I owe a lot to the discussions with the members of the Russia seminar of the Cicero Foundation. I want to thank in particular Albert van Driel, Peter Verwey, Ernst Wolff, Christiane Haroche, and Rona Heald for their continuous support. Not least am I indebted to my wife, Valérie, and my sons, Michiel and Cyrille, who gave me the necessary feedback during the whole project.

Glossary and Abbreviations

AfD	*Allianz für Deutschland* (German Eurosceptic political party)
AFP	*Agence France-Presse* (French news agency)
Agitprop	*Otdel agitatsii i propagandy* (Propaganda department of the Central Committee of the Communist Party of the Soviet Union)
ARD	Consortium of public broadcasters in Germany (operates the national First TV Channel, regional TV channels, and the international channel *Deutsche Welle*)
BBC	British Broadcasting Corporation
BDI	*Bundesverband der Deutschen Industrie* (German employers' organization)
BfV	*Bundesverfassungsgericht* (German Constitutional Court)
BIS	*Bezpečnostní informační služba* ("Security Information Service," counterintelligence service of the Czech Republic)
BMD	Ballistic Missile Defense
BRIC	Acronym of grouping referring to Brazil, Russia, India, and China
BRICS	Acronym of grouping referring to Brazil, Russia, India, China, and South Africa

CCFRC	*Conseil de coordination du forum des Russes de France* (Coordination Council of the Forum of Russians in France)
CCQS	*Conseil de coopération franco-russe sur les questions de sécurité* (French-Russian Cooperation Council on Security Questions)
CDU	*Christlich Demokratische Union Deutschlands* (Christian Democratic Party of Germany)
CFE	Conventional Forces in Europe Treaty
CGT	*Confédération Générale du Travail* (French trade union)
Cheka	All-Russian Extraordinary Commission for Combating Counter-Revolution and Sabotage (Soviet secret service December 1917–1922)
CIA	Central Intelligence Agency (USA)
CIS	Commonwealth of Independent States
CNN	Cable News Network
COPS	*Comité politique et de sécurité* (Political and Security Committee of the European Union)
CPSU	Communist Party of the Soviet Union
CSU	*Christlich-Soziale Union in Bayern* ("Christian Social Union in Bavaria," German political party)
DCRI	*Direction centrale du renseignement intérieur* (French counter-intelligence service)
DECR	Department of External Church Relations of the Russian Orthodox Church
DGAP	*Deutsche Gesellschaft für Auswärtige Politik* (German foreign policy think tank)
DPR	"Donetsk People's Republic" (self proclaimed "republic" by Russian and rebel militias in Eastern Ukraine)
DS	*Darzhavna sigurnost* ("State Security," Bulgarian secret service during communist rule)

DVU
Deutsche Volksunion
(German extreme right party)

EED
European Endowment for Democracy
(nonprofit organization, supports pro-democratic civil
society organizations)

EU
European Union

Euromaidan
pro-EU protest movement in Ukraine, named after the
Maidan Nezalezhnosti, the Independence Square in Kyiv

FAPSI
Russian Federal Agency for Government
Communications and Information

FBI
Federal Bureau of Investigation (USA)

FN
Front National (French extreme right party)

FSB
Federalnaya Sluzhba Bezopasnosti
("Federal Security Service," Russian secret service)

FSO
Federalnaya Sluzhba Okhrany
(Russian Federal Protective Service)

GDR
German Democratic Republic
(former communist Eastern Germany)

GONGO
Government-organized nongovernmental organization

GRU
Glavnoe Razvedyvatelnoe Upravlenie
("Main Intelligence Directorate," Russian Military
Foreign Intelligence Service)

G7
Intergovernmental forum of seven leading advanced
economies

G8
Intergovernmental forum of eight leading advanced
economies

G20
Intergovernmental forum of twenty leading advanced
economies

IDC
Institute for Democracy and Cooperation
(Russian think tank, based in Paris)

IFRI
Institut français des relations internationales
(French think tank)

IRIS
Institut des relations internationales et stratégiques
(French think tank)

ITAR TASS
Information and Telegraph Agency of Russia
(Russian news agency)

KAPO	Estonian counterintelligence agency
KGB	*Komitet Gosudarstvennoy Bezopasnosti* ("Committee for State Security," secret service of the Soviet Union)
Komintern	Communist International
LDPR	Liberal-Democratic Party of Russia
LGBT	Lesbian, Gay, Bisexual, Transgender
LKA	*Landeskriminalamt* (State Criminal Police Office in Germany)
LPR	"Luhansk People's Republic" (self proclaimed "republic" by Russian and rebel militias in eastern Ukraine)
Maidan	protest movement in Ukraine, named after the *Maidan Nezalezhnosti* (Independence Square) in Kyiv
MAP	NATO Membership Action Plan
MELS	Abbreviation of the names of Marx, Engels, Lenin, Stalin
MGIMO	Moscow State Institute of International Relations
MH17	Malaysian Airways passenger plane downed above Eastern Ukraine on July 17, 2014
MI5	Military Intelligence, Section 5 (British counterintelligence and security agency)
MI6	Military Intelligence, Section 6 (British foreign intelligence service)
NATO	North Atlantic Treaty Organization
NEP	New Economic Policy
NGO	Nongovernmental organization
NPD	*Nationaldemokratische Partei Deutschlands* ("National Democratic Party of Germany," German extreme right party)
Ofcom	Office of Communications (UK)
OSCE	Organization for Security and Co-operation in Europe
PACE	Parliamentary Assembly of the Council of Europe
PDS	*Partei des Demokratischen Sozialismus* ("Party of Democratic Socialism," German left-wing party, legal successor to the SED, the East German Communist Party)

PR	public relations
RF	Russian Federation
RIAC	Russian International Affairs Council
RIA Novosti	Russian news agency
ROC	Russian Orthodox Church
ROCA	Russian Orthodox Church Abroad
ROCOR	Russian Orthodox Church Outside Russia
Rosaviatsiya	Russian Federal Air Transport Agency
Roskosmos	Russian Federal Space Agency
RosPil	anti-corruption website, launched by Kremlin critic Aleksey Navalny
Rossotrud-nichestvo	Russian Federal Agency for the Commonwealth of Independent States, Compatriots Abroad, and International Humanitarian Cooperation
Roszarubezh-tsentr	organization of the Russian Foreign Ministry, tasked with the promotion of the Russian language and culture abroad
RSFSR	Russian Socialist Federative Soviet Republic
RT	New name of "Russia Today" (Russian international cable and satellite TV)
SCO	Shanghai Cooperation Organization
SED	*Sozialistische Einheitspartei Deutschlands* ("Socialist Unity Party of Germany," East German Communist Party)
SOVA Center	independent, Moscow-based, Russian sociological research center
Spetsnaz	*Voyska spetsialnogo naznacheniya* (Russian Special Forces)
SPD	*Sozialdemokratische Partei Deutschlands* ("Social Democratic Party of Germany")
SS-20	Russian middle-range missile
Stasi	*Staatssicherheit* ("State Security," East German secret service)
StB	*Státní bezpečnost* ("State Security," secret police in former communist Czechoslovakia)

SVR	*Sluzhba Vneshney Razvedki* (Russian Foreign Intelligence Service)
UK	United Kingdom
UN	United Nations
Unicef	United Nations International Children's Emergency Fund
UOC-KP	Ukrainian Orthodox Church—Kyivan patriarchate
UOC-MP	Ukrainian Orthodox Church—Moscow patriarchate
USA	United States of America
USAID	US government-sponsored international development assistance agency
USSR	Union of Socialist Soviet Republics
Vkontakte	Russian equivalent of Facebook
VSSE	Belgian counterintelligence agency
VTsIOM	Russian state pollster

Introduction

During the Russian intervention in Ukraine in 2014, the world was confronted by the Kremlin's most massive and incisive propaganda offensive of the past seventy years. The Russian propaganda machine dwarfed even that of Saddam Hussein, who, in 1991, before Operation Desert Storm, promised the Western coalition that it would be defeated in what the Iraqi leader then called "the mother of all battles." According to Lev Gudkov, the director of the Levada Center, an independent Russian polling organization, one can observe today in Russia "aggressive and deceptive propaganda . . . worse than anything I witnessed in the Soviet Union,"[1] an opinion, shared by Irina Prokhorova, a well-known publisher, who did not hesitate in calling Putin's propaganda "Stalinist," comparing it with the anti-Western hysteria that characterized the repression of the late 1940s.[2] We should not forget, however, that "good" propaganda is not simply a matter of persuading the nonbelievers or just telling untruths and lies. As David Welch—rightly—remarked, there exist

> two common misconceptions connected with the study of propaganda. There is a widely held belief that propaganda implies nothing less than the art of persuasion, which serves only to change attitudes and ideas. This is undoubtedly one of its aims, but often a limited and subordinated one. More often, propaganda is concerned with reinforcing existing trends and beliefs; to sharpen and focus them. A second basic misconception is the entirely erroneous conviction that propaganda consists only of lies and falsehood. In fact it operates with many different kinds of truths—from the outright lie, the half truth to the truth out of context.[3]

Especially the last two categories, half truths and truths out of context, played an important role in the disinformation campaign that accompanied

1

Moscow's aggression in Ukraine. They were reminiscent of the period in which *Pravda*, the official paper of the Communist Party of the Soviet Union, was considered in the West as quite the opposite of its title: *The Truth*. We should remind that even the word "disinformation" (in Russian, *dezinformatsiya*) seems to be a Russian invention. According to Michel Heller, "The word first appears in 1963, when the KGB creates a special section tasked with creating 'disinformation' about the real political objectives of the Soviet Union."[4] For the KGB, disinformation was not restricted to the dissemination of half truths: it also included "the distribution of documents, letters, and manuscripts, of falsified or forged pictures, the propagation of malicious or suggestive rumors and false intelligence by its agents, [as well as] deception of foreign visitors to the Soviet Union."[5] Disinformation in the Soviet Union was a tradition that can be traced back to Lenin, who founded the Cheka, the KGB's forerunner.[6] Interestingly, Lenin had already developed ideas that might have inspired Putin's tactic of sending anonymous "little green men" into Ukraine, wearing uniforms without insignia but apparently belonging to the Russian Spetsnaz troops. "During the war with Poland [in 1920]," writes Heller, "one can find, among other suggestions made by Lenin, a project that he himself calls a 'perfect plan.' . . . [He proposed] to cleanse that part of Polish territory which is occupied by the Red Army: 'We can do it by passing ourselves off as "Greens." . . . We hang the kulaks, the priests and the landowners.'" "The whole ingenuity of this plan," wrote Heller, "is to be found in the idea 'of being taken for Greens,' in other words for rebellious farmers, who supported neither the 'Whites,' nor the 'Reds.'"[7]

THE RETURN OF AGITPROP?

The early Bolsheviks were masters of modern propaganda. Their propaganda effort became more institutionalized with the establishment of an Agitation and Propaganda Department (*otdel agitatsii i propagandy*) in the Central Committee of the Communist Party. This department, the main organizer of Soviet agitprop, grew during the years of the New Economic Policy (1921–1928) "into an elaborate bureaucratic structure of more than thirty subdepartments of the press, publishing houses, science, schools, cadres training, cinema, the arts, theater, radio, and literature, to name only a few."[8] In the mid-1920s, "all these departments systematically monitored activities in their field."[9] In the beginning, the huge Bolshevik propaganda effort was directed primarily at the population of the Soviet Union, but soon it would be extended to foreign audiences as well. While propaganda was used to influence the mind, agitation worked on the emotions of the receiver and his or her propensity to act. The Bolsheviks were firm believers in the communist cause, and they thought that all means—including censorship, lies, the deception of others, as well as the production of fake realities—were permissible to force their ideas on the population. The Bolsheviks were early champions of modern propaganda and served as a model to be emulated by Joseph Goebbels, the Nazi minister of Popular Enlightenment and Propaganda.[10] A high-ranking Nazi, quoted by an American reporter in June 1933, admitted openly: "We National Socialists have learned much from the Russian Bolsheviki."[11] The same journalist observed "Nazi placards with striking and colourful pictures of farmers, housewives and workers. . . . Quite often the posters are copied outright from those of the Russian or German Communists."[12]

The Bolshevik propaganda might have been a new phenomenon, but this was less the case with censorship, the invention of lies, the deception of others, and the creation of fake realities. These were already well-established practices in tsarist Russia. According to an early witness, Marquis Astolphe de Custine, a French nobleman who visited Russia in 1839 and published a famous book, *Lettres de Russie* (*Letters from Russia*), lies and deception were an integral part of Russian society. "Social life in this country," he wrote, "is a permanent conspiracy against the truth. Anyone who is not duped is regarded there as a traitor . . . to refute a lie, to contradict a political claim . . . is an attack on the security of the state."[13] It is a country, he continued, "where from birth minds are adapted to dissimulation."[14] "Only the truth shocks."[15] And he concluded: "One word of truth launched in Russia is a spark landing on a powder keg."[16]

Without doubt Lenin's and Stalin's propaganda machines continued an old tsarist tradition, and Putin, in his turn, emulated these Soviet models. However, Putin did not simply copy existing models; he is also an important innovator: the contemporary Russian propaganda effort has a completely new character, taking into account four developments: first is the unprecedented *generous budgets* allocated by the Kremlin to its propaganda efforts; second is the profound *modernization* of the propaganda machinery that has taken place under Putin. In a highly professional way, all media—not only TV, radio, and the press but the Internet and social media also—are employed in the promotion of the Kremlin's message. A third innovation is the *psychological know-how* with which this new information warfare is conducted, which is far more sophisticated and elaborated than in Lenin's or Stalin's time. The Kremlin is able to adapt its message with great ingenuity and flexibility to respective audiences in different countries. Finally, in the post–Cold War world, the Kremlin is able to make use of the relative *openness* of the Western media world for the Russian propaganda offensive, something that was not the case during the Cold War (with the exception, of course, of the Western communist press). These four factors—the Kremlin's exceptionally generous budgets, the professional and concerted media effort, its new psychological approach, and Western openness—have provided the Kremlin with countless opportunities to expand its audience in the West.

THE "HYBRID" WAR IN UKRAINE: FROM DISINFORMATION TO MISINFORMATION

This is the reason why not only the Russian population but also a not insignificant section of the Western public tended to believe the Kremlin's message that the Maidan revolt in Ukraine was inspired and led by Western intelligence services, that the new Ukrainian government was illegal and full of fascists and anti-Semites,[17] and that in the Crimea and in the Donbas region there was no Russian military infiltration but a genuine local movement consisting exclusively of homegrown separatists. The Kremlin was able to present a shrewd mixture of real and invented "facts." Indeed, some Western politicians did visit the Maidan, and it was true that members of the fascist "Pravy Sektor" and the right-wing "Svoboda" party participated in the Maidan movement. It is equally true that there were Ukrainian separatists. However, by exaggerating the negative aspects beyond proportion and mixing them with invented "facts"—a tactic which is characteristic of disinformation—the Kremlin succeeded in convincing a section of the Western public of its version of the events. According to the Polish analyst Jolanta Darczewska,

> The Crimean operation has served as an occasion for Russia to demonstrate to the entire world the capabilities and the potential of information warfare. Its goal is to use difficult to detect methods to subordinate the elites and societies in other countries by making use of various kinds of secret and overt channels (secret services, diplomacy and the media), psychological impact, and ideological and political sabotage."[18]

As the conflict dragged on, the *dis*information campaign soon started to make way for plain *mis*information: the invention and dissemination of flagrant untruths and pure lies. One example of this misinformation is a news item broadcast on July 12, 2014, by the Russian Pervyy Kanal (First TV Channel). In an interview, a woman named Galina, who claimed to be a refugee from Slavyansk in eastern Ukraine, told how Ukrainian soldiers had taken a three-year-old boy and crucified him "like Jesus."

> One man nailed him, while two [others] held him. And all this happened before his mother's eyes. [Then] they took the mother. And the mother saw how the child bled. The child cried and screamed. . . . People fainted. When the child was dead after having agonized for half an hour, they took the mother, tied her unconscious to a tank and drove three times round the square. Each circuit of the square was one kilometer.[19]

This story led to great outrage in Russia, but it was soon exposed as pure make-believe.[20] Another example of such deliberate misinformation was an article in the Russian *Life News*, published immediately after the downing of the Malaysian Airline flight MH-17 over eastern Ukraine. A spokesman for Rosaviatsiya, the Russian Federal Air Transport Agency, said it was believed that the crash, in which 298 people were killed, was caused by a "Ukrainian missile" launched from the ground or by a plane and that the target "could have been the Russian president's plane."[21] The Malaysian Boeing and Putin's plane would supposedly have crossed at the same height through the same air corridor near Warsaw. There were, apparently, no limits to these morbid fantasies. On January 25, 2015, Aleksandr Zakharchenko, "head of state" of the "Donetsk People's Republic," said in an interview with First TV Channel that "Ukrainian forces had brought with them three portable crematoriums. They serve to burn the bodies. Afterwards they will say that your children have disappeared or have been taken prisoner."[22]

Confronted with the accumulation of lies, in March 2014 a group of Ukrainian journalists started a website, www.stopfake.org, run by the London-based Ukrainian Institute, with the aim of checking the facts and verifying the information disseminated by Russian news channels. One of the examples of misinformation they found was a video on YouTube of Russian soldiers throwing into a heap bodies of Dagestanis they had killed. This video was "recycled" and spread on YouTube with the text "Punitive Ukrainian National Guard Mission throwing dead bodies near Kramatorsk (Donetsk region) on 3 May 2014."[23] Another example was a report, shown in March 2014 in the United Kingdom on RT, the Russian cable TV channel, that Jews were fleeing Kyiv in fear of an anti-Semitic Ukrainian government. The report featured Rabbi Misha Kapustin explaining that he and his family were leaving for their personal safety. However, the truth was that Kapustin was fleeing not Kyiv, but Simferopol in the Crimea after the illegal Russian annexation of the peninsula.[24]

The Kremlin's information war machine was put into a higher gear after the annexation of the Crimea, when Russia started its offensive in the Donbas region. Unfortunately, however, Russian propaganda did not receive an adequate response from the West, where, during the past few decades, the foreign ministries of most countries—including the United States—had sharply reduced their media budgets. This was one reason for John Lenczowski complaining that "recent [US] administrations have failed to incorporate an adequate public diplomacy dimension into their strategies."[25] He added that "America's foreign policy and national security culture has rarely given public diplomacy a place of prominence in national strategy. Indeed . . . it has been systematically neglected and under-funded during lengthy periods of the post-World War II era."[26]

In 2011, then-secretary of state Hillary Clinton had already said that the United States had to do more to communicate its values and spread its influence to the rest of the world through government-backed media. "We are engaged in an information war and we are losing that war," she warned,[27] mentioning that China and Russia had started multilanguage television networks at the very moment that the United States was cutting back in this area. Hillary Clinton concluded that "we are paying a big price" for dismantling international communication networks after the end of the Cold War.[28] In December 2014, Peter Horrocks, former director of the BBC World Service, equally warned that Britain and the United States were losing the global information war. "We are being financially outgunned by Russia and the Chinese," he said, at the same time emphasizing that "the role we need to play is an even handed one. We shouldn't be pro-one side or the other, we need to provide something the people can trust."[29] Russia is not the only country where an increased interest in information and communication strategies is apparent. China, too, is actively preparing itself for forthcoming information wars. According to Stefan Halper, "The Chinese public information chief, Li Chang-Chun, explained his government's view that the global information space now ranks among the crucial battlegrounds for power in the twenty-first century." According to the Chinese official, "Communications capacity determines influence. . . . Whichever nation's communications capacity is strongest, is that nation whose culture and core values spread far and wide . . . with the most power to influence the world."[30]

THE START OF THE INFORMATION WAR
ACCORDING TO IGOR PANARIN

When did the Kremlin's preparations start for this new information war with the West? And how, so far, has it been conducted? After the demise of the Soviet Union and the proclamation of a new world order by US President George Bush Sr., information wars between Russia and the West no longer seemed necessary. The former Cold War enemies expressed their confidence that they had become "partners," stakeholders in a new European security system which was no longer based on adversity but on mutual trust and shared security. In the beginning of the 1990s there was much talk about the "peace dividend," and most Western governments started to reduce their defense budgets. For Russia, the 1990s was a difficult decade, characterized by political turmoil, economic crises, and an unsuccessful war in Chechnya. Only with the advent of Vladimir Putin was order restored and, helped by the raising of oil and gas prices, Russian citizens began to enjoy a certain economic prosperity. However, the first decade of the twenty-first century was for the Russians not only a period of newly found wealth, stability, and national pride, it was also a period in which suddenly the loss of empire was experienced with more intensity and grief than before. This post-imperial pain led in Russia to dreams of national greatness and restored imperial grandeur.[31]

During Putin's reign there took place a reinterpretation of the causes of the demise of the Soviet Union. There are different ways to explain the sudden breakup of the Soviet empire. One way is to consider the disintegration of this huge country as the result of a power struggle between the leading politicians of that time: a struggle between Mikhail Gorbachev, President of the Soviet Union, on the one hand, and Boris Yeltsin, President of the RSFSR—the precursor of the present Russian Federation—on the other. The Belavezha Accords signed on December 8, 1991, by Boris Yeltsin and the leaders of Ukraine and Belarus—Leonid Kravchuk and Stanislav Shushkevich—were, in this version of events, the instrument of a soft coup d'état staged by Yeltsin to remove Gorbachev and become himself the supreme and uncontested ruler of the Russian heartland. The loss of the non-Russian Soviet republics was according to this version the unintended consequence of this "soft coup"—a loss the instigators thought could be quickly recouped by founding a new organization: the Commonwealth of Independent States, an organization modeled after the British Commonwealth.

A second way of explaining the demise of the Soviet Union is to consider it the logical consequence of a historical process that other European nations had already gone through: namely, a process of *decolonization*. Lenin famously called tsarist Russia "the prison of peoples" (*tyurma narodov*), demanding the liberation of the colonized peoples. This did not prevent him and his successor, Joseph Stalin, from closing the doors of this huge prison once again after a short decolonization period following the October Revolution. Stalin even succeeded in expanding the empire and, additionally, in bringing a group of dependent countries into the Russian sphere of influence: the so-called Soviet bloc. Great Britain, France, the Netherlands, and Belgium had lost their colonial possessions after World War II. Even Portugal, lagging behind, had been forced to give up its colonies. Why wouldn't the Soviet Union also—proudly claiming to be the champion of the "anticolonial struggle"—be obliged in the end to accept the urge for freedom of its subjected peoples?[32]

However, there is yet another, a third and less obvious way to explain the demise of the Soviet Union: this is to consider it as the result of a *conspiracy* planned by hostile foreign powers. It is this third explanation that has won more and more adherents in contemporary Russia. The conviction that the Soviet Union has disappeared as the consequence of a secret plan by hostile powers is widespread. These conspiracy theories can be found not only among the uneducated but also in the writings of prominent intellectuals. One of these is Igor Panarin, a former KGB agent who is a professor at the

Diplomatic Academy of the Foreign Ministry in Moscow. Panarin considers the demise of the Soviet Union the outcome of "the First Global Information War" conducted by the United States and Great Britain against the Soviet Union. In his book, titled *The First Global Information War—The Collapse of the USSR*,[33] he accused the West of having planned this "global informa- tion war" as early as 1943 at a summit in Quebec. Its instigator was believed to have been Winston Churchill.[34] The objective of this information war was the "weakening of the competitor, [and] economic or geopolitical expansion, etc.,"[35] leading to "the destruction (disintegration) of its main ideological and geopolitical opponent—the USSR."[36] At first, however, this information war did not go well for the West, due to Joseph Stalin's successful resistance, for which Panarin praises the Soviet leader. Things began to change in 1953, when "the USSR began to lose the information war after the death of J. Stalin, the chief ideologist of the successful resistance to the ongoing infor- mation war against the USSR."[37]

According to Panarin, the second phase of the Western information war against the Soviet Union started after Stalin's death with the advent of Nikita Khrushchev. At that moment Allen Dulles, the head of the CIA, together with MI6, the British foreign intelligence service, allegedly started operation "Anti-Stalin." "Operation 'Anti-Stalin,'" wrote Panarin, "marked the begin- ning of the defamation of the history of our country. N. S. Khrushchev was a typical representative of the nomenclature's undereducated social climbers, who seemed to be the ideal target for psychological-informational manipula- tion by the Anglo-American intelligence services."[38] "The CIA and MI6 supported N. S. Khrushchev in his power struggle in the USSR," he contin- ued.[39] The efforts of the Western secret services were crowned with success: "See how in 1953, after the death of J. Stalin, it was not Stalin-2 that came to power, but the anti-Stalin," a fact which gave the Anglo-Americans "the opportunity to break up the USSR."[40] The West's final victory came a few decades later. "The greatest success in the information war for the enemies of the USSR was the election of M. S. Gorbachev as general secretary of the Central Committee of the CPSU. The promotion of Gorbachev was a strate- gic loss for the Central Committee of the CPSU, but at the same time it was a victory for those who put him forward."[41] The Western conspiracy worked, wrote Panarin, because "the directors of the information war against the USSR (A. Dulles, G. Kennan, D. Rockefeller, H. Kissinger, Z. Brzezinski, R. Reagan) were able to implement a strategic operation in order to promote the ascension in the USSR of the Trotskyites-globalists N. S. Khrushchev and M. S. Gorbachev."[42] In the end, it was Gorbachev, whose "cold eyes" the author evokes several times, who was to blame: "I consider that the key factor in the demise of the USSR is the anti-government course of M. Gorbachev."[43]

Panarin's book is a conspiracy theory *in optima forma*. According to Walter Laqueur, "The belief in conspiracy theory is much more widespread than generally assumed. It is usually present in paranoia—the assumption that there is a pattern (usually negative or hostile) in random events. Nothing in the world happens by chance; obvious motives of other persons are rejected, and in severe cases this mental attitude leads to vengeful attitudes and violent confrontation."[44] Conspiracy theory is "present in terrorist movements of the extreme right; the murderers of Rathenau (the German foreign minister) believed that he was one of the Elders of Zion; the doctrines of the American far right are constituted almost entirely of conspiracies against patriots—by the United Nations, by Freemasons, the Illuminati, and of course, Zionists as well as a hundred other evil forces. The same is true with regard to the ideology of the lunatic fringe of the Russian right."[45]

The problem is that in today's Russia, it is no longer only the "lunatic fringe" of the Russian right that develops these theories but analysts and ideologists who are taken seriously by the Russian intellectual elite, including government circles close to the Kremlin.

Another author who should be mentioned here is Aleksandr Dugin, the inspirator of Putin's "Eurasian Union" and referred to by some authors as "Putin's brain."[46] One of Dugin's main works is titled *Konspirologiya*, which leaves nothing to be guessed about how the author views the world.[47] This book is a potpourri of magical and mystical theories, mixed with fascistoid, neo-imperialist geopolitical ideas. In the table of contents one finds subjects such as "Count Dracula," "Against Demons and Democracy," "The Occult Sources of Feminism," "The Threat of Globalization," "The Economic Meaning of September 11," "Liberalism—A Totalitarian Ideology," and so on. According to this author, the KGB was infiltrated by "Atlanticists," and in the last chapter he calls Nikita Khrushchev—in the same vein as Igor Panarin—"an agent of Atlanticism," while Mikhail Gorbachev—nicknamed "Mister Perestroika"—is called a "double agent."

Theories like these form the background to the new information war started by Putin's Russia. The crux of these theories is that they don't consider the present Russian information and propaganda war as a new phase in the post–Cold War era, in which—after a period of relative rapprochement between Russia and the West—the Kremlin has changed its course and opted for a policy of aggressive territorial revisionism, internal authoritarianism, and ideological closure. On the contrary, both thinkers consider Russia's new information war as a *defensive maneuver*, accusing the West of being responsible for the breakup of the Soviet Union. According to Panarin, the "first information war" started in 1943, more than seventy years ago, and ended with the demise of the Soviet Union. Therefore, in another book, titled *Information War, PR, and World Politics*,[48] he calls the present information war the *second* information war. According to him, this war also was started by the West and began in the early 1990s. He predicts that it will be concluded in 2020 with a Russian victory. Such a positive outcome he deems possible on the condition that "the Russian political elite must become *passionate* and be prepared for a global uncompromising informational-psychological confrontation with the global elites [i.e., the United States and United Kingdom]."[49] This confrontation includes not only actions abroad but also "defending the *consciousness* of Russian citizens from negative information flows, i.a. during elections."[50] Panarin emphasizes that the information war has an *offensive* ("uncompromising confrontation") as well as a *defensive* side (defending Russian citizens from "negative information flows"). It is clear that measures taken by Putin after his return as president in 2012, such as strengthening the control of the internet, restricting the freedom of action of NGOs, and muzzling the independent media, fit into this last category. Apparently, freedom of the press and the social media is incompatible with the Kremlin's understanding of the information war.[51] The war in Ukraine was an occasion for the Kremlin to further increase its already impressive propaganda effort abroad. In the federal budget for the year 2015, an increase of 41 percent is earmarked for RT—the Kremlin's international cable TV.[52] Some of these funds will be used to launch German-language and French-language channels alongside the existing channels in English, Arabic, and Spanish. The new propaganda unit Rossiya Segodnya, which combines the former news agency RIA Novosti and the radio station Voice of Russia, is treated with even greater generosity: in 2015 its budget will be increased by 250 percent.[53] In December 2014, Russia Segodnya launched an English-language online and radio service to replace Voice of Russia.

STRUCTURE OF THE BOOK

This book consists of three parts.

Part I: The Search for Russian Soft Power (chapters 1–7)

This part takes as its point of departure the concept of "soft power," which is defined by Joseph S. Nye Jr. as "the power of attraction." I analyze the recent introduction of this concept in Russia's official political discourse. The Kremlin's analysts, estimating Russia's soft-power potential to be "near to zero," undertook a redefinition of the soft-power concept, transforming it into "hard power in a velvet glove." In this redefined "soft-power" concept, I distinguish three components: "mimesis," "rollback," and "invention." "Mimesis" consists of attempts to copy Western public diplomacy, "rollback" is a strategy of attacking Western public diplomacy initiatives, and "invention" includes new methods of information warfare. One of these inventions is the hiring of Western PR firms to improve the Kremlin's image in the West. Another innovation is the organization of international seminars by the Valdai Discussion Club in Russia and Kremlin-funded institutes abroad. These initiatives not only serve the goal of creating goodwill but are also used by the Kremlin as a testing ground for Russian diplomatic initiatives. Helped by its newly acquired wealth, the Kremlin was also able to buy itself a place in the Western media landscape. I provide a detailed analysis of the impact of new projects, such as "Russia beyond the Headlines," initiated by the official Kremlin paper *Rossiyskaya Gazeta*, which publishes monthly newspaper supplements with leading Western newspapers, and similar initiatives, such as RT (former Russia Today)—an international cable TV channel set up as a competitor of CNN and Al Jazeera, and "Rossiya Segodnya"—a revamped version of the news agency RIA Novosti, designed to make it the direct mouthpiece of the Kremlin's propaganda machine. I also discuss another new phenomenon, although it is probably not directly instigated by the Kremlin: Russian oligarchs who take over Western newspapers, such as *The Independent* (United Kingdom), which was bought by the ex-KGB agent Alexander Lebedev, and *France-Soir* (France), bought by Putin's banker Sergey Pugachev and his son Alexander. Attention is also paid to the growing grip of the Kremlin-friendly oligarch Alisher Usmanov on the social media in Russia, and the activities of Kremlin-inspired bloggers, the so-called "trolls," who are flooding the social media and Western discussion forums with pro-Putin comments. In a special chapter, I offer different examples of instances in which the Kremlin or Kremlin-related oligarchs were allegedly implicated in the financing of politicians and political parties abroad. The examples come from Britain, France, the Netherlands, the Czech Republic, Lithuania, and Estonia. This part concludes with a chapter on the recent increase in Russian espionage activities. Although in Western concepts of "soft power" there is no place for espionage, this is different in the Kremlin's "hard" soft-power definition. Recent efforts to place "agents of influence" in foreign governments and international organizations build on a well-established Soviet-era tradition.

Part II: Creating a New Missionary Ideology: The Role of the Russian Orthodox Church (chapters 8–11)

One of the Kremlin's most important new "soft-power" instruments is the Russian Orthodox Church (ROC). Orthodox notions such as "spiritual security" had already been introduced by Putin in 2000 in the National Security Concept. I analyze the close, not to say "cozy" cooperation that in recent years has been established between the Foreign Ministry and the Orthodox Church, which work hand in hand in an offensive against universal human rights in international fora, such as the UN, the OSCE, and the Council of Europe. Claiming the defense of "traditional values," the Kremlin uses the Russian Orthodox Church as an instrument to spread a new, messianic, Russian state ideology, which is homophobic, anti-democratic, and anti-Western.

A new fact is that the Kremlin is trying to expand the Russian Orthodox Church beyond its historical geographical boundaries, making it into a genuine *global* church. By replacing communism with Orthodoxy, a new form of Russian messianism is emerging. This messianism, however, is no less illiberal and anti-Western than the former creed. In this new messianic effort, Russian oligarchs play a major role, acting as active sponsors of the Orthodox Church abroad. In the last chapter of this section, I analyze and summarize the reasons why the Russian Orthodox Church could so easily be instrumentalized by the Kremlin in its ideological war with the West. There are five reasons: first, the fact that the church is not independent but closely linked to the Kremlin and the secret services; second, that the church is not acting as a universalist moral standard-bearer—eventually able and willing to stand up against the state; third, that it is an adversary of freedom of religion—especially of Protestant denominations; fourth, that it is an adversary of Western democracy and universal human rights; and fifth, that it wholeheartedly supports Putin's neoimperialist policy in the Russian Near Abroad—especially in Ukraine.

Part III: Undermining Atlanticism: Building a Strategic Triangle Moscow-Berlin-Paris (chapters 12–16)

In this part I analyze the success of Putin's information war in two leading EU countries: Germany and France. I chose these countries because they constitute the Kremlin's main target in its "Two Triangles" strategy to counter US global influence. The first strategic triangle the Kremlin wants to create consists of an axis of Moscow-Beijing-New Delhi. The second consists of the axis of Moscow-Berlin-Paris. Moscow's propaganda efforts in Europe, therefore, are in particular targeted at these two countries. I will show how Putin's efforts to promote a Moscow-Berlin axis were helped by a wave of "Germanophilia" in Russia and analyze the psychological, historical, cultural, philosophical, geopolitical, and economic reasons for this Germanophilia. These include the Russian admiration for typical "German" virtues and the "double amnesia" in Russia: the fact that Russians try to forget communism as well as bad memories of the Nazi era and want to reconnect with the nineteenth-century friendship between Bismarck's Germany and tsarist Russia. Also noteworthy is the continuing Russian appetite for German ideology. In Putin's Russia, Marx's "German" communism has been replaced by German *Geopolitik*—an influence which can be traced in the writings of the Eurasianist Aleksandr Dugin, who has been a great influence on Putin. Russian Germanophilia is met with German Russophilia in Germany: a majority of Germans have developed a positive view of the Russian-German relationship. What is surprising is the broad consensus in the German population: positive views can be found among parties of the right and the left, including the extreme left. What is interesting is the new, pro-Russian stance of extreme-right parties and the intellectual "New Right," which used to be vehemently anti-Russian and anti-Soviet. It is an indication that in recent years the Kremlin has become a beacon for Europe's extreme right. Apart from these ideological and psychological underpinnings, the Russian-German friendship also has solid economic foundations. The growing mutual economic interdependence (in German: *Verflechtung*) has led to the formation of a powerful pro-Russia business lobby in Germany, which influences Germany's foreign policy.

Russian efforts to build a European Moscow-Berlin-Paris triangle implied also a "soft-power offensive" in the direction of the EU's second-leading power: France. Under the presidencies of Jacques Chirac and of Nicolas Sarkozy, the Franco-Russian relationship began to blossom—in particular after Sarkozy's mediation in the Russian war with Georgia, which led to a personal relationship between the leading Russian "tandem" and the French president. Immediate outcomes were the organization in 2010 of a "Russian Year" in France and a "French Year" in Russia and the purchase of the "Mistral" helicopter carrier by Russia—the first important defense purchase ever made by Russia in a NATO country. Another Russian wish was fulfilled when Russia was able to buy a plot near the Eiffel Tower to build an Ortho-dox seminary and church for its Orthodox hub in Paris. France was even prepared to support the creation of an exclusive EU-Russia security commit-tee, an idea that was supported by Germany. Like in Germany, in France there exists a powerful pro-Russia lobby of French companies with business interests in Russia. Another interesting parallel is that in France, the extreme right Front National has become a staunch supporter of the Kremlin—a fact that can be explained by the ideological affinity between Putin's regime and the West European extreme right.

NOTES

1. Bridget Kendall, "Russian Propaganda Machine 'Worse Than Soviet Union,'" *BBC* (June 5, 2014).
2. Kendall, "Russian Propaganda Machine 'Worse Than Soviet Union.'"
3. David Welch, "Introduction," in *Nazi Propaganda: The Power and the Limitations*, ed. David Welch (London: Routledge, 2014), 2.
4. Michel Heller, "Analyse politique (physique et métaphysique)," in *La désinformation: arme de guerre*, ed. Vladimir Volkoff (Lausanne: L'Age d'Homme, 2004), 167.
5. John Barron, "Analyse par 'l'Ennemi principal,'" in *La désinformation: arme de guerre*, ed. Vladimir Volkoff, 179.
6. The Cheka was an abbreviation of the VChK (ВЧК), the All-Russian Extraordinary Committee (*Vserossiyskaya Chrezvychaynaya Komissiya*), founded by Lenin on December 20, 1917.
7. Michel Heller, "Analyse politique (physique et métaphysique)," 168.
8. Vladimir N. Brovkin, *Russia after Lenin: Politics, Culture, and Society, 1921–1929* (London: Routledge, 1998), 81.

9. Brovkin, *Russia after Lenin*.

10. The Bolshevik model of a propaganda department with many subdepartments might have inspired the Ministry of Popular Enlightenment and Propaganda, headed by Joseph Goebbels, which comprised five departments: radio, press, active propaganda, film, and theater and popular education.

11. Roger B. Nelson, "Hitler's Propaganda Machine," *The New York Times* (June 1933).

12. Nelson, "Hitler's Propaganda Machine."

13. Marquis de Custine, *Lettres de Russie: La Russie en 1839*, ed. Pierre Nora (Paris: Gallimard, 1975), 370.

14. Custine, *Lettres de Russie*, 367.

15. Custine, *Lettres de Russie*, 365.

16. Custine, *Lettres de Russie*, 370.

17. An example of this is an article, published in the *Huffington Post* one week after the annexation of the Crimea, in which the author wrote: "The Obama administration has vehemently denied charges that the Ukraine's nascent regime is stock full of neo-fascists despite evidence suggesting otherwise. Such categorical repudiations lend credence to the notions that the U.S. facilitated the anti-Russian cabal's [*sic*] rise."(Cf. Michael Hughes, "The Neo-Nazi Question in Ukraine," *The Huffington Post* (March 11, 2014), http://www.huffingtonpost.com/michael-hughes/the-neo-nazi-question-in_b_4938747.html.) Four days earlier, the BBC correspondent wrote: "[The far right's] role in ousting the president and establishing a new Euromaidan-led government should not be exaggerated. . . . Euromaidan officials are not fascists, nor do fascists dominate the government." (Cf. "Ukraine's Revolution and the Far Right," *BBC* (March 7, 2014), http://www.bbc.com/news/world-europe-26468720.)

18. Jolanta Darczewska, "The Anatomy of Russian Information Warfare—The Crimean Operation, A Case Study," *Point of View*, no. 42 (May 2014), Warsaw, Center for Eastern Studies, 5.

19. "Bezhenka iz Slavyanska vspominaet, kak pri ney kaznili malenkogo syna i zhenu opolchentsa," *Pervyy Kanal* (July 12, 2014).

20. During Putin's yearly news conference, Ksenia Sobchak from the Dozhd TV channel explicitly referred to this episode. "I get the sense that federal channels are deliberately fanning hatred in Russian society," she said. "Take for instance the episode about a crucified boy from Slavyansk that was shown on the first federal channel where the state has a controlling stake. This episode . . . was proved to be false, but nobody apologised for it." (Cf. "News Conference of Vladimir Putin," official site of the President of Russia (December 18, 2014), http://eng.news.kremlin.ru/news/23406/print.)

21. "Tselyu ukrainskoy rakety mog byt samolet Vladimira Putina—Po slovam istochnika v Rosaviatsii, bort rossiyskogo lidera i poterpevshego kryshenie 'Boinga' peresekalish na odnom echelone," *Life News* (July 17, 2014).

22. Cf. Isabelle Mandraud, "Télépoutine," *Le Monde* (February 12, 2015).

23. *Stop Fake*, http://www.stopfake.org.

24. *Stop Fake*, http://www.stopfake.org. Another example of misinformation took place on October 25, 2014—one day before the parliamenary elections in Ukraine, when pro-Russian hackers accessed electronic billboards in the streets of Kyiv and published images of alleged carnage wrought by Ukrainian troops in the east of the country. Russian state-owned Channel One broadcast a report on these photographs, describing them as "horrifying images of the events in Donbas." However, one of the pictures showed mass graves of civilians in Chechnya. The Russian soldier who figured in the original picture, taken in 1995, was removed. (Cf. Carl Schreck, "Ukraine Unspun: Chechnya War Pic Passed Off as Ukraine Atrocity by Hackers, Russian TV," *RFE/RL* (October 27, 2014).)

25. John Lenczowski, *Full Spectrum Diplomacy and Grand Strategy: Reforming the Structure and Culture of U.S. Foreign Policy* (Lanham, MD: Lexington Books, 2011), 9.

26. Lenczowski, *Full Spectrum Diplomacy and Grand Strategy*, 10.

27. Colby Hall, "Hillary Clinton: 'America Is Losing' an Information War That 'Al Jazeera Is Winning,'" *Mediaite.com* (March 2, 2011), http://www.mediaite.com/tv/hillary-clinton-claims-al-jazeera-is-winning-an-information-war-that-america-is-losing/.

28. Hall, "Hillary Clinton: 'America Is Losing.'"

29. Josh Halliday, "BBC World Service Fears Losing Information War as Russia Today Ramps Up Pressure," *The Guardian* (December 21, 2014).

30. Stefan Halper, *The Beijing Consensus: Legitimizing Authoritarianism in Our Time* (New York: Basic Books, 2012), 10.

31. For more on post-imperial pain in post-Soviet Russia, see Marcel H. Van Herpen, *Putinism: The Slow Rise of a Radical Right Regime in Russia* (Houndmills: Palgrave Macmillan, 2013), 76–97.

32. On the demise of the Soviet Union as a—late—process of decolonization, see my book *Putin's Wars: The Rise of Russia's New Imperialism* (Lanham, MD: Rowman and Littlefield, 2014), chapters 1 and 2.

33. Igor Panarin, *Pervaya Mirovaya Informatsionnaya Voyna: Razval SSSR* (Moscow: Piter, 2010).

34. Panarin is referring to the Quebec Conference, held in Quebec City between August 17 and August 24, 1943, with the code name Quadrant, in which Franklin D. Roosevelt, Winston Churchill, and Canadian Prime Minister Mackenzie King participated. According to Lawrence James: "[Churchill] was uneasy about Russia's long-term international ambitions. He confided his anxieties to Mackenzie King during the Quebec Conference. Soviet Communism exerted 'influence in all parts of the world' and Churchill believed that Russia was 'powerful enough to more than control the world'" (Lawrence James, *Churchill and Empire: Portrait of an Imperialist* (London: Phoenix, 2013), 313). However, the concerns expressed by Churchill on this occasion cannot be taken as proof of a secret Western plan to start an "information war" with the aim of dismembering the Soviet Union.

35. Panarin, *Pervaya Mirovaya Informatsionnaya Voyna*, 12.

36. Panarin, *Pervaya Mirovaya Informatsionnaya Voyna*, 12–13.

37. Panarin, *Pervaya Mirovaya Informatsionnaya Voyna*, 14.

38. Panarin, *Pervaya Mirovaya Informatsionnaya Voyna*, 123.

39. Panarin, *Pervaya Mirovaya Informatsionnaya Voyna*, 123.

40. Panarin, *Pervaya Mirovaya Informatsionnaya Voyna*, 144.

41. Panarin, *Pervaya Mirovaya Informatsionnaya Voyna*, 9.

42. Panarin, *Pervaya Mirovaya Informatsionnaya Voyna*, 247.

43. Panarin, *Pervaya Mirovaya Informatsionnaya Voyna*, 228.

44. Cf. Walter Laqueur, *No End to War: Terrorism in the Twenty-First Century* (New York: Continuum, 2003), 155.

45. Laqueur, *No End to War*, 155.

46. Anton Barbashin and Hannah Thoburn, "Putin's Brain—Alexander Dugin and the Philosophy behind Putin's Invasion of Crimea," *Foreign Affairs* 93, no. 2 (March/April 2014).

47. Aleksandr Dugin, *Konspirologiya*, available at http://epop.ru/sub/trash/book/konspy.html.

48. Igor Panarin, *Informatsionnaya Voyna, PR i mirovaya politika* (Moscow: Goryachaya Liniya, 2014).

49. Panarin, *Informatsionnaya Voyna, PR i mirovaya politika*, 133 (emphasis in original).

50. Panarin, *Informatsionnaya Voyna, PR i mirovaya politika*, 133–134 (emphasis in original).

51. As was made clear in February 2013 by Aleksey Wolin, the Russian deputy minister of mass communication, who explained to journalism students of Moscow State University that "any journalist must understand clearly that it is not his task to make the world better, to bring the light of the truth, to lead humanity into the right direction," adding, "we need to teach students clearly that they are going to work for the boss and the boss should tell them what to write, what not to write and how to write on these or other subjects, and the boss has this right because he pays them." (Cf. "Zaministr svyazi Aleksey Volin ustroil skandal na konferentsii v MGU," *AN-Onlayn* (February 11, 2013).)

52. "RT poluchit na 41% bolshe deneg iz byudzheta," Colta.ru (September 23, 2014). In 2015, RT will receive 15.38 billion rubles (approximately $365.1 million).

53. "RT poluchit na 41% bolshe deneg iz byudzheta," Colta.ru (September 23, 2014). The 2015 budget of Rossiya Segodnya is 6.48 billion rubles (approximately $153.8 million).

I

The Search for Russian "Soft Power"

Chapter One

Russian Soft Power

Hard Power in a Velvet Glove

INTRODUCTION: US SOFT POWER AND THE
FATHER OF PERESTROIKA

During Khrushchev's East-West thaw, US President Dwight Eisenhower made a proposal for something unheard of before: an academic exchange between the United States and the Soviet Union. The proposal was accepted by the Soviets and started in September 1958. One of the seventeen students sent by the Central Committee was Aleksandr Yakovlev. Yakovlev studied for one academic year at Columbia University. Later he would become Soviet ambassador to Canada and a close friend and source of inspiration of Mikhail Gorbachev, which earned him the nicknames *godfather of glasnost* and *father of perestroika*. According to his biographer, Christopher Shulgan,

> Yakovlev sometimes denied the influence of the West on his political thinking. At various times, in various ways, he insisted his time in the West did not change him. "It simply did not," he said on one occasion. This attitude seems like revisionism. Yakovlev acknowledged, in more conciliatory moods, that his time in the West influenced his reformist convictions. He was particularly reluctant to discuss America's influence on him. However, his year at Columbia seems certain to have helped forge the unusually democratic sentiments that defined his 1960's work in Propaganda [Department of the Central Committee of the Communist Party].[1]

Eisenhower's exchange program was certainly not set up to convert young Soviet academics (which, incidentally, would have proved difficult, since most of Yakovlev's Russian exchange colleagues were KGB spies). However, giving young Russians a rare chance of living in the United States for a year exposed them to the "soft power" of American society. In the modern world you don't need to *live* in another country to become attracted by its soft power. Hollywood movies that were watched in the 1950s in the local cinemas of small towns in Africa, Latin America, and Asia did a lot more to propagate the "American way of life"—including its values and aspirations—than any US government–sponsored initiative could have done. The same is true for music and fashion. In a Russian book with the telling title *Glyadya na Zapad* (*Looking West*), the authors describe the attraction of Western pop music and fashion for Russian youth. "At the end of the 1990s," they write, "the West continued to be the most important orientation point in the cultural identification of 'progressive' [Russian] youth."[2]

WHAT IS SOFT POWER?

Soft power is not only an important concept, it is also a rather *new* concept. It was used for the first time by the American political scientist Joseph S. Nye Jr., in his book *Bound to Lead*,[3] published in 1990. However, it only became a new catchword in the international political discourse after the publication, in 2004, of Nye's book *Soft Power: The Means to Success in World Politics*.[4] From that moment, "soft power" began to be used by a broader public. The new concept evoked what Germans call an *Aha Erlebnis*: it seemed to express exactly the meaning of an existing phenomenon for which one had not yet found an adequate description. Nye's introduction of the concept "soft power" resembled to some extent Freud's invention of the word "unconscious" in the nineteenth century. This, too, was a phenomenon many already had felt existed but for which they had not yet found an adequate expression. Why did this new concept of "soft power" find a worldwide reception so quickly? A key may well be found in the subtitle Joseph Nye gave his 2004 book: *The Means to Success in World Politics*. He presented soft power as a highly valuable and profitable asset for policy makers because of its purported impact on the success or failure of a country's foreign policy objectives. In the aftermath of the demise of the Soviet Union, it seemed one of the decisive factors that had contributed to the West's final prevalence over the Soviet bloc.

But what exactly *is* soft power? According to Nye, it is

> the ability to get what you want through attraction rather than coercion or payments. It arises from the attractiveness of a country's culture, political ideals, and policies. When our policies are seen as legitimate in the eyes of others, our soft power is enhanced. America has long had a great deal of soft power. Think of the impact of Franklin Roosevelt's Four Freedoms in Europe at the end of World War II; of young people behind the Iron Curtain listening

to American music and news on Radio Free Europe; of Chinese students symbolizing their protests in Tiananmen Square by creating a replica of the Statue of Liberty.[5]

The dynamic force of soft power, explained Nye, is *attraction*. This is, indeed, very different from more classical definitions of power. The sociologist Max Weber, for instance, defined power as "any opportunity to impose one's own will within a social relationship, even in the face of resistance, no matter what might be the basis of that opportunity."[6] For Weber, the essence of power is that one person prevails over the other *even in the face of resistance*. In a more extreme way, the same is expressed in the definition of power given by Mao Zedong, who said that "power grows out of the barrel of a gun." The characteristic of *soft* power is that there exists no resistance needing to be overcome, and certainly no guns have to be used: others adapt to our objectives because they feel sympathetic towards us and have interiorized our objectives as their own. This interiorization is based on the attraction of our political ideals and actual policies. On a lower level, soft power is based on the attraction of a country's culture, art, language, music, fashion, landscape, or cuisine.

Nye's concept has been criticized from many sides. David Marquand, for instance, called it "a slippery concept; and in real life the distinction between it and 'hard power' is apt to slither into a bog of semantic confusion."[7] Marquand added: "Mahatma Gandhi was perhaps the twentieth century's supreme exemplar of soft power in action, but as he himself acknowledged, his success in using it depended on British willingness to allow him to do so. He would not have got very far if India had been ruled by the Nazis."[8] This last observation may be true; however, it does not invalidate the concept. Its essential characteristic remains: that soft power is based on attraction, on exemplarity, on its model function for others, making it a source of inspiration beyond national borders.

SOFT POWER IS A VARIABLE CURRENCY

Soft power is generally considered a characteristic *par excellence* of Western societies, especially of the United States. We should not forget, however, that the—now defunct—Soviet Union also had, in its time, its own soft-power sources—a fact of which Nye is aware. "In terms of soft power," he wrote, "following World War II communist ideology was attractive in Europe because of its resistance to fascism and in the Third World because of its identification with the popular movement toward decolonization."[9] Successes in space exploration also played a role in boosting Soviet soft power. According to Innokenty Adyasov, a Russian analyst, "Yury Gagarin was the best instrument of Soviet soft power: never, perhaps, in the post-war world was sympathy towards the USSR so great and here also the personality of the earth's first cosmonaut had an impact."[10] This soft-power reservoir, however, was depleted when the Soviet leadership decided in 1968 to crush the Prague Spring and communism as an ideology gradually lost its appeal throughout the world. Soviet soft power reached its nadir in 1991 when the Soviet Union broke up and communism lost its status as official state ideology.

In 2009 Sergey Karaganov, a Russian analyst, wrote that Russia had to use "hard power, including military force, because it lives in a much more dangerous world and has no one to hide behind from it, and because it has little soft power—that is social, cultural, political and economic attractiveness."[11] And Konstantin Kosachev, a Russian Duma member, wrote: "We can say that practically the whole post-war period of our relationship with the U.S. and the West . . . took place under the banner of soft power. And clearly we should admit that, apparently, we were not up to the challenge—however, as concerns hard power, the field of *hard security* [English in the original] we were inferior to no one."[12] This assessment is shared by Joseph Nye in *The Future of Power*. "In terms of soft power," writes Nye, "despite the attractiveness of traditional Russian culture, Russia has little global presence."[13] Russians envied and resented Western soft power while at the same time criticizing it for its supposed hypocrisy. Yury Kaslev, for instance, in a book on the Helsinki process published in 1980, writes:

> In general, the discussion on human rights, artificially imposed by the American delegation during the meeting in Belgrado, showed, in the first place, that this was done for propagandistic reasons in the framework of the well-known policy of the administration in Washington to proclaim the United States "the champion of human rights in the world," secondly, that the United States in practice is not respecting human rights at home . . . , [and] was trying to use the human rights topic as a means to intervene in the internal affairs of other countries.[14]

In the 1970s and 1980s Soviet Russia was clearly on the defensive. However, soft power is not an asset that can be taken for granted. After the subprime crisis in 2008, which was followed by a worldwide financial and economic crisis, Western, and especially US, soft-power attractiveness suffered a severe blow. A Japanese commentator wrote: "The Japanese are less and less attracted by American culture. American *soft power* seems to have diminished and according to specialists such a phenomenon has never been known before."[15] American soft power, he continued, "is diminishing progressively in the archipelago, although for the Japanese the United States represented a dream, with its technology, its democracy, its egalitarian relationships between couples. They were not only attracted by the 'city on the hill,' but also by its counter-culture, for instance the protests against the war in Vietnam."[16]

This sentiment that US soft power has declined in the past decade was also expressed by Zbigniew Brzezinski, who said that due to the war in Iraq, "I do think that we have unfortunately delegitimized ourselves."[17] He added: "Then, the American dream was widely shared. Today, it isn't."[18]

Similar observations were made in the French daily *Le Monde*, but this time on the declining soft power of Europe. Under the title "Europe No Longer Makes Asians Dream,"[19] the story explains that Asian countries— due to the never-ending euro crisis—began to question Europe's proud soft-power model: European integration. The fact that the EU received the 2012 Nobel Peace Prize probably did little to compensate for this loss of soft power. Even if the combined soft-power potential of the United States and Europe still remains considerable, one has to admit that it is a far cry from its strength at the beginning of the 1990s. In this period the Soviet empire crumbled, the United States organized a broad international coalition under the aegis of the UN against Saddam Hussein's invasion of Kuwait, and in Maastricht the European Community transformed itself into a "European Union"—ready to expand with fourteen new countries and to make an important next step towards integration with the introduction of a single currency. "The end of history," announced in 1989 by Francis Fukuyama in an article in *The National Interest* and further elaborated by him in a book in 1992,[20] was in fact nothing else than a celebration of the West's soft-power dominance at that specific historical moment. Fukuyama could not imagine that any other political and economic system could, in the future, compete with the West. He was wrong. Now, in the present day, we are witnessing the emergence of competing political models, of which Putinism is a leading example. These models, although superficially resembling the Western model and presenting themselves as democratic market economies, are, in fact, authoritarian semi-state economies. Competition from these alternative models is taking place at a historical moment when the West's soft-power dominance is no longer self-evident. According to Moisés Naím, "Soft power is, at the very least, a volatile concept, highly vulnerable to short-term twists in world affairs, in an environment where news travels more rapidly than ever."[21] We should, indeed, not forget that soft power is a currency that—as any currency—has no constant and stable value but undergoes important variations.

HOW TO MEASURE SOFT POWER?

One of the problems with Nye's concept of soft power was that it remained, indeed, a rather vague concept. Jeanne Wilson spoke about "the amorphous nature of soft power as a concept, the absence of a set methodology for measurement, a lack of comparable data, and the inherently subjective nature of constructing indicators."[22] What also did not help was that Nye broadened his concept over the years. In his book *The Future of Power* (2008) he added economic resources and even military power as possible soft-power assets (the latter in the form of offering training facilities and disaster relief). The method most frequently used to measure soft power was through opinion polls. This was how Anholt-GfK Roper, for instance, composed its annual *Overall Nation Brands Index*. In the index for 2010, the United States ranked number one, followed by Germany, France, and the United Kingdom in second, third, and fourth places, respectively. Russia came in at twenty-first place, just before Luxembourg and China.

A more elaborate and objective method to measure soft power was developed by the London-based Institute for Government. In its 2010 report it weighed a number of objective criteria concerning culture, government, diplomacy, education, and business/innovation.[23] The outcomes of these objective criteria were complemented by a subjective evaluation by an experts' panel. In the resulting *Soft Power Index Results*, twenty-six countries were analyzed. The same four countries came on top as in the Overall Nations Brands Index, but in a different order: France was number one, the United Kingdom second, the United States third, and Germany fourth. Russia came in at the twenty-sixth and last place.[24] In the 2011 report the method was further fine-tuned and improved. Now the United States came in at number one, followed respectively by the United Kingdom, France, and Germany. Russia went down to the twenty-eighth place (of a total of thirty countries).[25] However, the author of the report warned against too much optimism. He wrote that

> Observed in isolation, the results of the index might produce a false sense of security for the world's developed countries. But comparing the recent approaches to soft power taken by the established and emerging powers throws up some interesting questions, namely how long can the West's soft-power hegemony last? In the current context of sustained fiscal austerity for the West, soft-power assets have been among the most tempting budget lines for governments to cut. [At the same time,] emerging powers have been investing in their capacity to generate and project soft power.[26]

"MYAGKAYA SILA": THE HISTORY OF THE SOFT-POWER DEBATE IN RUSSIA

In Russia the concept "soft power" attracted only little attention at first. Unlike in China, Nye's book *Bound to Lead*, in which the concept made its first appearance, was not translated. According to Jeanne Wilson, "The Eastview Universal Database, the largest repository of journals and newspapers available in the Russian language does not indicate a reference to soft power until 2000."[27] In the period 2000–2012, this database listed 334 articles that referred to "soft power" in the text and 32 articles that contained "soft power" in the title.[28] Neither Putin during his first two presidencies nor Medvedev during his presidency seemed to have used the concept.

Several factors point to why in Russia the debate on "soft power"—in Russian, *myagkaya sila*—started rather late. First was the fact that a concept such as "soft power" was completely at odds with the Russian tradition and the Russian way of thinking. In tsarist Russia as well as in the Soviet Union, power tended to be unilaterally defined as *zhestkaya sila*, or "hard power." The foreign policy of both regimes was characterized by their emphasis on military power while internally the authorities often resorted to brutal violence and police repression. To understand the new concept of "soft power," a complete reversal of these traditional ways of thinking was necessary.

A second reason for the late reception of the "soft-power" concept was the fact that Russians considered "soft power" a typical *American* concept. From Russia's perspective, it looked like a new fad, invented by American political scientists, which had, maybe, relevance for the United States but no direct implications for Russia's situation. A real interest in the new concept arose only after the "color revolutions" in the post-Soviet space: the 2003 Rose Revolution in Georgia and the 2004 Orange Revolution in Ukraine—popular movements which swept away corrupt and undemocratic regimes. At this point, the Kremlin woke up to the new reality that soft power could, eventually, be used as a very effective weapon.

HOW DID RUSSIA ASSESS ITS OWN SOFT-POWER POTENTIAL?

The color revolutions were a watershed moment in the Kremlin's thinking on soft power. Russian politicians and political analysts suddenly recognized that in the modern, globalized, and interconnected world of the twenty-first century, characterized by a growing role for the internet and social media, soft power had become an important strategic asset. For the Kremlin it was a rude awakening. Observations about the dire state of Russian soft power, made earlier in the West, now also began to surface in the Russian media. Alexander Lukin, director of the Center for East Asian Studies at the Moscow State Institute of International Relations (MGIMO), for instance, wrote:

> The Soviet Union offered an alternative to bourgeois civilization and quite a number of people would long view it as a rising ideal society, for which they were ready to sacrifice their lives. Today's Russia does not offer anything— apart from its mineral resources—that would deserve at least some interest, to say nothing of sacrificing one's life. Its soft power, nonaggressive attraction, and moral and ideological influence have dropped to zero. It does not promote either a democratic ideal (similar to the United States) or a fundamentalist

ideal (similar to some Islamic countries and movements). It does not serve as a
model of successful integration on the basis of democracy (like the EU) or a
pattern of speedy development (like China that has aroused global interest
with the so-called "Beijing Consensus" as an alternative to the "Washington
Consensus"). Russia is not a crucial and useful ally for anyone (the way Japan
is for the U.S.) or anyone's bitter enemy (like Iran is for the U.S.). Naturally,
someone can say that the world has a large number of countries that do not
offer anything special to mankind (e.g. the small states of Europe). But they do
not claim the role of independent centers of power, to say nothing of being
separate civilizations, since they are part of the European one. In the meantime, an attempt to integrate Russia into Europe flopped, and that is why
Russia must look for ways to consolidate its own soft power and seek things
that it could offer to the rest of the world, albeit not on the Soviet scale of the
past.[29]

Lukin's gloomy but realistic assessment was that Russia's soft power had
"dropped to zero." While Lukin still stuck to Nye's definition that soft power
is the power of attraction, this was no longer the case for two other Russian
authors, Latukhina and Glikin, who defined soft power as

> the ability to influence the development of a political situation abroad with the
> help of specially deployed experts and polit-technologists—sort of agents of
> influence. Russian political scientists like to give the example of the local
> branches of the Soros Foundation and the Carnegie Center, which are in an
> effective way active throughout the world, "spreading democracy." We don't
> have such agents of influence in whom we can put our hope and whom we
> could finance. Russian soft power is completely powerless, we might even say
> that such a power, in general, does not exist.[30]

While these authors shared Lukin's observation that Russian soft power
"dropped to zero," writing that it simply "does not exist," something else
here catches the eye. It is the explicit redefinition of soft power, which is
reduced to a simple tool of manipulation in the hands of hostile governments.
American NGOs are considered to be "agents of influence" sent abroad by
"polit-technologists." An "agent of influence" is defined by *Wikipedia* as "an
agent of some stature who uses his or her position to influence public opinion
or decision making to produce results beneficial to the country whose intelligence service operates the agent." Soft power here is put into a conspirational
context and becomes an instrument in the hands of hostile secret services.
Also the use of the word "polit-technologists" is telling. In Putin's Russia,
"polit-technologists" are those experts who, like Vladislav Surkov, the former deputy head of the presidential administration, manipulate the political
system, including the elections, in the Kremlin's favor.

THE TRIPLE REDUCTION: HOW THE "SOFT-POWER" CONCEPT WAS REDEFINED IN CONTEMPORARY RUSSIA

This trend of changing the content and meaning of Nye's soft-power concept has become mainstream in contemporary Russia. The concept underwent, in fact, a *triple* reduction. The first step was to reduce the broad concept of soft power to one of its constituent parts: public diplomacy. This means that soft power—which in Nye's definition is a power emanating from *both* civil society and the state—was reduced to an instrument used by the state to influence foreign governments and manipulate foreign public opinion. The fact that it is a country's civil society in particular that produces soft power was lost out of sight. By reducing soft power exclusively to a policy of the state, conducted with the aim to enhance its hard power, the *focus* of soft power also was changed.

This was the second reduction: from a non-zero-sum game, soft power became a zero-sum game with winners and losers. In Nye's definition, the soft power of one country does not hinder or diminish the soft power of another country. The four countries that are the world's soft-power champions, the United States, the United Kingdom, France, and Germany, do not fight a "soft-power war," nor do they "attack" the soft power of their "rivals" (assuming for a moment that this would be possible). The only way to become number one in the league of "soft-power champions" is to become more attractive. In this beauty contest, you don't become more beautiful by denigrating or attacking the other participants. You win because you have the best qualifications.

The reduction of soft power to political diplomacy, conducted by the state, led to an additional—third—reduction of Nye's original concept. Because the Kremlin regarded soft power exclusively as a constituent part of an overall hard-power game, the meaning of soft power became totally inverted, and even illegal activities, such as bribery and espionage abroad, could be presented as useful instruments of a country's "soft-power arsenal."

VLADIMIR PUTIN'S CONCEPT OF "SOFT POWER": HARD POWER IN A VELVET GLOVE

These three reductions of Nye's soft-power concept can clearly be observed in the way in which Vladimir Putin describes "soft power" in a manifesto for his third presidency published in the *Moskovskie Novosti* in February 2012:

> There is a concept, such as soft power, a complex of instruments and methods to achieve foreign policy objectives without the use of weapons, which include the use of information and other means. Unfortunately, these methods are often used to cultivate and provoke extremism, separatism, nationalism, ma-

nipulation of public opinion, [and] direct intervention in the internal politics of sovereign governments. The distinction must be made clearly between where there is freedom of expression and normal political activity, and where illegal instruments of "soft power" are used. . . . However, the activity of "pseudo-NGOs" [and] other structures which, with outside support, have the aim to destabilize the situation in this or that country, is unacceptable.[31]

Putin spoke here about the soft power of the West and the activities of what he called "pseudo-NGOs" working within Russia and receiving financial support from the West. He could not believe that the activities of these NGOs could be inspired by a genuine desire to promote the cause of democracy, to protect human rights, or to work for an independent judiciary. For him, these NGOs were all "foreign agents."[32]

All the elements of the redefined, reduced version of Nye's soft-power concept are present in Putin's text. Soft power is defined as "a complex of instruments and methods to achieve foreign policy objectives." Soft power is conceived, therefore, as an exclusively *state* affair. Soft power is for him also an integral part of a *hard*-power game. The message is that Russia should develop its own soft-power arsenal in order to prevail in this zero-sum power game. The weapons in this soft-power game include "the use of information and other means." For Putin, the former spy master, "information" has a broad meaning, and it includes, undoubtedly, the intelligence of the secret services. This vision is shared by a Russian analyst, who wrote: "Putin emphasizes that his understanding of 'soft power' includes, quite precisely, the use of illegal instruments, 'undercover work' (*rabotu pod prikrytiem*)."[33] On September 3, 2012, Prime Minister Dmitry Medvedev reiterated in a speech at the Russian Foreign Ministry the need for Russia to further develop its soft-power tools. This "may look to an outside observer like an optimistic signal and a long-awaited change in Russia's foreign policy," wrote Dumitru Minzarari. "This benign view, however, could not be more wrong. Rather, the Kremlin is seeking to exploit the Western concept of 'soft power' . . . and reframing it as a euphemism for coercive policy and economic arm-twisting."[34]

We find this reframing of the Western "soft-power" concept already in the "Basic Guidelines Concerning the Policy of the Russian Federation in the Sphere of International Cultural-Humanitarian Cooperation," an official document published in 2010 as a complement to the Foreign Policy Concept of 2008. These "Basic Guidelines" begin with the observation that "culture, in the realization of Russia's foreign policy strategy, plays a special role."[35] "It is increasingly evident," the text continues, "that the global competition takes on a cultural dimension. Among the fundamental games in the international arena the struggle for cultural influence is becoming more intense."[36] Therefore, write the authors, the government should not only "actively support the competitivity of the [different] branches of the national culture" but also take care that an "objective and favorable image of our country" will be formed, that "the number of Russia's friends grows," and that "anti-Russian political and ideological attitudes are neutralized."[37] According to the guidelines, "Cultural diplomacy becomes [also] increasingly important in efforts with the aim of actively counteracting the propaganda campaign [conducted] under the banner 'containment' of Russia."[38]

What immediately catches the eye here is the martial, almost warlike terminology that is used. One speaks about a "struggle" that is "becoming more intense," about "anti-Russian attitudes" that should be "neutralized," about a Western "propaganda campaign" that should be "counteracted." Apparently, the authors of this paper have sought their inspiration in Samuel Huntington's "Clash of Civilizations" rather than in Joseph Nye's soft-power concept. The authors claim to promote an "objective and favorable image" of Russia. A few lines further, they make this "objective image" more explicit, writing: "Making use of specific forms and methods of influencing public opinion, cultural diplomacy, as no other instrument of 'soft power,' convincingly expresses the rebirth of the Russian Federation as a free and democratic society."[39] The problem, however, is that neither foreigners, nor many Russians, consider today's Russian Federation "a free and democratic society." And only a few will agree with the statement that "Russia's dynamic cultural life [takes place] in conditions of pluralism and free creativity, pluralism of opinions, and absence of censorship."[40]

Putin, however, considers the negative image of Russia in the West not as a consequence of the immanent flaws of the Russian political system but rather as a result of actions of Western governments and the Western media to blacken Russia's reputation. In a speech to the ambassadors in July 2012, he said that

> Russia's image abroad is formed not by us and as a result it is often distorted and does not reflect the real situation in our country or Russia's contribution to global civilisation, science and culture. Our country's policies often suffer from a one-sided portrayal these days. Those who fire guns and launch air strikes here or there are the good guys, while those who warn of the need for restraint and dialogue are for some reason at fault. But our fault lies in our failure to adequately explain our position. This is where we have gone wrong.[41]

In the same vein, he stated in his concluding speech at the 2014 Valdai Club conference: "Total control of the global mass media has made it possible when desired to portray white as black and black as white."[42]

For the Kremlin, the solution seemed simple: Russian state agencies should get the task to debunk Western misinformation and to provide "real," "truthful" information. Giving truthful information on Russia is certainly desirable. As Greg Simons remarked, "Truth is the best propaganda and lies are the worst. To be persuasive, we must be believable; to be believable we must be credible; to be credible we must be truthful. It is as simple as that."[43] He added: "One of the problems encountered by Russian public diplomacy relates to the credibility, and therefore to the believability of the messenger. This is especially the case if the messenger is tied to the Russian authorities, owing in no small part to the strong anti-democratic reputation that has been gained in the post-Yeltsin era (from the year 2000)."[44]

NOTES

1. Christopher Shulgan, *The Soviet Ambassador: The Making of the Radical behind Perestroika* (Toronto, Ontario: McClelland & Stewart, 2008), 291.

2. Hilari Pilkington, "Pereosmyslenie 'Zapada': Stil i Muzyka v Kulturnoy Praktike Rossiyskoy Molodezhi," in Hilari Pilkington, Elena Omelchenko, Moya Flynn, Uliana Bludina, and Elena Starkova, *Glyadya na Zapad: Kulturnaya Globalizatsiya i Rossiyskie Molodezhnye Kultury* (Saint Petersburg: Aleteiya, 2004), 186.

3. Joseph S. Nye Jr., *Bound to Lead: The Changing Nature of American Power* (New York: Basic Books, 1990).

4. Joseph S. Nye Jr., *Soft Power: The Means to Success in World Politics* (New York: Public Affairs, 2004).

5. Nye, *Soft Power*, x. In *Bound to Lead*, Nye spoke also about "co-optive power": "Co-optive power is the ability of a nation to structure a situation so that other nations develop preferences or define their interests in ways consistent with one's own nation. This type of power tends to arise from resources as cultural and ideological attraction as well as the rules and institutions of international regimes" (191).

6. Max Weber, *Wirtschaft und Gesellschaft: Grundriss der verstehenden Soziologie*, Erster Halbband, herausgegeben von Johannes Winckelmann (Cologne and Berlin: Kiepenheuer & Witsch, 1964), 38 (my translation).

7. David Marquand, *The End of the West: The Once and Future Europe* (Princeton and Oxford: Princeton University Press, 2011), 154.

8. Marquand, *The End of the West*, 155.

9. Joseph S. Nye Jr., *The Future of Power* (New York: Public Affairs, 2011), 168–169. Cf. Nye, *Bound to Lead*, 188–189: "In the early postwar period, the Soviet Union profited greatly from such strategic software as Communist ideology, the myth of inevitability, and transnational Communist institutions."

10. Innokenty Adyasov, "Vozmozhnaya li rossiyskaya 'myagkaya sila'?" *Regnum* (May 7, 2012).

11. Sergei Karaganov, "Russia in Euro-Atlantic Region," *Rossiyskaya Gazeta* (November 24, 2009). English version available at http://karaganov.ru/en/news/98.

12. Konstantin Kosachev, "'Myagkaya Sila' kak faktor sblizheniya?" (May 18, 2012), http://baltija.eu/news/read/24577.

13. Nye, *The Future of Power*, 170, 209. In this book Nye introduces the new concept of "smart power," which combines hard- and soft-power strategies.

14. Y. B. Kashlev, *Razryadka v Evrope: Ot Helsinki k Madridu* (Moscow: Politizdat, 1980), 78.

15. "L'Amérique ne fait plus rêver" (originally published in *Tokyo Shimbun*), translated in *Courrier International* no. 1129 (June 21–27, 2012).

16. "L'Amérique ne fait plus rêver."

17. Zbigniew Brzezinski, "U.S. Fate Is in U.S. Hands," TNI Interview, *The National Interest* no. 121 (September/October 2012), 12.

18. Brzezinski, "U.S. Fate Is in U.S. Hands." 14.

19. François Bougon, "L'Europe ne fait plus rêver les Asiatiques," *Le Monde* (July 1–2, 2012).

20. Francis Fukuyama, *The End of History and the Last Man* (London and New York: Penguin, 1992).

21. Moisés Naím, *The End of Power: From Boardrooms to Battlefields and Churches to States, Why Being in Charge Isn't What It Used to Be* (New York: Basic Books, 2013), 148.

22. Jeanne L. Wilson, "Soft Power: A Comparison of Discourse and Practice in Russia and China," *Social Science Research Network* (August 2012), 3, available at http://ssrn.com/abstract=2134457.

23. Jonathan McClory, *The New Persuaders: An International Ranking of Soft Power* (London: Institute for Government, 2010). The culture subindex includes measures such as the annual number of incoming tourists, the global reach of the country's language, and Olympic sporting successes. The government subindex gives measures for the quality and effectiveness of the system of governance as well as for individual liberty and political freedom. The diplomatic subindex includes measures for the global perception of a country and its ability to shape a positive national narrative abroad. The education subindex gives measures for a country's ability to attract foreign students and the quality of its universities. The business/innovation subindex includes figures for openness and innovation, competitiveness, and corruption.

24. McClory, *The New Persuaders*, 5.

25. Jonathan McClory, *The New Persuaders II: A 2011 Global Ranking of Soft Power* (London: Institute for Government, 2011), 15.

26. McClory, *The New Persuaders II*, 20.

27. Jeanne L. Wilson, "Soft Power," 5–6.

28. Jeanne L. Wilson, "Soft Power," 6.

29. Alexander Lukin, "From a Post-Soviet to a Russian Foreign Policy," *Russia in Global Affairs*, no. 4 (October–December 2008), available at http://eng.globalaffairs.ru/print/number/n_11886.

30. Kira Latukhina and Maksim Glikin, "Politicheskie Zhivotnye," *Nezavisimaya Gazeta* (April 1, 2005).

31. Vladimir Putin, "Rossiya i menyayushchiysya mir" (Russia and the Changing World), *Moskovskie Novosti* (February 27, 2012).

32. It is interesting to compare Putin's attitude towards foreign-government-funded agencies with that of the Indian leader Nehru. John Kenneth Galbraith, who was US ambassador to India at the beginning of the 1960s, told how Sargent Shriver, the founding head of the US Peace Corps, came to visit Nehru. "I warned him," wrote Galbraith, "that in the Indian mood of the time, and that of Jawaharlal Nehru in particular, the Peace Corps would be regarded as a rather obvious example of the American search for influence." Shriver presented to Nehru a project which would "help the most needy of the Indian needy" in Punjab. "When he [Nehru] eventually replied, it was to ask why the enterprise had to be so small, why it had to be limited to only one Indian state. He thought the idea excellent, regretted only the evident limitations." John Kenneth Galbraith, *Name-Dropping: From F.D.R. On* (Boston and New York: Houghton Mifflin, 1999), 123–124.

33. Mikhail Moskvin-Tarkhanov, "Vladimir Putin i 'myagkaya sila,'" *Svobodnyy Mir* (February 27, 2012).

34. Dumitru Minzarari, "Soft Power with an Iron Fist: Putin Administration to Change the Face of Russia's Foreign Policy toward Its Neighbors," *Eurasia Daily Monitor* 9, no. 163 (September 10, 2012). We should emphasize, however, that this interpretation of soft power is that of the dominant *siloviki* faction of the political elite. Igor Yurgens, for example, the chairman of the board of the Institute of Contemporary Development, a liberal pro-business think tank, wrote: "Even if we . . . can tell the world about our culture, [and] historical heritage, we will not be attractive in Europe and North America if we have not completed the development of our democratic institutions and structures of civil society. Only these can become true ambassadors of Russian culture in the world." (Cf. Igor Yurgens, "Zhestkiy vyzov 'myagkoy sily,'" *Rossiyskaya Gazeta* (September 16, 2011).)

35. "Osnovnye napravleniya politiki Rossiyskoy Federatsii v sfere mezhdunarodnogo kulturno-gumanitarnogo sotrudnichestva" (Moscow, 2010), 1.

36. "Osnovnye napravleniya," 2.

37. "Osnovnye napravleniya," 3.

38. "Osnovnye napravleniya," 3.

39. "Osnovnye napravleniya," 3.

40. "Osnovnye napravleniya," 4.

41. "Meeting with the Russian ambassadors and permanent representatives in international organisations," *Official site of the President of Russia* (July 9, 2012).

42. "Vladimir Putin Meets with Members of the Valdai International Discussion Club. Transcript of the Final Plenary Session," *Valdai Discussion Club* (October 25, 2014), http://valdaiclub.com/valdai_club/73300/print_edition/.

43. Greg Simons, "Attempting to Re-Brand the Branded: Russia's International Image in the 21st Century," *Russian Journal of Communication* 4, no. 3/4 (Summer/Fall 2011): 329.

44. Simons, "Attempting to Re-Brand the Branded."

Chapter Two

The Three Components of the Kremlin's Soft-Power Offensive

Mimesis, Rollback, and Invention

Igor Ivanov, Russia's former minister of foreign affairs (1998–2004), wrote: "The fundamental question for twenty years to come is whether Russia will learn to use the tools political scientists refer to as 'soft power.' Being realistic in assessing the dynamics of global development, we have to admit that Russia's opportunities of using the traditional foreign policy tools (such as military or economic power) will most likely be shrinking."[1] Ivanov called for a "smart foreign policy" in which Russia "diversifies its assets," combining military and energy tools with "nonmaterial" dimensions. For him, as for the other members of Russia's foreign policy elite, the new Russian soft-power offensive is conceived as an integral part of a zero-sum hard-power game.

This Russian "soft-power offensive" has three components:

1. Mimesis
2. Rollback
3. Invention

The first component, "mimesis," refers to the fact that the Kremlin's actions in the field of soft power have a strong mimetic character. The Russian leadership tries to copy those Western strategies and institutions which it thinks are most effective. In the process of copying, however, it often gives its own initiatives a new twist, as a result of which the Russian clones differ in a fundamental way from their Western models.

33

The second component, "rollback," is a logical consequence of the Kremlin's vision that the soft-power game is an integral part of a zero-sum hard-power game. "Rollback" means curtailing, opposing, and possibly forbidding the activities of Western soft-power institutes inside Russia.

The third component of the Kremlin's soft-power strategy, "invention," is its most important part. It is a strategy to invent new soft-power strategies, making ample use of the possibilities offered by the open Western societies. It includes legal as well as illegal activities in order to enhance the Kremlin's influence abroad and ranges from hiring Western public relations firms to improve its image to setting up spy rings, illegally financing political parties, and directly "buying" people. This "innovative" part of the Kremlin's soft-power strategy—which is at odds with Western definitions of soft power—is in fact not so innovative because it often makes use of many techniques used in the past by the Soviet KGB. It is the main subject of this book and will be analyzed in detail in the following chapters. In this chapter, however, we look first at the other two components of the Kremlin's soft-power strategy: mimesis and rollback.

THE KREMLIN'S MIMETIC SOFT-POWER INSTRUMENTS: THE INSTITUTE FOR DEMOCRACY AND COOPERATION, ROSSOTRUDNICHESTVO, AND RUSSKIY MIR

From the start, the Kremlin's new initiatives to enhance its soft power had a strong mimetic character. In Russian publications, the activities of some Western NGOs and public diplomacy agencies, such as the British Council, the German Goethe Institut, the Alliance Française, and USAID (United States Agency for International Development), were presented as shining examples of how to promote the national language, culture, and interests abroad. It led in 2008 to the Kremlin's establishment of the Institute for Democracy and Cooperation (IDC) with offices in New York and Paris. Apparently, the institute was set up as a Russian equivalent of the American NGO Freedom House. However, according to Andranik Migranian, the director of the New York institute, its goal was not to compete against Freedom House but to help US citizens to understand Russia's position on human rights and democracy.[2] Officially, the institute's task was "to study democracy and human rights in Europe," but in practice it defended the Russian version of "managed democracy" and "human rights based on traditional values" (which means that human rights are not universal but have a locally variable application). The Paris office, l'Institut de la Démocratie et de la Coopération (http://www.idc-europe.org/), is headed by Natalya Narochnitskaya, a former Duma member for the ultranationalist Rodina (Fatherland) Party, founded by Dmitry Rogozin. Narochnitskaya shares the paranoid worldview of the Kremlin leaders. On her website (http://narochnitskaia.ru/) she has written that "in all Caucasian wars there are non-Islamic instigators." One of the speakers invited to her conferences in Paris in 2011 was General Alexander Vladimirov. In 2007 this general spoke about "the inevitability of war between Russia and the United States within 10 to 15 years."[3] "The two branches of IDC," wrote Andrey Makarychev, "are overwhelmingly perceived as propaganda platforms rather than as intellectual think tanks."[4]

In Russia there existed already an organization, called Roszarubezhtsentr (Russian Foreign Center), which was a government agency for friendship and cultural relations with foreign countries. It was subordinate to the Ministry of Foreign Affairs and dated back to 1925, early in the Soviet era. A press release, published in 2005 by the Foreign Ministry on the occasion of the eightieth anniversary of the organization, praised its many achievements. "World-famous local and foreign scientists, writers, painters, composers, and artists," said the release, "laid the foundation for the organization's high prestige in the world by their participation in the development of 'people's diplomacy.'"[5] The names of Albert Einstein, Marie Curie, Yury Gagarin, Vladimir Mayakovsky, Ernest Hemingway, Bernard Shaw, and Herbert Wells were mentioned. Its objectives included strengthening the Russian language and culture abroad, as well as "providing informational support for Russian foreign and domestic policies, and helping to shape in the world community a positive image of contemporary Russia." Recently, the organization also began to play a role in "assisting the development of compatriots' all-round relations with their historic homeland and engaging with Russian-speaking diasporas abroad." Roszarubezhtsentr had offices in sixty-five countries as well as "Russian Culture and Science Centers" in thirty-nine countries. It seemed to be one of the most successful Russian soft-power organizations.

Nevertheless, on September 6, 2008, a new organization, called Rossotrudnichestvo (Russian Cooperation Agency), was founded by a decree of President Medvedev. The new organization inherited the cultural centers from its predecessor, received additional funding, and got more autonomy from the Foreign Ministry. The reason was that the Kremlin had discovered that USAID, the foreign aid agency of the American government, was much more effective in increasing goodwill abroad than its Russian equivalent. USAID, which was created in 1961 by executive order of President John F. Kennedy, claims on its website that "the United States has a long history of extending a helping hand to people overseas struggling to make a better life."[6] USAID's website further states that

> spending less than 1 percent of the total federal budget, USAID works in over 100 countries [with the aim to promote] broadly shared economic prosperity; strengthen democracy and good governance; protect human rights; improve

global health; advance food security and agriculture; improve environmental sustainability; further education; help societies prevent and recover from conflicts; and provide humanitarian assistance in the wake of natural and man-made disasters.[7]

It is, indeed, an impressive US "soft-power" toolkit. As USAID's name already indicates, the organization was much more focused on providing direct, bilateral aid to foreign countries, working not only with governments but also with NGOs. The activities of the existing Russian Cultural Centers seemed in comparison to be too "elitist cultural" and too "top-down," as one can conclude from the impressive list of famous names mentioned in the Foreign Ministry's press release.

The Kremlin's purpose of founding the new organization Rossotrudnichestvo was not so much cultural as geopolitical. It was set up "to centralise activities undertaken with a view to maintaining Russian influence in the CIS area."[8] Its official name, "Federal Agency for the CIS, Compatriots Living Abroad and International Humanitarian Cooperation," indicates that its primary focus was the former Soviet space and the Russian-speaking minorities living there. The agency remained subordinated to the Ministry of Foreign Affairs and would operate abroad through delegations organized within diplomatic posts. Starting in January 2009, these delegations employed about six hundred staff members.[9] In the next three years, Rossotrudnichestvo grew exponentially—also outside the CIS—and was represented in Russian diplomatic missions in seventy-four countries, where it had established eighty-three subdivisions, including fifty-eight Russian centers for culture and science.[10]

On June 28, 2012, its newly appointed director, Konstantin Kosachev, revealed in a speech before the Federation Council his ambitious plans for the future. "My agency," he told the deputies, "operates Russian culture and science centres in 74 countries. By January [2013], the number is expected to rise to 83, and by 2018, to 104."[11] Kosachev, who had just returned from Bethlehem, where President Putin had opened a new Russian culture and science center, explained: "The Palestinian Autonomy is home to tens of thousands of ethnic Russians and Russian expats. The Russian Centre should be of help to them and also to Russia, as it continues to seek a stronger geopolitical clout in their area."[12] The goals of Rossotrudnichestvo were never more clearly expressed: spreading Russian culture and science was not the ultimate goal; what mattered was to give Russia and the Russian state "a stronger geopolitical clout." This stronger geopolitical clout was especially sought after in the former Soviet space where the Kremlin introduced new integration projects, latterly in the form of a megaproject called "Eurasian Union," targeting the Russian minorities in the former Soviet states as possible allies. On this matter, Kosachev said in an interview: "We have missed many opportunities. We could by now have been at a much higher level of reintegration of this post-Soviet space—please don't confuse it with a reconstruction of the Soviet Union. But what has been done abusively, remained in the past. We will learn from these mistakes and move forward. Thank god, the project of the Eurasian Union is now well elaborated and is moving forward with seven-mile strides."[13]

Similar geopolitical aims in the Kremlin's new soft-power strategy were assigned to another new institute, the Russkiy Mir Foundation. Vyacheslav Nikonov, its director, did not make a secret of the mimetic character of this organization. "We are far, far from what the Americans are doing," he said. "We are students, freshmen."[14] Like Rossotrudnichestvo, Russkiy Mir's main focus is on the countries of the former USSR. Georgi Bovt, editor in chief of the *Russkiy Mir Journal*, writes:

> Regrettably, the Russian language is on the defensive even in the territories of the CIS countries where, one would expect, the wealth of historical and cultural traditions could for decades to come serve at least to keep up the language inertia. However, the pressure to unseat it from public and cultural practice is too heavy. There is an impression that some sort of a plan is under way to uproot the Russian altogether, with a political motivation discernible behind it.[15]

Russian analysts often fall back on conspiracy theory to explain the reduced influence of the Russian language in the former Soviet space, the Baltic states in particular. However, this loss of influence is mainly a result of two factors: emigration[16] and cultural adaptation of Russian and Russian-speaking minorities. However, the activities of Russkiy Mir in the former Soviet space are not restricted to in itself praiseworthy efforts to promote the Russian language and culture abroad. These activities are often politically motivated, transforming Russian "compatriots" abroad into a virtual fifth column. Estonian analyst Juhan Kivirähk writes:

> The people whose interests the compatriots' policy allegedly protects are actually used as a tool for the realisation of Russia's imperialistic ambitions. The aim of Russia's efforts to consolidate the Russian-speaking population in Estonia is not to make them a part of Estonian society, but rather to push them outside society and to lead them into confrontation with it. Instead of making Russia's image more attractive (which would be in accordance with the nature of "soft policy"), the policy raises risk perceptions about Russia and increases tensions between nations.[17]

Russkiy Mir's main focus is the former Soviet space. However, this does not mean that it restricts its activities to this part of the world. On the contrary, the organization considers "the Russian World" as a *global* community that includes ethnic Russians as well as Russian speakers and Orthodox believers, *wherever they live.* Russkiy Mir, therefore, works hand in hand with Rosso-trudnichestvo in setting up Russian centers in universities abroad, an initiative which met with great success in recent years. Russian centers have been set up in many Western universities, such as in Leiden and Groningen in the Netherlands and in Durham, Edinburgh, and Glasgow in the United Kingdom. [18] On June 28, 2012, Russkiy Mir's director, Vyacheslav Nikonov, even received in Edinburgh an honorary doctorate. [19] This happened shortly after Russkiy Mir realized one of its greatest successes in Britain: the opening, on February 27, 2012, of a Russian center at St. Anthony's College of the revered Oxford University. [20] Other centers were opened on June 15, 2012, at the Minho University in the Portuguese city of Braga[21] and, on June 21, 2012, at the University of Kars in Eastern Anatolia in Turkey. [22] In each case, the Russkiy Mir Foundation provided books, disks, learning materials, and personnel. Despite a *prima facie* resemblance of this Russian cultural diplomacy with the work of the British Council, the Alliance Française, and the United States Information Agency's library program, there is, however, one great difference: neither the British Council, which operates in more than one hundred countries, nor any of the other Western institutes have established bases on university campuses. The Russian approach seems, therefore, to be inspired by the Chinese model. In 2004 China started setting up "Confucius Institutes" at foreign universities. There are now seventy of these institutes in the United States, fourteen in France, eleven in Germany, thirteen in Britain, and still others in Eastern Europe and Asia. [23] In the United States, the work of these institutes has led to critical comments. Arthur Waldron, a professor of international relations at the University of Pennsylvania, says:

> Once you have a Confucius Institute on campus, you have a second source of opinions and authority that is ultimately answerable to the Chinese Communist Party and which is not subject to scholarly review. You can't blame the Chinese government for wanting to mold discussion. But Chinese embassies and consulates are in the business of observing Chinese students. Should we really be inviting them onto our campuses?[24]

According to another critic, Teufel Dryer, who teaches Chinese government and foreign policy at the University of Miami, there were strings attached to the Chinese largesse. "You're told not to discuss the Dalai Lama—or to invite the Dalai Lama to campus. Tibet, Taiwan, China's military buildup, factional fights inside the Chinese leadership—these are all off limits."[25] These considerations led the University of Pennsylvania's East Asian Studies faculty to oppose unanimously an initiative to open a Confucius Institute. Similar concerns are certainly justified with regard to the opening of Russian centers, supervised by the Kremlin, at Western university campuses.

Other Mimetic Structures: The Russian International Affairs Council and the Gorchakov Foundation

Apart from the IDC, Rossotrudnichestvo, and Russkiy Mir, two other public diplomacy initiatives should be mentioned here: the Russian International Affairs Council, and the Gorchakov Foundation. The Russian International Affairs Council (RIAC) is modeled after the US Washington-based think tank Center for Security and International Studies (CSIS). In it government representatives, foreign policy experts, and representatives of business and civil society work together on foreign policy issues. The RIAC was founded by a decree by President Medvedev of February 2, 2010, with the mission "to facilitate the prospering of Russia through integration in the global world."[26] Its board of trustees includes political heavyweights, such as former prime minister Yevgeny Primakov, Foreign Minister Sergey Lavrov, Deputy Prime Minister Sergey Prikhodko, and Sberbank chairman German Gref. President of the presidium is former foreign minister Igor Ivanov. As of November 2013, the RIAC had 110 members. The RIAC organizes many seminars on international policy issues. Events in 2012 included subjects such as "Russia's Interests in the Arctic"; "Central Asia after the Withdrawal of Coalition Forces from Afghanistan"; "Public Diplomacy as an Instrument of Russia's Foreign Policy"; and "Russia and Arab Spring Countries: Opportunities for Soft Power and Traditional Cooperation Vehicles." An English-language website opened in March 2012.

The Gorchakov Foundation, another initiative of President Medvedev, opened in the same year (2010). It is named after Prince Aleksandr Gorchakov, who was foreign minister from 1856 to 1882 and is considered the architect of Russia's comeback as a major European power after the defeat in the Crimean War. Gorchakov is apparently considered a model to be emulated. The goal of the foundation is to support public diplomacy. On its website, the foundation's director, Leonid Drachevsky, writes in his welcome declaration that "in international life so-called 'soft power' has begun to play a more important role," and he welcomes the fact that Russian NGOs "begin to play an important role in the realization of [Russia's] foreign policy strategy."[27] The Gorchakov Foundation, he continues, has been set up "to strengthen the international activity of Russian NGOs." He emphasizes, not without pride, that "in contemporary Russia our Foundation is the first and only government-civil society partnership in the sphere of foreign policy," and expects that "with shared efforts we can reach a synergetic effect."[28]

Against the background of the Russian tradition with its strong state and its relatively weak civil society, a Western observer may ask whether Russian NGOs are really "helped" by this initiative or whether it may rather enable the state to control and monitor NGOs that deploy activities which have an impact on Russian foreign policy. The massive presence of the state becomes clear from the important personal overlap and cross memberships among the different soft-power agencies. For instance, Igor Ivanov, president of the RIAC, together with Foreign Minister Sergey Lavrov, are members of the administration of the Gorchakov Foundation. The Gorchakov Foundation's "Expert's Council" has only one member, Igor Ivanov. In his turn, Leonid Drachevsky, the director of the Gorchakov Foundation, is a member of the board of trustees of RIAC. Konstantin Kosachev, the director of Rossotrudnichestvo, is also a member of this board.

"ROLLBACK": THE ASSAULT ON THE RUSSIAN NGOs

The second component of the Kremlin's soft-power offensive, we mentioned, was a "rollback" strategy directed at curtailing the influence of not only Western NGOs within Russia but also Russian NGOs that are partially funded by Western sources. Although this strategy was not new, it moved up a gear in the summer of 2012—immediately after Putin's re-election. Russian authorities established a precedent in December 2007, when they ordered the regional offices of the British Council to be closed. The official reason was that the British Council was alleged to have violated Russian tax regulations—a classic pretext the Russian authorities use when they wanted to harass an institution. The action followed Britain's expulsion of four Russian diplomats in connection with the murder of the dissident Alexander Litvinenko in London.[29] At that time this—temporary—measure could be considered a simple "tit-for-tat" action. In 2012, this was no longer the case. A frontal attack began on Russian NGOs that received funding from Western sources. Both houses of parliament adopted a law in the first weeks of July 2012, signed by President Putin on July 21, that forced NGOs receiving funding from abroad and engaging in "political activity" to register with the Justice Ministry as an *inostrannyy agent* (foreign agent). The new law was preceded by attacks by Vladimir Putin on the work of NGOs in his February article in *Moskovskie Novosti* and in a speech in December 2011 in which he attacked "so-called grant recipients," adding, "Judas is not the most respected biblical figure among our people,"[30] apparently having in his sights the election-monitoring organization Golos, which had denounced irregularities in the December 2011 Duma elections.

The new law, in fact, had three objectives:

- to discredit these organizations
- to impose new burdens on their activities
- to criminalize their activities

The label "foreign agent" was meant to discredit these organizations in the eyes of the population, demonizing their members as local representatives of foreign powers, if not treating them as outright traitors. The bill would make it obligatory for foreign-funded NGOs involved in political activities to add to all publications and websites the label "foreign agent." About one thousand NGOs were targeted by the law.[31] The head of the well-known human rights organization "Moscow Helsinki Group," the eighty-four-year-old Lyudmila Alekseeva, did not hide her rage. She said her organization would not register. "If they want, let them close us," she said. "That will mean that the whole world will know that they closed the MHG [Moscow Helsinki Group] that has existed for thirty-six years and survived the Soviet regime."[32] A similar reaction came from the human rights defender Oleg Orlov, head of the organization Memorial. "We will never declare ourselves 'foreign agents,'" he said.[33] Orlov announced that he would appeal to the European Court of Human Rights in Strasbourg.

The threat, however, was real. Annual audits were announced, as well as unannounced checks for the use of "extremist speech" in published materials. Those found guilty could face fines up to one million rubles ($30,000). According to a Justice Ministry spokesman, under the new law, NGOs that failed to comply with the new requirements would be suspended for a maximum of six months; if they failed to comply again, the organization could face prosecution. The same spokesman warned that if an NGO is suspended for noncompliance of the law, it will be prohibited "from holding mass rallies and public events, [as well as] using bank accounts except for routine payments."[34]

The new law on "foreign agents" led to another rollback move when, in September 2012, the Russian government ordered the US development agency USAID to leave the country by October 1. USAID had been present in Russia for twenty years. It not only funded the Moscow Helsinki Group, Memorial, and the election watchdog Golos, but also engaged in charity, offering aid to children's homes and disabled children. According to Victoria Nuland, the spokesperson for the US Department of State, even "United Russia," the official Kremlin party, received USAID grants for years.[35] USAID spent nearly $3 billion in Russia on aid and democracy programs over the past twenty years.[36] Another victim of the Kremlin's rollback strategy was UNICEF, which was expelled at the end of 2012. Many foreign donors, including the International Red Cross, World Wildlife Fund, and the Ford Foundation, had already lost their tax exempt status in 2008.[37] On June 6, 2013, the vote monitoring agency Golos was dissolved. It had improperly failed to register as a foreign agent. Its director fled the country.[38]

Putin's government, however, not only wanted to harass critical NGOs and take their funding away, it especially wanted to *criminalize* their activities. This was put into effect by the adoption by the Duma, on October 23,

2012, of amendments to articles 275 and 276 of the criminal code. These amendments introduced a much broader definition of "treason." Treason was no longer limited to illegally handing over secret information to foreign governments; it now also included "providing assistance in the form of information, funds and consultation to Western and international organizations." These "Western and international organizations" also meant Western NGOs. The amendment was proposed by the FSB, the Russian secret service. In his presentation of the draft bill before the State Duma, Yuriy Gorbunov, deputy director of the FSB, declared that an amendment to the criminal code was

> due to a change in tactics by foreign intelligence services that actively make use of international organizations in their operations. . . . We propose that article 275 of the Criminal Law of the Russian Federation ("High Treason") includes international organizations in the list of destinations of treason as (foreign secret services) actively make use of them as cover, and they independently conduct intelligence activities.[39]

Also the definition of "security" was broadened in the amended article. Where the old article only mentioned "external security," the new article 275 spoke about "activities directed against the security of the Russian Federation, including its constitutional order, sovereignty, territorial and state integrity."[40] The Russian SOVA Center commented: "Criminalization of any given 'act directed against the constitutional order,' presents a very serious danger, as such acts could on a whim be made to include virtually any form of political or social activism. What is 'state integrity' is left to the imagination, as is how it differs from territorial integrity."[41] This opinion was shared by Rachel Denber, deputy director for Europe and Central Asia at Human Rights Watch, who wrote:

> Now, if this proposed definition becomes law . . . even advocacy to promote change could land you in jail. . . . The law would also open the way for the FSB to carry out surveillance on nongovernmental groups in the name of investigation—tapping phones, bugging offices and lodgings, with practically no time limitations. They'd be able to open a criminal case into alleged treason and use it to keep the Kremlin's adversaries under surveillance for years. So any kind of advocacy with foreigners about the need for fair elections, the electoral process, or for example even the separation of powers and the need for an independent judiciary could be off limits.[42]

For Denber it was clear. "I can't help," she wrote, "but hear the faint but creepy echo of the old article 58 of the Soviet criminal code, which was commonly used against dissidents. Article 58 made offering assistance to the 'international bourgeoisie' . . . a treasonous offense."[43] In the week after the adoption of the amendments, the head of the European diplomacy, Catherine Ashton, also expressed her deep concern.[44]

This rollback strategy of Western soft power can sometimes take unexpected and even ridiculous forms. When, in the summer of 2014, Russia was hit by Western economic sanctions after its aggression in Ukraine, the Kremlin retaliated by shutting down the McDonald's restaurant in Moscow's Pushkin Square for "sanitary reasons." Masha Gessen pointed out that the Kremlin's action was meant less as an economic reprisal than as an attack on a symbol of US soft power. McDonald's, she wrote, "was a unique place in several ways: It was a public space where ordinary people could have a private conversation while eating food they could afford, sold to them by a polite staff."[45] The American fast-food restaurant promised its Russian clients "a public sphere, which had not and could not have existed in a totalitarian society." Therefore, she concluded, "the Russian government is shutting down a symbol [of American soft power], not a business."[46]

INVENTION: NEW TOOLS FOR THE KREMLIN'S SOFT-POWER OFFENSIVE

We have, so far, spoken about two of the three components of the Kremlin's new "soft-power" strategy: mimesis and rollback. Both are characterized by different timetables. The mimesis started in 2008 with the foundation of Russian GONGOs (government-organized nongovernmental organizations), such as the Institute for Democracy and Cooperation, Russkiy Mir, and Rossotrudnichestvo. The rollback was given a powerful push after Putin's return to the Kremlin in May 2012, when the government started a massive crackdown on the activities of Western and Russian NGOs. The third component of the Kremlin's new soft-power strategy, *invention*, which will be analyzed in the following chapters, started earlier. Its beginnings can be traced back to the "color revolutions" in Georgia and Ukraine in 2003 and 2004. It was during the second presidency of Vladimir Putin (2004–2008) that the Kremlin began to implement a "grand strategy," designed to build, to reinforce, and to activate all possible soft-power sources that the Russian state had at its disposal (without, at that time, using the concept "soft power"). This "soft-power offensive" was not a hotchpotch of isolated, individual measures but, on the contrary, a large-scale, centrally led and coordinated effort by the Russian state with the aim of creating the maximum possible impact. All available assets that could possibly play a role in this strategy have been assembled and brought together. Helped by its huge oil profits, the Kremlin has invested billions of dollars in this unprecedented "soft-power offensive." A small part of this offensive consisted of an effort to build authentic soft power.[47] The main part, however, consisted of building *hard* soft power. In the following chapters we will explore how this offensive was organized: how Western PR firms were hired to improve Russia's image, how influence was bought in the Western media, how Russia set up its own media facilities, including a multilingual international cable television network, how Kremlin "trolls" began to flood the internet, how rings of "sleeper" spies were installed in Western cities to infiltrate leading Western political circles, and how political parties and politicians were financed in an effort to influence the policies of Western governments. Normally, in the Western sense, most of these activities do not qualify as "soft power." However, in the Russian context, soft power is considered to be a manipulatable asset, which is an integral part of a zero-sum hard-power game, a strategy in which the Kremlin not only buys influence but also uses other vectors for its soft-power projection. One of these vectors is the activation of the Russian diaspora abroad—not only in the CIS, but also in the West, where this strategy is facilitated by the fact that post-Communist Russia has access not only to the recently established diaspora but also to old émigré communities of White Russians who immigrated to the West after the Bolshevik Revolution. A second, important vector is, as we will see, the Russian Orthodox Church, which is closely related to the Kremlin and the FSB, the follow-up organization to the KGB. The Kremlin actively supports claims by the Russian Orthodox Church for the restitution of church properties in the West. More important, however, is that the Kremlin—together with the patriarchate—has initiated plans to give the Orthodox Church a global reach, making the church the vector of a new Russian messianism, which replaces the obsolete communist messianism. This new Orthodox messianism offers a strongly conservative and antidemocratic worldview which directly challenges the liberal values of the West. It is deeply anti-Western and critical of Western democratic standards and universal human rights. Universal human rights are attacked in international forums, such as the UN, the OSCE, and the Council of Europe.

NOTES

1. Igor Ivanov, "What Diplomacy Does Russia Need in the 21st Century?" *Russia in Global Affairs* (December 29, 2011).

2. Cf. Andis Kudors, "'Russian World'—Russia's Soft Power Approach to Compatriots Policy," *Russian Analytical Digest*, no. 81 (June 16, 2010), 3.

3. Cf. Theo Sommer, "Moscow Is Elbowing into Its Place in the Sun," *The Atlantic Times* (August 2007).

4. Andrey Makarychev, "Hard Questions about Soft Power: A Normative Outlook at Russia's Foreign Policy," *DGAPanalyse kompakt*, no. 10 (October 2011), Deutsche Gesellschaft für auswärtige Politik, Berlin, 3.

5. "Press release—80th Anniversary Celebrations of Roszarubezhtsentr," *Official Site of the Ministry of Foreign Affairs of the Russian Federation* (October 19, 2005).

6. "Who We Are," USAID, http://www.usaid.gov/.

7. "Who We Are."

8. "The Kremlin Reinforces Russia's Soft Power in the CIS," Centre for Eastern Studies, Warsaw (September 17, 2008).

9. Andrey Kazantsev, "'Rossotrudnichestvo' vo glave s Kosachevym budet rabotat na razvitie dobrososedstva," MGIMO (March 19, 2012).

10. Kazantsev, "Rossotrudnichestvo."

11. "Head of Rossotrudnichestvo Konstantin Kosachev speaks to the State Duma on Diaspora Issues," *Fond Russkiy Mir* (June 28, 2012).

12. "Head of Rossotrudnichestvo Konstantin Kosachev speaks to the State Duma."

13. "Konstantin Kosachev: Reputatsiya Rossiya za rubezhom otkrovenno zanizhena," *Fond Russkiy Mir* (April 9, 2012).

14. Quoted in Peter Finn, "Russia Pumps Tens of Millions into Burnishing Image Abroad," *The Washington Post* (March 6, 2008).

15. Georgi Bovt, "Soft Power of the Russian Word," Russian International Affairs Council (October 2, 2013).

16. Between 1989 and 2011, the percentage of Russians in Lithuania went from 9.4 to 5.4 percent; in Latvia, from 34 to 26.9 percent; and in Estonia, from 30.3 to 25.5 percent. (Cf. Vadim Smirnov, "Russia's 'Soft Power' in the Baltic," Russian International Affairs Council (May 4, 2012).)

17. Juhan Kivirähk, "How to Address the 'Humanitarian Dimension' of Russian Foreign Policy?" *Diplomaatia*, no. 90, International Centre for Defence Studies, Tallinn (February 3, 2010).

18. Cf. "Alexei Gromyko Discusses Opening of Russian Centers with Representatives of UK Universities," *Russian Centre in Scotland "Haven"* (November 16, 2009).

19. "Vyacheslav Nikonov Receives Honorary Doctorate from University of Edinburgh," *Fond Russkiy Mir* (June 28, 2012).

20. "Russkiy Mir Program Officially Inaugurated at University of Oxford," *Fond Russkiy Mir* (February 27, 2012).

21. "Nadejda Machado: The Russkiy Mir Cabinet Will Help Promote the Russian Language and Culture among the Portuguese," *Fond Russkiy Mir* (June 18, 2012).

22. "Russkiy Mir Cabinet Opens at Kafkas University in Kars, Turkey," *Fond Russkiy Mir* (June 29, 2012).

23. Cf. D. D. Guttenplan, "Critics Worry over Chinese Largess in U.S.," *International Herald Tribune* (March 5, 2012).

24. Guttenplan, "Critics Worry over Chinese Largess in U.S."

25. Guttenplan, "Critics Worry over Chinese Largess in U.S."

26. "What Is RIAC? General Information," RIAC, retrieved November 8, 2013, http://russiancouncil.ru/en/about-us/what_is_riac/.

27. L. V. Drachevsky, "Obrashchenie Ispolnitelnogo direktora fonda," Gorchakov Foundation, retrieved November 8, 2013, http://gorchakovfund.ru/about.

28. Drachevsky, "Obrashchenie Ispolnitelnogo direktora fonda."

29. Cf. Luke Harding, "Russia Orders British Council to Be Shut Down," *The Guardian* (December 13, 2007).

30. Ellen Barry, "Foreign-Funded Nonprofits in Russia Face New Hurdle," *The New York Times* (July 2, 2012).

31. Miriam Elder, "Russia Plans to Register 'Foreign Agent' NGOs," *The Guardian* (July 2, 2012).

32. "Alekseeva: MKhG ne budet registrirovatsya kak inosstrannyy agent," *Grani.Ru* (July 2, 2012).

33. "Oleg Orlov: 'My nikogda ne obyavim sebya inostrannymi agentami,'" *Novaya Gazeta* (October 8, 2012).

34. "Russian NGOs Threaten to Boycott Foreign Agent Law," *RT* (July 25, 2012).

35. Jadwiga Rogoża, "Russia Expels USAID," *Centre for Eastern Studies* (September 26, 2012).

36. Robert Orttung, "Kremlin Nationalism versus Russia's NGOs," *Russian Analytical Digest*, no. 138 (November 8, 2013), 9.

37. Orttung, "Kremlin Nationalism versus Russia's NGOs," 9.

38. Orttung, "Kremlin Nationalism versus Russia's NGOs," 10.

39. "FSB predlagaet uzhestochit zakon o 'Gosudarstvennoy izmene,'" *Politikus.ru* (September 21, 2012).

40. Cf. "Duma Adopts Expansion of Criminal Code Articles on Treason, Espionage at First Reading," SOVA Center for Information and Analysis (September 28, 2012).

41. "Duma Adopts Expansion of Criminal Code Articles."

42. Rachel Denber, "The Kremlin May Call It Treason," *The Huffington Post* (September 28, 2012).

43. Denber, "The Kremlin May Call It Treason."

44. "Sovet Federatsii Rossii odobril zakon o gosudarstvennoy izmene," *Golos Ameriki* (October 31, 2012).

45. Masha Gessen, "The Other Big Mac Index—Russia Goes to War with McDonald's, Soviet Style," *The New York Times* (August 28, 2014), available at http://www.nytimes.com/2014/08/29/opinion/masha-gessen-russia-goes-to-war-with-mcdonalds-soviet-style.html?_r=0.

46. Gessen, "The Other Big Mac Index."

47. As, for instance, plans to promote the Russian language in the CIS or to have five Russian universities in the world's top hundred by 2020—which will require a huge effort given the fact that in the QS World University Ranking 2012, only one Russian university had a place in the top 200 (the Lomonosov Moscow State University, at place 116). (Cf. "Rossiya nuzhna 'myagkaya sila,'" *Narodnaya Gazeta* (September 6, 2012).) In a critical article, Irina Dezhina expresses her doubts about these plans in the light of the Kremlin's attacks on the autonomy of Russian scientists. "Creating a positive image of science is problematic," she writes. "The whole world has been watching the battle between the leadership of the Russian Academy of Sciences and the Ministry of Education and Science for a long time, and this does not add respect for the country as a whole." (Cf. Irina Dezhina, "The Russian Science as a Factor of Soft Power," *Russian International Affairs Council* (June 21, 2012).

Chapter Three

"Reputation Laundering"

How Western Communication Firms Help Improve the Kremlin's Image

Mimesis and rollback are only two of the three strategies used by the Kremlin to foster Russian soft power. Of particular interest is a third strategy developed by the Kremlin: innovation. This innovation strategy has been made possible by the end of communism, the reintegration of Russia into the capitalist world economy, and its claim to be a genuine, Western-style democracy. While the Western world was a closed territory for inhabitants of the former Soviet Union, this changed after 1991. The Russian government got access to Western political fora, such as the G7 (which became the G8), Russian firms became active actors and investors on Western markets, Russian oligarchs bought expensive mansions in London or Paris and sent their children to elite Western schools, and Russian citizens traveled freely all around Europe. This opened up many new opportunities for a Kremlin-inspired soft-power strategy. Not only could the post-communist regime reconnect with the heirs of the White Russians who had fled after the Bolshevik Revolution and with communities of Orthodox believers in Western countries, it also had access equally to the services of Western companies that before 1991 would have refused to work for the Kremlin. This was the case, in particular, of Western PR and lobbying firms. Using PR firms was in itself not new. Already in the 1930s "in the United States, Hitler and Goebbels hired public relations firms in an attempt to secure favorable press coverage of the regime."[1] However, it was something completely new for post-Soviet Russia.

HIRING WESTERN LOBBYING FIRMS: THE CASES OF KISSINGER ASSOCIATES AND KETCHUM

According to Thomas Hammes, lobbying is not a neutral activity. He calls it an integral part of "fourth generation warfare": an indirect strategy to reach one's goal, which is often used by liberation movements. "A prudent planner," wrote Hammes, "will assume that parliaments and congresses of democratic nations will be natural targets. . . . Just as clearly, non-governmental groups—churches, business groups, and even lobbying firms—can be major players in shaping national policies. President Dos Santos of Angola actually hired a U.S. lobbying firm to prevent Jonas Savimbi of Unita from meeting the president of the United States."[2] In Soviet times, it would have been unthinkable that the Kremlin would—or could—hire Western lobbying firms to promote its interests. This is no longer the case. In the "normalized" post-Soviet world, the Kremlin gained access to the most prestigious lobbying and communication firms. It was also able and ready to pay the often expensive bills. These firms are highly interesting, not only because they possess the necessary know-how, but also—and maybe even more so—because they often employ former politicians, ambassadors, and other highly placed officials, who have direct personal access to government circles. Former politicians can fulfill political missions and at the same time serve the interests of their clients. Some years ago Zbigniew Brzezinski was already warning:

> It is only a question of time before a Hindu-American, Chinese-American, or Russian-American lobby also deploys substantial resources to influence congressional legislation. . . . The Russian press, for example, has candidly speculated on the potential advantages for Russia of a well-oiled Russian-American foreign policy lobby, capable of hiring lobbying firms, sponsoring research institutes, and engaging in various other promotional activities designed to advance Russian interests.[3]

Since he wrote these words, Brzezinski's prediction seems to have been fully materialized. "Moscow has already enlisted extremely influential lobbyists," writes Gregory Feifer, "including former Secretaries of State Henry Kissinger and James Baker, who has worked as a consultant for Gazprom and Russia's pipeline monopoly Transneft."[4] The case of Henry Kissinger is particularly interesting. Kissinger, a former secretary of state, has become a prominent lobbyist. He heads Kissinger Associates, an international consulting firm he founded in 1982. Kissinger is an ideal lobbyist for the Kremlin because he abstains from asking annoying questions about democracy and human rights. On China, for instance, he writes: "Western concepts of human rights and individual liberties may not be directly translatable . . . to a civilization for millennia ordered around different concepts."[5] This value relativism is highly appreciated by the Kremlin, which since Putin's rise to power has shown no special interest in promoting human rights. In 2007—one year before the Russian invasion of Georgia—Kissinger formed with former Russian prime minister Yevgeny Primakov a Russian-US working group to improve relations. This private-public initiative got the green light from the Kremlin and the Bush administration.[6] The frequency of Kremlin-sponsored efforts to hire Western communication firms only increased after Obama started his "reset" policy. Andrei Piontkovsky, a Kremlin critic and director of the Moscow-based think tank Strategic Studies Center, comments:

> The Kremlin's achievements in securing the help of Americans willing to offer their influence are equally impressive. Indeed, the Obama administration's Russia policy is being nurtured with advice from people who have no official position in the administration but close business ties to Russia and the Kremlin: Henry Kissinger, James A. Baker, Thomas Graham, and Dimitri Simes. Like [former German chancellor] Schroeder, all these people are not economically disinterested. Baker is a consultant for the two companies at the commanding heights of the Russian economy, Gazprom and Rosneft. The Kissinger Associates lobbying group, whose Russian section is headed by Graham, feeds in to the Kissinger-Primakov working group, a quasi-private-sector effort, blessed by Putin, to deepen ties between Russia and the US. It is highly instructive to read the recommendations of these people and groups, as they unobtrusively render the objectives of their Kremlin clients into a language familiar to American leaders.[7]

The "private" Kissinger-Primakov working group was established in July 2007, when it gathered for a whole day behind closed doors in Putin's presidential residence near Moscow. There was no doubt who was the initiator. "Addressing the panel's first meeting," one could read in a press release, "Putin thanked its participants for their quick response to the idea to set up such a high-level group, first aired during his April meeting with Kissinger and Primakov."[8] Apart from Kissinger, the American group consisted of former secretary of state George Schulz, former treasury secretary Robert Rubin, former senator Sam Nunn, Chevron CEO David O'Reilly, and Thomas Graham, head of the Russian department of Kissinger Associates.

In the beginning of the 1990s, between Putin and Kissinger there developed a strange kind of mutual understanding after Kissinger visited Saint Petersburg. In this period, Kissinger came to Saint Petersburg to participate in the Kissinger-Sobchak Commission, set up to attract foreign investment. "Once I met him at the airport," one can read in Putin's autobiographical book, *First Person*, "we got into the car and went to the residence. On the way, he asked me where I was from and what I was doing. He was an inquisitive old fellow."[9] Kissinger was, indeed, so inquisitive that after some questioning, he found out that Putin had worked for the KGB. Kissinger then said, reassuringly, "All decent people got their start in intelligence. I did, too."[10] Putin continued:

> Then he said something that was completely unexpected and very interesting. "You know, I am very much criticized for the position I took regarding the USSR back then. I believed that the Soviet Union should not abandon Eastern Europe so quickly. We were changing the balance in the world very rapidly, and I thought it could lead to undesirable consequences. And now I'm being blamed for that position. People say, 'See, the Soviets left, and everything's normal. You thought it was impossible.' But I really did think it was impossible." Then he thought a while and added, "Frankly, to this day I don't understand why Gorbachev did that." I had never imagined I might hear something like that from the lips of Henry Kissinger. I told him what I thought, and I will repeat it to you right now: Kissinger was right. We would have avoided a lot of problems if the Soviets had not made such a hasty exit from Eastern Europe.[11]

In that car in Saint Petersburg we could witness the meeting of two minds: on the one hand, the KGB agent who regretted the loss of empire and would make it his life's vocation to repair "the greatest geopolitical catastrophe of the twentieth century," and on the other hand, the former secretary of state to Richard Nixon, who, as an admirer of Metternich, seemed to prefer the stability of a repressive and totalitarian empire to a rapid decolonization and democratic change.[12] The mutual admiration between Putin and Kissinger was still intact in February 2012, when Putin, in an article in the *Moskovskie Novosti*, wrote: "Not long ago I spoke with H. Kissinger. We meet him regularly. And I share completely this great professional's thesis that in periods of international turbulence especially, a close and trusting collaboration between Moscow and Washington is required."[13]

Thomas Graham, head of the Russian department of Kissinger Associates, was the author of the report *Resurgent Russia and U.S. Purposes* that was published in 2009. This report was full of good advice for the new Obama administration. Graham started with an attack on Georgian President Mikheil Saakashvili. He criticized Saakashvili's "vitriolic anti-Russian rhetoric" and mentioned "Georgia's reckless military operation last August" as one of the reasons for the new administration to "cease U.S. pressure for the near-term expansion of NATO."[14] Graham also advised the Obama administration to react positively to Medvedev's proposal for a new European security architecture, adding, "If this ultimately leads to the subsuming of NATO into a larger structure over the long term, we should be prepared to accept that. America's essential goal is not securing NATO's long-term future as the central element of our engagement with Europe, no matter how valuable an instrument of U.S. policy in Europe NATO has been in the past."[15] The reader might feel an urge to rub his eyes in disbelief. But the text is unequivocal: Thomas Graham seemed not only to be ready to give the Kremlin a veto over NATO decisions but was even prepared to sacrifice NATO for an illusory entente with the Kremlin bosses. It came as no surprise, then, when on the next page he declared himself to be in favor of "Finlandizing" Ukraine.[16] The United States, he continued, should also stop criticizing Russia on human rights and the lack of democratic standards. Issues of democratic development should be "raised in a non-confrontational and non-accusatory manner," because Russia "is deeply sensitive about any appearances of interference in its domestic affairs."[17] The best way to raise these issues would be to abstain from public declarations and instead organize "discussions among experts." Thomas Graham's report is an indication of how successful the Kremlin's strategy of hiring Western lobbyists had, by now, become: the report could have been written by Vladislav Surkov or another Kremlin pundit, if not by Putin himself.

The idea of hiring Western lobbyists had already emerged in 2001 when Mikhail Lesin, the Russian media minister, declared that the country needed to groom its image abroad, unless, in his words, Russians wished to "always look like bears."[18] However, it took another five years before the idea materialized. The actual occasion was the Russian presidency of the G8 in 2006. To improve its PR, the Kremlin hired the New York–based firm Ketchum together with its Brussels-based sister organization GPlus Europe, both owned by the parent firm Omnicom. The $2 million contract was meant to improve the Kremlin's image when it was at a historical low: in January of the same year, Russia had started its gas war with Ukraine and cut off the gas supplies to that country, while in May, Moscow banned a gay march and homosexuals were beaten up by nationalists. This led to calls by US senator John McCain to boycott the Petersburg G8 summit. Ketchum sent twenty-five people to St. Petersburg to arrange interviews for journalists with Russian government leaders. They established podcasts featuring Russian officials and made a webcast of the summit with the BBC. Ketchum was satisfied with the results. The firm proudly declared that it "succeeded in helping . . . shift global views of Russia to recognize its more democratic nature."[19] Ketchum's effort in shifting the world's views of Russia's "more democratic nature" apparently boosted its reputation: the firm won a "Silver Anvil" prize from the Public Relations Society of America and a *PRWeek* Global Campaign of the Year Award for its work.

The Kremlin also was satisfied.[20] Eager to continue the collaboration, it signed in January 2007 a two-month contract worth $845,000 with Ketchum and the Washington Group, another subsidiary. The latter was the lobbying arm of Ketchum with good contacts in the US government and Congress. One of the persons involved was John O'Hanlon, a former fund-raiser for the Democratic Party. Ketchum organized interviews with Russian government officials for journalists like David Remnick, editor of the *New Yorker*, or a meeting between the editorial board of the *Wall Street Journal* and top executives of Gazprom. The apotheosis of Ketchum's efforts, however, was its successful lobbying on behalf of Putin, elected in 2007 by *Time Magazine* as "Person of the Year." (Later, *Time*'s managing editor, Richard Stengel, emphasized that being *Time*'s Person of the Year "is not and never has been an honor.") As in the case of Kissinger, the lobbying soon became overtly political, especially one year later, during the war in Georgia. "In the midst of the conflict between Russia and Georgia," writes James Kirchick, "employees for the Washington Group, including former Republican congresswoman Susan Molinari, then CEO of the firm, contacted Representative Ileana Ros-Lehtinen, her former colleague and ranking Republican member on the House Committee on Foreign Affairs, as well as staffers for Representative Joe Crowley and then-Senator Joe Biden, according to documents filed with the Department of Justice."[21] Ketchum's policy of "business as usual" with a country that in Georgia had committed a flagrant breach of international law led to internal criticism. "During Russia's war with Georgia in 2008," wrote the *New York Times*, "there was a movement in Ketchum's New York office to drop Russia as a client, according to a former Ketchum employee who requested anonymity because he was not authorized to discuss the firm."[22] The protesters did not succeed: "Those who expressed concern were placated by the Washington office, the employee said."[23] Ketchum was also helpful in setting up a web platform, called ModernRussia, the name of which was later changed to ThinkRussia (http://www.thinkrussia.com). Its home page announced that it contained material disseminated by Ketchum Inc. on behalf of the Russian Federation. After the annexation of the Crimea and the creeping invasion into eastern Ukraine in 2014, Ketchum's relationship with the Kremlin again came into the limelight. According to Kathy Jeavons, a Ketchum partner in Washington who heads Russia's account, in the summer of 2014 the number of employees working for this account had diminished from three dozen to "about ten," but the firm had no plans to stop its collaboration. According to Angus Roxburgh, a former Ketchum consultant, Ketchum's aim was to make Russia more attractive to investors, which "means helping them disguise all the issues that make it unattractive: human rights, invasions of neighboring countries, etc."[24]

The goal of the Kremlin was not only to improve its PR and communications; it had a keen interest especially in *political* lobbying. This became clear in the choice of Ketchum's Brussels-based sister organization, GPlus Europe. GPlus Europe was founded by Peter Guilford and Nigel Gardner, two former European Commission trade spokespersons. On its website, the firm claims to have a team of over fifty experts of whom "several have held senior posts in the European Commission, European Parliament or national governments." In France, GPlus is represented by Bernard Volker, who, as a former TV news presenter, is a well-known face in that country. According to the French weekly *Le Nouvel Observateur*, Volker is

> one of the key personalities of Russian propaganda in France. He is one of the representatives in Paris of GPlus, a British-Belgian firm that since 2006 has been taking care of public relations and lobbying for the Kremlin and Gazprom in Europe. For them Bernard Volker writes or rewrites Russian officials' articles in the French press, advises the Kremlin on the strategies to adopt vis-à-vis Parisian journalists, waits for interviews at the Ministry of Foreign Affairs and organises meetings between French ministers (for instance Christine Lagarde) and the chiefs of Gazprom. And in his spare time he teaches at *Sciences-Po*. On what subject? Journalism. [25]

On January 25, 2009, during the Russian-Ukrainian gas war, GPlus was suspended from the EU's lobbying register for refusing to disclose the identity of three clients. Peter Guilford, one of the founders, said the firm had confidentiality agreements with these clients. [26] In London, GPlus subcontracts to Portland, led by Tim Allan, the former deputy of Tony Blair's spin doctor Alastair Campbell, and Angus Roxburgh, the former Moscow correspondent for the BBC. [27] In his book, *The Strongman*, Roxburgh gives an *oratio pro domo* for his work for the Kremlin:

> Much of Ketchum's work involved the kind of things that most governments get done internally, by their embassies and foreign ministry—in whom the Kremlin evidently had little faith. We organised press conferences for government ministers when they travelled abroad, and provided briefing papers for them with the questions they were likely to be asked (and sometimes with the answers we thought they ought to give—though they rarely used them). We drafted articles for ministers (and even the president) which were generally redrafted out of all recognition in Moscow and became so unreadable that they were difficult to place in any newspaper. [28]

Roxburgh's narrative resembles that of a teacher complaining about a bad pupil. But was the PR work for the Kremlin as innocent and politically neutral as he suggests? In January 2012 in the United Kingdom, a controversial debate emerged in a four-part BBC2 documentary series entitled "Putin, Russia and the West." According to Vladimir Bukovsky, a former Soviet dissident who spent twelve years in Soviet prisons and who has lived in Britain since 1976, the series had a clear pro-Putin bias. The film did not discuss painful events, such as the 1999 apartment bombings in which the FSB was suspected of being involved, nor the savage war in Chechnya. No representatives of the opposition were featured in the series. Luke Harding, former correspondent of the *Guardian* in Moscow, drew attention to the link with Ketchum. The series consultant, he pointed out, was Angus Roxburgh, who worked for Ketchum between 2006 and 2009. The documentary's producer, Norma Percy, "told the *Guardian* that her production team had hired Roxburgh 'to get a foot in the door' and to persuade the notoriously suspicious Kremlin that the BBC series would be genuinely fair-minded."[29] The end result seemed, indeed, to be fair-minded enough for Moscow. In *Russia in Global Affairs*, the leading Russian foreign policy magazine, Fyodor Lukyanov writes: "The series, shown on BBC2, is good in that—in a calm and objective fashion—it shows the real person of Vladimir Putin." He does not hide his satisfaction when he concludes: "And generally the creators of 'Putin, Russia and the West' may be congratulated on the excellent work which, I hope, will also be shown on Russian television at some point. As an example of genuine objectivity and professionalism."[30]

The Kremlin's great satisfaction with the work of Western PR firms became clear from the fact that between 2006 and 2009 it paid Ketchum and the Washington Group at least $14 million for their services. Gavin Anderson, a London-based financial PR firm, was paid $5 million for representing the state gas giant Gazprom. Even the "governments" of the Georgian breakaway provinces South Ossetia and Abkhazia followed in the Kremlin's footsteps and hired their "own" PR firm: Saylor Group, based in the California city of Pasadena. It has been suggested that the fee was paid by the Kremlin.[31] Individual Russian oligarchs have also found their way to Western PR firms. When Oleg Deripaska, said to be Russia's richest oligarch and a prominent friend of Putin, was denied a visa for entry to the United States due to alleged shadowy business dealings, he hired the Global Options Group Inc., a Washington, DC–based private company, which, in turn, hired Alston and Bird, a law firm whose special counsel was former Republican presidential candidate Bob Dole. "New documents," write Mark Hollingsworth and Stewart Lansley, "obtained by the authors shed light on Dole's lobbying services for Deripaska. One invoice, dated 15 April 2004 was sent by Alston and Bird to Deripaska himself in Moscow for £45,000. The invoice was submitted for 'legal services in connection with . . . immigration' while 'Robert Dole' was the designated lawyer. In 2008 Dole himself was still actively lobbying on the oligarch's behalf."[32]

On September 12, 2013, Vladimir Putin published an op-ed in the *New York Times* titled "A Plea for Caution from Russia,"[33] warning the United States against intervening in Syria and at the same time ridiculing Obama's remark that America's ability to act against injustice around the globe was what makes the United States "exceptional." It was an important "soft-power" coup. In the article, Putin poses as a peace apostle, lecturing the United States for its tendency to use "brute force" abroad. The paper had received the article the day before, on Wednesday, September 11 (a strange coincidence: exactly the anniversary of 9/11). Eileen Murphy, a spokesperson for the *New York Times*, said that the newspaper was approached by Ketchum. The PR firm confirmed that "the opinion piece was written by

President Putin and submitted to the *New York Times* on his behalf by Ketchum for their consideration."[34] According to files of the US Department of Justice, Ketchum received $1.9 million in the first half of 2013 for promoting Russia "as a place favorable for foreign investments."[35] Apparently, for Ketchum, helping Putin in publishing this highly political op-ed was part of the package. It is telling that Putin's article, which was reproduced by many newspapers and news sites over the world, got positive reactions elsewhere. A commentator from Pakistan called it an example of how "soft power overpowers hard power."[36] For Putin, to be seen as an example of "soft power" reigning in American "hard power" must have been music to his ears.

Tim Allan, head of Portland, who admitted giving advice to Vladimir Putin, said: "All organisations are professionalising the way they communicate. When governments which have previously been secretive do that, it is not an affront to democracy. In many cases, communicating more professionally is an essential part of that process. And getting good professional ethical advice is part of it as well."[37] It is hard to see, however, how Portland's "ethical advice" did support democracy in Russia. Ultimately, not only are Western PR firms communication coaches to their dubious clients, but they become instrumental in selling their dubious policies to Western governments and audiences. *How* instrumental they can become can be seen in a peculiar case in which the French PR firm Euro RSCG played a dubious role.

A FRENCH PR FIRM AND THE POISONING OF VIKTOR YUSHCHENKO

In 2004, a very special case of intervention by a Western lobbying firm took place after the poisoning of Ukrainian presidential candidate Viktor Yushchenko during the election campaign. At that time, the French firm Euro RSCG had Viktor Pinchuk as a client. Pinchuk, a Ukrainian oligarch, is one of the richest men in Ukraine. He is married to the daughter of Leonid Kuchma, a former Ukrainian president. Pinchuk's holding, Interpipe, has a steel division that produces gas and oil pipes. Its important clients include the Russian state firms Gazprom and Rosneft. Outgoing President Kuchma and his son-in-law Pinchuk supported the pro-Russian candidate Viktor Yanukovych. The Kremlin considered these elections crucial, and there was a lot of Russian meddling. On September 5, 2004, after a meal with the head of the Ukrainian secret service, Yushchenko suddenly became severely ill. In haste he was flown to the Rudolfinerhaus, a specialized clinic in Vienna. According to Taras Kuzio, an expert, "Yushchenko's near-fatal poisoning on September 5–6, 2004, nearly succeeded as Yushchenko arrived at the Vienna clinic where he was treated with only 12 hours to spare before he could have died."[38] Professor Abraham Brouwer of the Free University of Amsterdam, where blood samples were sent, claimed that "the concentration of dioxin found in Mr Yushchenko's blood was the second highest recorded in human history."[39] On September 21, 2004, back in Kyiv, in a speech to parliament, Yushchenko declared that he had been poisoned. To refute these allegations, Viktor Pinchuk traveled to the clinic in Vienna. But he was not alone. According to the *Financial Times,*

> A team of public relations experts from Euro RSCG, part of the Paris-based Havas Group, also came to Vienna, headed by Yffic Nouvellon, who had worked with Mr Pinchuk and Ms Franchuk [Pinchuk's wife, daughter of former Ukrainian President Kuchma] in Kiev. Mr Nouvellon's team arranged a press conference where Lothar Wicke, the Rudolfinerhaus's general manager, contradicted Mr Yushchenko's poisoning allegations. Mr Nouvellon also contacted international media, including the *Financial Times,* offering evidence that Mr Yushchenko had not been poisoned. Mr Nouvellon did not reveal his connection to Mr Pinchuk, and when confronted about it insisted he did not know Mr Pinchuk and that he had never been to Kiev. Michael Zimpfer, the Rudolfinerhaus's president, said he had cut the clinic's contact with Mr Nouvellon's team after Mr Yushchenko had informed him of Euro RSCG's ties with the Kuchma family.[40]

Nouvellon was accompanied by a colleague, Ramzi Khiroun. It was Khiroun who, on September 28, 2004, organized a press conference in the private clinic. In the press release one could read that "the allegations that Viktor Yushchenko has been poisoned are totally unfounded in medical terms."[41] This was taken over by Reuters and disseminated by Reuters to the international press. "It is Yffic Nouvellon and Ramzi Khiroun, sent to Vienna by Euro RSCG, who have written this much discussed press release."[42] Viktor Pinchuk, the financier and supporter of the pro-Russian candidate Viktor Yanukovych, as well as his friends in the Kremlin knew very well the truth of the proverb "Whose bread I eat, his song I sing."

Euro RSCG worked not only for Kremlin-friendly oligarchs but also directly for the Kremlin itself. In December 2006 the Moscow correspondent of the French paper *Le Monde* reported a strange meeting. Foreign correspondents were invited to be informed about the launch of a new political party, called "A Just Russia," headed by Sergey Mironov, president of the Federation Council and a friend of Putin. The meeting was organized by two French PR firms, Euro RSCG and Bernard Krief. The new party, created in October 2006, was set up as an "opposition party" while at the same time supporting Putin. The goal of this fake opposition party was to attract leftist voters from the Communist Party. "It is a very interesting project," one of the PR people is quoted. "Because in Russia a real opposition would have no chance at all of having access to the media, you must take into account the framework created by the government."[43] The "framework created by the government" in which the French consultants were ready to work was that of Putin's fake democracy. Ultimately, it is profit and money and not morality or democratic principles that are the overriding factors. Against the background of the flexibility of Euro RSCG—its *souplesse* in accepting the conditions imposed by the Kremlin—it was no wonder that the firm was chosen to organize the communication for the "Exchange Year France-Russia" (L'Année Croisée France-Russie), a series of cultural events, organized in 2010 in both countries, which had, according to its organizer, Nicolas Chibaeff, the aim of "overcoming the clichés."[44]

However, even the most professionally conducted PR campaign cannot take away the fundamental bias in Moscow's approach: the Kremlin's efforts to build a good reputation with the help of Western communication firms is constrained by the reality on the ground. People may be duped by state-sponsored propaganda, but not indefinitely, no matter how cleverly packaged. In the end, therefore, Moscow's manipulation of the "soft-power" concept tends to turn against the masters of the Kremlin, because even the most professional PR campaign cannot circumvent the fact that the essence of "soft power" is and remains the power of *attraction*. An example of this "revenge" of real soft power was the unwillingness of Western investors to invest in Russia, despite Putin's announcement in 2012 of a bold $33 billion privatization program. Moreover, Putin's desire to turn Moscow into a financial center did not prevent Russian companies from bringing their initial public offerings to London. Andrey Kostin, chairman of the VTB group, the second-largest bank in Russia, was candid about the reasons why. He said the country was undervalued "because of its image of corruption and lack of necessity to comply with the law."[45] In the "Global Financial Centers Index 2012,"[46] Moscow ranked 64, and in the "Doing Business" ranking, published by the World Bank, the Russian Federation occupied a poor 112th place among a total of 185 countries.[47] However, this performance was still better than its results in the "Corruption Perceptions Index 2012" of Transparency International, where Russia ranked 133 among 176 countries.[48] One would expect that the Russian government would give priority to enhancing its *real* soft power by tackling the endemic corruption and by reinforcing the rule of law. Instead, it decided to do more of the same: it hired Goldman Sachs to polish Russia's image abroad. In February 2013 the bank signed a three-year contract with the Economy Ministry of the Russian Federation. Its task was "to advise on issues such as communicating government decisions and setting up meetings with investors."[49]

A PERSONAL EXPERIENCE

Let me tell here a personal experience with the work of these firms. On July 3, 2012, I published a paper on the website of the Cicero Foundation. In this paper I warned that the massive Kavkaz-2012 exercise, organized by Moscow in September 2012 in the Caucasus, could have a destabilizing effect on the countries in the region. I mentioned in this article the upcoming parliamentary elections in Georgia in which the new "Georgian Dream" coalition was participating, led by the Georgian oligarch Ivanishvili. I wrote: "The election campaign will be rude. A new opposition coalition has emerged: 'Georgian Dream,' led by Bidzina Ivanishvili, a Georgian oligarch who has made his fortune in Russia with his Unikor holding and who is an important stakeholder of Russia's gas giant, Gazprom. Ivanishvili, who has returned from Russia in 2004, has more than doubled his worth since 2004–2005 and is recently estimated by Forbes to possess \$6.4 billion. The oligarch has started to sell some assets in Russia for liquidity to pay for his political campaign."[50] Nine days later, on July 12, 2012, I received a call at the Paris bureau of the Cicero Foundation. The telephone screen showed a Brussels number. The man at the other end started speaking in French but then asked whether he could continue in Dutch. He introduced himself as Aart Van Iterson, working at Cambre Associates, a Brussels-based public relations and public affairs consultancy. His firm worked for Ivanishvili, he explained. He told that my article on Georgia had led to "a lot of email traffic between Georgia and Brussels." "In your article there are inaccuracies," he said, and he asked me whether he could meet me so that he could give me the correct information. He was even ready to come to Paris. I told him that I was willing to meet him, but not immediately. "You write that he is an important stakeholder of Gazprom," Van Iterson said. "However, he owns scarcely 1 percent of the shares." "But that 1 percent has a value of about one and a half billion dollars," I answered. "It represents a quarter of his fortune." I knew that Ivansihvili had hired communication firms in the United States and Europe to improve his image in the West, and apparently he was not happy with my article. "I am not a political adviser," Van Iterson tried to reassure me. "I work as a media adviser." He proposed again to arrange a meeting and when I said that I could not meet him because I would be traveling abroad, he suddenly asked: "Maybe you are going to Berlin?" "No," I said. "Why?" "There will be a meeting of a number of advisers," he answered, "also from Georgia." He did not give any more details. I told Van Iterson that I would be glad to receive more information and that he could send me the documentation by mail or email. I never received any documentation. Ivanishvili's "Georgian Dream" coalition won the elections. It was considered a sign of the maturity of Georgia's democracy. Possibly, it was also a sign of the effectiveness of the work of the PR firms hired by Ivanishvili.

THE VALDAI DISCUSSION CLUB: HOW IT IS USED
BY THE KREMLIN

Hiring lobbying firms has become a well-established method used by the Kremlin to influence Western elite opinion. Another method is the organization of international forums. One of these forums is the Valdai Discussion Club. On its website (http://www.valdaiclub.com) it presents itself as a "global forum for the world's leading and best-informed experts on Russia to engage in a sustained dialogue about the country's political, economic, social and cultural development." The Valdai Club, named after the Valdai Hills, a district between Moscow and Saint Petersburg, was organized for the first time in 2004 on the initiative of the Kremlin. Its objective is to invite Western "Russia experts," let them meet with their Russian counterparts, and organize "an open dialogue" with the Russian leadership. This initiative served three objectives:

- To create goodwill in Western intellectual circles
- To create an opportunity for the Russian elite for networking with Western opinion leaders
- To create a testing ground for the Kremlin's foreign policy initiatives

The first objective, *to create goodwill*, is realized by inviting Western scholars and analysts for a week in pleasant Russian surroundings and letting them mix socially with Russian colleagues. During the Valdai conference that took place from August 31 to September 7, 2010, for instance, participants enjoyed a five-day cruise aboard a ship that brought them to two islands in Northern Russia. Although the visit to the island of Valaam had to be canceled because of a storm on Lake Ladoga, there was plenty of time to socialize on board. After the cruise, the group went to Saint Petersburg and was then flown to the Black Sea tourist resort of Sochi to meet with Prime Minister Putin. This "holiday atmosphere" is an excellent means to create personal relationships between the participants, and it is certainly conducive to bringing even the fiercest critics of the Russian regime to a more positive assessment of the situation in Russia. Because the Western participants are opinion leaders in their respective countries, this will have a positive influence on the way Western publics are informed.

A second objective of the Valdai meetings is *networking*: by forging direct, personal, face-to-face contacts with Western analysts, it will be easier to contact them later for other initiatives. A third objective is to use the conference *as a testing ground*. The Kremlin is not interested in diplomatic, superficial, polite discussions. On the contrary, it wants the Western experts to express themselves freely and without any constraint. Only if Western experts say what they *really* think can the Kremlin adapt and *fine-tune* its arguments in the international arena in order to make its diplomacy more effective. For this reason, both Putin and Medvedev participated in the conferences, often in lengthy question-and-answer sessions. Undoubtedly, these sessions were afterwards meticulously analyzed by the presidential staff. The Western analysts were unconsciously being used as valuable guinea pigs and—ironically—it was especially those who were most critical of the Kremlin who were most helpful in making the Kremlin's diplomacy more effective. In order to make the Valdai conferences attractive to Western participants, some conditions had to be fulfilled. All appearance of authoritarianism and ideological one-sidedness had to be avoided. The conferences would have to be organized completely "in Western style," with "open" discussions that would come close to the ideal discussion situation, described by the sociologist Jürgen Habermas as *herrschaftsfreie Diskussion*—the unforced power of the better argument. This "openness" is achieved by inviting selected critical voices to these conferences. This might be a journalist of the *Novaya Gazeta* or a politician of the opposition, such as Vladimir Ryzhkov, who was invited to the 2009 conference. During the 2014 Valdai conference, Putin openly boasted about this "openness," telling the audience: "I hope the 'Valdai spirit' will remain—this free and open atmosphere and chance to express all manner of very different and frank opinions."[51] The Valdai formula resembles the creation of small artificial islands of "open discussion" amidst a repressive society. Creating such small islands, which operate differently from the surrounding society, is not new in Russia. During the Soviet era, centers for nuclear research and weapons development were organized in a similar way. These centers were *zakryt* (closed), completely shielded from the rest of society. Employees had high salaries and enjoyed many privileges. Another example is the new high-tech zone Skolkovo near Moscow, the pet project of former president Dmitry Medvedev, which was equally destined to be become such an artificial island. Unlike in the rest of the country, property rights of foreign investors would be guaranteed in order to attract Western capital.[52] The creation of these small islands in a repressive society—a mini *Rechtsstaat* in Skolkovo or the "free discussion" in the Valdai seminars—is, of course, as deceptive as the fake villages Prince Potemkin is said to have built to please tsarina Catherine the Great: they are not real and will function only as long as they serve the interests of the ruling elite in the Kremlin.

That the Valdai seminars *did* serve the interests of the ruling Kremlin elite became clear in September 2008, a few weeks after the Russian invasion of Georgia. Anatol Lieven, a prominent Valdai participant, writes: "During two lunches over the course of the conference, the president and prime minister of Russia spoke with us for a total of almost seven hours, answering unscripted questions without the help of aides. The foreign minister, deputy prime minister and deputy chief of the general staff spoke with us for several more hours. The chances of this happening in George Bush's Washington, or indeed most other Western capitals, are zero."[53] It seems, in my opinion, at least a little *strange* for a British analyst to accept an invitation from the Russian government only a few weeks after the Russian invasion of Georgia and only a few days after the unilateral recognition of the independence of South Ossetia and Abkhazia. Even more so since the conference included meetings with the "presidents" of the two breakaway provinces. Lieven's unequivocal pro-Kremlin stance becomes clear when, in the same article, he calls the negative US reaction to the Russian aggression "mass hysteria."[54] Other participants also mentioned the opportunity to have "open discussion" with the Russian leaders as one of the attractive aspects of the Valdai discussions. The American analyst Ariel Cohen said, for instance: "I practically do not know of a similar situation in world practice, for heads of state and governments, people so responsible and busy, to spend so much time and explain the policy of their country in such detail."[55] After the Valdai conference of 2011, Tim Wall, editor in chief of the English-language paper the *Moscow News*, wrote, in the same vein:

> It may seem sometimes to the casual observer that Vladimir Putin does not have a very high regard for the opinion of outsiders. But in fact, the opposite is true. When the prime minister outlined his vision for Russia to the Valdai Club . . . he was following an important tradition of his rule. While he may agree or disagree with his interlocutors at these dinner-inquisitions, there is plenty of evidence that Putin cares what the West thinks about Russia. . . . Putin likes to keep dissenting voices around.[56]

The participants of the Valdai conferences are clearly flattered. The Kremlin appeals to the vanity and narcissism of analysts, who dream that the prince listens to their advice—a dream that, in reality, seldom comes true. But even greater than their narcissism is their naïveté: their firm belief that the interest shown by the Kremlin in the opinions of Western analysts is a sign that the Russian leaders want to *learn* from these opinions. If the Russian leaders are eager to listen to these analysts and are prepared to discuss with them for hours, seemingly open to hearing all kinds of possible criticisms, this is only because they have a clear *interest* in these discussions. And this interest is not so much to change their policies but first to influence their Western audience and second to get a very precise and detailed picture of the prevalent Western elite opinion, which can help them to improve and fine-tune the arguments for selling their diplomatic initiatives on the Western political market.[57] Angus Roxburgh, who worked for the Kremlin as a consultant from the American PR consultancy firm Ketchum, writes: "My criticism of the participants is not that they fall for the propaganda, but that few of them—perhaps being too much in awe of him—take this unique opportunity to *argue* with Putin."[58] Roxburgh adds: "I know privately from Dmitry Peskov [Putin's spokesman] that Putin himself (who quite clearly enjoys an argument) despairs at the lack of combative questioning."[59] Roxburgh does not ask, however, *why* Putin is so interested in this "combative questioning."

I certainly do not want to call into question the moral and intellectual integrity of the majority of the Western Valdai participants. However, I would like them to consider for a moment the question addressed to them by Nikolay Petrov of the Carnegie Moscow Center: "How justified from the moral point of view is it for Western analysts to participate in Valdai, a project used as blatant propaganda by the Kremlin? . . . I hope that many participants in the Valdai meetings will decline the next Kremlin invitation."[60] In an article in the Polish paper *Gazeta Wyborcza* with the title "Putin's Useful Idiots," the Russian sociologist Lilia Shevtsova, a colleague of Petrov, criticizes the Valdai conferences, in which Western participants "wine and dine with Russia's leading 'tandem' [Putin and Medvedev]" as "one of the most effective tools for brainwashing the Western intelligentsia while using it for the Kremlin's propaganda goals." Shevtsova continued: "I think all the Valdai Club invitees must understand what kind of spectacle they are participating in. They are not stupid, after all. Some may be naïve, but not so naïve that they don't understand the purpose of the show they are taking part in and their role in it."[61]

Valdai's success seemed to be a good occasion for taking a new initiative. In 2012 the Youth Association for a Greater Europe (http://www.greater-europe.com) was founded, a nonprofit organization with "the aim to strengthen Europe's dialogue with Russia." From July 29 to August 4, 2013, the association organized its first summer seminar in Strasbourg. Almost two hundred students and graduates participated. Guest of honor was Alexander Orlov, ambassador of the Russian Federation in France. The 2014 seminar took place in Paris, while Vienna will be the venue for the meeting in 2015.

NOTES

1. Anthony Pratkanis and Elliot Aronson, *Age of Propaganda: The Everyday Use and Abuse of Persuasion* (New York: Holt, 2002), 319.

2. Thomas X. Hammes, *The Sling and the Stone: On War in the 21st Century* (St. Paul, MN: Zenith Press, 2004), 213.

3. Zbigniew Brzezinski, *Second Chance: Three Presidents and the Crisis of American Superpower* (New York: Basic Books, 2007), 197.

4. Gregory Feifer, "Why the Russia Spy Story Really Matters," *rferl.org* (July 9, 2010).

5. Henry Kissinger, *On China* (London and New York: Penguin, 2011), 426.

6. "Kissinger, Primakov to head Russia-U.S. working group-1," *RIA Novosti* (April 26, 2007).

7. Andrei Piontkovsky, "It's All Business between US and Russia," *Gulfnews.com* (June 2, 2009).

8. "Kissinger-led U.S. Group Attends Closed Debate at Putin Home," *RIA Novosti* (July 13, 2007).

9. Vladimir Putin, *First Person: An Astonishingly Frank Self-Portrait by Russia's President Vladimir Putin* (New York: Public Affairs, 2000), 80.

10. Putin, *First Person*, 81.

11. Putin, *First Person*, 81.

12. In the 1970s, Kissinger's boss, Richard Nixon, was already arguing that "the only time in the history of the world that we have had any extended periods of peace is when there has been a balance of power. It is when one nation becomes infinitely more powerful in relation to its potential competitors that the danger of war arises." (Quoted in Joseph S. Nye Jr., *The Paradox of American Power: Why the World's Only Superpower Can't Go It Alone* (Oxford and New York: Oxford University Press, 2002), 12.) Joseph Nye comments: "But whether such multipolarity would be good or bad for the United States and for the world is debatable. I am skeptical."

13. Vladimir Putin, "Rossiya i menyayushchiysya mir," *Moskovskie Novosti* (February 27, 2012).

14. Thomas Graham, "Resurgent Russia and U.S. Purposes: A Century Foundation Report," Century Foundation, New York and Washington (2009), 23.

15. Graham, "Resurgent Russia," 24.

16. Graham, "Resurgent Russia," 25. Graham's plea in favor of a Finlandization of Ukraine was only a consequence of his opinion that "a robust Russian presence throughout the former Soviet space serves U.S. interests in building stable balances." (Cf. Thomas Graham, "U.S.-Russian Relations: Towards a Strategy beyond the Reset," *Expert* (September 6, 2010).) In an article in *The American Interest* in 2012, Graham repeats this wish for a "robust Russian presence" in the former Soviet space. "To ease Moscow's concerns," he writes, "Washington would have to acknowledge that the threat to its own interests is not Russia's resurgence, but rather Russia's withdrawal from the former Soviet space." (Thomas Graham, "Putin, the Sequel," *The American Interest* 7, no. 4 (March/April 2012), 57.)

17. Graham, "Resurgent Russia," 30.

18. Quoted in Claire Bigg, "Russia: Kremlin Hoping to Speak West's Language," *RFERL* (June 9, 2006).

19. Quoted in James Kirchick, "Pravda on the Potomac," *The New Republic* (February 18, 2009).

20. However, not all Russian analysts shared the Kremlin's satisfaction with the results obtained by Ketchum. Georgy Filimonov, for instance, wrote: "Also, the foreign public relations agencies hired under state contracts were not very effective. In particular, this applies to the agency Ketchum. Which the Russian presidential staff in 2006 asked to provide a positive news background during Russia's presidency of the Group of Eight in 2006." (Georgy Filimonov, "Russia's Soft Power Potential," *Russia in Global Affairs* (December 25, 2010).)

21. Kirchik, "Pravda on the Potomac." In November 2008, the Washington Group merged with Clark & Weinstock, another Washington-based lobbying firm owned by the Omnicom Group. In a Ketchum news release, the new firm is said to create "an extraordinary package of Democratic and Republican advocates with experience in the House, Senate and executive branch." ("Clark & Weinstock and The Washington Group Merge," Ketchum, news release (November 14, 2008).)

22. Ravi Somaiya, "P.R. Firm for Putin's Russia Now Walking a Fine Line," *The New York Times* (August 31, 2014).

23. Somaiya, "P.R. Firm for Putin's Russia."

24. Somaiya, "P.R. Firm for Putin's Russia."

25. Vincent Jauvert, "Nos amis du Kremlin," *Le Nouvel Observateur* (February 25, 2010).

26. Roman Kupchinsky, "Russia's Hired Lobbies in the West," *Eurasia Daily Monitor* 6, no. 148 (August 3, 2009).

27. Cf. David Teather, "PR Groups Cash In on Russian Conflict," *The Guardian* (August 24, 2009).

28. Angus Roxburgh, *The Strongman: Vladimir Putin and the Struggle for Russia* (London and New York: I.B. Taurus, 2012), 186.

29. Luke Harding, "BBC Criticised over 'Pro-Putin' Documentary," *The Guardian* (February 1, 2012).

30. Fyodor Lukyanov, "Putin, Russia and the West: Beyond Stereotype," *Russia in Global Affairs* (February 12, 2012).

31. Teather, "PR Groups Cash In on Russian Conflict."

32. Mark Hollingsworth and Stewart Lansley, *Londongrad: From Russia with Cash—The Inside Story of the Oligarchs* (London: Fourth Estate, 2010), 335–336.

33. Vladimir V. Putin, "A Plea for Caution from Russia," *The New York Times* (September 12, 2013).

34. Alec Luhn and Adam Gabbatt, "Vladimir Putin Wrote 'Basic Content' of New York Times Op-Ed, Spokesman Says," *The Guardian* (September 12, 2013).

35. Luhn and Gabbatt, "Vladimir Putin Wrote 'Basic Content.'"

36. Alauddin Masood, "Soft Power Overpowers Hard Power," *weeklypulse.org* (October 14, 2013), retrieved October 30, 2013.

37. Quoted in Gideon Spanier, "Reputation Launderers: The London PR Firms with Their Own Image Problem," *London Evening Standard* (March 30, 2011).

38. Taras Kuzio, "State-Led Violence in Ukraine's 2004 Elections and Orange Revolution," *Communist and Post-Communist Studies*, no. 43 (2010).

39. Cf. Tom Warner, "Yushchenko Links Poison to Meal with Secret Police," *Financial Times* (December 16, 2004).

40. Warner, "Yushchenko Links Poison to Meal."

41. Cf. Ariane Chemin, "Quand Khiroun 'niait' l'empoisonnement de Ioutchenko," *Le Nouvel Observateur* (April 22, 2010).

42. Chemin, "Quand Khiroun 'niait.'"

43. Millot Lorraine, "Une Opposition Russe . . . Pro-Poutine," *Le Monde* (December 6, 2006).

44. "Quand les Etats font leur pub," *France 24* (December 11, 2010).

45. Jason Corcoran, "Russia Hires Goldman as Corporate Broker to Boost Image," *Bloomberg* (February 5, 2013).

46. "The Global Financial Centres Index 12" (September 2012), available at http://www. longfinance.net/Publications/GFCI%2012.pdf.

47. "Doing Business 2013—Comparing Business Regulations for Domestic Firms in 185 Economies" (Washington, DC: International Bank for Reconstruction and Development/The World Bank), 190.

48. "Corruption Perceptions Index 2012," Transparency International.

49. Jason Corcoran, "Russia Hires Goldman as Corporate Broker to Boost Image."

50. Cf. Marcel H. Van Herpen, "2012: A New Assault on Georgia? The Kavkaz-2012 Exercises and Russian War Games in the Caucasus," Cicero Foundation Great Debate Paper No. 12/04, (July 2012), available at http://www.cicerofoundation.org/lectures/Marcel_H_Van_ Herpen_2012_ASSAULT_ON_GEORGIA.pdf.

51. "Vladimir Putin Meets with Members of the Valdai International Discussion Club: Transcript of the Final Plenary Session," *Valdai Discussion Club* (October 25, 2014), http:// valdaiclub.com/valdai_club/73300/print_edition/.

52. Medvedev spoke, for instance, about "the possibility of establishing a special intellectual property rights court within our arbitration court system and have it located at Skolkovo." See "Joint Meeting of Commission for Modernisation and Skolkovo Fund Board of Trustees," official site of the President of Russia (April 25, 2011), http://eng.special.kremlin.ru/state/ news/2126.

53. Anatol Lieven, "Lunch with Putin," *The National Interest* (September 17, 2008).

54. In another article, Lieven wrote that "US policy has encouraged Georgia to attack Russia and thereby endanger and destabilize itself." (Anatol Lieven, "How Obama Can Reform Russia Policy," *The Nation* (January 12, 2009).) Here, Lieven's Kremlin-friendly attitude brings him to write an outright lie. How could Georgia "attack" Russia when there was not one single Georgian soldier in Russia but thousands of Russian troops in the territory of Georgia? It is no wonder that shortly after its publication, this article was reproduced by an official, Kremlin-related Abkhaz website. Cf. http://www.abkhazworld.com/articles/analysis/162-obama-russia-policy.html.

55. Quoted in Lilia Shevtsova, *Lonely Power: Why Russia Has Failed to Become the West and the West Is Weary of Russia* (Washington and Moscow: Carnegie Endowment for International Peace, 2010), 101.

56. Tim Wall, "Putin's De Gaulle Moment," *The Moscow News* (November 14, 2011).

57. Two Valdai participants from the United States, Fiona Hill and Clifford Gaddy, seemed to grasp this when they wrote: "He [Putin] . . . views other individuals as sources of raw intelligence. He does not seem to rely on others for direct counsel or interpretation of people or events." (Fiona Hill and Clifford Gaddy, "Putin and the Uses of History," *The National Interest*, no. 117 (Jan./Feb. 2012), 31.) They added that Putin acts according to the principles: "Don't destroy your enemies. Harness them. Control them. Manipulate them, and use them for your own goals" (30).

58. Roxburgh, *The Strongman*, 195.

59. Roxburgh, *The Strongman*, 195.

60. Lilia Shevtsova, *Lonely Power*, 98.

61. Lilia Shevtsova, "Pożyteczni idioci Putina," *Gazeta Wyborcza* (September 6, 2010).

Chapter Four

The Propaganda Offensive in the Western Media, Part I

The Creation of Russia Today (RT), Russia beyond the Headlines, and Rossiya Segodnya

OVERT AND COVERT PROPAGANDA

In the Soviet era, the Kremlin was already making use of different channels to disseminate its overt and covert propaganda. The official channels were radio broadcasts in foreign languages by Radio Moscow, press releases distributed by the Soviet press agencies TASS and RIA Novosti, publications of books and brochures in foreign languages, and the distribution of cheap, glossy magazines. One of these was *Soviet Union*, which had editions in several languages. The magazine proudly presented the achievements of state socialism and showed full-color pictures of pretty blonde Komsomol girls with red neck scarves in impeccable uniforms. One could read reportages on model *kolchoz* farms accompanied by photos of endless fields of waving, ripe corn. There were also stories on Russian *kosmonavty*, these latest "Soviet hero" specimens, floating weightlessly in their mighty Soyuz spaceships. The problem with this kind of propaganda was that it was consumed by those who did not need to be converted. The same was true of another, more indirect means of propaganda: the communist press in Western Europe. It was read by those who were supposed to be susceptible to its message. More interestingly, therefore, was *covert* propaganda, which was disseminated by front organizations that were not openly communist but were controlled by the Soviet Union or by communist "sister" parties. These organizations worked under the guise of innocent labels, such as "World Peace Council" or

"Medical Committee Vietnam," which ensured that the identity of those who provided the information remained unknown.

However, the best propaganda was that of so-called fellow travelers: notorious noncommunists—often liberal, individualist intellectuals and artists—who, although critical of their own governments, displayed a great naïveté vis-à-vis the Soviet regime, for which they functioned as "useful idiots." A well-known example of this category was George Bernard Shaw, a British author and Nobel laureate in literature, who visited Stalin's Soviet Union in 1932—precisely at the time of the Holodomor in Ukraine, a manipulated famine in which millions of people, many of them young children, died. After his return to Britain, Shaw attacked "the intensity of the blind and reckless campaign to discredit [Russia]." This "lie campaign" was, according to Shaw, far from deserved: "Everywhere we saw hopeful and enthusiastic working-class, self-respecting, free up to the limits imposed on them by nature . . . , developing public works, increasing health services, extending education, achieving the economic independence of woman and the security of the child . . . setting an example of industry and conduct which would greatly enrich us if our systems supplied our workers with any incentive to follow it."[1] Winston Churchill commented on Shaw's visit to Stalin's Russia with cold irony: "Here was the World's most famous intellectual Clown and Pantaloon in one," he wrote, "and Arch Commissar Stalin, 'the man of steel,' flung open the closely-guarded sanctuaries of the Kremlin, and pushing aside his morning's budget of death warrants, and *lettres de cachet*, received his guests with smiles of overflowing comradeship."[2] In 1935 two other famous Britons, Shaw's fellow Fabian socialists Sydney and Beatrice Webb, followed in his steps and published a booklet entitled *Soviet Communism: A New Civilization?* In this pamphlet they denied that Stalin was a dictator. However, one should note that at that time, apart from the support of these individuals and the local communist parties, Soviet propaganda had practically no access to the Western mass media.

This situation changed dramatically after the fall of communism. Because of its conversion to capitalism and a Western-style democracy, Russia was no longer an international outcast. It became overnight—if not an ally and completely friendly power[3]—a more or less "normal" country. It gained almost unrestricted access to Western markets and—helped by its newly acquired wealth—it was soon able to buy itself a place in the Western media landscape. Agitprop (agitation and propaganda) was one of the main departments of the Central Committee of the Soviet Communist Party. Putin had no known equivalent of this *otdel agitatsii i propagandy*,[4] this former Soviet propaganda department, but propaganda remained one of the spearheads of his regime. The ideological supremacy of the Western world and of the United States in particular during the Cold War had convinced the Russian leadership of the importance of soft power. At home, as well as in the Warsaw Pact countries, the Soviet Union had always relied disproportionately on its military might. The concept of "soft power" was then still unknown. According to Nye, "A country may obtain the outcomes it wants in world politics because other countries want to follow it, admiring its values, emulating its example, aspiring to its level of prosperity and openness."[5] "This aspect of power," he writes, "getting others to want what you want—I call soft power."[6] Soft power is for Nye not the exclusive trump card of the rich and democratic Western countries. He admits that "the Soviet Union had a good deal of soft power, but," he adds, "it lost much of it after the invasions of Hungary and Czechoslovakia. Soviet soft power declined even as its hard economic and military resources continued to grow. Because of its brutal policies, the Soviet Union's hard power actually undercut its soft power."[7] He concludes: "A closed system, lack of an attractive popular culture, and heavy-handed foreign policies meant that the Soviet Union was never a serious competitor with the United States in soft power during the Cold War."[8] What came closest to soft power during the Soviet era was the communist ideology. However, after the public denunciation of Stalinist atrocities by Khrushchev, this ideology gradually lost its attractiveness. During Brezhnev's reign it had become an obsolete legitimation theory totally unrelated to the bureaucratic reality of a semitotalitarian state.

When Putin became president, the soft-power potential of Russia had reached its nadir. The country was virtually bankrupt. In the North Caucasus it was confronted with an unruly and de facto independent Chechen Republic. The Russian population was plagued by alcoholism and a rampant AIDS epidemic, resulting in demographic decline. However, when oil and gas prices went up, the newly acquired wealth offered new chances. Moreover, Russia fully took these chances. In the first decade of the twenty-first century, one could witness one of the most impressive soft-power offensives ever conducted by the Kremlin. Russia, write Popescu and Wilson, "not usually considered particularly adept at the use of soft power—has learned the power of incentives as well as of coercion."[9] They add: "Its soft power is built on a bedrock of historical and cultural affinity—the presence of Russian minorities in neighbourhood countries, the Russian language, post-Soviet nostalgia and the strength of the Russian Orthodox Church."[10] These authors rightly emphasize that the turning point came with the Orange Revolution in Ukraine in 2004, which triggered a fundamental tactical rethink by Russia: "Drawing its lessons from the central role played by civil society groups and NGOs in the Orange revolution, Russia began developing a rival 'counter-revolutionary' ideology, supporting 'its' NGOs, using 'its' web technologies, and exporting its own brands of political and economic influence. Gleb Pavlovsky [a Kremlin adviser] described the Orange revolution as 'a very useful catastrophe for Russia. We learnt a lot.'"[11]

In the previous chapter we have already seen how the Kremlin contracted Western PR firms and began to organize the Valdai series of high-level seminars and conferences for international experts. However, in order to conduct its propaganda offensive, the Kremlin had a much broader panoply of instruments at its disposal. These included:

- Disseminating official Russian state propaganda *directly* abroad via foreign-language news channels, making use of TV and the internet;
- Disseminating official Russian state propaganda *indirectly* via *Western* media;
- Takeovers of Western papers;
- Gaining a hold over the new social networks and setting up Kremlin-friendly websites;
- An active presence in blogs and discussion forums, as well as the publication of organized postings by "Kremlin trolls" on the websites of Western papers;
- Financing Western politicians and/or political parties;
- Reactivating spy rings, which had the task to penetrate influential political circles; and
- Activating the Russian Orthodox Church as a soft-power tool.

In this chapter we will analyze the first five of the above-mentioned strategies, which all had the task to influence—directly or indirectly—the Western media landscape.

RUSSIA TODAY (RT): CONSPIRACY THEORIES AND WEIRDLY CONSTRUCTED PROPAGANDA

In May 2005, just one month after Putin had delivered his famous speech in which he called the demise of the Soviet Union "the greatest geopolitical catastrophe of the twentieth century," the Kremlin announced the launch of a new Kremlin-sponsored international TV news channel. The idea came from Putin's press minister, Mikhail Lesin. This new twenty-four-hour English-language channel, called "Russia Today"—later known by the abbreviation RT—had the task of becoming a global competitor of CNN, BBC World, and Al Jazeera. The newly appointed editor in chief was Margarita Simonyan, a twenty-five-year-old ethnic Armenian born in Krasnodar in southern Russia. Between 2002 and 2005, Simonyan was a member of the prominent Kremlevskiy Pul, the "Kremlin Pool"—a Russian equivalent of the US White House Press Corps—where she represented Rossiya, the second-largest state television network. To become a member of this press pool, a journalist was not expected to excel at critical thinking nor even set himself or herself the minimum professional goal of impartial, objective fact finding. On the contrary, one had to be extremely loyal and trustworthy. Journalists who were admitted to this exclusive inner circle had completely interiorized the objectives of their Kremlin masters. They were convened every Friday by Vladislav Surkov, the deputy chief of the presidential administration, to discuss and "prepare" the news for the coming week.

The newly appointed Simonyan, helped by a team of equally young journalists, started her new job with great energy. After three months of rehearsal, the channel went live on December 10, 2005. The Kremlin was ready for a huge effort and assigned large sums to the project. In 2005, $23 million were invested in launching the channel, with an additional budget of $47 million. In 2007, the budget went up to $80 million. In 2008, this was increased by 50 percent to $120 million. In 2011, this already sizable sum more than *tripled* when $380 million were assigned.[12] The Russian opposition politician Garry Kasparov commented: "There are certain rules of any dictatorship: never save money on police or propaganda."[13] The results of this "propaganda war effort" were, indeed, impressive. In 2011 RT had grown into an organization with a staff of two thousand employees worldwide, reporting from twenty bureaus. Amongst this staff was included an office with about one hundred personnel in Washington. RT's global staff had become larger than that of Fox News, which has worldwide a staff of about 1,200. In 2009 Nielsen Media Research found that viewers in the Washington, D.C., area preferred to watch prime-time news on Russia Today rather than on other foreign English-language networks, including Al Jazeera, France 24, and Deutsche Welle.[14] In 2013 two million Britons watched RT regularly, and its online presence was "more successful than those of all its competitors. What's more, in June [2013], Russia Today broke a YouTube record by being the first TV station to get a billion views of its videos."[15] RT did not confine itself to broadcasting in English but also offered programs in Arabic and Spanish. After the annexation of the Crimea in March 2014 and the Russian invasion of eastern Ukraine in August 2014, the Kremlin decided to focus on the two leading European countries, Germany and France. A German-language channel was planned for launch in 2015, and RT's budget was increased by $39 million to fund its expansion into French.[16] "The focus on Germany and France," writes the *Wall Street Journal*, "reflects the Kremlin's attempts to open a gap between Europe and the U.S., and between the European public and its governments, over how to respond to the Ukraine crisis."[17]

But what about the *contents* of RT's programs? In the first years of its existence, Russia Today aimed at improving Russia's image abroad and concentrated on information programs about Russia. These programs stressed Russia's positive points: its unique culture, its ethnic diversity, its role in World War II, and so on. RT also reported on Russia's "modernization," featuring new shopping malls and newly built highways. However, most of the time viewers would seek in vain for reliable information on more critical subjects, such as election fraud, corruption by government officials, the repression of demonstrations, the frequent murders of journalists, the lack of independence within the judiciary, and the HIV epidemic. This absence of reliable, balanced, and objective information turned into active disinformation during the Russian invasion of Georgia in August 2008. Julia Ioffe writes: "Russia Today correspondents in Ossetia found that much of their information was being fed to them from Moscow, whether it corresponded to what they saw on the ground or not. Reporters who tried to broadcast anything outside the boundaries that Moscow had carefully delineated were punished."[18] She continues: "Another correspondent, whose reporting departed from the Kremlin line that Georgians were slaughtering unarmed Ossetians, was summoned to the office of the deputy editor in chief in Moscow, where they went over the segment's script line by line. 'He had a gun on his desk,' the correspondent says."[19] Shaun Walker, the Moscow correspondent of the *Independent*, gives the following opinion on RT's coverage of the war in Georgia: "The channel's coverage of Russia's war with Georgia was particularly obscene. With Western TV networks hooked on a 'New Cold War' headline and often not too well versed in the nuances of the region, there was a gap in the market for a balanced view of the conflict that explained Russia's position. Instead, RT blasted 'GENOCIDE' across its screens for most of the war's duration, produced a number of extraordinarily biased packages, and instructed reporters not to report from Georgian villages within South Ossetia that had been ethnically cleansed."[20]

From 2009 onward, the focus of Russia Today began to change. From a *defensive* soft-power weapon, RT began to develop into an *offensive* weapon. RT began to report on the negative sides of the West, especially of the United States. Favorite news items included the growing social inequality, the fate of homeless people, mass unemployment, human rights violations, and the consequences of the banking crisis. Anchors of RT programs (such as Peter Lavelle) did not hide their explicit anti-American views. RT also started inviting representatives of marginal, often extreme right antigovernment groups, who were presented as "experts." One of these groups was the so-called 9/11 truthers, people who believe that the 9/11 attacks were not the work of al-Qaeda terrorists but a US government conspiracy. Luke Rudkowski, the founder of We Are Change, who purports "to seek the truth" behind 9/11, was invited for an extensive interview. "Truthers" like him were invited on several occasions. Another group was the "birthers," people who doubted—against all evidence—that President Obama was born in the United States and denied that he was eligible to be US president. One of these was James David Manning, a pastor of a Harlem church, who saw "pure evil" in Obama.[21] RT's "experts" also included Malik Zulu Shabazz, the leader of the New Black Panther Party, a hate group. Another invited pundit was Daniel Estulin, who considered the European Union to be the realization of a secret plan invented by the Bilderberg Group and who also claimed that the US government was building thirteen secret bases in Afghanistan for the forward push to an eventual war against Russia.[22] The same penchant for conspiracy theories was revealed in the RT program *The Truthseeker*, which suggested that the US government was behind the terrorist attack on the Boston Marathon in April 2013, in which two ethnic Chechens killed three people.[23] Manuel Ochsenreiter, a guest speaker about German affairs on RT's English-language channel, is actually the editor of the neo-Nazi magazine *Zuerst!*, a monthly radical-right magazine that pledges "to serve German—not foreign—interests" and speaks out against "de-nazification."[24]

For James Miller this is problematic, "as RT used Ochsenreiter to defend Russia's invasion of Crimea, an invasion which the Kremlin said was done to defend the peninsula against neo-Nazis."[25] Another RT guest, Ryan Dawson, who was presented as a "human rights activist," was in reality a Holocaust denier who wrote blogs about anti-Semitic ideas.[26] The *Economist*, in an article with the title "Russia Today Goes Mad," does not hesitate to qualify RT's programs as "weirdly constructed propaganda," characterized by "a penchant for wild conspiracy theories."[27] To attract new viewers, the channel also did not hesitate to use methods that were far from subtle. It was, for instance, running full-page ads featuring Josef Stalin in a general's uniform, armed with a writer's quill in his hand. "Stalin wrote romantic poetry," the ad states. "Did you know that?" The German magazine *Der Spiegel* comments: "It's about as subtle a message as a scenario in which German international broadcaster Deutsche Welle were to advertise with Hitler and the question: 'Did you know that Adolf Hitler also painted?'"[28] On another occasion, RT published ads on billboards in the United Kingdom featuring the face of Barack Obama morphing into that of Iranian President Mahmoud Ahmadinejad with the text: "Who poses the greater nuclear threat?" In US airports these ads were banned. In August 2014, during the crisis in Ukraine, another aggressive poster campaign was launched around New York, featuring the text: "In case they shut us down on TV—Go to RT.com for the second opinion." The poster was accompanied by a second one, denouncing the former US government's claims that Saddam Hussein possessed weapons of mass destruction.[29]

One may conclude that RT has become a full-fledged propaganda tool of the Kremlin. It has acquired free access to Western audiences without being bothered by Western nations' regulations which prescribe impartiality rules (in Britain, for instance, Ofcom's Broadcasting Code, section 5, on Due Impartiality and Due Accuracy and Undue Prominence of Views and Opinions). In 2012, despite its lack of impartiality and its reputation for being a

Kremlin mouthpiece, RT succeeded in hiring WikiLeaks founder Julian Assange to present a series of talk shows. In May 2013 RT even signed a contract with former CNN anchor Larry King to present two programs.[30] RT's propaganda is supported by other media, such as *Russia Profile*, an internet paper. The Kremlin's international radio station, the Voice of Russia, a revived version of Radio Moscow of Soviet times, also got a facelift. By presidential decree of December 9, 2013, it was merged with the news agency RIA Novosti and became part of a new entity called Rossiya Segodnya. The new international radio station was rebaptized into "Radio Sputnik" and became part of a broader platform, "Sputnik News," which has also an online presence. The new radio station began to broadcast on November 10, 2014. The Kremlin's propaganda effort, however, is not restricted to these initiatives. It has found other and quite unexpected ways of influencing Western public opinion, as we will see below.

RUSSIA BEYOND THE HEADLINES: NEW METHODS TO BUILD SOFT POWER

Apart from RT, another important project to disseminate official Russian state propaganda in the West is "Russia beyond the Headlines" (http://www.rbth.ru), which started in 2007. It consists of the publication of newspaper supplements by the *Rossiyskaya Gazeta* (*Russian Paper*). This is the official Kremlin paper in which laws and decrees are published and the official views of the regime are ventilated. From the beginning, the propaganda project was very ambitious. Once a month, an eight-page supplement is added to a group of highly influential Western papers, including the *Washington Post* (United States), the *New York Times* (United States), the *Daily Telegraph* (United Kingdom), *Le Figaro* (France), *Repubblica* (Italy), *El Pais* (Spain), and the *Süddeutsche Zeitung* (Germany). There are also arrangements with leading papers in India, Brazil, Argentina, Bulgaria, and Serbia. The title of this paid supplement is *Russia Now* in the United States and the United Kingdom, *La Russie d'Aujourd'hui* in France, *Russland Heute* in Germany, *Russia Oggi* in Italy, and *Rusia Hoy* in Spain. The supplements' titles are in fact the same as the former full name of the Kremlin's TV channel RT. The different supplements have their own websites, which can be reached via links on the official websites of the respective papers. When the project started in 2007, an American journalist made an ironical comment. He wrote that "it's a bad sign for the Putin regime if it thinks this expensive PR exercise will elicit anything but laughter from the West."[31] But in the meantime, the Kremlin has not only learned a lot, it has also begun *to spend* a lot. "In 2011," writes Luke Harding, "the Russian government will spend $1.4 billion on international propaganda—more than on fighting unemployment."[32] And one has to admit that this spending spree is beginning to show an impact.

The supplements of *Russia Now* have an attractive layout and offer a mix of sport, culture, *faits divers*, Russian cuisine, and serious information. The most important lesson the publishers have learned is to make the supplement resemble a Western newspaper. This means that you will not find any straightforward Kremlin propaganda in it. On the contrary, criticism of the Kremlin leaders sometimes takes a prominent place. Difficult topics, such as the Khodorkovsky trial or the suppression of demonstrations by the opposition, are not avoided. In the February 2011 supplement to the French *Le Figaro*, for instance, the opposition politician Vladimir Ryzhkov is quoted, and, similarly, one could find an interview with the Russian writer Lyudmila Ulitskaya, who talks about her correspondence with the jailed oligarch Mikhail Khodorkovsky and praises him as "brilliant" and "an outstanding businessman," qualifications normally rather found in the Russian opposition paper *Novaya Gazeta*. After the rigged Duma elections of December 2011 and the subsequent massive protest rallies, in the December supplement of that year political life in Russia was said to have "become more lively" because of these events, a description that would certainly not have the same positive connotations in the Kremlin as in the West. A Western reader could, therefore, easily get the impression of reading a "normal" paper. And that is what it is all about. The "critical" texts in the supplement are meant to mollify the Western reader so that he is also ready to take in the other texts.

In fact, here two stratagems are used to manipulate Western readers. The first stratagem is to diminish their cognitive dissonance by adapting the contents and the style of the articles to fit their "critical" Western mind.[33] The second stratagem is an application of the *two-step flow of communication* theory of the sociologist Paul Lazarsfeld. This is the theory that information delivered by the mass media does not find its way *directly* to the broader public but is rather channeled *indirectly* to it via opinion leaders. For this reason, it is especially the Western quality newspapers that are targeted by the Kremlin's soft-power offensive. In fact, it is a modern form of the old agitprop. The project "Russia beyond the Headlines" is, as in former Soviet times, a living example of "active disinformation." The "critical" articles that are published in the supplements for a Western public would never stand a chance of being published in their mother paper, *Rossiyskaya Gazeta*. Their only function is to give the Kremlin a "liberal" image—an old strategy of which the KGB has always been a real master: for instance, after the repressive KGB chief Yury Andropov was appointed general secretary, the KGB presented him as a modern, Western-style, jazz-loving whisky drinker. Andropov had kidney problems and drank no alcohol.

THE KREMLIN ASSAULT ON RIA NOVOSTI

On Monday, December 9, 2013, President Putin issued a decree ordering the liquidation of RIA Novosti, the state-owned Russian news agency. According to the *Moscow Times*, Sergey Ivanov, the head of the Kremlin administration, "justified the decision to shut the agency on financial grounds, while also admitting to the 'soft power' purposes behind its replacement."[34] It is interesting that Ivanov also mentioned "soft power" as one of the reasons for this Kremlin "coup." It reveals—once more—the Kremlin's idiosyncratic way of defining "soft power": rather as official state propaganda than as the result of attractive policies. "Russia is pursuing an independent policy, firmly protecting its national interests and explaining this to the world is not easy, but it can and must be done," said Ivanov.[35] Explaining that a country is "firmly protecting its national interests and [is] explaining this to the world" has not much to do with soft power. Vladimir Zhirinovsky, the leader of the extreme-right Liberal-Democratic Party, came closer to the truth when he said that what was at stake here was building "more powerful ideological centers, propaganda centers."[36]

In actual fact, RIA Novosti, despite being a state-owned news agency, had a reputation for being quite objective as a news provider—which was not to the liking of the Kremlin, which needed a more powerful Kremlin voice in the international arena. RIA Novosti employed about 2,300 staff and had offices in sixty-nine Russian cities. It had an international presence in forty-nine countries. The agency, as such, did not disappear. It was simply renamed and revamped. The new name is Rossiya Segodnya, which means "Russia Today." This is also the former name of the Kremlin's international cable TV station RT. There were, however, no plans to merge RIA Novosti with RT (only with the international radio station the Voice of Russia). RIA Novosti's new name is, therefore, in effect the product of a lack of imagination on the part of the Kremlin bureaucrats. Svetlana Mironyuk, RIA Novosti's editor in chief, who, over the past decade, built the agency into a modern and highly professional organization, has been replaced by Dmitry Kiselyov, a popular television host on Russia's state-owned Channel One. Kiselyov, who presents the talk show *The National Interest*, certainly in the eyes of the Kremlin is the right man for the Kremlin's new soft-power offensive. A loyal Putin supporter, he is known for his praise of Stalin and his homophobia. In 2012 he said the hearts of gay organ donors collected after fatal car crashes should be "buried or incinerated as unsuitable to prolong someone's life."[37] In late June 2014, Kiselyov cast the Ukraine conflict as an echo of the run-up to World War I, which he described as engineered by Washington and London to decimate their adversaries on the continent. "Now, just as back then, the English and the Americans have the common goal of making enemies of Germany and Russia and thus to exhaust them," Kiselyov told his viewers.[38]

These remarks came after having reminded his audience already in March 2014 that Russia was capable of "turning the U.S. into radioactive ash."[39] It is telling that a news agency which, on the basis of its objectivity and professionalism, has succeeded in building real soft power abroad was replaced by the Kremlin with a clone of the former Soviet agitprop agencies.

This policy of creeping resovietization of Russia's media sphere was also evident when, on September 1, 2014, the director of the news agency ITAR-TASS, Sergey Mikhailov, announced that the agency would return to its historical name TASS (without the prefix ITAR), a strange decision because the acronym TASS stood for Telegraph Agency of the *Soviet Union* and the Soviet Union no longer exists. To give this former mouthpiece of Soviet state propaganda a new credibility, the acronym ITAR (Information Telegraph Agency of Russia) was added in 1992. According to Jefim Fistein, former director of Radio Free Europe/Radio Liberty's Russian Service, this odd name change is deliberate: "For many people now, the Soviet past, paradoxically, reflects the happy future of present-day Russia. . . . They don't expect a happy future to come in the form of modernization or in the form of approaching the Westernized world. For them, the future lies in the Soviet past of Russia."[40] This return to the Soviet past could also be observed in the attack in 2014 on one of the remaining independent media, Dozhd (Rain) TV. On the seventieth anniversary of the lifting of the siege of Leningrad, the station organized a debate on the question of whether the surrender of Leningrad would have saved millions of lives—a debate which is legitimate, because Stalin's decision to defend the city to the bitter end, notwithstanding the tremendous civilian death toll, is criticized by many historians. However, in the Russian national consciousness, the siege of Leningrad has become an epic event of mythical proportions, and a debate on this question is taboo. The public outrage was a good pretext for the authorities to curtail this independent news outlet: "Major cable and satellite TV operators began to pull the plug. The station's audience fell from 20 million to just 2 million, as broadcasters abandoned the channel."[41] According to Mikhail Zygar of Dozhd TV, "The owners of all those companies, operators, told us privately that that's not their wish. . . . They were asked to do it by phone call, by someone from the Kremlin."[42]

NOTES

1. George Bernard Shaw, "Social Conditions in Russia—Recent Visitor's Tribute," Letters to the Editor, *The Manchester Guardian* (March 2, 1933), Gareth Jones Memorial Website, available at http://www.garethjones.org/soviet_articles/bernard_shaw.htm.

2. Winston Churchill, "George Bernard Shaw," in *Great Contemporaries* (London: Thornton Butterworth, 1937), 55.

3. In a Gallup poll conducted in 2010, a majority of respondents in Germany, Italy, the Netherlands, Spain, Greece, Cyprus, and Bulgaria considered Russia to be a "partner" of their

country. However, a majority of respondents in the United Kingdom, France, Belgium, Finland, Sweden, Portugal, Poland, Lithuania, Latvia, Hungary, Czech Republic, Romania, Slovenia, and Malta considered Russia rather to be their country's "frenemy." (Quoted in Ivan Krastev and Mark Leonard, "The Spectre of a Multipolar Europe," policy report (London: European Council on Foreign Relations, 2010), 30.)

4. However, even in this respect, Russia is still haunted by a return of the old Stalinist ghosts. On October 20, 2012, President Putin signed a decree creating a new subdivision within his presidential administration, which intended to "work on the strengthening of patriotic education and the spiritual-moral foundations of Russian society." The department, headed by Pavel Zenkovich, will have a full-time staff of thirty to thirty-five people. *Nezavisimaya Gazeta* did not hesitate to label this initiative as "the Kremlin's agitprop." (Cf. Aleksandra Samarina, "Kremlevskiy Agitprop," *Nezavisimaya Gazeta* (October 22, 2012).)

5. Joseph S. Nye Jr., *The Paradox of American Power: Why the World's Only Superpower Can't Go It Alone* (Oxford and New York: Oxford University Press, 2002), 8.

6. Nye, *The Paradox of American Power*, 9.

7. Joseph S. Nye Jr., *Soft Power: The Means to Success in World Politics* (New York: Public Affairs, 2004), 9.

8. Nye, *Soft Power*, 75.

9. Nicu Popescu and Andrew Wilson, "The Limits of Enlargement-Lite: European and Russian Power in the Troubled Neighbourhood," policy report (London: European Council on Foreign Relations, June 2009), 27.

10. Popescu and Wilson, "The Limits of Enlargement-Lite," 29.

11. Popescu and Wilson, "The Limits of Enlargement-Lite," 29.

12. Cf. Marcin Maczka, "The Propaganda Machine," *New Eastern Europe* 3, no. 4, New Europe, Old Problems (July–Sept. 2012).

13. Andrew E. Kramer, "Russian Cable Station Plays to U.S.," *The New York Times* (August 22, 2010).

14. Sonia Scherr, "The Conspiracy Channel," *UTNE Reader* (January–February 2011), available at http://www.utne.com/media/conspiracy-channel-russia-today-anti-american-propaganda.aspx.

15. Benjamin Bidder, "Putin's Weapon in the War of Images," *Spiegel Online* (August 13, 2013).

16. Anton Troianovski, "Russia Ramps Up Information War in Europe," *The Wall Street Journal* (August 21, 2014).

17. Troianovski, "Russia Ramps Up Information War."

18. Julia Ioffe, "What Is Russia Today?" *Columbia Journalism Review* (September/October 2010).

19. Ioffe, "What Is Russia Today?"

20. Ian Burrell, "From Russia with News," *The Independent* (January 15, 2010).

21. Cf. Scherr, "The Conspiracy Channel."

22. Scherr, "The Conspiracy Channel."

23. Bidder, "Putin's Weapon in the War of Images."

24. Gianluca Mezzofiore, "RT Host Manuel Ochsenreiter Exposed as Neo-Nazi Editor," *IB Times* (March 24, 2014).

25. James Miller, "Throwing a Wrench in Russia's Propaganda Machine," *The Interpreter* (June 18, 2014), available at http://www.interpretermag.com/throwing-a-wrench-in-russias-propaganda-machine/.

26. Miller, "Throwing a Wrench."

27. "Airways Wobbly—Russia Today Goes Mad," *The Economist* (July 6, 2010).

28. "Using Stalin to Boost Russia Abroad," *Spiegel Online* (November 20, 2007).

29. Catherine Taibi, "Russia Today Launches Provocative New Ad Campaign," *The Huffington Post* (August 18, 2014).

30. Charles Clover, "Talk Show Host Larry King to Present Russia Today Programme," *Financial Times* (May 29, 2013).

31. Jack Shafer, "Hail to the Return of the Motherland-Protecting Propaganda! The Russians and Their Unintentionally Hilarious *Washington Post* Ad Supplement," *Slate* (August 30, 2007).

32. Luke Harding, *Mafia State: How One Reporter Became an Enemy of the Brutal New Russia* (London: Guardian Books, 2011), 115.

33. In fact, the Kremlin is using the tactics of the "indirect strategy," as described by the French strategist General André Beaufre, who wrote that "the propaganda can be very different at home and in the outside world." (André Beaufre, *Introduction à la stratégie*, with a preface by B. H. Liddell Hart (Paris: Librairie Armand Colin, 1965), 106.)

34. Gabrielle Tétrault-Farber, "Putin Shuts State News Agency RIA Novosti," *The Moscow Times* (December 10, 2013).

35. Tétrault-Farber, "Putin Shuts State News Agency."

36. Quoted in "Kiselyov: narabotki RIA Novosti v novom agenstve budut vostrebovany," *RIA Novosti* (December 11, 2013).

37. Paul Sonne, "Putin Shakes Up Russian Media Landscape," *The Wall Street Journal* (December 9, 2013).

38. Quoted by Troianovski, "Russia Ramps Up Information War."

39. Troianovski, "Russia Ramps Up Information War."

40. Charles Recknagel, "ITAR-TASS Looks Ahead by Traveling Back to Soviet-Era Name," *Radio Free Europe/Radio Liberty* (September 2, 2014).

41. Mary Gearin, "Vladimir Putin Accused of Using Soviet-Style Propaganda Strategy to Control Russian Media," *ABC News* (September 17, 2014).

42. Gearin, "Vladimir Putin Accused of Using Soviet-Style Propaganda."

Chapter Five

The Propaganda Offensive in the Western Media, Part II

Buying Western Newspapers, the Increasing Grip on the Social Media, the "Kremlin School of Bloggers"

BUYING WESTERN NEWSPAPERS, PART I: THE CASE OF *FRANCE-SOIR* IN FRANCE

Buying advertising space in Western papers and reformatting RIA Novosti and ITAR-TASS into Soviet-style agitprop agencies were not the only strategies the Kremlin used to influence Western public opinion. There were other, more indirect ways already exploited by the KGB in Soviet times. For instance, in the 1970s, the KGB already had contacts with two important journalists of the French paper *Le Monde*. At that time, the French news agency AFP would also have been infiltrated.[1] Pierre-Charles Pathé, the son of a prominent French film tycoon, working for the KGB, launched a biweekly magazine, *Synthesis*, in this period. The first issue, published in June 1975, was sent to five hundred opinion leaders, including deputies, senators, and journalists. "Pathé is finally arrested by the DST [French counter intelligence] in 1979," writes Andreï Kozovoï, and "in 1980 the journalist is condemned to five years prison."[2] Pathé was to be released one year later, thanks to an amnesty by President François Mitterrand, who had communist ministers in his government.

This old KGB tradition of influencing Western public opinion[3] indirectly seemed to have made a glorious comeback in the first decade of the twenty-first century, when a totally new phenomenon began to develop: Russian oligarchs started buying important stakes in what in Soviet times would have been called "the bourgeois press." One example was the French daily *France-Soir*. *France-Soir*, a popular paper, was founded in 1944. It had its time of glory in the 1960s, when it employed four hundred journalists and sold about one million copies. At the end of 2008, its circulation had gone down to 23,000 copies. A company called "Sablon International," registered in Luxembourg, which had a stake of 19.9 percent in the capital, made an offer to raise its stake to 85 percent. On January 16, 2009, it became known that the Commercial Court of Lille had given the offer the green light.[4] But who was behind Sablon International? Its owner was Alexander Pugachev, then twenty-three years old, the youngest son of the Russian oligarch Sergey Pugachev. Young Alexander had just received a French ID card from the prefecture of Alpes-Maritimes—a necessary condition for the transaction because according to French law, a foreigner cannot own more than 20 percent of a French paper. Pugachev is a famous family name in Russia. It was a Pugachev who, in the eighteenth century, led a powerful peasants' rebellion against tsarina Catherine the Great. But the Russian oligarch Sergey Pugachev, whose fortune in 2008 was estimated by *Forbes* at $2 billion, was not, like his eighteenth-century namesake, a Kremlin critic. On the contrary, as the owner of the Mezhprombank (International Industrial Bank IIB), he had the nickname "Putin's banker."[5] According to *Paris Match*, "Some have also christened him the 'Orthodox banker' because of his close relationship with the Orthodox Church and with nationalist circles that are in favor of the return of 'Holy Russia.'"[6] The man himself, with a big black beard, resembles an Orthodox priest and calls himself a *francophile*. He is the owner of a château near Nice and two villas in the jet-set resort of Saint-Jean-Cap-Ferrat, known as the "billionaires' peninsula." Pugachev, who was also the owner of the Severnaya Verf shipyard in Saint Petersburg, had good personal contacts with Putin, whom he knew from the days when the latter was deputy mayor in Saint Petersburg. He also knew personally French President Nicolas Sarkozy and his presidential adviser Claude Guéant, who, in 2009, started negotiations with the Kremlin on the sale of four French Mistral helicopter carriers, two of which would be built at Pugachev's shipyard.[7]

However, is being a *francophile* in itself a reason to buy the loss-making *France-Soir*? Certainly not. The real objective was to make this paper into a popular, mass-selling French tabloid, similar to the British *Sun* or the German *Bild*. The political impact of these popular tabloids is well known. Tony Blair's election and reelection was, for instance, at least partly a result of the support he received from Rupert Murdoch's *Sun*. Similarly, *Bild*'s support for German Chancellor Helmut Kohl was legendary. Pugachev's son Alexander, who was in charge of *France-Soir*, took Holger Wiemann as an adviser. Wiemann was a former manager of Gruner and Jahr, the largest European printing and publishing firm, which is 74.9 percent owned by the Bertelsmann media group. Pugachev Jr. reputedly said: "If, in order to make money, I have to make a *trash* paper, I will make a *trash* paper."[8] He is also quoted as having said that his favorite headline would be: "All Arabs are rapists,"[9] something he later denied. According to a blog by the French weekly *L'Express*, the editor of *France-Soir* was seriously concerned about what it called Alexander Pugachev's "extreme right-wing stance that would not be challenged by a Le Pen."[10] Alexander Pugachev openly aired his extreme-right sympathies. "I like the ideas of Le Pen," he said. "There is more and more immigration and insecurity in France."[11] This bias in favor of the extreme right became even more clear in March 2011, when, just two days before the second round of the regional elections, on the first three pages of *France-Soir* the results of an opinion poll on the Front National were published. The poll was commissioned by the paper. Marine Le Pen, wrote the paper, "is changing the image of the FN." And in an editorial comment, Gérard Carreyrou (a journalist who replaced star reporter Anne Sinclair in 1988 on *7/7*, a famous TV program, when she refused to interview Jean-Marie Le Pen) wrote that "the Front National, having become the party of Marine Le Pen, is tending towards becoming, little by little, a party just like the others."[12] This overt attempt to make the extreme-right party more acceptable to a broader public was a welcome boost for the Front National, just two days before the election, at a moment when political leaders of the democratic left and right called for a "republican front" to isolate the party.

In the fall of 2011, young Pugachev exposed his views with more clarity. Asked on November 11, 2011, in a TV program for whom he would vote in the presidential elections of 2012, he declared: "I am tempted by Marine Le Pen." When the journalist asked whether he was serious, he answered: "In any case there are 20 percent who want to vote for her." He added: "There are not many people who openly declare themselves [in favor], but I don't know why, she is not a fascist."[13] The interview led to loud protests from the trade unions Comité Inter CGT and Info'Com CGT, which declared that they "will never accept that *France-Soir* should become a new channel for the theses of the extreme right." The Society of Journalists of the paper equally expressed its "vivid outrage" and emphasized "its will to preserve a form of neutrality and political equilibrium."[14]

How did the paper develop? Christian de Villeneuve, a newly appointed chief editor, succeeded in more than tripling the circulation from 23,000 copies in January 2010 to 87,000 in June of the same year. Despite these positive results, he was fired by his young boss, who had set a target of 150,000 sales by the end of that year. And even 150,000 copies was still a far cry from his two great models: three million sales of *Bild* in Germany and about two million of the *Sun* in Britain. However, the real reason to fire his chief editor was a disagreement about the political line of the paper. "He is leaving," said Pugachev Jr. in an interview with *Le Figaro*, "because we have certain points of disagreement together, especially as concerns the image and

the editorial line of the paper."[15] The identity of the new editor, Rémy Dessarts, left no doubts about Pugachev's plans. In the past, Dessarts had led a
Springer project to launch a French version of *Bild*. Despite positive results
from the market analysis, this project was ultimately abandoned in 2007 due
to logistical reasons, such as the fact that there were not enough newspaper
kiosks in France and that printing and distribution were controlled by unruly
trade unions.[16] Pugachev hoped to circumvent these problems by concentrat-
ing on the regions outside greater Paris.

The German weekly *Der Spiegel* writes about *Bild* that it "serves up tripe,
trash, tits and, almost as an afterthought, a healthy dose of hard news seven
days a week."[17] *Bild* is known for its nationalist, anti-EU, and anti-immigrant
stance and clearly has political aspirations. *Der Spiegel* writes that *Bild* "in
fact is taking on the role of a right-wing populist party that has always been
lacking in German politics."[18] This opinion was shared by a former editor of
Bild am Sonntag who said that by its campaigns, "the red carpet is being
rolled out for a party that has not yet been founded, led by a German Jörg
Haider [an Austrian extreme-right politician]."[19] In the 1970s, Heinrich Böll,
a German Nobel Prize winner for Literature, accused *Bild* of "naked fascism,
agitation, lies and dirt."

The fate of *France-Soir* took a new turn at the end of 2011. The number
of copies sold, still at 75,000 in 2010, was more than halved. In October
2011, only 36,074 copies found a buyer.[20] In the first six months of 2011, the
paper had generated a loss of almost 13 million euro. Alexander Pugachev,
who had already invested about 70 million euros in three years, had to make
a decision. Rumors claimed that he was prepared to sell the paper for a
symbolic price of one euro. But he was not yet willing to give up his hold
over a French media outlet. On December 13, 2011, the last paper edition
appeared. Pugachev fired eighty-nine people but used the remaining staff to
continue with an internet edition of the paper.[21] This initiative, however, was
short-lived. When the website did not attract enough advertisers, the young
owner threw in the towel, and on July 23, 2012, the Commercial Court of
Paris announced the liquidation of the paper.[22] The remaining forty-nine
personnel were fired. The attempt to create a popular, extreme-right,
Kremlin-friendly paper in France had failed.[23]

BUYING WESTERN NEWSPAPERS, PART II:
THE CASE OF THE *LONDON EVENING STANDARD* AND THE
INDEPENDENT IN BRITAIN

There was, however, another example of a Russian oligarch who had become
the owner of a Western paper. It was Alexander Lebedev, a former lieutenant
colonel of the KGB, whose fortune was estimated at $3.1 billion before the

credit crunch and at $2.5 billion thereafter. In January 2009, Lebedev bought 75.1 percent of the loss-making *London Evening Standard* from its parent company, Daily Mail & General Trust, for the symbolic price of £1. The paper is widely regarded as "the voice of London" and had a circulation at that time of just under three hundred thousand. "The purchase will be an astonishing moment in British press history," wrote the *Guardian* at that time, "the first time a former member of a foreign intelligence service has owned a British title."[24] Lebedev said that it was his task to read the *Evening Standard* and other British newspapers when he was a young spy at the Soviet embassy in London in the late 1980s. To reassure some Tory MPs who had expressed reservations about the takeover, Lebedev came up with the names of Tony Blair and Jacques Chirac, who would, he said, be invited onto the advisory board, together with "leading Russian editors."[25] The name-dropping also included Harry Potter author J. K. Rowling. Later, however, the names of Blair, Chirac, and Rowling were no longer mentioned. Lebedev denied that he had immediate plans to buy other papers, saying, "I can help one newspaper but not 10."[26] Despite guarantees that editorial independence would be safeguarded, doubts remained, especially when it was confirmed "that the transaction had been authorized by the Kremlin."[27] Also, the ex-KGB billionaire's statement that he could "help one newspaper but not 10" was relative: at that moment, he had already tried—in vain—to buy the old and venerable *Times*.

A former KGB agent gaining hold over an important paper in the British capital led to concerned comments. John Lloyd writes in the *Guardian*, "He [Lebedev] has done good works. His proprietorship of Novaya Gazeta means he has lent his wealth and protection to the most radical oppositionists among Russia's journalists. He has offered the equivalent of £1m for the capture of the assassin of Anna Politkovskaya, the paper's famed writer on Chechnya. He has remained faithful to the (unpopular, in Russia) Gorbachev, bankrolling many of his political initiatives."[28] Lloyd concedes that Lebedev might "indeed be a better man than many of his proprietor colleagues, past and present." However, he adds, "the appearance in their ranks of a former lieutenant colonel in an organisation with the blood of millions (of Russians, mostly) on its books should give us a pause."[29] Lloyd continues, "Ownership of a newspaper is different from other ownerships. It is to have a position of power over the minds of men and women—not so much in telling them what to think, but what to think about."[30]

One year later, in March 2010, Lebedev bought the loss-making quality newspaper the *Independent*—again for the symbolic price of £1. His twenty-nine-year-old son Yevgeny became the official owner. The *Independent*, which sold four hundred thousand copies in 1989, was, with a circulation of 92,000, at the brink of collapse. Again one could hear concerned voices. The *Times* wrote that "the elder Lebedev's relationship with the Russian Government was called into question in January after he received a huge cash injection in a deal personally sanctioned by Vladimir Putin, the Prime Minister. The sale of Mr. Lebedev's £450 million stake in the airline Aeroflot and other assets back to the Russian Government led some to question his reputation as a critic of the Kremlin as well as his motivation for buying the newspaper titles."[31]

Indeed, some interesting parallels are evident between the acquisition of the *Evening Standard* and the *Independent* in London and the acquisition of *France-Soir* in Paris:

- First, the initiatives concerned *loss-making newspapers that were bought for a symbolic price* against the promise to invest in the paper. In all three cases, the acquisition by a Russian oligarch was welcomed by the personnel and the editors of the respective newspapers, who were delighted with the rescue actions. The new owners both pretended to be simply rich "hobbyists," not interested in making money but wanting to spend money "to help" the press. "As far as I'm concerned this has nothing to do with making money," Lebedev told the *Guardian*. "There are lots of other ways. This is a good way to waste money."[32] As concerns "wasting money": Alexander Pugachev also seemed—at the outset—not to be easily dissuaded. In January 2011 he declared that he had already invested about 60 million euros since he bought *France-Soir* in 2009. He announced an additional investment of 20 million euros in 2011, hoping "to reach a break-even point at the end of 2012."[33]
- A second similarity is that both new owners worked with "father-and-son" formulas. In France, oligarch Sergey Pugachev had made his youngest son the paper's manager; in Britain, oligarch Alexander Lebedev made his son Yevgeny senior executive director of the *Evening Standard* and owner of the *Independent*.[34]
- A third similarity is that both families had *no known journalistic or media traditions* or foreign media projects *before* the takeover of the papers. When asked what profession he dreamed of as a boy, young Alexander Pugachev answered: "Rather a job where one produces something."[35] In another interview he confessed: "I have never felt like working in the press."[36]
- A fourth similarity is—at least in the beginning—the clear objective expressed by both oligarchs *to expand their press empire*. Asked whether he would be interested in buying the paper *Le Parisien*, Alexander Pugachev answered: "I would have liked to, but the group has not felt inclined to inform me [about the sale]," adding, "but I have recently studied the dossier of a regional paper and remain very interested in the opportunities that the regional press might offer."[37]

There were, however, also some differences. Alexander Lebedev was an ex-KGB lieutenant colonel who, as such, had even been expelled from Britain. Alexander Pugachev's father, Sergey Pugachev, had no KGB past. The fact that Lebedev was a former KGB agent was a disadvantage. But it was balanced by the fact that he—together with Gorbachev—owned 49 percent of the shares of *Novaya Gazeta*, Russia's famous opposition paper. Lebedev liked to present himself as a kind of semidissident. In reality, however, he always had a rather close relationship with the Russian leadership. The question was whether or not there existed an unspoken partition of tasks. The Kremlin needed *Novaya Gazeta* for its image abroad: it was its *fig leaf* to show its democratic credentials. This ambiguous relationship between the Russian leadership and the opposition paper became, for instance, clear in April 2009, when President Medvedev granted *Novaya Gazeta* a long interview—the first of its kind to a Russian paper. Undoubtedly, Lebedev's image as a "semidissident" has helped him to buy the British newspapers. "Against him," writes François Bonnet, "many Russian observers quote the old principle: 'Once a KGB man, always a KGB man.'"[38] And he adds: "Mr. Lebedev's boldness is said to be limited. He would know to stop when the Kremlin whistles. The proof? He closed overnight the Moscow daily paper 'Moskovskii Korrespondant' which had published an article that criticized the ruling elite."[39] (The paper had written about Putin's purported secret liaison with Alina Kabayeva, a former Olympic gymnast.)

Equally, Luke Harding, who was the *Guardian*'s Moscow correspondent, remarked that "in Moscow, Lebedev's position is of someone who is inside the political elite rather than outside it."[40] From 2002 to 2007 he was a Duma deputy of the pro-Kremlin party United Russia. Having refused in 2008 to join Garry Kasparov's opposition movement Solidarity, he announced in May 2011 that he would endorse Putin's Popular Front. The Popular Front, however, did not want Lebedev as a member. "To critics," wrote Harding, "the move is proof that Lebedev is in bed with the Kremlin."[41] At the same time, Lebedev still upheld his reputation as a semidissident. In June 2012 he helped the anti-corruption blogger and opposition leader Aleksey Navalny become a member of the board of directors of Aeroflot. He also launched a debit card, issued by his National Reserve Bank. One percent of all purchases would go to RosPil, a fund launched by Navalny to expose government corruption.[42] Had Lebedev at that point overstepped the mark and evoked the wrath of the Kremlin? This seemed the case when, in September 2012, the billionaire was charged with hooliganism and battery for punching a businessman in the face live on television one year earlier.[43] He could face up to seven years in prison. His son Yevgeny expressed his concern, saying his father could be murdered in prison by "some sinister elements that he's crossed in the past with his anti-corruption campaign. We believe there's been a contract taken out on his head."[44] However, when, on July 2, 2013, the verdict came, Lebedev avoided jail and was instead ordered to do 150 hours of community service.[45] He was, apparently, not considered a *real* enemy of the state.

What is the impact, so far, of the Russian influence on Western media? We have already discussed Alexander Pugachev's open support for the extreme right Front National, which is, one should not forget, an anti-EU, anti-NATO, and openly pro-Putin party.[46] In 2010 the French weekly magazine *Le Nouvel Observateur* hinted at a possible *political* outcome from the Russian ownership of *France-Soir*: an eventual deal between the owner and Nicolas Sarkozy to support the latter in the presidential elections of 2012 in exchange for the sale of French Mistral helicopter carriers to Russia. Pugachev, wrote the magazine, "prepares to relaunch the right-wing paper mid-March [2010], between the two rounds of the regional elections. A deal?"[47]

In the British case, however, there were no signs of direct interference of the Lebedevs in the editorial policy of the *Independent* or the *Evening Standard*. Alexander Lebedev and his son Yevgeny also showed themselves more astute managers than the Pugachevs. The loss-making *Evening Standard*, which in 2009 was turned into a free paper distributed at London metro stations, made for the first time a (modest) profit of £82,000 in the year September 2011–September 2012.[48] Not only did the circulation grow from 250,000 to 700,000 copies, but the paper succeeded in upholding its reputation of being a quality paper, preferred by the young, well-educated, urban commuters. In February 2013 the Lebedevs managed to get a license for a local twenty-four-hour TV information channel, London Live, which was launched in March 2014. The editors of the *Evening Standard* and the *Independent* are responsible for its programs.[49] This channel, however, had a difficult start: in May 2015 it was announced that London Live had to cut twenty jobs, one third of the total. So far, the hands-off approach of the Lebedevs, who—unlike Alexander Pugachev—did not interfere in their papers' editorial policies, has paid off. The oligarch and his son have become respected members of the British media establishment. How respected becomes clear from the fact that they have direct access to the British government. The influence of the media tycoon Rupert Murdoch on British politics is legendary. It is telling that during the hearings of the Leveson government inquiry, held after the telephone hacking scandal by Murdoch's *News of the World*, Lebedev's son, Yevgeny, testified that he had met with British Prime Minister David Cameron on four occasions—a number of personal meetings a simple Russian or British citizen could only have dreamed of.[50]

Suspicions that the takeovers of Western news media are motivated by the strategic interests of the Kremlin are also aired elsewhere. In August 2008, one week after the Russian war against Georgia, the German paper *Frankfurter Allgemeine Zeitung*, for instance, wrote about the sale of the Czech publishing house Economia by its German owner Handelsblatt, a division of the German Holtzbrinck group. Economia is the editor of *Hospodářské noviny*, a renowned Czech economic paper. The Italy-based bank UniCredit acted as a trustee for anonymous buyers. "The lack of transparency," wrote the *Frankfurter Allgemeine*, "is feeding fears that investors from Russia want to obtain the quality newspaper in order to influence public opinion in the Czech Republic in the Kremlin's interests. Apparently the anonymous investors are even prepared to pay Holtzbrinck about twenty million euro more than one could get for 'Hospodářské noviny' from serious publishing houses."[51]

During the November 2013 EU summit in Vilnius, Bulgarian President Rossen Plevneliev told a presummit meeting of the European People's Party (EPP) that "90% of the media in Bulgaria work for Russian masters."[52] In August 2014, the website of the Bulgarian Defense Ministry published a fourteen-page report—*Outlook 2020*. The report, meant to be presented by Bulgarian President Rossen Plevneliev and the caretaker defense minister Velizar Shalamanov at the NATO summit on September 4–5, 2014, in Cardiff, Wales, warned that the main risks for Bulgaria were "the new hybrid war, which combines conventional methods with guerrilla, cybernetic and information war."[53] Heavily criticized by parties of the left, the report was withdrawn.[54]

Are suspicions of a Kremlin-inspired *prise d'influence* in Western news media exaggerated? Maybe. However, there remain many questions—many *unanswered* questions—such as the fact that these takeovers of Western news media seem to be motivated less by economic than by *strategic* reasons. In November 2012, the Russian magazine *Russkiy Reporter* published an interesting article in which the economic liberalization of Russia was presented as a KGB project, masterminded by general secretary and former KGB chief Yury Andropov. It is no secret that Andropov was Gorbachev's mentor. Gorbachev started the perestroika. In the transformation of Russia's planned state economy into a private-market economy, the KGB is thought not only to have played a leading role but also to have provided the initial capital and picked the individuals who were to become the new owners of the country's huge natural resources and economic infrastructure. "In this way," wrote the magazine, "the present oligarchs would, indeed, only be hired managers controlled by the real owners. . . . According to this model the oligarchs would be simple 'operators,' people who, it was decided, would manage assets acquired with money that did not belong to them."[55] The magazine also mentioned "the strange story of the sudden prosperity of the banker Alexander Lebedev, that many in bankers' circles cannot explain other than by the legendary 'gold of the Communist Party,' as regards the short time he needed, in the middle of the 1990s, to find himself sitting on top of huge sums. In the past Lebedev worked in the secret service and he worked undercover at the Soviet embassy in Great Britain."[56] In this version of the facts, Lebedev acted as a "manager" of money "that did not belong to him." It is, therefore, not at all counterintuitive that the master of the Kremlin—himself a former KGB chief—could have asked him to show his patriotism by expanding into Western media. However, another possibility for the emergence of Russian "oligarch-tycoons" is suggested by *Novaya Gazeta* reporter Yuliya Latynina. According to her, "Pugachev has bought *France-Soir* because he belongs to a category of [Russian] businessmen, who have developed a passion for foreign media, wanting to rebuild their image and to prove their importance to the Russian authorities."[57] In this scenario, the oligarchs' initiative of buying Western papers would have completely been their own, without interference from the Kremlin. Particularly in the case of the Lebedevs this last interpretation seems rather plausible.

GAINING A HOLD OVER THE SOCIAL NETWORKS: THE CASE OF FACEBOOK AND VKONTAKTE

The Kremlin's interest is not restricted to the print media. It also has a growing appetite for gaining a hold over the social media. In the aftermath of the mass protests against Putin in the winter of 2011–2012, the Kremlin began to tighten its grip on the internet. The Russian government introduced a blacklist of banned websites, supposedly to protect minors, but according to human rights advocates, intended to attack free speech.[58] The technology required to enforce the blacklist would make it possible for the government to closely monitor the internet. Additionally, it took other repressive measures. Libel has been redefined as a crime. "High treason" also has been redefined, making it easier for the state to bring charges against regime critics. A law against "blasphemy" is under consideration. However, the Kremlin has not only legal means at its disposal. It can also rely on the cooperation of Kremlin-friendly oligarchs. In this context, the role played by the oligarch Alisher Usmanov deserves our special attention. Usmanov is the king of the Russian internet, of which he controls about 70 percent. He has stakes in Mail.ru—the Russian equivalent of Yahoo!—as well as in Yandex, a search engine, and in Vkontakte, a Russian equivalent of Facebook. Usmanov was ranked by *Forbes* in 2010 as the hundredth-richest fortune holder of the world with $7.2 billion—ahead of Rupert Murdoch ($6.3 billion) and Apple's Steve Jobs ($5.5. billion).[59] Usmanov's curriculum vitae is very special. Born in 1953 in Uzbekistan to a Muslim family, the son of the public prosecutor in the capital Tashkent, Usmanov studied at the Moscow State Institute of International Relations, or MGIMO. He returned to Tashkent to work for the local branch of the Soviet Peace Committee, a KGB front organization, which, at that time, was headed by the later SVR (Foreign Intelligence Service) chief Yevgeny Primakov. Usmanov's career took an unexpected turn when he was arrested and sent to jail for six years for alleged fraud and embezzlement. But his prison past was not an impediment to a fast-rising career. Apparently, Usmanov had powerful friends. In 2000 he was appointed director of Gazprominvestholding, the investment branch of Gazprom, and in 2005 he became the main shareholder of Metalloinvest, a gigantic iron and steel company with fifty thousand employees. Shortly afterwards, Usmanov started his expansion into the Russian internet and began to build his internet empire. Usmanov liked to show off his success. He took a 28 percent stake in the British soccer club Arsenal and bought a 110-meter yacht as well as a Tudor manor in Surrey and a property in Sardinia with direct access to the golf course. Usmanov is certainly no friend of press freedom. On December 13, 2011, he fired Maxim Kovalsky, the editor in chief of *Kommersant Vlast*, a paper of which he is the owner. Kovalsky had attracted Usmanov's ire after publishing a photograph critical of Putin.[60]

Usmanov has shown himself a shrewd investor. When, in 2009, during the financial crisis, Mark Zuckerberg, the CEO of Facebook, turned to Russian investors because other sources of financing were drying up, Mail.ru Group, the leader of the Russian internet, took, via its international investment vehicle Digital Sky Technologies (DST), a 2 percent stake in Facebook for $200 million. In September 2010, DST became an independent company with the name DST Global. In January 2011, Mail.ru Group had invested $310 million in Facebook. Together with DST Global, it possessed 10 percent of Facebook's shares.[61] Rumors soon emerged that the Kremlin had succeeded—via Usmanov—in gaining a hold over Facebook, the world's most important social networking site. It became, indeed, a cause for concern. The *New York Times* wrote on Usmanov's financial stake in Facebook: "His ties to the Kremlin and Facebook have stirred concerns that he might influence the company's policies in subtle ways to appease governments in markets where Facebook is also an important tool of political dissent, such as Russia."[62] There was, however, one caveat. The Russian owners had been able to invest in Facebook only by transferring their voting rights to Zuckerberg. Therefore, Usmanov would have no direct influence on Facebook's policies in Russia.

In effect, it was in Russia where Usmanov's main interests lay. In 2010, an IPO of Mail.ru allowed Usmanov to gain a voting majority in this company.[63] In October 2012, Mail.ru sold an important stake in Facebook, cashing in about $320 million and keeping only 0.75 percent of the shares.[64] Usmanov needed this money for his next move: the control of Vkontakte. Vkontakte is the Russian equivalent of Facebook and the biggest social network there. Mail.ru already owned 40 percent. However, two other investors, Vyacheslav Mirilashvili and Lev Leviev, holding 48 percent of the shares, said that they had no plans to sell their shares to Mail.ru.[65] Usmanov thereupon began to woo a third owner, Pavel Durov, the founder and CEO of Vkontakte, who owned 12 percent, proposing to buy his stake. This would give Usmanov a majority vote in Vkontakte, a move that was fully supported by the Kremlin.[66] Durov was accused of playing a dubious role in the Russian social media world. In March 2013, the opposition paper *Novaya Gazeta* published a letter supposedly written in December 2011 by Durov to Vladislav Surkov, then first deputy chief of the presidential administration, in which he wrote that "we have already worked together for some years with the FSB and the 'K' department of the Ministry of Internal Affairs, engaged in supplying information on thousands of users of our site."[67] In the letter Durov boasted that Vkontakte had actively countered opposition initiatives during the December 2012 anti-government rallies in Moscow by creating fake profiles on the site of purported "opposition groups." By receiving false information on imminent fake rallies, potential protesters were redirected away from the real rallies. However, Vkontakte's spokesman, Georgy Lobushkin, denied that Durov had sent this letter.[68] Doubts remained, in particular because in 2012 Usmanov—instead of buying Durov's shares—handed Durov the control of Mail.ru's 40 percent stake, which seemed rather to confirm the version given by *Novaya Gazeta*. In April 2013, Mirilashvili and Leviev, the two remaining shareholders, sold their 48 percent shares to United Capital Partners (UCP), an investment fund headed by Ilya Shcherbovich, who is a board member at the state-owned oil giant Rosneft, which is headed by Igor Sechin, an ally of Vladimir Putin. From that moment, 88 percent of the shares of Vkontakte seemed to be in Kremlin-friendly hands.[69]

In January 2014, Pavel Durov sold his 12 percent stake to Ivan Tavrin, CEO of MegaFon, a mobile phone operator controlled by Mail.ru Group's main shareholder, Alisher Usmanov. Usmanov seemed now to control a majority of the shares. On April 21, 2014, Pavel Durov, who had remained Vkontakte's CEO, was dismissed. He left Russia immediately. In his own words, he left Russia "for ever." On his Vkontakte page he recounted how he had come under increasing pressure from the FSB, which sent him an order in December 2013 to hand over the personal details of the members of Vkontakte's Euromaidan group, which supported the protests in Ukraine against President Yanukovych.[70] Durov refused. On his Vkontakte page, Durov explained: "Our answer was and remains a categorical no—Russia's jurisdiction does not extend to Ukrainian users of Vkontakte."[71] The FSB also ordered him to shut down the Vkontakte group dedicated to anti-corruption activist Aleksey Navalny—an order he equally refused. He said that this pressure from the FSB was the reason he had sold his stake in the company.[72] After Durov's departure, the new owners could not agree on the company's strategy. The conflict was resolved when, on September 16, 2014, UCP sold its stake in the company to Mail.ru for $1.47 billion.[73] Alisher Usmanov's grip on Russia's most important social media group seemed to be complete. From now on, the FSB would be able to monitor Vkontakte without restraint, and its surveillance was not restricted to the territory of the Russian Federation. Because Vkontakte also has millions of users in the former Soviet republics, it offers the FSB unprecedented opportunities to watch closely—and subsequently manipulate—events in the neighboring republics. Taking control of the most important social media, however, seemed not to be enough to satisfy the Kremlin's appetite for strengthening its grip on the internet community. On July 1, 2014, the Duma passed a law at first reading on *blokirovka*, which made it possible to block the World Wide Web in order "to rescue Russian transmissions from enemy intelligence services." From September 2016 onward, sites that store data on Russian citizens on servers outside Russia can be "blacklisted." According to Andrey Mima, a Russian internet expert, "Protecting data from Western intelligence services simultaneously means feeding these data to Russian intelligence."[74]

TROLLS AND KREMLIN BLOGGERS

Finally, we should mention here the activities in the blogosphere, where a close and almost symbiotic cooperation has been developed between Russia's secret services and the youth movement Nashi. In 2009 a project was set up, called the "Kremlin School of Bloggers." It was organized by Gleb Pavlovsky's Foundation for Effective Politics. The "Kremlin School of Bloggers" sells the Kremlin's policies to the young internet community by writing blogs, attacking opposition websites, and posting ideological YouTube videos.[75] The name of its website (liberty.ru) is *Free World* (*Svobodnyy Mir*), and its motto is—why not?—"Freedom is better than unfreedom." The Russian bloggers post comments on the websites of Western papers and think tanks, attacking articles and analyses which are critical of the Kremlin or the Russian leadership.[76] "Some observers believe that the bloggers are simply a spontaneous group of patriotic enthusiasts," wrote Luke Harding. "More convincing, though, is the view that the Kremlin discreetly funds these anonymous pro-government commentators, in order to discredit opponents and to promote Moscow's authoritarian agenda."[77] In times of increased tension with the West, these activities reach new heights. In May 2014, for instance, during the Ukraine crisis, the British paper the *Guardian* received an overwhelming number of pro-Russian comments. A moderator said: "Zealous pro-separatist comments in broken English claiming to be from western countries are very common."[78] Although there was no conclusive evidence about who is behind these actions, the *Guardian*'s readers' editor Chris Elliott believed "there was an orchestrated campaign."[79] Ilya Klishin, the editor in chief of the (opposition) Dozhd television website, was able to give more information on these practices:

Two weeks ago, the moderators for the website of The Guardian warned their readers that they were dealing with an "organized pro-Kremlin campaign" to place pro-Russian comments on the newspaper's website, using a practice called "trolling." According to my near-Kremlin sources, many of the pro-Putin messages have been posted by Russian expats in Germany, India and Thailand. Hackers from Anonymous, a vigilante activist network, hacked the e-mail account of one "trolling" group that is charged with running the campaign in the U.S. and gave me some of the information they discovered. . . . Russia's "Internet trolling squad" made detailed studies of such sites as The Blaze, The Huffington Post and Fox News, including their audiences, owners, official and actual editorial policies, as well as their attitudes toward Russia and Obama. Screenshots show comments posted in English with serious grammatical errors. [80]

According to the *Ukrainskaya Pravda*, the Kremlin bloggers were also active in Ukraine. They were said to be paid twenty-four euros per day for their activities. [81]

NOTES

1. Cf. Andreï Kozovoï, *Les services secrets Russes: Des tsars à Poutine* (Paris: Talandier, 2010), 229.

2. Kozovoï, *Les services secrets Russes*, 230.

3. This strategy may even predate the KGB and the Soviet Union. Marquis Astolphe de Custine wrote in 1839: "For many years Paris is reading revolutionary papers, revolutionary in any sense, paid by Russia." (Marquis de Custine, *Lettres de Russie: La Russie en 1839*, ed. Pierre Nora (Paris: Gallimard, 1975), 369.) The Russian government's objective, wrote Custine, was fomenting "anarchy, hoping to profit from a destabilization, which was caused by her . . . it is the history of Poland over again, but now on a great scale." (Ibid.)

4. "*France Soir* racheté par Sablon International," *Le Nouvel Observateur* (January 16, 2009).

5. Pauline Delassus, "Alexandre Pougatchev, l'apprenti Tsar de 'France-Soir,'" *Paris Match* (October 4, 2010).

6. François Labrouillère, "Sergueï Pougatchev: avis de tempête pour l'oligarque francophile," *Paris Match* (November 20, 2010).

7. However, Sergey Pugachev lost his two shipyards in the fall of 2010, when his bank, unable to repay $200 million in debts to the Central Bank, lost its registration. The shipyards, which were offered as collateral for the loan, were sold for $500 million to United Shipbuilding Corporation, at that time headed by Igor Sechin. The estimated real value of the shipyards was $3.5 billion.

8. Marie-Pierre Subtil, "'France soir' est secoué par le raidissement éditorial de son propriétaire russe," *Le Monde* (August 14, 2008) (emphasis and English word in the original).

9. Renaud Revel, "Nouvelle crise à France Soir: Pougatchev, qui veut du trash, menace de virer le patron de la rédaction," *L'Express Blogs* (August 11, 2010), http://blogs.lexpress.fr/media/2010/08/11/nouvelle_crise_a_france_soir_p/.

10. Revel, "Nouvelle crise à France Soir."

11. Frédérique Roussel, "Russie-Soir," *Libération* (February 17, 2011).

12. Gérard Carreyrou, "Le FN n'est plus ce qu'il était," *France-Soir* (March 25, 2011).

13. "La CGT craint que 'France Soir' ne devienne un organe du FN," *Le Monde.fr* (November 11, 2011).

14. "La CGT craint que 'France Soir' ne devienne un organe du FN."

15. Delphine Denuit, "Pugachev: '*France-Soir* ne sera pas un quotidien trash,'" *Figaro* (August 23, 2010).

16. "Der 'France Soir' wittert Morgenluft," *Frankfurter Allgemeine Zeitung* (August 26, 2010).

17. "Bild Zeitung Rules Germany," *Spiegel Online* (April 25, 2006).

18. "Im Namen des Volkes," *Der Spiegel*, no. 9 (February 28, 2011), 132.

19. "Im Namen des Volkes," 135.

20. Alexandre Debouté, "Clap de fin pour 'France-Soir,'" *Le Figaro* (December 15, 2011).

21. Guy Dutheil, "A 67 ans, 'France Soir' abandonne le papier pour le tout-numérique," *Le Monde* (December 16, 2011).

22. "France Soir est liquidé," *Libération* (July 23, 2012).

23. Sergey Pugachev, Alexander's father, fared hardly better. After having been forced by the Kremlin to sell his St. Petersburg shipyards at an undervalued price, his Mezhprom bank went bankrupt in 2010. Accused of having taken more than one billion euros from the bank before it went bankrupt, Interpol issued a red notice. The Russian billionaire, fallen from grace with the Kremlin, is hiding in London. (Cf. Benoît Vitkine, "La disgrâce d'un oligarque," *Le Monde* (January 20, 2015).)

24. Luke Harding, "Russian Oligarch Alexander Lebedev to Buy London Evening Standard," *The Guardian* (January 14, 2009).

25. Harding, "Russian Oligarch Alexander Lebedev to Buy London Evening Standard."

26. Harding, "Russian Oligarch Alexander Lebedev to Buy London Evening Standard."

27. "GB: Un milliardaire russe, ancien du KGB, rachète l'Evening Standard," *AFP* (January 21, 2009).

28. John Lloyd, "Why Nobody Lords It Over the Press Barons," *The Guardian* (January 29, 2009).

29. Lloyd, "Why Nobody Lords It Over the Press Barons."

30. Lloyd, "Why Nobody Lords It Over the Press Barons."

31. Alexi Mostrous, "Former KGB Spy Alexander Lebedev Buys Independent for £1," *The Times* (March 26, 2010).

32. Harding, "Russian Oligarch Alexander Lebedev to Buy London Evening Standard."

33. "'France-Soir': nouvelle formule et investissements supplémentaires," *Le Monde* (January 18, 2011). However, on August 29, 2011, the paper was placed under supervision by the Commercial Court of Paris, which decided to impose a preservation plan (*plan de sauvegarde*). An administrator was appointed who was given four months to make the paper profitable. "Today the daily is losing 1 million euro per month," wrote *Le Figaro*, "and there remain 5 million euro to hand." Of Alexander Pugachev, who had already invested 50 million euros, it was said that "he no longer has the intention of losing money." (Cf. "'France-Soir': 4 mois pour changer de modèle," *Le Figaro* (August 30, 2011).)

34. Stephen Brook and Mark Sweney, "Alexander Lebedev's Evening Standard Takeover: Dacre Announces Sale to Staff," *The Guardian* (January 21, 2009).

35. Roussel, "Russie-Soir."

36. Delassus, "Alexandre Pougatchev, l'apprenti Tsar de 'France-Soir.'"

37. Delphine Denuit, "Pugachev: '*France-Soir* ne sera pas un quotidien trash.'"

38. François Bonnet, "La presse et les gentils," *Mediapart* (January 21, 2009).

39. Bonnet, "La presse et les gentils."

40. Luke Harding, *Mafia State: How One Reporter Became an Enemy of the Brutal New Russia* (London: Guardian Books, 2011), 109.

41. Harding, *Mafia State*, 114.

42. Miriam Elder, "Alexander Lebedev Launches New Project against Russian Corruption," *The Guardian* (July 11, 2012).

43. "Alexander Lebedev Says Hooliganism Charge Is Revenge," *The Guardian* (September 27, 2012).

44. "Russian Tycoon Alexander Lebedev 'Expects Jail' over Punch-Up," *BBC News Europe* (November 25, 2012).

45. "Russian Tycoon Lebedev Avoids Jail over TV Brawl," *Reuters* (July 2, 2013).

46. On the close ideological affinity between Putinism and the Front National and other radical-right movements in Europe, see Marcel H. Van Herpen, "Putinism's Authoritarian Allure," *Project Syndicate* (March 15, 2013), http://www.project-syndicate.org/commentary/putinism-as-a-model-for-western-europe-s-extreme-right-by-marcel-h--van-herpen.

47. Vincent Jauvert, "Nos amis du Kremlin," *Le Nouvel Observateur* (February 2, 2010).

48. Marc Roche, "L' 'Evening Standard' est bénéficiaire, quatre ans après son passage à la gratuité," *Le Monde* (June 30–July 1, 2013).

49. Roche, "L' 'Evening Standard' est bénéficiaire."

50. Charles Clover, "Lunch with the FT: Alexander Lebedev," *Financial Times* (July 27, 2012).

51. "Russen ante portas? Dubioser Verlagskauf in Tschechien," *Frankfurter Allgemeine Zeitung* (August 16, 2008).

52. "Official Report: Russia Is a Threat to Bulgaria," *EurActiv* (August 27, 2014).

53. "Official Report: Russia Is a Threat to Bulgaria."

54. "Bulgaria Govt Withdraws Outlook 2020: Bulgaria and NATO in European Defence Document," *Focus News Agency* (August 28, 2014).

55. Dmitry Kartsev, "Plan Andropova—Plan Putina: Kak Chekisty poluchili kontrol nad stranoy," *Russkiy Reporter* 43, no. 272 (November 1, 2012). This is confirmed by an insider who quoted Putin as saying: "A chicken can exercise ownership of eggs, and it can get fed while it's sitting on the egg . . . but it's not really their egg." (Cf. Steven Myers and Jo Becker, "Even Loyalty No Guarantee against Putin," *The New York Times* (December 26, 2014).)

56. Dmitry Kartsev, "Plan Andropova—Plan Putina."

57. Millot Lorraine, "Pougatchev se paie une image," *Libération* (January 14, 2009).

58. "Russia's Big Leap in Internet Control," *The Washington Post* (November 13, 2012).

59. Guillaume Grallet and Katia Swarovskaya, "L' 'ami' russe de Facebook," *Le Point* (January 27, 2011).

60. Miriam Elder, "Russian Editor Fired over Anti-Putin Jibe," *The Guardian* (December 13, 2011).

61. "Au coeur de l'explosion du Web social, un géant russe," *Le Monde* (February 24, 2011).

62. Andrew E. Kramer, "A Russian Magnate's Facebook Bet Pays Off Big," *The New York Times* (May 15, 2012).

63. Ilya Khrennikov and Alex Sazonov, "Usmanov Spurns IPO for Grip on Technology," *Bloomberg* (November 30, 2012).

64. Ilya Khrennikov and Amy Thomson, "Usmanov's Internet Company Sold $320 Million Facebook Stake," *Bloomberg* (October 25, 2012).

65. Amy Thomson, "Mail.ru Seeks Deal for Russian Social Network Operator VKontakte," *Bloomberg* (November 15, 2012).

66. Ilya Khrennikov, "Billionaire Usmanov Seeks to Boost Stake in VKontakte Next Year," *Bloomberg* (December 21, 2012).

67. "Rukovodstvo 'VKontakte': 'My uzhe neskolko let sotrudnichaem s FSB i otdelom "K" MVD, operativno vydavaya informatsiyu o tysyachakh polzovateley nashey seti,'" *Novaya Gazeta* (March 27, 2013).

68. "Vkontakte Manipulated Web Content to Counter Opposition, Report Says," *The Moscow Times* (March 27, 2013).

69. Simone Foxman and Gideon Lichfield, "Putin's Friends Now Own 88% of Russia's Facebook," *Quartz* (April 18, 2013).

70. Jennifer Monaghan, "Vkontakte Founder Says Sold Shares Due to FSB Pressure," *The Moscow Times* (April 17, 2014).

71. Pavel Durov's Vkontakte page (April 16, 2014), http://vk.com/durov?z=photo1_327778155%2Falbum1_00%2Frev.

72. "Vkontakte Founder Pavel Durov Learns He's Been Fired through Media," *The Moscow Times* (April 22, 2014).

73. Mark Scott, "Mail.ru Takes Full Ownership of VKontakte, Russia's Largest Social Network," *The New York Times* (September 16, 2014).

74. Andrey Mima, "Zapretit Internet," *TJournal* (July 3, 2014), http://tjournal.ru/paper/mima-servers.

75. Cf. Evgeny Morozov, "What Do They Teach at the 'Kremlin's School of Bloggers'?" *Foreign Policy* (May 26, 2009).

76. To give one example: an article critical of Putin, published in October 2012 on the website of the French paper *Le Figaro*, received forty-five comments, of which thirty-three were in favor of Putin and his version of democracy. Is this really representative of the readership of this paper? Several pro-Putin commentators, writing in impeccable French, presented themselves as Russians living in Russia. (Cf. Pierre Avril, "Vladimir Poutine, le poignard et le goupillon," *Le Figaro* (October 5, 2012), retrieved November 6, 2012, available at http://www.lefigaro.fr/international/2012/10/05/01003-20121005ARTFIG00630-vladimir-poutine-le-poignard-et-le-goupillon.php.

77. Harding, *Mafia State*, 116.

78. William Turvill, "Guardian Fears 'Orchestrated' Pro-Kremlin Campaign in Website Comments," *The Guardian* (May 6, 2014), http://www.pressgazette.co.uk/guardian-fears-orchestrated-pro-kremlin-campaign-website-comments.

79. Turvill, "Guardian Fears 'Orchestrated' Pro-Kremlin Campaign in Website Comments." On August 22, 2014, the Dutch internet paper *De Correspondent* published an interview with me on my book *Putin's Wars*. The following days the paper received more than 150 comments. About 75 percent of these comments were pro-Putin and anti-US/EU. In these comments, the integrity of the reporter and the interviewee were put in doubt and the paper was accused of receiving financial support from dubious sources. See Tomas Vanheste, "Na jaren van wegkijken zien we nu Vladimir Poetin's ware gezicht," *De Correspondent* (August 22, 2014), https://decorrespondent.nl/1618/Na-jaren-van-wegkijken-zien-we-nu-Vladimir-Poetins-ware-gezicht/160548549810-f249e501. This wave of pro-Putin comments, accompanied by a slur campaign against the paper, was a reason for the chief editors to publish a declaration in which they distanced themselves from these comments, considering them "unfounded, [while] expressing conspiracy theories which cast doubt on the integrity, independence, or transparency of correspondents." They also rejected "allegations of double agendas, as if we were being 'paid' to present this perspective." See Karel Smouter and Rob Wijnberg, "Een hoofdredactionele reflectie op het artikel over Vladimir Poetin," *De Correspondent* (August 23, 2014), https://decorrespondent.nl/1626/Een-hoofdredactionele-reflectie-op-het-artikel-over-Vladimir-Poetin/161342362170-f4b2132b.

80. Ilya Klishin, "The Kremlin's Trolls Go West," *The Moscow Times* (May 21, 2014).

81. Cf. Antoine Arjakovsky, *Russie Ukraine: De la guerre à la paix?* (Paris: Parole et Silence, 2014), 63. In June 2015 more information became available on the activities of the Russian "troll farms" when Lyudmila Savchuk, a former employee, sued her purported former employer, a company based in St. Petersburg called "Internet Research," for having failed to provide her any contract. The firm employed an estimated workforce of four hundred employees, who worked around the clock in two twelve-hour shifts. They were paid high salaries of about 41,000 rubles ($777) a month for posting comments on Facebook, Twitter, and other social media. (Cf. Viktor Rezunkov, "Whistle-Blowing Russian 'Troll' Gets Her Day In Court," *RFERL* (June 1, 2015); and Adrian Chen, "The Agency," *New York Times Magazine* (June 2, 2015).)

Chapter Six

Financing Politicians and Political Parties

INTRODUCTION: THE SOVIET LEGACY

During Soviet times, the Kremlin was already secretly giving financial support to foreign political parties and governments. A famous case is that of Finnish President Urho Kekkonen, the father of what has been called "Finlandization." At the beginning of the 1990s, a former KGB agent resident in Helsinki revealed that Kekkonen had received millions of dollars from Moscow for his reelection and, in effect, for his private expenditure also. These transfers were confirmed when Moscow opened the archives of the International Department of the Central Committee of the Communist Party. At that moment it became clear that, far from protecting the Finns from Russian interference, "Finlandization" had offered the Soviets a unique opportunity to meddle constantly in Finnish internal affairs.[1] Apart from the Finnish president, foreign communist parties were also supported. In each "sister party," one prominent member acted as a contact person for the Soviet secret service. The name of this person was known only to the secretary of the party and to one or two members of the Central Committee—to avoid the party becoming involved in spy scandals.[2]

Through the communist parties Moscow was able to influence the political landscape in other countries. After 1991, the new post-Soviet Russia had lost this capacity. It was no longer the center of the world communist movement, and many communist parties abroad disintegrated, merged with other political parties, or simply disappeared. However, this did not mean that the Kremlin leaders no longer had the capability to influence political parties abroad: the loss of control over the communist parties was largely compensated by the availability of new targets—the so-called "bourgeois" political parties—which in Soviet times had been more difficult to approach. These new ways of influencing the political systems of the West available to the Kremlin were less visible and even more secretive than in Soviet times. They were, however, often not less effective.

SUSPICION IN FRANCE AND THE NETHERLANDS

Two French analysts, Hélène Blanc and Renata Lesnik, confirm that "the [Russian] infiltration is intensifying equally via the political world. It is more urgent [than ever] to open one's eyes because it is gaining ground."[3] They cite the example of François Bayrou, the centrist candidate in the French presidential elections of 2002. "At that time via a French personality above any suspicion, who acted as an intermediary, unknown Russians had offered to pay for the complete campaign expenditure. The message was explicit: 'We have been following your career for a long time, we believe in your political future. And we are ready to finance you.'"[4] Bayrou, who refused the generous offer, was alerted to "certain influences that could exist about which no one would be aware."[5] Indeed, as concerns the funding of political candidates, controls over the origin of the funding are, in general, rare. In an interview, Hélène Blanc emphasized that according to Interpol, "next to terrorism, infiltration by dubious businessmen who have come in from the cold, ex-Soviet and especially Russian, is the second scourge threatening the [European] Union. A danger that is most of the time hidden. These individuals are weakening our democracies. Their strength is based mostly in our weakness and our blindness. I am convinced that as well as the economic and financial power, they also want here the same political power they already possess in Russia. From well informed sources I know that elected politicians have been approached in other countries of Europe."[6] And she continued, "these generous donors are not stupid: the money will be transferred via a European bank, not from Moscow but from Monaco, from Luxembourg, Austria, or Malta, or even Cyprus where 4,000 Russian companies are registered."[7]

The lack of strict regulations concerning party funding, in particular, creates an area of weakness. This was the case, for instance, in the Netherlands, where, on April 3, 2008, former Dutch immigration minister Rita Verdonk started a new right-wing populist party with the name Trots Op Nederland (Proud of the Netherlands). For a new party, there was no obligation to publish the sources of its funding.[8] When the list was leaked, it came out that one of the top funders was "Pershore," an unknown company registered in Cyprus, which had donated 100,000 euros. The party did not want (and, unfortunately, was not obliged) to provide any details about this mysterious sponsor. There were suspicions that the money might have come—

directly or indirectly—from a Russian source. There was, however, no proof. If it had been true, then it would have been, at that time, a good investment. The polls predicted that the new party would get 22 out of the 150 seats in the Dutch parliament.[9]

AN EU COMMISSAR, BRITISH POLITICIANS, AND A RUSSIAN OLIGARCH

In Britain there were also rumors of Russian political influence and illegal party funding. A key role in these rumors was attributed to Oleg Deripaska, an aluminium magnate and Russia's richest oligarch. Deripaska is married to Polina, the daughter of Valentin Yumashev, former chief of the presidential administration of Boris Yeltsin. Because Yumashev remarried with Yeltsin's daughter Tatyana, Deripaska became a member of the influential Yeltsin "family." He is a close ally and protégé of Vladimir Putin, completely loyal to the master in the Kremlin. Deripaska presents himself not as a tycoon but rather as a custodian of (former) Russian state property. In July 2007 he said, for instance: "If the state says we need to give it up, we'll give it up. I don't separate myself from the state. I have no other interests."[10]

A strange story began on Friday, August 22, 2008, when European trade commissioner Peter Mandelson and conservative MP and shadow chancellor George Osborne were on the Greek island of Corfu to celebrate the fortieth birthday of Elisabeth Murdoch, daughter of media mogul Rupert Murdoch. Oleg Deripaska also happened to be there, and the oligarch invited both men onto his yacht, the *Queen K*, for drinks. Two days later, Osborne returned to Deripaska's yacht, accompanied by Andrew Feldman, the Conservative Party's fund-raiser, and the banker Nat Rothschild, heir to the famous Rothschild banking dynasty and a personal friend and business associate of Deripaska. On October 5, 2008, there was an unexpected sequel to this private meeting when Osborne leaked to the *Sunday Times* that in Corfu, Mandelson had made derogatory remarks about Prime Minister Gordon Brown. It was apparently a political coup by the Conservatives, meant to destabilize the Labour government. A few days earlier, Mandelson had been appointed by Gordon Brown as business secretary in his cabinet. Nat Rothschild, Deripaska's business partner, reacted with a letter to the *Times*. His letter was a bombshell. Rothschild wrote:

> George Osborne . . . found the opportunity of meeting with Deripaska so good that he invited the Conservatives' fundraiser Andrew Feldman, who was staying nearby, to accompany him onto Deripaska's boat to solicit a donation. Since Deripaska is not a British citizen, it was suggested by Feldman, in a subsequent conversation at which Deripaska was not present, that the donation

was "channelled" through one of Deripaska's British companies (Leyland DAF). Deripaska declined to make any donation. [11]

Osborne and Feldman vehemently denied these allegations. However, in a commentary, the BBC's Robert Peston observes that Rothschild "does not make allegations lightly," adding, as a kind of understatement: "I would not have described him as a Labour supporter." [12] "So," he continued, "these allegations are not going to vanish into thin air as quickly as they've come." As concerns the sum in question (£50,000): "The Tories have said they did not solicit such a donation. I suspect that much will hinge on that word 'solicit'—whether the donation was sought or simply offered." [13] Osborne and Feldman were not able to dismiss these allegations.

This was not the end of the "Corfu story." It would soon lead to other revelations which were equally surprising and potentially extremely embarrassing. Commentators began to take a closer look at the relationship between Peter Mandelson, then European trade commissioner, and Oleg Deripaska. They highlighted the fact that Commissioner Mandelson, five weeks after the yacht meeting and just before leaving office in Brussels, announced new European trade rules which were extremely profitable for Deripaska, whose aluminum companies benefited from lower EU tariffs. The British *Independent* published an article with the title "A Final Favour? How Mandelson's Last Act in Brussels Boosted Russian Oligarch." [14] According to the author, political editor Jane Merrick, "critics said that the announcement of new trade rules, five weeks after the yacht meeting and five days before he became Secretary of State for Business, fuelled the suspicion of a conflict of interest." Mandelson denied any wrongdoing. When doubts surfaced about the frequency of Mandelson's contacts with the oligarch, European Commission officials suggested that the two men had met "at a few social gatherings in 2006 and 2007." [15] Mandelson, however, had to admit that he had already met Deripaska in Moscow in 2004 and 2005. A key role in arranging a meeting in Moscow was said to have been played by Valery Pechenkin, the head of security at Deripaska's holding company Basic Element. Pechenkin, the oligarch's right hand, is not an ordinary security man but a former high-ranking officer in the KGB and a former FSB colonel general. He is called "one of Deripaska's strongest links to the Kremlin." [16] The veteran spy would have organized an instant entry visa for Mandelson when he arrived in Moscow in the Rothschild executive jet for his meeting with Deripaska.

An article in the *Guardian* ended with the following "remaining questions": "Did Lord Mandelson meet Oleg Deripaska before a 2004 Moscow dinner? Was he aware that the oligarch had been barred from entering the US and of allegations that he had been associated with alleged organized criminals? How many times has he been on board Deripaska's private jet or his yacht? Did Mandelson and Deripaska discuss aluminium tariffs at any of their meetings? . . . Did he arrive in Corfu aboard Deripaska's yacht, or board it on the island?"[17] Important questions indeed. They were—partly—answered some years later when Deripaska's friend Nat Rothschild sued the owner of the *Daily Mail* over an article published in this paper in May 2010. Rothschild lost the case. Feldman, the Conservative Party's fund-raiser, told the High Court that he "had never approached Mr. Deripaska for a donation, but said Mr. Rothschild had made the suggestion twice during the summer of 2008." Feldman said: "Mr. Rothschild asked about my involvement in the Conservative Party and suggested that his friend, Mr. Deripaska, could be interested in making a party donation."[18] This testimony confirms that an offer was made rather than a gift solicited. How serious this offer was becomes clear from the fact that three weeks later, Rothschild is alleged to have told Feldman that "[Deripaska's British firm] Leyland DAF was interested in making a donation."[19] This gift, however, was ruled out by senior party officials because of its "political sensitivity." Rothschild, for his part, "denied the suggestion that it was an example of Mr. Deripaska 'seeking political influence.'"[20]

In May 2013, yet another unexpected sequel to the Mandelson story emerged, when Mandelson followed in the footsteps of another high-level European politician, Gerhard Schröder, and the *Guardian* announced that he had been offered a place on the board of directors of the Russian conglomerate AFK Sistema.[21] The *Guardian* accused Sistema—a Fortune Global 500 business with a reported revenue of $34.2 billion in 2012—of links with organized crime. According to a cable released by WikiLeaks, Sistema is allegedly linked to one of the biggest organized crime gangs of Russia, Solntsevo. The cable alleges that Evgeny Novitsky, the former president of Sistema, "controlled the Solntsevo criminal gang." According to Mark Galeotti, an expert on organized crime, the gang was based in Moscow but had links in Israel, the United States, and Europe. "It's so large that it's a stretch to call it a gang. It doesn't really have a leadership or a hierarchy, it's more like a criminal club full of regional clubs."[22]

Despite these *liaisons dangereuses* of the Russian oligarchs, other highly placed British officials also seem to have exercised little self-restraint and let themselves be easily seduced by these new, generous bosses. In 2011, for instance, Sir Michael Peat, the former principal private secretary to Prince Charles, was appointed to the board of Evraz, Roman Abramovich's steel and mining group, on a salary of £250,000 a year. One year later, in March 2012, Peat appointed Eugene Shvidler, Abramovich's right-hand man who is himself a billionaire with a personal fortune of £1.5 billion, to the board of his stockbroking company MC Peat & Co.[23] Another oligarch, Boris Berezovsky, even had no problem in hiring the services of "real" blue blood when he recruited the Prince of Kent, a member of the royal family. It is telling also that Tony Blair Associates, a counseling firm founded by the former Labour prime minister, had among its clients oligarchs from Kazakhstan who were close to the autocratic president, Nursultan Nazarbayev.[24]

CONSERVATIVE FRIENDS OF RUSSIA

In August 2012 in London, a new club was launched, called the Conservative Friends of Russia. This was an initiative of the diplomat Sergey Nalobin, first secretary in the political section of the Russian embassy in London. Nalobin had a solid KGB/FSB family background. Both his brother and his father worked for the secret service. His father, Nikolay Nalobin, a former KGB agent, became an FSB general and was said to have been the former boss of Alexander Litvinenko, the dissident spy who was allegedly killed by the FSB in London with radioactive polonium-210. The Conservative Friends of Russia was inaugurated on August 21, 2012, at a garden party at the Kensington residence of the Russian ambassador, Alexander Yakovenko. About 250 guests, including Tory MPs and Tory peers, attended the party. The guests were served vodka, champagne, and shashlik and received a biography of Vladimir Putin as a present. The festive inauguration of the Conservative Friends of Russia, coming only a few days after the verdict in the "Pussy Riot trial," met with critical reactions. Labour MP and former minister for Europe Denis MacShane called it "inappropriate" to accept hospitality from the Kremlin just a few days after this crackdown.[25] However, Sir Malcolm Rifkind, a former Conservative foreign secretary, saw no problem in accepting the honorary presidency of the new group. Richard Royal, a PR consultant who worked at Ladbrokes, a betting and gaming enterprise, became its chair. On the website of Ladbrokes, Richard Royal was cited as the contact for information about "political betting, betting and gaming policy, governmental liaison, security issues."[26] One month later, in September 2012, Richard Royal and other members of the Conservative Friends of Russia were invited to Moscow and St. Petersburg, where they visited the Hermitage museum and the state ballet and participated in gala dinners. In between, they had meetings with politicians of Putin's United Russia Party. Their ten-day trip was paid for by Rossotrudnichestvo, the Kremlin's new soft-power organization.

The idea of setting up Conservative Friends of Russia as an instrument to influence elite political opinion in Britain came directly from the Kremlin. The *Guardian* published an e-mail sent by Sergey Nalobin to Sergey Cristo, a Russian-born Tory and fund-raiser, in which Nalobin wrote: "We've received instructions from Moscow to discuss the perspective of co-operation between British Conservatives and United Russia in the parliamentary assembly of the Council of Europe."[27] The two parties both belong to the

European Democrat Group (EDG) in the council's parliamentary assembly, with Tory members often voting with their Russian colleagues against motions condemning Moscow. Sergey Cristo said Nalobin had already approached him in December 2010, seeking introductions to top Conservative Party figures. According to Cristo, Nalobin also offered to make donations to Conservative Party funds via UK-registered, Russian-owned companies. "No companies were named, however, and the offer never materialized."[28] In November 2012, the Conservative Friends of Russia published a controversial photo of the Labour MP Chris Bryant in his underpants on its website. Chris Bryant, a former minister for Europe and chairman of the All Party Parliamentary Group on Russia, was an outspoken critic of Putin whom the Russian embassy wanted removed. The homophobic attack on Bryant led Malcolm Rifkind and two other Tory MPs, Nigel Evans and Robert Buckland, to quit the Conservative Friends of Russia.[29] These complications, however, did not cause Russian diplomats to tone down their efforts to influence British politics. Emma Reynolds, a Labour MP, told the *Guardian* that she had met Nalobin at a Labour party conference. "The Russian diplomat suggested it would be a good idea to set up a Labour Friends of Russia. She declined."[30]

In July 2014, the *Guardian* published details of the Conservative Party's fund-raising dinner which was organized the year before. The dinner, on June 24, 2013, was said to have attracted 449 attendees who had a combined wealth of £11 billion. "One of the most surprising guests," wrote the paper, "was Vladimir Putin's judo partner, Vasily Shestakov, who was introduced to the prime minister. The Russian president's key aide had been tasked with improving Russia's reputation in the UK and the handshake was 'to make wheels go round,' a member of the Russian's party said."[31] Shestakov, a Duma member for United Russia, is a long-time friend of Putin and Putin's coauthor on several books, including *Learn Judo with Vladimir Putin* and *Judo: History, Theory, and Practice*. During the fund-raising dinner, Shestakov was introduced to David Cameron by David Burnside, director of the PR firm New Century Media, a firm which in the years 2009 and 2010 donated £91,000 to the Conservative Party. In June 2013, the same month in which the fund-raising dinner took place, David Burnside founded with Tim Lewin, a colleague, the Positive Russia Foundation. This seemingly "British" initiative was Kremlin inspired. The Russian news agency ITAR-TASS presented Vasily Shestakov as "one of the head officials of the new foundation," adding that the plans to create the foundation "were approved by Prince Michael of Kent and British Prime Minister David Cameron."[32] Its purpose was to combat "'anti-Russian propaganda' in the British media."[33] In an interview, Shestakov described the Positive Russia Foundation "as a new variant of RT, but under the patronage of English aristocrats."[34] Labour MP Chris Bryant, former chairman of the all-party parliamentary Russia group, said: "This shows the utter hypocrisy of David Cameron's Tory party and explains Cameron's spinelessness in relation to Putin. Voters will think that it's not just bizarre but despicable that Cameron will shake hands with, sit down to dinner with, and quite possibly take the money off, people such as these—the very people he is pretending to criticize over Crimea."[35] The Conservative Party's spokespersons did not react and apparently agreed with the old adage: *pecunia non olet*.

Conservative justice minister Chris Grayling also rejected criticisms of a £160,000 donation to the party from Lubov Chernukhin, the wife of Vladimir Chernukhin, a former deputy finance minister in Putin's government. She had paid this sum in a fund-raising auction in the summer of 2014 to play tennis with David Cameron. Minister Grayling insisted: "When you contribute money to the Conservative party, you don't buy policy decisions."[36] He was certainly right that buying political influence is often not a question of giving *A* in exchange for *B*. However, Francis Fukuyama rightly points out that such an explicit exchange need not be a necessary condition for effective lobbying: "Interest groups are able to influence members of Congress legally simply by making donations and waiting for unspecified return favors."[37] It is, indeed, the *unspecified* return favors in which the generous donors could be interested.[38]

BUYING INFLUENCE IN THE FORMER SOVIET BLOC: THE CASES OF LITHUANIA, ESTONIA, AND THE CZECH REPUBLIC

The Kremlin's efforts in buying political influence are probably even more successful in the countries of the former Soviet bloc. In 2004 the president of Lithuania, Roland Paksas, was removed from office after being impeached for having accepted $400,000 from a Russian businessman, Yury Borisov. "According to the parliamentary inquiry," wrote the *Economist*, "Mr. Borisov was linked to a Russian lobbying firm probably tied to Russia's security services."[39] Borisov was granted Lithuanian nationality by President Paksas in return but made threats against Paksas when he did not get a government position.

Another case is that of the Centre Party in Estonia. The Centre Party is an opposition party of which 80 percent of the electorate consists of Russophones. According to information from the Kapo, the Estonian intelligence service, published at the end of December 2010, the leader of the Centre Party, Edgar Savisaar, who is mayor of the capital, Tallinn, had asked for financial support from Russia: 1.5 million euros for the party and 1.5 million euros for the construction of an Orthodox church in a suburb of Tallinn. The Kapo had observed several meetings between Savisaar and Vladimir Yakunin, president of the Russian railways and a well-known Russian oligarch.

He is the son of a pilot with the Soviet Border Troops of the KGB and during his youth lived in Estonia, a country he knows very well. Since the beginning of the 1990s he has been a very close friend of Vladimir Putin. Both men had a dacha at the shore of Lake Komsomolskoye near Saint Petersburg and were members of Ozero (Lake), the cooperative society of dacha owners. Yakunin, who between 1988 and 1991 was first secretary of the Soviet diplomatic mission to the UN, worked according to some sources as a KGB officer under diplomatic cover in the First Chief Directorate (for foreign espionage)—the same directorate as Putin.[40] The contacts between Savisaar and Yakunin were a reason for Estonian Prime Minister Andrus Ansip to warn Savisaar. "It is not a secret," he said, "that there exist in Russia forces that still seek to bring Estonia into their sphere of influence. Unfortunately, Savisaar is lending them a helpful hand."[41] An officer of the Estonian intelligence service told *Le Monde* that they had met with Savisaar on November 4, 2010. "We drew his attention to the fact that he risked being compromised if his party received money from abroad and that that could represent a national security risk."[42]

The Kremlin is also active in the former satellite states. In the Czech Republic, rumors concerning former president Vaclav Klaus circulate. "Klaus has backed Moscow so consistently over the years that jokes in Prague about his being a Russian agent prompt chuckles tinged with more than a little nervousness," wrote two experts on Central Europe.[43] Klaus, who long opposed signing the Lisbon Treaty, putting him in step with "one of Moscow's biggest foreign-policy goals: splitting European unity," in the 1990s promoted gas and oil deals with Russia while opposing a deal to buy gas from Norway. Lukoil, the Russian oil company, paid for the translation of an anti-global-warming book written by him. "There are worries," wrote the authors, "that Klaus . . . is just the tip of the iceberg. A growing number of Czech politicians across the spectrum appear to have ties to Russia in one or another form, and it's setting off alarm bells. Twenty years after the end of communism—and four decades after the Red Army crushed the Prague Spring in 1968—a few lonely voices are warning that the Czech Republic and its neighbors are in danger of falling under Moscow's influence once again."[44] Former President Vaclav Havel warned that Russian state-controlled and private enterprises that play a role in the Kremlin's foreign policy are "undoubtedly influencing the behavior of various Czech political parties and politicians. . . . I've seen several cases where the influence started quietly and slowly began projecting onto our foreign policy."[45]

The Kremlin is not only interested in enhancing its influence in the national parliaments of Europe, it is equally interested in enhancing its influence in the European Parliament. The Russian Orthodox Church, acting as one of the agencies of the Russian Foreign Ministry, "is expressing open support for assisting ethnic Russians in election campaigns to legislative bodies in the European Union."[46] The Russian Orthodox Church also acts as an intermediary in establishing contact between United Russia and conservative parties in the West.[47] (The prominent role assigned by the Kremlin to the Russian Orthodox Church in projecting soft power abroad is discussed in more detail in part II of this book.)

The Kremlin cultivates its relations with Western politicians not only directly but also indirectly via Russian firms or Kremlin-friendly oligarchs. In the Czech Republic, for instance, the Russian oil giant Lukoil cultivates its ties with leading Czech politicians with the help of lobbyists. Contacts include not only the Russia-friendly President Vaclav Klaus but also former prime minister Miloš Zeman, who left the Social Democratic Party and started his Party of Civic Rights. This party "admits taking money from Russian-connected lobbyists. Chief among them is Miroslav Slouf, a former communist youth leader whose Slavia Consulting company brokered the Lukoil deal to supply Prague's airport. Slouf, who is known to be Lukoil's main promoter in the Czech Republic, also happens to be Zeman's right-hand man."[48] On January 26, 2013, Miloš Zeman won the presidential elections. According to Riikka Nisonen, an analyst, "Zeman's presidential campaign received money from the head of Lukoil's Czech office. Zeman claims the money was a personal donation."[49] It may seem an exaggeration to call Zeman "Moscow's man." However, the Kremlin had every reason to be satisfied. As Corinne Deloy of the French think tank Fondation Robert Schuman reminds us: "If Milos Zeman can be expected to bring Prague closer to its European partners, the new president could also do the same with Russia with which he entertains a close relationship."[50] Some months later, this prophecy seemed to be vindicated when the president—apparently drunk—attended an official ceremony at the Prague Castle. He had spent the day at a reception at the Russian embassy, where there was no shortage of vodka. Zeman was not only accused of "grave disrespect for the presidential institution and his ceremonial duties"[51] but was also criticized for something perhaps much more disturbing: his "overt inclination toward Russia."[52]

In July 2009 a group of leading East European politicians[53] published in the Polish paper *Gazeta Wyborcza* an "Open Letter to the Obama Administration." In this letter they expressed their concern, writing that "Russia is back as a revisionist power pursuing a 19th century agenda with 21st-century tactics and methods. . . . It uses overt and covert means of economic warfare, ranging from energy blockades and politically motivated investments to bribery and media manipulation in order to advance its interests and to challenge the transatlantic orientation of Central and Eastern Europe."[54] The signatories also warned that "there is a danger that instead of being a pro-Atlantic voice in the EU, support for a more global partnership with Washington in the region might wane over time," due to a leadership change and the fallout from the global economic crisis, which "provide additional opportunities for the forces of nationalism, extremism, populism, and anti-Semitism."[55] In September 2014 these words seemed almost prophetic when, at the NATO summit in Wales, Miloš Zeman declared his government to be opposed to sanctions against Moscow because there was not yet "clear proof" of Moscow's intervention in Ukraine. Zeman was supported by Slovakia and by Hungary, whose prime minister, Viktor Orbán, openly rejects the principles of liberal democracy, opting for an "illiberal" democracy along Putinist lines.[56] Alexandr Vondra, former minister of defense of the Czech Republic and one of the signatories of the "Open Letter," wrote: "Five years have passed since 2009. One can easily reach the conclusion that the reset policy was a failure. . . . Russia annexed Crimea. . . . Ukraine is in a *de facto* state of war with Russia. The art of Russian propaganda has reached Goebbelsian proportions—and celebrates a successful road show in many European capitals. The Russian espionage and intelligence services are active in the West as never before. . . . Rereading the 2009 open letter five years after, I would not change a word of it. . . . All our arguments remain valid."[57]

CORRUPTION RISKS IN EUROPE

In 2012, Transparency International published a report on corruption risks in Europe. The report identified political parties, public administrations, and the private sector "as the weakest forces in the promotion of integrity across Europe."[58] One of the report's conclusions was that "political parties and businesses exhibit the highest risks of corruption across Europe; with few exceptions they are rated among the weakest sectors when it comes to anti-corruption safeguards. One of the intersections at which parties and businesses meet—political party financing—is a particularly high-risk area, which even countries often described as 'low corruption contexts' have not managed to insulate themselves against."[59] Another conclusion was that "lobbying remains veiled in secrecy: In most European countries, the influence of lobbyists is shrouded in secrecy and a major cause for concern. Opaque lobbying rules result in skewed decision-making that benefits a few at the expense of the many."[60] It is precisely by making use of these weak spots of Western democracies that the Kremlin tries, often successfully, to influence the decision making of Western governments.

NOTES

1. Cf. Walter Laqueur, *Mein 20. Jahrhundert: Stationen eines politischen Lebens* (Berlin: Propyläen, 2009), 129.
2. Cf. Thierry Wolton, *Le KGB en France* (Paris: France Loisirs, 1986), 22–23. This system was installed by Leon Trotsky as early as 1924.

3. Hélène Blanc and Renata Lesnik, *Les prédateurs du Kremlin (1917–2009)* (Paris: Seuil, 2009), 330–331.

4. Blanc and Lesnik, *Les prédateurs*, 331.

5. Blanc and Lesnik, *Les prédateurs*, 331.

6. Hélène Blanc, "Les mafias russes menacent l'Europe," *L'Express* (June 28, 2004).

7. Blanc, "Les mafias russes."

8. A report of Transparency International judged the Netherlands' regulations concerning party financing to be "wholly inadequate, as the rules only apply to political parties at the central level who have chosen to receive state subsidy. For all other political parties (those not receiving a subsidy and those at the regional or local levels) no rules on political financing exist." (Suzanne Mulcahy, "Money, Politics, Power—Corruption Risks in Europe," Transparency International (2012), 23.) A new law, adopted by the Dutch parliament in 2012, made it obligatory for all parties operating at the national level to reveal gifts of more than €4,500 (even for those not receiving a state subsidy) but failed to impose the same regime for local parties and local party branches, thereby making it possible for national parties to circumvent the new regulations. The new liberal-socialist coalition government, installed in November 2012, promised to extend the new legislation to the local level.

9. When, in June 2010, the parliamentary elections were held, the party failed to gain a single seat. It was the populist Party for Freedom (PVV) of competitor Geert Wilders that got twenty-four seats.

10. Quoted in Mark Hollingsworth and Stewart Lansley, *Londongrad: From Russia with Cash—The Inside Story of the Oligarchs* (London: Fourth Estate, 2010), 342.

11. Nathaniel Rothschild, "Letter to the Editor," *The Times* (October 19, 2008).

12. Robert Peston, "Rothschild v Osborne," *BBC* (October 21, 2008).

13. Peston, "Rothschild v Osborne."

14. Jane Merrick, "A Final Favour? How Mandelson's Last Act in Brussels Boosted Russian Oligarch," *The Independent* (October 26, 2008).

15. Merrick, "A Final Favour?"

16. Keith Dovkants, "Veteran KGB Spy Revealed as Deripaska's Right-Hand Man," *London Evening Standard* (October 29, 2008).

17. Tom Parfitt, "Mandelson Silent on Deripaska," *The Guardian* (October 28, 2008).

18. Vanessa Allen, "Rothschild 'Suggested Russian Oligarch Could Become a Tory Donor,'" *Mail* online (January 24, 2012).

19. Allen, "Rothschild 'Suggested.'"

20. Allen, "Rothschild 'Suggested.'"

21. "Peter Mandelson Joins Board of Russian Firm 'with Organised Crime Links,'" *The Guardian* (May 30, 2013). The article was taken down from the *Guardian*'s website on June 1, 2013, "pending an investigation."

22. Quoted in "Peter Mandelson Set to Join 'Mafia-Linked' Russian Firm," *The Week* (May 31, 2013).

23. Tim Walker, "The Queen's Man Sir Michael Peat Strengthens His Ties to Roman Abramovich," *The Telegraph* (March 13, 2012).

24. Marc Roche, "Ces politiques qui cèdent aux sirènes des oligarques russes," *Le Monde* (June 2–3, 2013).

25. Luke Harding and Nicholas Watt, "Conservative Friends of Russia under Fire for Launch after Pussy Riot Verdict," *The Guardian* (August 22, 2012).

26. Ladbrokes website, retrieved on December 12, 2012, http://news.ladbrokes.com.

27. Luke Harding, "How Kremlin Got Diplomats to Woo Tories," *The Guardian* (November 30, 2012).

28. Harding, "How Kremlin Got Diplomats to Woo Tories."

29. Andy McSmith, "Chris Bryant Accuses Russian Officials of 'Smear Campaign,'" *The Independent* (November 24, 2012).

30. Luke Harding, "Tory Blushes Deepen over Activities of Conservative Friends of Russia," *The Guardian* (November 30, 2012).

31. Robert Booth, Nick Mathiason, Luke Harding, and Melanie Newman, "Tory Summer Party Drew Super-Rich Supporters with Total Wealth of £11bn," *The Guardian* (July 3, 2014),

http://www.theguardian.com/politics/2014/jul/01/-sp-tory-summer-party-drew-super-rich-supporters-with-total-wealth-of-11bn.

32. Lyudmila Alexandrova, "Russia Takes New Steps to Improve Its Image Abroad," ITAR-TASS (July 9, 2014).

33. Booth et al., "Tory Summer Party."

34. Booth et al., "Tory Summer Party."

35. Booth et al., "Tory Summer Party."

36. Rajeev Syal, "PM's Tennis Match with Wife of Former Putin Minister Will Go Ahead, Say Tories," *The Guardian* (July 31, 2014).

37. Francis Fukuyama, "America in Decay—The Sources of Political Dysfunction," *Foreign Affairs* 93, no. 5 (September/October 2014): 15–16.

38. According to the BBC, since 2010 the Conservative Party has received at least £1,157,433 from British citizens who were formerly Russian citizens or are married to Russians or from their associated companies. This sum does not include donations from companies with links to Russia or who deal with the country but whose owners and directors cannot be verified. It was emphasized that "Labour and the Lib Dems have not received any donations from Russians over the same period." Cf. "UK-Based Russians Donating Large Sums to Tories," *BBC* (July 23, 2014), http://www.bbc.com/news/uk-politics-28450125?print=true.

39. "Muddling On," *The Economist* (January 8, 2004).

40. Cf. "Antikompromat," http://www.anticompromat.org/yakunin/yakunbio01.html.

41. Olivier Truc, "La présence russe au coeur des législatives en Estonie," *Le Monde* (March 5, 2011).

42. Truc, "La présence russe."

43. Gregory Feifer and Brian Whitmore, "Czech Power Games: How Russia Is Rebuilding Influence in the Former Soviet Bloc," Radio Free Europe/Radio Liberty (September 25, 2010).

44. Feifer and Whitmore, "Czech Power Games."

45. Feifer and Whitmore, "Czech Power Games."

46. Robert C. Blitt, "Russia's 'Orthodox' Foreign Policy: The Growing Influence of the Russian Orthodox Church in Shaping Russia's Policies Abroad," *University of Pennsylvania Journal of International Law* 33, no. 2 (December 2011): 426.

47. "Russian Church to Help Expand Dialog between United Russia and Western Conservatives," Interfax (May 31, 2010).

48. Feifer and Whitmore, "Czech Power Games."

49. Riikka Nisonen, "Miloš Zeman Is the New President of the Czech Republic," *Baltic Worlds* (January 31, 2013), http://balticworlds.com/new-president-of-the-czech-republic/.

50. Corinne Deloy, "Milos Zeman, nouveau président de la République tchèque," Fondation Robert Schuman, Observatoire des Elections en Europe (January 28, 2013), available at http://www.robert-schuman.eu/oee.php?num=818.

51. Jan Hornát, "Russian Vodka and Czech Crown Jewels," openDemocracy (May 17, 2013).

52. Hornát, "Russian Vodka."

53. The group included Valdas Adamkus, Emil Constantinescu, Vaclav Havel, Alexander Kwasniewski, Vaira Vike-Freiberga, and Lech Walesa, respectively former presidents of Lithuania, Romania, Czechoslovakia/Czech Republic, Poland, Latvia, and Poland.

54. Cf. "An Open Letter to the Obama Administration from Central and Eastern Europe," Radio Free Europe/Radio Liberty (July 16, 2009).

55. "An Open Letter to the Obama Administration."

56. Cf. Harold Meyerson, "Hungary's Prime Minister a Champion for Illiberalism," *The Washington Post* (August 6, 2014).

57. Alexandr Vondra, "Letter to Obama: Five Years Later," Center for European Policy Analysis (July 10, 2014).

58. "Money, Politics, Power—Corruption Risks in Europe," 3.

59. "Money, Politics, Power—Corruption Risks in Europe," 22.

60. "Money, Politics, Power—Corruption Risks in Europe," 5.

Chapter Seven

Spies and Spooks as Soft-Power Instruments?

WILLY BRANDT AND THE GUILLAUME AFFAIR: A MODEL?

Spies and spooks are normally not considered as a constitutive part of a country's soft-power arsenal, and they certainly do not fit into Nye's definition of soft power as "power of attraction." However, they deserve a place here because they fit very well within Putin's definition of soft power as an integral part of an overarching hard-power game—a zero-sum game in which the influence of one party is detrimental to the influence of the other—adversarial—party. One might expect that the Russian government—the highest leader and core officials of which have a KGB/FSB background—would give the secret services an important role in the realization of Putin's soft-power offensive. Moreover, they can fall back on an old tradition developed during the Soviet era, when the Kremlin was not in a position to contract the services of Western PR firms or to buy advertising space in Western papers. At that time, however, it had other means of influencing Western public opinion and Western political leaders.

A famous example is the case of Günter Guillaume, an agent of the Stasi, the secret service of the former German Democratic Republic. Guillaume became a close aide to German Chancellor Willy Brandt—so close, indeed, that he even accompanied Brandt on his holidays. Due to the "Guillaume Affair," Brandt had to resign in 1974. For Brandt, the father of Germany's Ostpolitik who sought a rapprochement with Moscow and the leaders in East Berlin, it was an extremely traumatic and humiliating event. "Almost for a year he travelled with this Judas through Germany, they ate and drank together. Guillaume was his paymaster, he paid the bills, small things of which the chancellor often was not aware, in the saloon carriage [of Brandt's special train] he laid out his clothing and prepared his shoes for the next day. The traitor assisted at many confidential discussions of the party."[1] It is striking that in his autobiography, *Begegnungen und Einsichten: Die Jahre 1960–1975* (*Meetings and Insights: The Years 1960–1975*), a book of 647 pages, Brandt mentions the name of Guillaume only *once*, writing: "I have to disappoint readers who expected from this book revelations on the 'Guillaume Affair'. The competent court and a parliamentary inquiry commission have dealt with that. I have nothing to add here to what I said there to the best of my knowledge and belief."[2] He added, tellingly: *"It is certain that I accepted advice that, looking back, I should not have accepted."*[3] Brandt here openly admits that some of his decisions in his function as German chancellor were influenced by the Stasi, the KGB's East German sister organization.

1991: THE TAMING OF THE BEAST

The East German Stasi disappeared definitively with German reunification, which brought about the end of the German Democratic Republic. The situation, however, was different in Russia, the successor state to the Soviet Union. After the KGB-inspired coup d'état of August 1991 and the subsequent breakup of the Soviet Union in December of that year, Russian President Boris Yeltsin did not disband the KGB but sought only to weaken it by splitting it into different independent agencies. In this way the old KGB gave birth to five children: the Foreign Intelligence Service SVR, the internal counterintelligence service FSB, the Border Guard Service PSR, the Federal Protective Service FSO (responsible for the protection of government buildings and highly placed persons), and FAPSI (a service tasked with secure communications and cryptography). However, this "taming of the beast" did not last long. Under Putin there began a new centralization. By presidential decree of March 11, 2003, the FSB absorbed the PSR and the FAPSI. It is not excluded that—in time—the FSB will also try to bring the foreign intelligence branch (SVR) back under its wing, which would come close to restoring the near-monopoly of the former KGB.[4] For the moment, however, there remain two secret services tasked with working abroad. These are the SVR and the GRU. The latter is the Russian military intelligence service, responsible for military espionage. Both services have four functions: intelligence gathering and analysis, industrial and military espionage, dissemination of disinformation, and infiltration of foreign governments and international organizations. It is especially the last function—the infiltration of foreign governments and international organizations—which interests us here.

STATIONING "ILLEGALS" IN FOREIGN COUNTRIES: THE CHAPMAN STORY

Russian espionage activities in the West, having declined in the early 1990s, are now back to their former Cold War levels. Not only do the Russian secret services place their spies under diplomatic cover in embassies abroad, but they also invest heavily in "human relations" by stationing so called "illegals" or "sleepers" in foreign countries, a practice that was already widespread in Soviet times. "Illegals" live for many years in the target country, often under a false identity, unnoticed by their colleagues and neighbors. Target countries are especially the United States and Western Europe. The French analyst Thierry Wolton estimates that in 1984 about one hundred illegals were living in France alone. [5]

A reminder of the persistence of this strategy was the arrest by the FBI on June 27, 2010, of a Russian spy ring in the United States. An eleven-strong team of "deep cover" agents with mostly faked names and false passports had been living in the United States for many years, some of them for almost two decades. They were leading normal lives in the suburbs of New York, Boston, and Washington. Some couples even had children together. Their mission was not only to gather information on nuclear plants, the CIA, and US foreign policy but also to infiltrate circles close to the government. On July 8, 2010, ten captured spies were exchanged in Vienna for four US agents. In Moscow the Russian spies were welcomed like heroes. They were the invitees of Putin and sang patriotic songs with him. After receiving medals from President Medvedev, they were offered prestigious positions in state firms. One of them was a young woman named Anna Chapman. (Her own name was Kushchenko, Chapman being her former British husband's name.) She had her photo, showing her in sexy black underwear, published on the cover of *Maxim*, a glossy men's magazine. Chapman got a job as adviser to the director of the Moscow FundServiceBank FSB, a bank linked with Roskosmos, the Russian space agency. (Ironically, the bank name's abbreviation FSB was the same as that of the KGB's successor organization FSB.) This new job was a reason for Chapman to fly to Baikonur, Kazakhstan, for a photo session with Russian cosmonauts, evoking memories of the glorious days of the Soviet past. The former spy also got a leading position in the Molodaya Gvardiya, the youth organization of the ruling United Russia Party, and in January 2011 she was invited to present her own TV show on REN TV. Anna Chapman-Kushchenko is a pure KGB product. She is the daughter of Vasily Kushchenko, a high-ranking officer of the secret services who worked in the Russian embassy in Zimbabwe. Coming from an authentic "KGB nest," Chapman represents for the Putin regime the new Russian heroine of the modern epoch: the "Chekist" (member of the secret service) who, motivated by deep patriotic feelings, is ready to do anything for his or her country.

Chekists are characterized by almost unlimited commitment, similar to that of monks and nuns in religious orders. However, their loyalty is not to a heavenly god but to the earthly hierarchy of their organization and to what they consider to be their country's interests. "Illegals" are prepared to live double lives: to enter into fake marriages, including having children together while the children are not informed about their parents' real activities. One of the illegals in Chapman's spy ring, living under the adopted name of Juan Lazaro, confirmed this explicitly. He declared that he had "sworn loyalty to the Russian intelligence service. He even explained that this oath was more important than everything else, including his wife and his children."[6] After the arrest of the members of the spy ring, the *Economist* wrote that Moscow was embarrassed not so much "because Russia was spying on America, but because it did it so clumsily."[7] Maybe so. But one could ask why the Russian government continues to invest so much money and energy in a kind of espionage that requires a real *long-term* investment, including agent training, the creation of phony identities, the purchase of cars and houses, buried money, bank accounts, encrypted Wi-Fi connections, and more. The reason is that in the past, illegals have often been very effective. They have succeeded in infiltrating the highest levels of foreign governments.

The dismantling of Chapman's spy ring in the United States had a spin-off in Europe. After a tip-off from the FBI, a German couple, Andreas and Heidrun Anschlag, were arrested on October 18, 2011, in Germany, accused of having been working for the SVR for more than twenty years. They had passed on secret information about the EU and NATO via "dead letter boxes" to their spy masters and were paid €100,000 per year for their services.[8] When the police raided their home, Heidrun was caught sending coded messages to Russia with her shortwave radio. From October 2008 to August 2011, the couple had been managing another agent, Raymond Poeteray, an official of the Dutch Foreign Ministry, who had worked as vice-consul in Hong Kong and had access to highly confidential information. Poeteray was arrested on March 24, 2012.[9] Another diplomat, this time from Belgium, was recalled from the Belgian embassy in Copenhagen at the end of 2011. The man, who had worked in embassies in Japan, India, Portugal, and the United States, was accused of working for the KGB and its successor organizations since the late 1980s.[10] The man was suspected of setting up false identities for Russian spies in Belgium. It came, therefore, as no surprise when, in October 2012, the FBI discovered another extended spy ring in the United States, again composed of eleven people. This time it concerned a conspiracy to export cutting-edge microelectronics to Russia via a Houston-based company called Arc Electronics Inc. This firm had been set up by Alexander Fishenko, a recently naturalized American, born in Soviet Kazakhstan. Between 2002 and October 2012, the firm exported approximately fifty million dollars' worth of microelectronics to Russia, which could be used in a wide range of military systems, including radar and missile-guidance systems. The firm allegedly evaded the US government's licensing system and export controls by providing false end-user information and using intermediary procurement firms. The end users allegedly included the Russian military and Russian intelligence agencies. To American suppliers, the firm reportedly produced benign products such as traffic lights. On its website, the firm—Arc Electronics Inc.—claimed to be a traffic-light manufacturer.[11] Houston FBI special agent in charge, Stephen L. Morris, commented: "In this day and time, the ability of foreign countries to illegally acquire sensitive and sophisticated U.S. technology poses a significant threat to both the economic and national security of our nation. While some countries may leverage our technology for financial gain, many countries hostile to the United States seek to improve their defense capabilities and to modernize their weapons systems at the expense of U.S. taxpayers."[12]

THE "MAGNIFICENT FIVE" AND THEIR HEIRS

Russian spy rings are not new. A famous example is that of the Magnificent Five, a spy ring set up by Kim Philby in Britain. The members of this group were recruited in the 1930s when they were still students at Cambridge University. They succeeded in penetrating the Foreign Office and MI5 and MI6—respectively, the internal and foreign branch of the British secret service. One of them, Donald Maclean, was the son of Sir Donald Maclean, a former liberal cabinet minister and leader of the parliamentary opposition after World War I.[13] Attempts by the KGB to recruit members of the British elite continued well into the 1980s. To this day rumors persist in Britain that British Prime Minister Harold Wilson resigned from office on March 16, 1976, because of presumed links with members of the secret services from the Soviet bloc. In his book *The Defence of the Realm: The Authorised History of MI5*, the British historian Christopher Andrew refutes these allegations.[14] However, having had full access to the British counterintelligence service files, he discovered a secret permanent file for Harold Wilson, created when he entered the House of Commons in 1945. The file, in which Wilson was given the code name Norman John Worthington, was kept throughout Wilson's two premierships (1964–1970 and 1974–1976). It was kept secret, including from the prime minister himself, which led to allegations of an MI5 plot to topple his government.

The defection of Josef Frolik, a Czechoslovak spy, to the United States in 1969, where he joined the CIA, had more serious consequences. In 1975 Frolik, who had worked as a spy for the Czechoslovak secret service StB in the London embassy in the guise of a diplomat, published a book titled *The Frolik Defection: The Memoirs of an Intelligence Agent*. In this book he accused three Labour MPs of being Soviet agents. The names of the accused were Will Owen, Bob Edwards, and John Stonehouse. The last one was postmaster general in Wilson's government. Will Owen was tried for spying for the Czechoslovak StB but was acquitted. However, according to Christopher Andrew, "he was, almost certainly, guilty as charged."[15] Another revelation in Frolik's book was a plot of the StB to seduce and then blackmail Edward Heath, who would later become British prime minister (1970 to 1974). Heath, a lifelong bachelor, was suspected of being gay. The StB's plan was to invite Heath, who had a love of classical music, to a concert in Prague, where—according to the blueprint—a romantic affair would ensue, which would be filmed by the agents of the StB. Eventually, the MI5 warned Heath that a trip to Czechoslovakia could expose him to blackmail by the StB. The trip did not take place.[16]

How persistent these attempts to engage members of the British political elite were becomes clear from remarks made by British Prime Minister David Cameron during a speech to students at Moscow State University in September 2011. Cameron told his audience:

> I first came to Russia as a student on my gap year between school and university in 1985. I took the Trans-Siberian railway from Nakhodka to Moscow and went on to the Black Sea coast. There two Russians, speaking perfect English, turned up on a beach mostly used by foreigners. They took me out to lunch and dinner and asked me about life in England and what I thought about England.[17]

The naïve Cameron did not immediately realize what was happening until he returned to England and reported the event to his tutor at the university. It was considered serious enough for Cameron to disclose the incident to MI5 when he applied for a job as a special adviser to Norman Lamont in the Treasury.[18]

HIGH-LEVEL INFILTRATION IS REACHING UNPRECEDENTED HEIGHTS

In the first decade of the twenty-first century, Russian espionage activities continued unabatedly—possibly even at a higher level than during the Cold War. This is the case not only in the United States but also in Europe. In Germany, memories of the Guillaume Affair were reawakened in March 2010, when it became known that the Verfassungsschutz, the German counterintelligence service, had unmasked two high-ranking civil servants in the state chancellery of Brandenburg, a German *Land* (state) in the former

East German part of the country.[19] The spies had free access to circles close to Matthias Platzeck, the president of the federal state of Brandenburg. One of them, a doctor of law, already had close contacts with the StB, the KGB's Czechoslovak sister organization, before the fall of the Berlin Wall. The other, a woman, may have been engaged by the Russian KGB when she studied in Moscow. A third person, a business adviser, who organized Brandenburg President Platzeck's visits to Moscow, was similarly unmasked as a collaborator with the FSB. At the same time, it became known that the Brandenburg bureau of criminal investigation LKA had been infiltrated by two members of the GRU, the Russian military secret service. These were not "illegals" with fake identities but people working for the Russian secret services under their own identity.

In the United Kingdom in June 2008, Andrew MacKinlay, a Labour MP and member of the influential Foreign Affairs Committee, received a warning after the British counterintelligence MI5 discovered that he was meeting a suspected Russian spy. He even had tea with the agent at the House of Commons. His contact, Alexander Polyakov, worked as a counselor at the Russian embassy and was suspected to be one of the senior Russian SVR agents in the United Kingdom.[20] MacKinley, despite the warnings, continued to meet Polyakov and present a series of parliamentary questions on Russia-related matters. One of his questions concerned why Britain had granted political asylum to Putin critic Boris Berezovsky. MacKinlay's "tea at the Commons" came at the height of Britain's argument with the Kremlin over Andrey Lugovoy, who was suspected of killing the former KGB agent Alexander Litvinenko in London with the radioactive substance polonium-210.

In the United Kingdom in December 2010, another spy affair came out into the open when the British counterintelligence MI5 asked for the deportation of Katia Zatuliveter, the twenty-five-year-old Russian assistant of Mike Hancock, a British Liberal Democrat MP for Portsmouth South. Hancock's constituency, Portsmouth, is an important British naval base, and Hancock himself is a defense specialist. As a member of the Defence Select Committee he received classified briefings from military sources and secret papers. Chris Bryant, Labour's former minister for Europe, said he had ousted Hancock as chairman of the all-party Russian group because he was too lenient towards Moscow. "We were concerned by Mike Hancock's pro-Putin and pro-Medvedev position," said Bryant. "That is why I stood against him and ousted him. . . . The combination of being on the delegation to the Western European Union, the Council of Europe, his membership of the common defence select committee and his position as Portsmouth MP: you can see how he was attractive. Russian secret operatives are working as assiduously now as they did 30 years ago."[21]

Suspicions arose because Hancock had tabled a series of parliamentary questions about Britain's Trident nuclear deterrent and the Atomic Weapons

Establishment at Aldermaston. Hancock insisted, however, that "there was nothing unusual about asking for the locations of berths for submarines."[22] Oleg Gordievsky, a former KGB officer who defected to Britain, claimed that Britain was under attack from Russian spies. "They're spying on all western countries like mad. It's just their psychology and their tradition." The news story explains, "Mr. Gordievsky said the Russians were spying just as much as they always had but that now it was easier to do so in the west. . . . In the past it would have been impossible for Russia to be able to infiltrate the House of Commons so easily."[23]

In December 2010, Mikhail Repin was expelled from Britain after he was caught trying to recruit politicians and civil servants as agents. "Young, good looking and articulate," writes the *Telegraph*, "he introduced himself as 'Michael' at events at Westminster think tanks and embassy receptions."[24] Repin, a junior officer in the SVR, was operating under diplomatic cover from the embassy. His job was apparently to "cultivate" individuals who might be of value to the Kremlin and recruit them as agents. Repin attended events organized by think tanks, such as the International Institute of Strategic Studies, Chatham House, and the Royal United Services Institute, where he was certain to meet MPs, civil servants, and executives from defense firms. "An annual fee of a few hundred pounds got him access to private lectures by senior military and intelligence officials and the chance to mingle with them at the drinks parties and finger food buffets that often followed the talks. This so-called 'overt information gathering' is often the first step in identifying individuals for cultivation."[25]

In 2014 in France, a similar case was reported. It concerned a certain Colonel Ilyushin, deputy air attaché of the Russian embassy, who had the task to place a "mole" in the heart of the French government. Like his colleague in London, the young Russian colonel, who worked for the GRU, the intelligence service of the Russian army, participated in seminars organized by the École Militaire, the Institut de l'Armement, or the Fondation pour la Recherche Stratégique, where he tried to make contact with officers, researchers and journalists. *Le Nouvel Observateur* writes:

> It worked dangerously well. He was interested in certain journalists who were defense specialists. Before approaching them he knew everything about them. Their family, their preferences, their weaknesses also. . . . Every two weeks he invited them for lunch, that is a rule in the Russian secret services. And while sitting around a well-filled dish he gave them unknown information on the Russian army or the defense relations between Paris and Moscow. In the beginning he did not ask anything in return. On the contrary. To strengthen his grip on them he offered an initial present: a Montblanc pen or a bottle of whisky of a good brand—which are the first standard presents of the ex-KGB, expensive enough to be a bit compromising, but not enough to be considered

corruption. Then he observed the reaction. If one of the targets took the pen or the bottle it meant that he or she was ripe for phase 2: recruitment.[26]

With one of the journalists, who could give intimate information on a close aide of French President François Hollande, the approach entered phase 2. However, the reporter contacted the DCRI, the French counterintelligence service, and told H4, the department for Russia, about his experiences. After the Russian colonel had received a warning that he was being observed, he left for Moscow. However, this does not mean that these activities stop, but only that the personnel rotates across the different Russian embassies. Etienne de Durand, a researcher for the French think tank IFRI who is a specialist on military affairs, is said to have been contacted at least four times.[27]

The level of Russia's spying activities can be inferred from the number of personnel staffing its embassies. In 1982 the Soviet embassy in Paris had about seven hundred personnel, of whom at least 10 percent were suspected of working for the secret services.[28] Between 1960 and 1986, France expelled eighty-three KGB and GRU officers from its territory—which is an average of *more than three per year for a quarter of a century*.[29] At present, not only West European states are targeted, but also, and possibly even more so, post-Soviet states and former satellite states. A famous case is that of Herman Simm, an Estonian security expert who worked at the Estonian Defense Ministry from 1995 to 2006. Simm, who had access to top-secret documents, participated in international meetings and commissions of the EU and NATO concerning bolstering information security.[30] He handed over more than two thousand pages of information to his Russian bosses. These included many classified NATO documents.[31] In a report NATO would later conclude that Simm's activities made the alliance "more vulnerable to cyber threats and attacks" because "our weak points are now well-known by our adversaries."[32] These vulnerabilities were apparently exploited during the three weeks of cyberattacks on Estonia in 2007 that all but paralyzed this small Baltic country. The *Economist* called Simm "a potential European equivalent of Aldrich Ames," who was once Russia's top spy in the United States. For years Ames headed a CIA counterintelligence department and is now serving a life sentence in jail after his conviction in 1994.[33] The NATO report called "particularly worrisome" Simm's participation in the annual security conferences organized at the NATO military headquarters in the Belgian town of Mons, as well as his participation in 2006 and in 2007 in two counterespionage conferences. During a conference in the Dutch town of Brunssum in 2006, attendees received a CD containing the names of all known and suspected Russian NATO spies, including detailed information on double agents. According to Sergei Yakovlev, the SVR agent who was Simm's contact person, the compact disk "landed directly on Putin's desk" and "caused quite a stir" in Moscow.[34] Simm would have received a €5,000 bonus above his regular salary. On February 25, 2009, Simm pleaded guilty and was jailed for twelve and one-half years.

Estonia was not the only weak spot in the former Soviet bloc. After the eviction in 2009 of two alleged Russian agents from the embassy in Prague, the Czech domestic intelligence service BIS published in June 2010 a report in which it warned that up to 150 people were working for the Russian secret services.[35] A recent affair that attracted much publicity was that of Robert Rakhardzho, a prison psychologist who started a relationship with a female army major who was chief of staff to three senior generals. The first of these, Josef Sedlak, was a military representative to the NATO command in Europe, the second, Josef Proks, was deputy general for the chief of staff, and the third, Frantisek Hrabal, head of the military office of the president. All three resigned. The alleged spy, son of a Russian mother and an Indonesian father, was believed to have been recruited by the Russian secret service while on vacation in Crete in 2003. His mission was to gather *kompromat* (compromising information) on leading Czech personalities that could be used for blackmail. The man fled to Moscow in September 2009, leaving his wife and two children behind. In its 2011 report, the Czech intelligence service stated "that Russian spies work under different covers, mainly at Russian diplomatic missions, and in numbers that are utterly unjustified given the current status of Czech-Russian relations."[36]

In the 1980s, when Putin worked for the KGB in the German Democratic Republic, his cover job was deputy director of the House of German-Soviet Friendship in Leipzig. There he did not use his own name but was known as Mr. Adamov. Mr. Adamov's task was mainly to recruit agents for espionage in West Germany. Using a "cultural" cover is not new for Russian spies. It came, therefore, as no surprise when, in October 2013, the American magazine *Mother Jones* revealed that the FBI was investigating Yury Zaytsev, the head of the Russian Center for Science and Culture in Washington, for alleged spying activities.[37] The center, set up by Russia's new soft-power agency Rossotrudnichestvo, organized all-expenses-paid trips to Russia for young professional Americans. One of these had been an adviser to an American governor. It was suspected that these trips were used in an effort to cultivate young Americans as intelligence assets (an "asset" could be someone who actively works with a foreign service as well as someone who provides information without realizing that it is being used). The participants of the June 2012 trip were treated as VIPs. They stayed in St. Petersburg at the Sokos Hotel Palace Bridge, a luxury hotel that has hosted delegations for the G8 and G20 summits. They met with the governors of the Moscow and Leningrad regions and with Aleksander Torshin, a prominent member of Putin's United Russia Party. In the years 2011–2013, Rossotrudnichestvo has organized six trips, most of which included about twenty-five people. The

FBI agents, interviewing Americans who participated in the program, would have discovered that Zaytsev or his associates had built files on the participants. The Russian embassy in Washington dismissed the accusations.[38]

The Russian embassy in the Austrian capital Vienna, where many international organizations are based, employs 116 diplomats. This is almost *double* the number of diplomats employed by the US embassy and almost four times the number employed by the French embassy.[39] One might ask: Why? According to Hans-Georg Maaßen, director of the BfV, the German counterintelligence office, one third of the Russian diplomats stationed in Berlin are spies.[40] Brussels also is an important European capital. According to Alain Winants, the head of Belgium's State Security Service, VSSE, in Belgium "Russian espionage . . . [is] at the same level as the Cold War. . . . We are a country with an enormous concentration of diplomats, businessmen, international institutions—NATO, European institutions. So for an intelligence officer, for a spy, this is a kindergarten. It's the place to be."[41] Winants describes their approach as follows: "They make friends with officials at seminars or social events in the EU capital. EU security staff use an acronym for the kind of people they target: Mice (money, ideology, compromise, ego)—people who are greedy or in debt, who have radical ideas, who have guilty secrets or who want to be James Bond."[42]

According to the American security expert Mark Galeotti, "It would be easy to write off Western concerns as an anachronistic relic of the Cold War, but they are genuine. Of course, the West also spies on Russia, but across the board they are reporting a pattern of not just sustained but actually increasing Russian espionage, which is now as extensive and as aggressive as at the height of the Cold War."[43] This view is shared by Edward Lucas. "For the *Siloviki* in Moscow," he writes, "Western society is a spies' paradise. . . . To worry about Russian spies still counts as almost comically paranoid. The popular assumption is that we have no secrets worth stealing. . . . [However], Russia is not like other countries, as the case of Sergei Magnitsky demonstrates. It uses its intelligence agencies as part of a broad and malevolent effort to penetrate our society and skew our decision-making."[44] Lucas adds: "Russian spies' activities are not just a lingering spasm of old Soviet institutions. . . . They are part of a wider effort to penetrate and to manipulate, which targets the weakest parts of our system: its open and trusting approach to outsiders and newcomers."[45] According to Western standards, these activities would certainly not be subsumed under the term "soft power." In the Kremlin's mindset, however, they are valuable assets in its information warfare.

NOTES

1. Peter Merseburger, *Willy Brandt 1913–1992: Visionär und Realist* (Berlin: Pantheon, 2013), 727.

2. Willy Brandt, *Begegnungen und Einsichten: Die Jahre 1960–1975* (Hamburg: Hoffmann und Campe, 1976), 586.

3. Brandt, *Begegnungen und Einsichten*, 586 (emphasis mine).

4. This scenario was predicted by the Russian security expert Pavel Felgenhauer. He expected that the mass spy exposure in the United States in the summer of 2010, due to betrayal in the SVR headquarters, might "lead to serious changes in personnel and possibly in the organization of the intelligence community in Moscow, namely the subordination of the SVR to the FSB, to root out negligence and corruption." (Pavel Felgenhauer, "Russian 'Illegal' Spies in the US Were Betrayed by a Double Agent," *Eurasia Daily Monitor* 7, no. 210 (November 18, 2010).) However, it is not clear whether such a consolidation of the different branches of the secret services is in the interests of the political leadership.

5. Thierry Wolton, *Le KGB en France* (Paris: France Loisirs, 1986), 280.

6. Olivier O'Mahony, "Anna: le visage d'ange du nouveau KGB," *Paris Match* (July 9, 2010).

7. "Spies Like Us," *The Economist* (July 3, 2010).

8. Jorge Benitez, "Germany Charges 2 Alleged Russian Spies Accused of Snooping on EU, NATO Strategy," *Atlantic Council* (September 27, 2012).

9. Jorge Benitez, "Dutch Arrest Foreign Ministry Official for Spying for Russia," *Atlantic Council* (April 2, 2012).

10. Jorge Benitez, "Belgium Suspends Senior Diplomat Suspected of Being a Russian Spy," *Atlantic Council* (October 11, 2012).

11. "Russian Agent and 10 Other Members of Procurement Network for Russian Military and Intelligence Operating in the U.S. and Russia Indicted in New York," *FBI, Houston Division* (October 3, 2012).

12. "Russian Agent and 10 Other Members of Procurement Network."

13. Cf. Christopher Andrew and Vasili Mitrokhin, *The Mitrokhin Archive: The KGB in Europe and the West* (London and New York: Penguin, 2000), 75–88; and Vladimir Fédorovski, *Le roman du Kremlin* (Paris: Éditions du Rocher, 2004), 115–141.

14. Christopher Andrew, *The Defence of the Realm: The Authorised History of MI5* (London: Penguin, 2010).

15. Andrew, *The Defence of the Realm*, 413.

16. Joseph Fitsanakis, "Did Czechoslovakian Spies Plan to Blackmail British Leader?" *Intelnews.org* (January 26, 2012), http://intelnews.org/2012/06/26/01-1020/.

17. Robert Winnett, "David Cameron Tells Russian Hosts: KGB Tried to Recruit Me but I Failed the Test," *The Telegraph* (September 12, 2011).

18. Winnett, "David Cameron Tells Russian Hosts."

19. "Russischer Geheimdienst Spione in Potsdam," *Focus Online* (March 13, 2010).

20. Glen Owen, "Labour MP Pulled before Chief Whip for Inviting 'Russian Spy' to Tea in the Commons," *Daily Mail Online* (June 28, 2008).

21. Nicholas Watt and Luke Harding, "Mike Hancock, His Russian Assistant and Questions on Trident," *The Guardian* (December 5, 2010).

22. Mike Hancock was still involved in other affairs. According to the BBC, "Mr. Hancock was arrested in 2010 after a complaint was made about his behaviour towards a vulnerable constituent who had a history of mental health problems, but no charges were brought." ("Mike Hancock MP Resigns from Liberal Democratic Party," *BBC* (September 18, 2014), http://www.bbc.com/news/uk-england-27909267.) In June 2014 the complainant agreed to a confidential settlement and the MP issued an apology over an "inappropriate and unprofessional friendship." Being already suspended by his party, he resigned from the party in September 2014.

23. Victoria Ward, "Russian Spy Echoes Anna Chapman," *The Telegraph* (December 6, 2010). After Hancock, Katia Zatuliveter had an affair with another older high-ranking defense

expert: a NATO official dealing with Ukraine and Russia. When the British home secretary ordered her deportation, she appealed and won. The reason was insufficient evidence.

24. Jason Lewis, "Mikhail Repin: The Perfect Party Guest Who Was Whitehall Spy for the Russians," *The Telegraph* (December 10, 2011).

25. Lewis, "Mikhail Repin: The Perfect Party Guest." SpyBlog.org asks, "Will *The Independent* or the *London Evening Standard* newspapers keep silent about this story, given that their proprietor Alexander Lebedev is a former KGB diplomat/spy who was stationed at the Russian Embassy in London?" ("Daily Telegraph Names Last Year's Expelled Russian Diplomat/Spy as Mikhail Repin," *Spy Blog* (blog) (December 11, 2011).)

26. Vincent Jauvert, "Révélations sur les espions russes en France," *Le Nouvel Observateur* (July 24, 2014), 12.

27. Jauvert, "Révélations sur les espions russes."

28. Jean-Dominique Merchet, "Paris en guerre froide," *Libération* (November 9, 2009).

29. A list with the names of the expelled KGB and GRU officers can be found in Wolton, *Le KGB en France*, 294. He adds that even this long list is "incomplete" (286).

30. Cf. Vladimir Vodo, "Estoniya vychislila pervogo shpiona," *Kommersant* (September 23, 2008).

31. Cf. Tony Barber, "NATO Expels Russian Envoys," *Financial Times* (April 29, 2009).

32. Fidelius Schmid and Andreas Ulrich, "New Documents Reveal Truth on NATO's 'Most Damaging' Spy," *Spiegel Online* (April 30, 2010).

33. "Estonian Spies: Fog in the Baltic," *The Economist* (November 6, 2008).

34. Fidelius Schmid and Andreas Ulrich, "New Documents Reveal Truth on NATO's 'Most Damaging' Spy."

35. Dan Bilefsky, "Russian Spy Tale Rattles Czechs," *The New York Times* (December 23, 2010).

36. "Russia's Spy Services Identified as 'the Most Active Espionage Organizations' in the Czech Republic," *Atlantic Council* (August 22, 2012).

37. Molly Redden, "FBI Probing Whether Russia Used Cultural Junkets to Recruit American Intelligence Assets," *Mother Jones* (October 23, 2013).

38. "Russia Rejects US Allegations That Russian Cultural Exchange Director Was Spying against US," *The Washington Post* (October 24, 2013).

39. Joëlle Stolz, "Vienne, nid d'espions," *Le Monde* (November 17, 2010).

40. Jauvert, "Révélations sur les espions russes," 13.

41. Jorge Benitez, "Intelligence Chief: 'Brussels Is One of the Big Spy Capitals of the World,'" *Atlantic Council* (September 17, 2012).

42. Benitez, "Intelligence Chief."

43. Mark Galeotti, "Keeping Tabs on Putin's Spooks," *The Moscow News* (December 26, 2011).

44. Edward Lucas, *Deception: Spies, Lies and How Russia Dupes the West* (London and Berlin: Bloomsbury, 2012), 311–312.

45. Lucas, *Deception*, 22.

II

Creating a New Missionary Ideology: The Role of the Russian Orthodox Church

Chapter Eight

The Russian Orthodox Church: The Kremlin's Secret Weapon?

According to the British author Martin Amis, "The twentieth century, with its scores of millions of supernumerary dead, has been called the age of ideology. And the age of ideology, clearly, was a mere hiatus in the age of religion, which shows little sign of expiry."[1] How true these lines are when one considers what is happening currently in a country that was, probably, the most important producer and bulwark of ideology in the twentieth century: Russia. From being the herald of a millenarian, atheist ideology, communism, it transformed itself overnight into a staunch defender of the Christian Orthodox religion. This phenomenon is at first sight certainly surprising. However, it is, maybe, less remarkable when one takes the historical context into consideration. When one looks at the long-term evolution of the Russian state, it is rather the seven decades of communism that are the exception. Throughout history there has always existed a close relationship between the Russian Orthodox Church and the Russian state. In the West, the state and the (Catholic) church each jealously defended their respective power bases. This led to constant struggles and a never-ending rivalry, but it had the positive result that the state emancipated itself from religious tutelage and that equally the church emancipated itself from political tutelage. In Russia, on the contrary, the two remained completely intertwined. "The Orthodox religion," writes Cornelius Castoriadis, "is the true Christian religion in the sense that it is theocratic, which means that nothing can be said against what the emperor says because the emperor is the incarnation of Christ on earth."[2] The Russian Orthodox Church has always been subservient to the Russian state, and since tsar Peter the Great it was even led by a special ministry. This tutelage did not change even during the communist era, when, after a period of repression, the state began to use the Orthodox Church as a foreign policy

129

instrument. Under Putin, the cooperation between the state and the church has reached a new high. Not only has the church been restored to its former tsarist glory, but it has become, maybe even more so than under the tsars, a "soft-power" tool of the Kremlin's foreign policy. A good example of how this new "religious" foreign policy was conducted can be found in Ukraine during the last year of the presidency of Viktor Yushchenko, the Kremlin's declared archenemy.

PATRIARCH KIRILL'S VISITS TO UKRAINE: AN INVERTED "POPE JOHN PAUL II EFFECT"?

Conscious of the role played by Pope John Paul II in supporting the Solidarity movement in Poland, thereby contributing to the demise of the Soviet empire, the Russian leadership started using the same weapon, but this time the other way around, against Ukraine. From July 27 to August 5, 2009, Kirill, the Patriarch of Moscow, visited Ukraine. His tour brought him not only to the pro-Russian eastern part but also to the western part of the country. One of his objectives was to suppress the pro-independence mood of the local church.[3] The Ukrainian government was clearly embarrassed by this self-invited "apolitical" visitor, who was briefed before and after his visit by the Kremlin and who in his speeches talked a lot about the "common heritage" and "common destination" of Ukraine and Russia. Kirill's intervention went further than merely delivering a spiritual message. According to Pavel Korduban, "One of his [Kirill's] chief ideologists, Andrey Kuraev, was more outspoken, threatening Ukraine with a civil war should a single church fully independent from Moscow ever be established."[4] Viktor Yanukovych, at that time leader of the opposition pro-Russian Party of the Regions, used Kirill's visit to boost his image. After meeting with Kirill in Kyiv, he accompanied him on a tour to Donetsk, his political stronghold. Olexandr Paliy, a historian at the Diplomatic Academy of the Ukrainian Foreign Ministry, comments: "We've seen more of a Russian state official than a religious figure. . . . The Church is being used as an instrument in the Kremlin's game."[5] Oleh Medvedev, adviser to Yulia Tymoshenko, then Ukrainian prime minister, was more outspoken. He described Kirill's tour "as a visit of an imperialist who preached the neo-imperialist Russian World doctrine."[6]

Kirill's visit to Ukraine copied Pope John Paul II's visits to Poland in the 1980s, but this time the other way around: instead of weakening the Russian empire, his visit was meant to strengthen it. However, we have to qualify this prima facie resemblance. The pope is an independent spiritual leader, answerable to no one. This is completely different in Russia. It is a well-known fact that in Soviet times, the Russian Orthodox Church was totally infiltrated by the KGB. According to Hélène Blanc and Renata Lesnik, "From 1922 to

1991, the year of its 'official abolition' and its rebirth from its ashes in the Kremlin, the KGB traversed the decades as the Siamese twin of the Patriarchate of Moscow. No appointment, not even an assistant, was decided without the blessing of the Soviet secret services, whose priests, with dual identities, also infiltrated European and international institutions, notably Unesco."[7] Since the demise of the Soviet Union, the Orthodox Church has acquired the status of a quasi-official state church, and relations between the hierarchy and the political leadership have become closer than they were even in tsarist times. The KGB code name of Patriarch Aleksey II was "Drozdov." Kirill's KGB code name was "Mikhailov."[8] Kirill was elected on January 27, 2009, as the successor to Patriarch Aleksey II. Before his election, he was the head of the Department of External Church Relations (DECR), which functions as a foreign ministry of the Moscow Patriarchate. It was established after World War II under Stalin's guidance. The new church leader, who is 100 percent loyal to the Kremlin and has extensive international experience, was Putin's man of choice. He was expected to be capable of giving a new élan to the church's foreign policy in former Soviet bloc countries.

FINDING GOD: THE MIRACULOUS CONVERSION OF PUTIN AND OTHER FORMER KGB CHEKISTS

The prominent role for the Russian Orthodox Church has been emphasized by Putin right from the beginning of his first presidency. Putin not only visited churches and monasteries regularly to show his interest in religious affairs, but he was also keen to show everyone that he himself was a true Orthodox believer. In his biography *First Person* he told how his mother and a religious woman who lived in the same apartment block had him baptized after his birth.

> They kept it secret from my father, who was a party member and secretary of the party organization in his factory shop. Many years later, in 1993, when I worked on the Leningrad City Council, I went to Israel as part of an official delegation. Mama gave me my baptismal cross to get it blessed at the Lord's Tomb. I did as she said and then put the cross around my neck. I have never taken it off since.[9]

There is no reason to doubt Putin's words. But one should note that his religious *coming out* took place in 1993, when he was already thirty-five or thirty-six years old, two years after the failed KGB coup that caused the demise of the Soviet Union and the end of communist rule. Putin was not the only ex-communist who suddenly found God. In the same period there was a complete—one would almost say "miraculous"—wave of religious conversions of former communists. Not only Yeltsin had found God, but equally Aleksandr Rutskoy, the Russian vice president, who during the standoff between President Yeltsin and the Duma in the autumn of 1993 supported the KGB-inspired coup against the president. In the same year that Putin decided to keep his baptismal cross around his neck, Rutskoy published an article with the title "Without Orthodoxy We Don't Revive the Fatherland."[10] Even the leader of the communist Duma faction, Gennady Zyuganov, displayed "a curious mix of Orthodox piety, Russian chauvinism and communist nationalism."[11] What was taking place during these years, however, was not so much a miraculous mass conversion of former atheist communists to the belief of their ancestors, it was rather a calculated search for a strong conservative and anti-Western ally by the former power elite in an attempt to survive.

> Events of the late 1980s produced a reconfiguration of the relations between the communist elite and the Orthodox church. The unsettling forces of advancing perestroika and the unleashing of divisive nationalist forces that tore apart the soviet system injected profound changes into the relationship between the Orthodox church and important elements inside the communist party. As the party's longstanding and constitutionally guaranteed monopoly on power slipped away, and pluralism in politics and society proliferated, the convergence of interests and energies between pristine stalinist communism and traditionally Russian elements within Orthodoxy. . . came to the fore.[12]

Putin's late conversion, therefore, should be placed in this context. His ostentatious display of a newly found religiosity was presumably less a question of deeply felt religious feelings than of a calculated attempt to improve his career prospects in a fluid and uncertain situation.[13] However, the possible influence of his religious mother cannot be ruled out.[14] In 1999, when he became prime minister and subsequently acting president, in addition to what may have been personal motives came new, *political* motives. From this point, for the new Kremlin leader the alliance with the church was also dictated by the raison d'état, and this for two reasons. The first reason was that when he acceded to the supreme power of the state, Putin instinctively followed Machiavelli's precept that it was useful for a ruler to behave *as if* he were religious without necessarily *being* religious.[15] The second reason was that he understood full well the useful role the Russian Orthodox Church could play in the reconstitution of the lost empire. This element was new. In the perestroika period, the new freedom given to the church by Gorbachev was justified by the fact "that Christians had high moral standards. Rampant alcoholism, prostitution, drug use, rising crime and other negative social developments indicated that there was something amiss in the degree of morality the Soviet regime inspired."[16] Putin saw also in the church an instrument of moral regeneration. But that was not the only role he ascribed to it. In his eyes, the Orthodox Church's vocation was to become the privileged instrument of a new *soft-power* offensive of the Russian state in the service of the reconstitution of the former empire.

HOW PATRIARCH KIRILL LEARNED TO LOVE THE BOMB

Putin has praised the positive role of the church and the virtues of the Ortho-dox religion often and on diverse occasions. In August 2001, after a visit to a monastery in the Solovki Islands in the White Sea, he said that Russia is "the guardian of Christianity," and he recalled that his country was traditionally known as "Holy Russia."[17] Without the Orthodox religion, he said, "Russia would have difficulty in becoming a viable state. It is thus very important to return to this source."[18] Three months later, visiting New York just after the 9/11 attacks, he took part in a short requiem service in Manhattan in the St. Nicholas Russian Orthodox Cathedral, built in 1902 by tsar Nicholas II. Putin emphasized that after the events, the American nation needed moral support, consolation, and encouragement. He added: "The Russian Orthodox Church provides this kind of support."[19]

Four months later—on March 6, 2002—a unique ceremony took place in Moscow when Patriarch Aleksey II consecrated the Church of St. Sofia of God's Wisdom, located on Lubyanka Square in the courtyard of the head-quarters of the FSB, the successor organization to the KGB. Among the officials who attended the ceremony was Nikolay Patrushev, then director of the FSB. The church, a historic building dating from 1480, had been used during the Soviet period as a storehouse. It had been meticulously restored, funded by donations from FSB staff and unknown sponsors.[20] The ceremony was kept low key. None of the three national TV channels covered the event in the evening news, probably because showing the Patriarch handing over a church near to Russia's most infamous jail to the successors of former perse-cutors was a sensitive subject. But others said that showing the Patriarch inside the former KGB headquarters had to be avoided for other reasons. Had not the Patriarch himself, according to Soviet-era records, worked for the KGB under the code name "Drozdov"? He was therefore, in a sense, "at home."[21] Since Stalin had given more freedom to the church during the war to boost Russian nationalism and the people's morale, the church and the secret service had worked in complete harmony. This close cooperation be-tween the local Orthodox Church and the communist secret services was not confined to the Soviet Union. It took place also in the satellite states—for instance, in Bulgaria, where in January 2012 the so-called Files Commission, a special panel investigating the secret files of the former communist regime, exposed eleven out of a total of fifteen Orthodox Metropolitan bishops as former agents of the DS, the Bulgarian KGB.[22]

The close cooperation between the church and the secret service under Putin was, therefore, not new.[23] What *was* new was the religiosity of former KGB personnel. "Putin and the New KGB Eventually Found God," is the ironic title of an article in the *Times* of London. "In March 2002," writes the paper, "the FSB (Putin's domestic security and intelligence service) at last found God."[24] "Though the FSB has not, of course, become the world's first intelligence agency staffed only or mainly by Christian true believers, there have been a number of conversions to the Orthodox Church by Russian intelligence officers past and present."[25] When the Patriarch was consecrating the private church of the FSB, the religious needs of the two other branches of the *siloviki*, the Ministry of Defense and the Ministry of the Interior, had already been met: they had gotten their own churches before the FSB. Moreover, the church already had a presence in the military bases of the army. "In mid-1997 it was reported that Orthodox churches existed on the territory of 88 military units."[26] The relationship between the *siloviki* and religion became so close that Putin had no hesitation in likening Russia's "traditional religions" to its nuclear shield, declaring that "both traditional faiths of the Russian Federation and its nuclear shield are the elements strengthening Russian sovereignty and creating the necessary prerequisites for maintaining our country's internal and external security."[27] Here, Putin was being very prudent in speaking about "traditional faiths," which in Russia—apart from Orthodoxy—include Islam, Judaism, and Buddhism.

However, Putin was not alone in comparing religion with Russia's nuclear deterrent. When, in August 2009, Patriarch Kirill visited the northern shipyard in Severodvinsk, he went aboard a nuclear submarine and presented the crew with an icon of Mary, Mother of God. "He later said Russia's defense capabilities need to be bolstered by Orthodox Christian values. You should not be ashamed of going to church and teaching the Orthodox faith to your children, the Patriarch told the Severodvinsk workers. Then we shall have something to defend with our missiles."[28] "Kirill's comments," writes Brian Whitmore, "linking sacred Christian faith and secular nuclear might raised eyebrows, particularly among Russia's religious minorities."[29] Patriarch Kirill developed a special relationship with the guardians of Russia's nuclear deterrent bordering on a deep personal affection. In December 2009, in a ceremony during his visit to the Academy of the Strategic Missile Forces in Moscow, he presented its commander, Lieutenant General Andrey Shvaychenko, with a pennant of the Holy Great Martyr Barbara, considered to be the heavenly protector of the Russian nuclear deterrent, this being the occasion of its fiftieth-year jubilee. The Patriarch said, in the translation of Interfax, he was convinced "such dangerous weapon can be given only to clean hands—hands of people with clear mind, ardent love to Motherland, responsibility for their work before God and people."[30]

Cooperation between the Orthodox Church and the Strategic Missile Forces started in the early 1990s. "Patriarch Kirill reminded that a faculty of Orthodox culture had existed in the Academy for 13 years and over 1600 officers and members of their family had become its graduates." When he left, Kirill wished the soldiers "courage, strength, and spiritual power."[31] But Kirill showed a special affection not only for the guardians of Russia's nuclear deterrent, he displayed a special reverence also for the deterrent itself. "Thus, under Putin, practices including the blessing of the President's nuclear launch code briefcase and the sprinkling of holy water by an ROC [Russian Orthodox Church] priest on an S-400 Triumph surface-to-air missile system during a ceremony broadcast on national television became commonplace, ostensibly to strengthen statehood and state security."[32] While Putin compared religion with a nuclear shield, Kirill blessed the nuclear deterrent and said he wanted to bolster Russian defense capabilities through Orthodox Christian values. The views of the Kremlin leader and the church leader seemed to coincide completely. When Putin stressed the role of religion in strengthening the state, he disclosed what he considered the *real* importance of the church: to act as a shield behind which the nation could hide. This is also the reason that the keyword used by the Kremlin to put forward its new, state-sponsored religiosity was neither "piety" nor "devoutness" but *security*. To be more precise: *spiritual security*.

"SPIRITUAL SECURITY": A SHARED CONCERN OF THE ORTHODOX CHURCH AND THE KREMLIN

At the root of this religious revival, closely linking the Russian Orthodox Church with the Kremlin and the "power ministries," lies the concept of *spiritual security*. This concept has become as central to the Putin regime as was the concept of class struggle for the former Soviet Union. The rationale behind the concept of "spiritual security" is that after the demise of the Soviet Union and the end of communism, Russian citizens were suffering from an ideological and spiritual void. The country was confronted with a multitude of economic, psychological, and social problems, which expressed themselves in widespread corruption, growing criminality, rampant alcoholism, drug abuse, and an expanding HIV and AIDS epidemic. Russia was not a healthy nation but a country characterized by a diminishing life expectancy and rapid demographic decline. The Russian leadership's new emphasis on "spiritual security" and "spiritual values" evokes at first sight memories of the Moral Re-Armament movement that emerged in Western Europe between the two world wars. Moral Re-Armament was also a Christian-inspired movement. It grew out of the Oxford Group, led by the Reverend Frank Buchman (1878–1961). The movement emphasized not so much the necessity for social or political change as the necessity for *personal* change. It was an elite movement and had the support of politicians, captains of industry, and members of the nobility. In 1938 Queen Wilhelmina of the Netherlands openly voiced her sympathy for the movement. Frits Philips, the CEO of the Dutch Philips electronics concern, was a prominent lifelong member. But this prima facie resemblance of the Moral Re-Armament movement in the West to the "spiritual revival" in Russia disappears on closer inspection. This is mainly because Moral Re-Armament, although it had a Christian inspiration, was associated neither with a particular church nor with a particular government. It was certainly not associated with the church and government of *one* country. Russia's "spiritual security," on the contrary, is a joint project of the Russian state and the Russian Orthodox Church, and it is this joint endeavor that defines its uniqueness.

"SPIRITUAL SECURITY": AN INTEGRAL PART OF THE 2000 RUSSIAN NATIONAL SECURITY CONCEPT

Putin's strategy to use the Russian Orthodox Church as a soft-power instrument of the Kremlin's policies predates his election to president in 2000. The concept of "spiritual security" had already emerged in the National Security Concept of the Russian Federation. This concept was approved by Yeltsin by presidential decree no. 1300 of December 17, 1999. It was one of the last decrees he signed. Two weeks later, he would abdicate in favor of Putin. The National Security Concept is noteworthy not only because of its contents but also because it was one of the first official strategy documents on the formulation of which Putin, in his capacity as secretary to the National Security Council, had a considerable influence. In a concept on national security, one might expect to find detailed information on a country's general security situation, on imminent threats, as well as the government's proposals to counter these threats. In the National Security Concept, this information is certainly available. However, there are also quite unexpected passages, such where the authors write that

> safeguarding the national security of the Russian Federation also includes the protection of the cultural, spiritual and moral heritage, historical traditions and norms of social life, the preservation of the cultural heritage of all nations of Russia, the elaboration of a state policy in the sphere of spiritual and moral education, the introduction of a ban on the use of air time of the electronic mass media for showing programs that popularize violence and exploit base instincts, as well as resistance to the negative influence of foreign religious organizations and missionaries.[33]

Apart from this appeal to resist "the negative influence of foreign religious organizations and missionaries," one could further read that the interests of society boil down to "the spiritual renewal of Russia"[34] and that "national interests in the spiritual life boil down to maintaining and developing the moral values of society, the traditions of patriotism and humanism, and the cultural and research potential of the country."[35] "Economic disintegration, social differentiation of society and devaluation of spiritual values," the text continues, "contribute to the growth of tensions."[36] The authors are said to regret "the dwindling spiritual and moral potential of society"[37] and "the fall of the spiritual, moral and creative potential of the population,"[38] warning that "the deepening of the crisis in the domestic political, social and spiritual spheres can result in the loss of democratic achievements."[39] The conclusion is that "the state should encourage the . . . spiritual and moral development of society"[40] as well as "the education of law-abiding citizens."[41]

In the space of a few pages the authors mention the following concepts: *a spiritual and moral heritage, spiritual renewal, spiritual life, spiritual values, spiritual and moral potential* (twice), *spiritual spheres*, and *spiritual and moral development*. Rather than a government strategy paper, one gets the impression one is reading a church manual. But this is only the way it appears. In fact, this National Security Concept is highly strategic, as will become clear from the way this concept has been implemented during Putin's reign. Putin's personal influence on the formulation of this concept, apparently, was immense. In the autobiographical interview published in 2000, shortly after his nomination to acting president by Yeltsin, he formulated concerns similar to those expressed in the concept. "We will fight to keep our geographical and *spiritual* position,"[42] he said, expressing his great admiration for the German politician Ludwig Erhard, because "his entire conception for the reconstruction of the country began with the creation of *new moral values* for society."[43] This search of Putin and the Russian leadership for new moral values was, in itself, not new. The leaders of the perestroika period had emphasized similarly the need for moral reform.[44] In their case, the intended moral reform was due to bring more glasnost—openness—and democratization. However, the "spiritual renewal" advocated by their retrograde KGB successors could not be more different. Instead of promoting open and critical minds, they preached uncritical submission to the leader and ultranationalist chauvinism while elevating an obscurantist and reactionary Russian Orthodox Church to a semiofficial state church.[45]

THE ORTHODOX CHURCH AND THE FOREIGN MINISTRY: "WORKING HAND IN HAND"

The close cooperation between the Russian Orthodox Church (ROC) and the Kremlin in the field of foreign policy was formalized for the first time in 2003, when, after a visit of Patriarch Aleksey II to the Ministry of Foreign Affairs, a standing working group was established, consisting of representatives of the church and the ministry. "The meetings serve as strategy sessions that address the planning of the Patriarch's international travels and evaluate the ROC's activities in international organizations as well as developments in its inter-religious relations, including with the Vatican."[46] Speaking in a press conference on the occasion of the tenth meeting of this working group, Foreign Minister Sergey Lavrov made no secret of the close cooperation between state and church. Having stressed that "Orthodox values formed the basis of Russian culture and Russian statehood," the minister noted with satisfaction that "the Church engages in tackling the same tasks as does diplomacy." His ministry and the church, he said, were "working hand in hand." "We do one big work very necessary for the country."[47] Tackling *the same tasks* as the ministry, working *hand in hand* with the ministry, doing together *one big work*. . . . The church seemed to be restricting itself no longer to its specific, religious domain but, on the contrary, to be assuming increasingly political, diplomatic, and patriotic roles no different from the ones assigned to the Foreign Ministry. Both work hand in hand to defend the geopolitical interests of Russia. In his press conference, Lavrov made no secret of this symbiotic relationship, using words of praise for "the role which the Church plays in solving the tasks of strengthening our Fatherland and establishing the most favorable conditions for the further development of the country."[48] Putin made a similar remark on the occasion of the enthronement of Kirill as Patriarch on February 3, 2009. "The Patriarch will contribute to the strengthening of Russia," Putin said. And he added that the Orthodox Church had always played a "special role" in Russia, different from the role of religion in other countries: "It was a source of Russian statehood." It was obvious that this "source of Russian statehood" should operate in tandem with the Kremlin to advance the state's foreign policy goals.[49]

NOTES

1. Martin Amis, *The Second Plane: September 11: 2001–2007* (London: Jonathan Cape, 2008), 13.

2. Cornelius Castoriadis, *Une société à la dérive: Entretiens et débats 1974–1997* (Paris: Seuil, 2005), 219.

3. Since 1992 there exists in Ukraine, alongside the official Orthodox Church that recognizes the Patriarch of Moscow, a rival independent Orthodox Church of the Kyiv Patriarchate (UPTs-KP), led by Patriarch Filaret.

4. Pavel Korduban, "Russian Orthodox Patriarch Kirill Visits Ukraine," *Eurasia Daily Monitor* 6, no. 155 (August 12, 2009), 5.

5. James Marson, "Faith or Politics? The Russian Patriarch Ends Ukraine Visit," *Time* (August 4, 2009).

6. Korduban, "Russian Orthodox Patriarch Kirill Visits Ukraine."

7. Hélène Blanc and Renata Lesnik, *Les prédateurs du Kremlin (1917–2009)* (Paris: Seuil, 2009), 260–261. According to the authors, in Vancouver in 1983, "at the 6th General Assembly of the World Council of Churches, for instance, the religious delegation of the USSR had no fewer than forty-seven KGB agents, which was the totality of the delegates."

8. Blanc and Lesnik, *Les prédateurs*, 263.

9. Vladimir Putin, *First Person: An Astonishingly Frank Self-Portrait by Russia's President* (New York: PublicAffairs, 2000), 12.

10. Aleksandr Rutskoy, "Bez pravoslaviya otechestvo ne vozrodim," *Blagovest*, no. 7 (1993), 3, quoted in Paul D. Steeves, "Russian Orthodox Fascism after Glasnost," paper presented to the Conference on Faith and History, Harrisburg, Pennsylvania (October 8, 1994), 9, note 20, http://www2.stetson.edu/~psteeves/rusorthfascism.html.

11. Zoe Knox, "The Struggle for Religious Pluralism: Russian Orthodoxy and Civil Society in Post-Soviet Russia," PhD diss., Centre for European Studies, Monash University, Victoria (Australia), (March 2002), 204, http://arrowprod.lib.monash.edu.au:8080/vital/access/manager/Repository/monash:6093.

12. Paul D. Steeves, "Russian Orthodox Fascism after Glasnost," paper presented to the Conference on Faith and History, Harrisburg, Pennsylvania (October 8, 1994), 6, http://www2.stetson.edu/~psteeves/rusorthfascism.html.

13. This impression that Putin's display of religiosity is rather instrumental than authentic is shared by other authors. Zoe Knox, for instance, wrote about "Putin's efforts to promote a pious image." (Knox, *The Struggle for Religious Pluralism*, 182.) Even Kirill, in an interview for the German *Spiegel* magazine, did not hide a certain doubt vis-à-vis the depth of Putin's religious feelings. When the interviewer asked him: "Vladimir Putin says that he often reads the Bible on the presidential plane during long trips. He and his ministers and his officials like to be seen attending church services, despite the fact that many of them were staunch supporters of atheism during the Soviet era. Does this make you happy or angry?" Kirill answered: "Most of the believers we encounter in church today were atheists yesterday. If an engineer can undergo this transformation, why shouldn't it work for a politician? *Unfortunately, they rarely attend church. I would like to see the president and the ministers go to church every Sunday and not just one or two times a year.*" ("The Bible Calls it a Sin: Interview with Russian Orthodox Metropolitan Kyrill," *Spiegel Online* (October 1, 2008) (emphasis mine).)

14. A totally unexpected explanation for Putin's religiosity may, in the end, be found in his sportive activities as a judo champion. In chapter 12 ("Devout Observances") of Thorstein Veblen's classic book *The Theory of the Leisure Class*, Veblen observed "that the habituation to sports, perhaps especially athletic sports, acts to develop the propensities which find satisfaction in devout observances." (Thorstein Veblen, *The Theory of the Leisure Class: An Economic Study of Institutions*, with an introduction by C. Wright Mills (New York and Scarborough, Ontario: Mentor, 1953), 197.) Veblen, who considered devoutness "a mark of arrested spiritual development" (200), wrote that "the religious zeal which pervades much of the college sporting element is especially prone to express itself in an unquestioning devoutness and a naïve and complacent submission to an inscrutable Providence" (196).

15. In chapter 18 of *Il Principe* (*The Prince*), Niccolò Machiavelli wrote that it was not necessary, and could even be harmful, for a ruler always to be merciful, loyal, human, honest, and religious. "Therefore," he writes, "it is not necessary for a ruler to have all these above mentioned qualities, but it is certainly necessary to appear to have them." (*A uno principe, adunque, non è necessario avere tutte le soprascritte qualità, ma è bene necessario parere di averle.*) Cf. Niccolò Machiavelli, *Il Principe e Discorsi sopra la prima deca di Tito Livio* (Milan: Feltrinelli Editore, 1971), 73. This urge, to appear to be religious, undoubtedly must also have inspired the final phrase in Putin's op-ed in the *New York Times* in September 2013 during the Syria crisis, when he wrote: "We are all different, but when we ask for the Lord's

blessings, we must not forget that God created us equal." (Vladimir Putin, "A Plea for Caution from Russia," *The New York Times* (September 12, 2013).)

16. Cf. Knox, *The Struggle for Religious Pluralism*, 86.

17. "Putin Says Russia Is the 'Guardian of Christianity,'" *Pravoslavie.ru* (August 21, 2001).

18. "Putin Says Russia Is the 'Guardian of Christianity.'"

19. "Vladimir Putin Visited St. Nicholas Cathedral in New York," *Pravoslavie.ru* (November 16, 2001).

20. Natalia Yefimova, "FSB Gets Its Own Place to Worship," *The Moscow Times* (March 7, 2002).

21. David Satter, a specialist on the KGB, wrote: "According to material from the Soviet archives, Kirill was a KGB agent (as was Alexei). *This means he was more than just an informer, of whom there were millions in the Soviet Union. He was an active officer of the organization.* Neither Kirill nor Alexei ever acknowledged or apologized for their ties with the security agencies." (David Satter, "Putin Runs the Russian State—And the Russian Church Too," *Forbes.com* (February 20, 2009) (emphasis mine).)

22. Cf. "Bulgaria's High Clergy Infected with Ex-Communist Spies," *Sofia News Agency* (January 17, 2012); and "Bulgarian PM Stunned by No. of Ex-Communist Spies among Clergy," *Sofia News Agency* (January 20, 2012).

23. "It is only the Moscow church that was and still is the slave and servant of the state," wrote Pavlo Shtepa, a Canadian-Ukrainian émigré writer. "Little wonder, when the Ukrainian National (Autocephalous) Church was revived in the 20s, ALL—without any exception—Moscow bishops and priests in Ukraine volunteered to serve in [the] Cheka [the KGB's forerunner] . . . to exterminate the separatist traitors." (Pavlo Shtepa, *Moscovism: Origin, Substance, Form, and Historical Continuity* (Toronto: S. Stasyshin, 1968), 20–21.)

24. "Putin and the New KGB Eventually Found God," *The Times* (September 19, 2005).

25. "Putin and the New KGB Eventually Found God."

26. Knox, *The Struggle for Religious Pluralism*, 181.

27. "Putin regards the nation's traditional religions and nuclear shield equally important for its security," *Interfax* (February 9, 2007).

28. Brian Whitmore, "Russia's Patriarch Increasingly Becoming Major Force in Politics," *RFE/RL* (September 6, 2009), http://www.rferl.org/content/Russias_Patriarch_Increasingly_Becoming_Major_Force_In_Politics/1815832.html.

29. Whitmore, "Russia's Patriarch Increasingly Becoming Major Force."

30. "Patriarch Kirill Awarded Strategic Missile Forces to St. Barbara Pennant," *Interfax* (December 8, 2009).

31. "Patriarch Kirill Awarded Strategic Missile Forces."

32. Robert C. Blitt, "One New President, One New Patriarch, and a Generous Disregard for the Constitution: A Recipe for the Continuing Decline of Secular Russia," *Vanderbilt Journal of Transnational Law* 43 (2010), 1353, http://works.bepress.com/robert_blitt/7/. When Kirill in the *Spiegel* interview was asked: "But you have no qualms about blessing all kinds of weapons: tanks, ships and guns," Kirill even seemed not to understand the problem. He answered: "priests do that when they are asked." (Cf. "The Bible Calls it a Sin: Interview With Russian Metropolitan Kyrill," *Spiegel Online*).

33. "National Security Concept of the Russian Federation," full English translation from *Rossiyskaya Gazeta* (January 18, 2000), 10, http://www.fas.org/nuke/guide/russia/doctrine/gazeta012400.htm.

34. "National Security Concept," 2.

35. "National Security Concept," 3.

36. "National Security Concept," 4.

37. "National Security Concept," 4.

38. "National Security Concept," 5.

39. "National Security Concept," 5.

40. "National Security Concept," 8.

41. "National Security Concept," 9.

42. Putin, *First Person*, 169 (emphasis mine).

43. Putin, *First Person*, 194 (emphasis mine).

44. "A new moral atmosphere is taking shape in the country," Gorbachev told the Central Committee at the January 1987 meeting . . . . A reappraisal of values and their creative rethinking is under way." (Quoted by Leon Aron, "Everything You Think You Know about the Collapse of the Soviet Union Is Wrong," *Foreign Policy* (July–August, 2011).)

45. This preoccupation of Putin's with "spiritual values" reappeared with the creation, in October 2012, of an agitprop office in the presidential administration. This office, tasked with organizing patriotic education, had the explicit goal of "strengthening the spiritual and moral foundations of Russian society." (Cf. "Kremlin to Create Office of Public Projects," *RIA Novosti* (October 20, 2012).)

46. Robert C. Blitt, "Russia's 'Orthodox' Foreign Policy: The Growing Influence of the Russian Orthodox Church in Shaping Russia's Policies Abroad," *University of Pennsylvania Journal of International Law* 33, no. 2 (May 2011), 382.

47. "Opening Remarks by Foreign Minister Sergey Lavrov at Press Conference after Tenth Meeting of Working Group on MFA-Russian Orthodox Church Interaction, November 20, 2007," Ministry of Foreign Affairs of the Russian Federation, *Info-Digest* (November 22, 2007), Permanent Mission of the Russian Federation to the United Nations Office and other International Organizations in Geneva, available at http://www.geneva.mid.ru/digests/digest-nov2007-6.doc.

48. "Opening Remarks by Foreign Minister Sergey Lavrov."

49. "Russian Orthodox Church to Work for Russian Identity—Putin," *Interfax* (February 3, 2009). Two years later, Putin repeated his words of praise for the church. "The Church is always with us," he said, "it has a huge influence on the moral atmosphere in society." ("Putin Says Orthodox Church Has Huge Influence," *Ria Novosti* (February 1, 2011).)

Chapter Nine

Attacking Universal Human Rights in the International Forums

This special role assigned to "traditional" religious values (in the Kremlin's jargon: *spiritual values*) by the Russian Foreign Ministry and the Orthodox Church is part of a joint *anti-Helsinki offensive* intended to undermine the validity of universal human rights. This offensive is fought on different fronts: in the UN General Assembly, in the UNESCO, in the UN Human Rights Council, in the OSCE, and in the Council of Europe. This offensive must not be underestimated. After having abandoned communism, Russia hesitated for a while about how to position itself in the new global ideological battlefield. But with Putin, these hesitations have disappeared. We can even see a surprising ideological *continuity* between the Soviet Union and post-Soviet Russia because the main targets of the ideological attacks—democracy, individual freedom, and universal human rights—remain essentially the same. Russia's activities in the UN Human Rights Council especially need to be mentioned here. The Russian Foreign Ministry arranged that on March 18, 2008, Kirill—at that time still head of the Department of External Church Relations (DECR)—could deliver a speech before the Human Rights Council. In his speech, Kirill attacked abortion and euthanasia, as well as the "strong influence of extreme feministic views and homosexual attitudes to the formulation of rules, recommendations and programs in human rights advocacy."[1] He pleaded for the installation of an "Advisory Council of Religions" in the UN. The idea behind this was that the implementation of human rights should be subsumed under so-called traditional values. This was necessary, said Kirill, because "various countries can implement them taking into account the cultural distinctive features of a particular people." This would make an end, he added, to the "quite undemocratic behavior . . . exhibited by some countries who consider their own system of human rights implementation to be universal. Directly or indirectly they seek to impose their own standards on other nations or become the only judge in the matter of human rights."[2] Kirill went on to say that human rights had also been used "to justify outrage against and distortion of religious symbols and teachings," implying that the defamation of religion should be forbidden, which would open the way for arbitrary restrictions on the right to freedom of expression. Some months later, on June 26, 2008, the Orthodox Church would formalize its criticism of universal human rights in an official document, "The Foundations of the Teaching of the Russian Orthodox Church on Dignity, Freedom and Human Rights," which said that "it is not tolerable and dangerous to interpret human rights as the highest and universal foundation of social life, under which religious views and practices should be subsumed."[3] Kirill blamed the former Soviet negotiators who had signed human rights agreements while lacking "any ideological outlook."[4]

TOUTING SO-CALLED TRADITIONAL VALUES

Kirill's speech before the Human Rights Council was a deliberate move within a broader strategy of the Russian Foreign Ministry. The event was part of a carefully planned sequence with the aim of attacking head-on the universal character of human rights. The opening move in this sequence was made on September 28, 2007, by Foreign Minister Lavrov in a speech before the sixty-second session of the UN General Assembly in which he proposed the setting up of a consultative Council of Religions in the UN. It was followed on October 3, 2007, with a speech by Patriarch Aleksey II before the Parliamentary Assembly of the Council of Europe. In this speech Aleksey II told the parliamentarians that "today there occurs a break between human rights and morality, and this break threatens the European civilization,"[5] claiming the moral high ground for religion against "amoral" human rights. The next move in this Russian offensive against human rights came on October 2, 2009, when the Russian Federation submitted resolution A/HRC/RES/12/21 to the UN Human Rights Council. The resolution, titled "Promoting Human Rights and Fundamental Freedoms through a Better Understanding of Traditional Values of Humankind," asked the Office of the High Commissioner for Human Rights to organize a workshop on traditional values and human rights. Human Rights Watch warned at that time that the resolution "does not acknowledge that many harmful practices such as female genital mutilation are justified by invoking 'traditional values.'"[6] But the resolution was accepted and the workshop was organized on October 4, 2010. Representatives of the Russian Orthodox Church played a prominent role in the workshop. Philip Riabykh, speaking for the Moscow Patriarchate, "stated that international authorities, while making human rights interpretations regarding specific countries, should make a thorough examination of the national context."[7]

Against these attempts to contextualize and relativize human rights, denying their universal validity, Ms. Navanethem Pillay, the UN high commissioner for human rights, took a stance. She rejected attempts to set traditional values against human rights. In no country, she said, has "any single woman, man or child ever stood to demand the right to be tortured, summarily executed, starved or denied medical care in the name of their culture."[8] The US representative emphasized that

> the concept of Traditional Values, without reference to human rights law, can undermine the universal principles enshrined in international human rights instruments with regard to the rights of women, minorities, LGBT individuals [lesbian, gay, bisexual, transgendered people], and other vulnerable groups. . . . The term has thus far been so vague and open-ended that it could be used to legitimize human rights abuses.[9]

How true these words were was proved some months later when, on May 28, 2011, the Moscow city government, despite having already been condemned by the Council of Europe for a similar decision, once again forbade the organization of gay pride. Gay and lesbian activists who took to the street were beaten by young extremists of the Orthodox Brotherhood. Archpriest Vsevolod Chaplin, head of the Synodal Department for Church and Society of the Orthodox Church, said he hoped that the authorities "will listen to the voice of their own people, the majority of whom do not accept the propaganda of homosexuality."[10] "All the people are against this monstrous immorality," he said.[11] Archpriest Chaplin's rejection of homosexuality, however, was not a question of personal opinion. It was fully in line with the "Bases of the Social Concept of the Russian Orthodox Church," a kind of new catechism adopted by the church in 2000. In this document one can read that homosexuality is a "sinful distortion of human nature" and that "homosexual desires, just as other passions torturing fallen man, are healed by the Sacraments, prayer, fasting, repentance, reading of Holy Scriptures and patristic writings, as well as Christian fellowship with believers who are ready to give spiritual support."[12] The events in Moscow were a clear example how "traditional values" could be invoked to repress the human rights of minorities.[13]

The Orthodox Church and the Russian authorities are here working closely hand in hand. When Russia was attacked in the OSCE—another international forum—for its repressive policies against homosexuals, Andrey Kelin, the Russian permanent representative, drily answered "that the concepts of 'sexual orientation' and 'gender identity' are not mentioned in universal international treaties or among the commitments of the OSCE itself. There is therefore no basis for requesting that Russia meet any commitments whatsoever in this area."[14] He added, clearly pleased at finding some minimal support for his theses in the audience: "We are in full agreement with the representative of the Vatican that these subjects are not within the OSCE's competence."[15] The answer of the US ambassador, Ian Kelly, however, was unambiguous: "We remain concerned by proposed local legislation in Russia that would severely restrict freedoms of expression and assembly for lesbian, gay, bisexual, and transgender (LGBT) individuals, and indeed all Russians. As Secretary Clinton has said, gay rights are human rights and human rights are gay rights."[16]

The decision of the Moscow city government, in May 2011, to forbid gay pride came just two months after Russia succeeded in having a second resolution adopted in the UN Human Rights Council. Resolution A/HRC/16/L.6, titled "Promoting Human Rights and Fundamental Freedoms through a Better Understanding of Traditional Values of Humankind" was adopted on March 24, 2011. In this resolution the Human Rights Council "confirmed that dignity, freedom and responsibility are traditional values shared by humankind as a whole and fixed in the universal treaties on human rights. The Council noted an important role for the family, community, society and educational institutions in maintaining and passing [on] traditional values and called upon all states to strengthen this role through adopting adequate positive measures."[17] The *Voice of Russia* wrote in a commentary that the proposal "is to change the international community's approach towards human rights. . . . The West has discredited the noble idea by meddling in the internal affairs of other countries under the pretense of protecting human rights and taking the idea of tolerance to absurdity."[18]

Eighteen months later—on September 27, 2012—the Kremlin notched up a new success when the UN Human Rights Council adopted resolution A/HRC/21/L.2 on collecting examples of *best practice*. In this resolution the UN high commissioner for human rights was requested "to collect information from States Members of the United Nations and other relevant stakeholders on best practices in the application of traditional values while promoting and protecting human rights and upholding human dignity."[19] With scarcely concealed satisfaction, the *Voice of Russia* wrote: "The co-authors of the resolution include representatives of more than 60 countries, including members of the Organization of Islamic Cooperation and the Arab League."[20] The resolution was adopted by a vote of 25 to 15, with seven abstentions. The United States and the European Union voted against. In the resolution, "traditional values were defined as 'dignity, freedom and responsibility,' with equality conspicuously absent."[21]

It was telling that this Russian "victory" in the UN Human Rights Council came in the same week that Sergey Naryshkin, Speaker of the State Duma, canceled his address to the Parliamentary Assembly of the Council of Europe (PACE), scheduled for October 1, 2012.[22] In the 2012 October part-session of PACE, a report was to be discussed on Russia's honoring of its obligations as a member of the Council of Europe, the Europe-wide human rights organization. It was the first such report in seven years. The Russian human rights record—notwithstanding the Kremlin's enthusiasm for "traditional values"—was far from exemplary. In 2011 the Russian Federation was, after Turkey, the most serious human rights offender. Of the 133 judgments of the European Court of Human Rights concerning Russia, the Russian state was condemned in 121 cases for at least one violation.[23] On December 31, 2011, 151,624 applications were still pending. Of this number, 40,250 concerned Russia. This means that out of a total number of forty-seven European states, Russia *alone* accounted for 26.6 percent of the cases pending.[24] During the debate on the report about Russia, one of the co-rapporteurs, Romanian member Gyorgy Frunda, strongly criticized new laws that had been adopted by the Duma shortly before. "The law on 'foreign agents,' the protest law, the law on the criminalization of defamation, and the federal law on protecting children from information harmful to their health and their development, contradict the minimum standards of the rule of law and human rights," Frunda said.[25] One might wonder why Naryshkin thought it better to cancel his participation.

While Russia was obliged to keep a low profile in the Council of Europe, the situation was different in Geneva, where the UN Human Rights Council convened. So far the joint attack of the Kremlin and the Russian Orthodox Church on the UN human rights regime seems to have been surprisingly successful, and it will depend on the firmness and cohesion of the West and like-minded countries to what degree Russia will succeed in creating a legal justification for repressive governments to implement human rights differently, in a "sovereign" way, according to so called traditional values. The crux of the problem is a clash over fundamental values. Terry Nardin writes:

> A pervasive assumption in discussions of religion is that religion is intrinsically moral. But there are reasons to doubt this assumption. Common sense suggests that religious practices can be immoral and religious beliefs false."[26] Sometimes "religions teach doctrines and practices that are not morally justifiable according to the precepts of natural law or common morality. Slavery, torture, conquest, terrorism, and genocide have all found warrant in religious traditions, but such practices have no place in natural law (. . .). Morality, so understood, must condemn any action or practice that fails to respect human beings as rational beings equally entitled to think and choose. *When religion and morality clash, it is religion that must give way if its claim to be moral is to be sustained.*[27]

In a similar way Michael Blake argued that even "traditional values" held in all societies at all times, are not above suspicion. "All cultures, at all times," he wrote, "have had some traditions best described as marginalizing to the experience and lives of women. Our response to this, of course, is not—and should not be—to validate the marginalization of women as morally sacred. The response is, instead, to say that women's lives have traditionally been blighted, and that this should change. . . . 'Traditional values' would be, if integrated into human rights practice, a political disaster, gutting the core of what human rights demand; they would also be, I think, a *moral* disaster, in that there are no good arguments in favor of such integration."[28]

In November 2013, the Russian Federation was elected for another three years to the UN Human Rights Council.[29] One may, therefore, expect the Russian assault on human rights to continue and intensify.

RUSSKIY MIR: THE "RUSSIAN WORLD" PROJECT

The Russian Foreign Ministry and the Orthodox Church work in tandem not only in international organizations to realize Russian foreign policy objectives. Their cooperation is, in fact, much more encompassing. Another channel for this close cooperation is the Russkiy Mir Foundation. This foundation was created by Vladimir Putin in 2007 by presidential decree with the purpose of promoting the Russian language and Russian culture abroad. This new GONGO (government-organized nongovernmental organization) seems to have been inspired by the example of the British Council, whose Russian offices were harassed by the Kremlin between 2004 and 2008. *Russkiy Mir* means "Russian World" (because *mir* in Russian can also mean "peace," there is also a connotation of a *peaceful* Russian world). It is a joint project of the Ministry of Foreign Affairs and the Ministry of Education and Science, financed with public and private funds. The official purpose of the foundation is cultural and not spiritual. However, the emphasis has gradually changed, and the promotion of the "spiritual heritage" of the Orthodox religion has become one of its most important functions. The privileged position of the Russian Orthodox Church can be deduced from the fact that only the ROC has a representative on the board of trustees. There are no representatives of the three other official religions (Islam, Judaism, Buddhism). Since the end of 2009, the cooperation between the church and Russkiy Mir has been formalized. A permanent working group has been installed, which had its first meeting in April 2010. Robert C. Blitt writes:

> Russkiy Mir's newly minted and far-reaching formal alliance with the ROC places the government into a constitutionally untenable position. In light of its direct financial and political support for the foundation, the government has in essence created and sanctioned a proxy body that represents nothing less than a fusion of Orthodox and state institutions. This chimera, originally tasked with the modest goal of showcasing examples of Russian art and culture, is now the perfect embodiment of how gravely secularism and religious equality have deteriorated in Russia's foreign policy today. Not surprisingly, at least

one media source has labeled Russkiy Mir "one of the structural divisions of Russia's Foreign Intelligence Service." Notably, Vyacheslav Nikonov [Molotov's grandson], the foundation's director, has a personal connection to Russia's secret service: According to his official biography, he served as advisor to the director of the KGB in the early 1990s.[30]

Russkiy Mir is part of a much more ambitious project that aims to give the Kremlin—again—the global ideological influence it had lost with the end of communism. In a Nietzschean *Umwertung aller Werte* (reassessment of values), Orthodoxy is destined to take the place of "godless" communism. At first glance this seems to be a complete volte-face, but the ideological reversal is less fundamental than one might be inclined to think. Both Soviet communism and Russian Orthodoxy share a set of the same underlying convictions, such as Russian nationalism, Russian imperialism, anti-liberalism, a deep-rooted traditionalism and conservatism, an aversion to human rights policies, and a deep dislike of Western democracy. In this sense, the Kremlin's ideological embracing of Russian Orthodoxy is a linear continuation of the age-old Russian "fear of freedom" that characterized both Soviet and tsarist Russia. In the words of Patriarch Filaret of the Ukrainian Orthodox Church and a declared enemy of the Moscow Patriarchate: "'Russkiy Mir' is the same shiny coin that 'A bright future with Communism' once was. Patriarch Kirill invented this concept to spur spiritual unification around Moscow first, followed by political and territorial unification. This is essentially reviving the Russian empire."[31] Seen against the background of Russia's aggression against Ukraine in 2014 and 2015, these words are prophetic.

For the Kremlin to become again a global ideological center is, however, more difficult today than it was in 1917, immediately after the Bolshevik October Revolution. After the October Revolution, the Kremlin had the support of a wide range of communist parties in many countries of the world, organized in the Moscow-controlled Komintern. The members of these parties came from the local populations. Communism was not an exclusive, parochial, Russian affair but a genuine *international* movement. By choosing Orthodoxy as its official ideology, the Kremlin's perspective is completely different from that of the young Soviet Union. The primary target groups of the Kremlin's ideological outreach are not the different national communist parties, but the *Russian diaspora*. The first layer of these diaspora consists of the ethnic Russian and Russian-speaking minorities in the ex-Soviet republics. The second layer consists mainly of the descendants of Russian émigrés who fled to the West during the civil war after the October Revolution.[32] They are complemented by a third layer of former dissidents who went to the West in the 1970s and 1980s. Finally, a fourth layer consists of new emigrants (such as rich oligarchs) who have left Russia in recent years to work and live abroad.[33] The fact that the target group of Russkiy Mir primarily consists of Russian and former Russian nationals and their descendants restricts its potential. However, this may soon change. This is because under Putin, Orthodox expansionism has become an important part of Russia's foreign policy. This finds expression in the three objectives the Kremlin and the ROC pursue outside Russia:

- First, to bring Orthodox parishes abroad back under the aegis of the Moscow Patriarchate.
- Second, to reclaim former church property abroad that belonged to tsarist Russia.
- Third, to create a wider group of supporters of a "Russian world" abroad, expected to become loyal defenders of the Kremlin's policies.

In the next two chapters we will see how far these objectives have been realized.

NOTES

1. "The Address of Metropolitan Kirill of Smolensk and Kaliningrad, Chairman of the Moscow Patriarchate DECR on the Panel Discussion on Human Rights and Intercultural Dialogue at the 7th Session of UN Human Rights Council," Geneva, March 18, 2008, *Interfax* (March 22, 2008), available at http://www.interfax-religion.com/print.php?act=documents&id=121.

2. "The Address of Metropolitan Kirill."

3. Patriarchate of the Russian Orthodox Church, "Osnovy ucheniya Russkoy Pravoslavnoy Tserkvi o dostoynstve, svobode i pravakh cheloveka," Moscow (June 26, 2008), http://www.patriarchia.ru/db/print/428616.html.

4. Svetlana Solodovnik, "Rossiya: ofitsialnaya tserkov vybiraet vlast," *Pro et Contra* (May–August 2013), 11.

5. "The Address of Patriarch Alexy II of Moscow and All Russia to the PACE" (October 3, 2007), available on the website of *Orthodoxy and the World*, http://www.pravmir.com/article_246.html.

6. "UN Human Rights Council: 'Traditional Values' Vote and Gaza Overshadow Progress," *Human Rights Watch* (October 2, 2009).

7. "Workshop on Traditional Values of Humankind," United Nations High Commissioner for Human Rights, UN General Assembly (December 13, 2010), 7, http://www2.ohchr.org/english/bodies/hrcouncil/docs/16session/A-HRC-16-37.pdf.

8. "Seminar on Traditional Values and Human Rights," Office of the High Commissioner for Human Rights, International Service for Human Rights, Geneva (October 4, 2010), http://www.ishr.ch/archive-council.

9. "Item 8: U.S. Explanation of Vote on the Traditional Values Resolution," Human Rights Council (March 23, 2011).

10. "Church Grateful to City Authorities for Preventing Moscow Gay Parade," *Interfax* (May 30, 2011).

11. Tom Washington, "Rival Rallies over Gay Rights in Russia," *The Moscow News* (May 23, 2011).

12. "Bases of the Social Concept of the Russian Orthodox Church," Department for External Church Relations of the Moscow Patriarchate, Moscow (2000), http://orthodoxeurope.org/print/3/14.aspx. In the same paragraph, the church condemns transsexuality as a "rebellion against the Creator."

13. This is not to say that no connection exists between religion and human rights. Such a connection is possible, but not necessarily so. The only clear guide, therefore, are human rights *as such* and not "religious" or "traditional" values. As Friedrich Hayek rightly remarked: "The undoubted *historical* connection between religion and the values that have shaped and furthered our civilisation . . . does not of course mean that there is any *intrinsic* connection between religion as such and such values." (Friedrich A. Hayek, "Religion and the Guardians of Tradition," in *The Collected Works of Friedrich August Hayek*, ed. W. W. Bartley III, vol. 1, *The Fatal Conceit: The Errors of Socialism* (London: Routledge, 1988), 137.)

14. "Statement by Mr. Andrey Kelin, Permanent Representative of the Russian Federation, at the Meeting of the OSCE Permanent Council, Delegation of the Russian Federation to the OSCE, Vienna" (February 16, 2012).

15. "Statement by Mr. Andrey Kelin."

16. "Statement on LGBT Legislation in the Russian Federation as Delivered by Ambassador Ian Kelly to the Permanent Council," United States Mission to the OSCE, Vienna (February 16, 2012).

17. "UN Human Rights Council Passes a Resolution on Traditional Values," *Russian Orthodox Church—Official Website of the Department for External Church Relations* (March 25, 2011), http://www.mospat.ru/en/2011/03/25/news38696/.

18. Natalya Kovalenko, "Human Rights Are Based on Traditional Values," *The Voice of Russia* (March 25, 2011).

19. UN Human Rights Council resolution of September 27, 2012 (A/HRC/21/L.2).

20. "UN Adopts Russian Version of Resolution on Human Rights," *The Voice of Russia* (September 27, 2012).

21. Cai Wilkinson, "Putting Traditional Values into Practice: Russia's Anti-Gay Laws," *Russian Analytical Digest*, no. 138 (November 8, 2013), 5.

22. Council of Europe, Parliamentary Assembly, "'It Takes Two to Hold a dialogue' Says PACE President, Following the Announcement That Sergey Naryshkin, Speaker of the State Duma, Will Not Be Coming to Strasbourg," Strasbourg (September 27, 2012).

23. European Court of Human Rights, *Annual Report 2011*, Registry of the European Court of Human Rights, Strasbourg (2012), 157.

24. European Court of Human Rights, *Annual Report 2011*, 152–153.

25. Rikard Jozwiak, "PACE Report Strongly Criticizes Russia," *RFERL.org* (October 2, 2012).

26. Terry Nardin, "Epilogue," in Fabio Petito and Pavlos Hatzopoulos, *Religion in International Relations—The Return from Exile*, (New York: Palgrave Macmillan, 2003), 273.

27. Nardin, "Epilogue," 274. (My emphasis, MHVH).

28. Michael Blake, "'Traditional Values' and Human Rights: Whose Traditions? Which Rights?" Cicero Foundation Great Debate Paper no. 13/06 (December 2013), 5, 10, http://www.cicerofoundation.org/lectures/Michael_Blake_Traditional_Valuesx.pdf.

29. Nikolay Surkov, "Russia to Rejoin the UN Council on Human Rights," *Russia beyond the Headlines* (November 18, 2013).

30. Blitt, "Russia's 'Orthodox' Foreign Policy: The Growing Influence of the Russian Orthodox Church in Shaping Russia's Policies Abroad," *University of Pennsylvania Journal of International Law* 33, no. 2 (May 2011), 390.

31. Olena Chekan, "When Evil Turns to Good: Filaret, Patriarch of Kyiv and All Rus-Ukraine, Talks about Raider Attacks on Churches Belonging to the Kyiv Patriarchate and the Delusion of a 'Russian World,'" *Ukrainian Week* (March 14, 2011).

32. For instance, in the summer of 2011, Dmitry Rogozin, Russia's envoy to NATO, announced a plan to set up a Congress of Russian Communities, meant to attract representatives of the old nobility, living outside Russia. The ancestors of families such as Trubetskoy, Pushkin, and Krylov fled to the West after the October Revolution. On September 21, 2011, Prince Alexander Trubetskoy, a French citizen, addressed the Congress. In October 2011, he was appointed chairman of the board of directors of the Russian telecom conglomerate Svyazinvest. (Cf. "Noble Aims: Rogozin Resurrects Nationalist Project," *rt.com* (September 6, 2011).)

33. This last group is the subject of the book by Mark Hollingsworth and Stewart Lansley, *Londongrad: From Russia with Cash—The Inside Story of the Oligarchs* (London, Fourth Estate, 2010).

Chapter Ten

A Global Church for the Kremlin?

On May 17, 2007, Ascension Day, the bells of Moscow's Cathedral of Christ the Savior rang out loud and clear over the Moskva River. Crowds gathered in the heavy rain outside the church and admired the splendid gilded domes. It was a memorable day: the celebration of the renaissance of the Russian Orthodox Church (ROC). On the one hand it was its *material* renaissance: the cathedral itself, demolished by Stalin in 1931, had been completely rebuilt in the 1990s. On the other hand, it was also a celebration of its *institutional* renaissance. On this memorable day an extraordinary event took place: the reconciliation between the Moscow Patriarchate and the US-based Russian Orthodox Church outside Russia (ROCOR), which was founded by Russian émigré communities who had fled their country after the October Revolution. Metropolitan Laurus, the head of the ROCOR and archbishop of New York, had especially come over to Moscow, accompanied by hundreds of faithful, to sign the Act of Canonical Communion during a ceremony attended by church dignitaries and Russian government officials. Also President Vladimir Putin was present. The act would end an eighty-six-year-old schism. The spectacle was reminiscent of Rembrandt's famous masterpiece *The Return of the Prodigal Son*, which can be admired in the Saint Petersburg Hermitage Museum.

MERGERS AND ACQUISITIONS: THE KREMLIN CLAIMS ORTHODOX CHURCH BUILDINGS IN THE WEST

Apart from this being an emotional and religious event, it was also—and by no means least—a *political* event. Putin had personally invested much time and effort into obtaining this result. He had made the first overtures to the church abroad in September 2003, when he met with Metropolitan Laurus in

New York.[1] "Indeed," writes Yuri Zarakhovich, "rather than first give thanks to God in his speech, the head of the ROC, Patriarch Alexy, paid homage to Russian President Vladimir Putin. The Patriarch emphasized that the reunification could happen only because the ROCOR saw in Putin 'a genuine Russian Orthodox human being.'"[2] For Putin, therefore, it was a day of great satisfaction and personal triumph. Nadia Kizenko, a professor of history at New York State University and herself the daughter of an émigré ROCOR priest, is less enthusiastic. She writes:

> Mr. Putin needs friends anywhere he can find them. Having a ready-made network of 323 parishes and 20 monasteries in the U.S. alone, and over a million church members in 30 countries, will offer Russia greater influence abroad. This is particularly true because, according to the terms of the agreement, Moscow regains control over bishops' appointments and the right to open or close all parishes. . . . Many in the Church Abroad wonder how this merger went through at all. The process was secretive, and there has even been speculation that some American businessmen with Russian ties helped to push it along. But now having accepted Moscow's authority, the former Church Abroad faces many questions. Can its leaders press Moscow to reject the church's tradition of collaborating with both the Kremlin and the KGB? Can they hold on to the church properties they have maintained for the past 80 years? Will the Moscow Church dispatch pro-Kremlin clergy to promote political aims? And, above all, can the leaders of the Church Abroad stem the tide of defection from the disappointed faithful that has already begun?[3]

These were, indeed, pressing questions. The most important question, however, was whether the ROCOR had not too easily accepted its reunification with the Moscow Patriarchate, taking into account the close, not to say cozy, relationship of the latter with the Kremlin and the KGB in the past, a relationship that seemed to be continuing into the present. The ROCOR was not particularly known for being a progressive organization. The French historian Antoine Arjakovsky calls it "a Church which rejects all modernity and ecumenical movement, which pushes this Church increasingly into the swamp of an apocalyptic and paranoid mythology."[4] Irina Papkova, a researcher born in the United States into an émigré family which counted four generations of Orthodox priests, observes

> A strong tendency, . . . particularly among the relatively younger clergy and parishioners, to idealize the situation over there [in Moscow], especially the Putin/Medvedev years. I think this has to do in part, at least, with the fact that many people of this category have been able to live in Russia and sometimes to work there (usually in wealthy Moscow-based firms) and that the Russian circles they've been in contact with have generally been well-to-do, well-connected with the government and also with the powers-that-be within the Moscow Patriarchate. So there is some blindness induced by being too close to the sources of power and influence over in Russia. Also, especially after the

reunion with the Patriarchate, you can see some clergy members frankly losing some of their objectivity and blindly accepting as truth any information they are given by their Moscow counterparts, especially in terms of church-state relations over there.[5]

USING HEAVY-HANDED METHODS

Despite this "tendency in ROCOR to view the present day Russian situation through rose-colored glasses,"[6] not all newly won parishioners overseas were convinced of the blessings of this merger with the Moscow Patriarchate. When the Russian government started to reclaim church property (this was a *government* affair and not a church affair because in tsarist times churches abroad were the property of the state), this led to court cases in New Jersey and in California. Three months after the merger, 100 of the 340 clergy of the church abroad had broken away.[7] It was not only church property in the United States that was on the wish list of the Kremlin and the Moscow Patriarchate. In 2001 Kirill had already made a tentative list of church build-ings in Europe which could be reclaimed. These churches, he said, could be found in "Stockholm, Copenhagen, Paris, Nice, Cannes, Biarritz, San Remo, Florence, Vienna, and Baden-Baden,"[8] a list that was still far from complete. The Saint Nicholas Basilica in the Italian town Bari, for instance, was not on this list, nor the Orthodox cathedral in Budapest. Moscow would later claim these church buildings also. In Budapest, however, the Patriarch of the Greek Orthodox Church of Constantinople, under whose jurisdiction the cathedral in the Hungarian capital fell, resisted Moscow's claims and went to court. The Greek Patriarch argued that in 1949, when the parish entered the juris-diction of the Moscow Patriarchate, this was not an act of free choice but one imposed by the Red Army.[9] In Italy things went more smoothly for the Kremlin. In April 2008 the church building in Bari was returned to the Russian government by the outgoing Prodi government.[10]

Aleksandr Soldatov, a journalist of the opposition paper *Novaya Gazeta*, describes how the Moscow Patriarchate together with the Ministry of Foreign Affairs was able to lay its hands on "Russian churches in Biarritz (France), Bari (Italy), Hebron and Jericho (Palestine), Ottawa (Canada), which before fell under other jurisdictions."[11] This was brought about, he writes, "by using sometimes heavy-handed methods." The Moscow Patriarchate claimed church property not only abroad but also within Russia. After a law passed in 2010 approved the restitution of church property to the Orthodox Church, the church immediately showed its great appetite. "The Moscow Patriarchate," writes the *New York Times*, "has taken over hundreds of religious buildings that were never Russian Orthodox but belonged to other denominations be-fore the 1917 Bolshevik revolution."[12] This led to a conflict with Poland because "some of those buildings belonged to the Catholic Church, and most

Roman Catholic clerics in Russia and the former Soviet republics are ethnic Poles."[13]

COURT CASES IN FRANCE, CONFLICTS IN BRITAIN AND UKRAINE

Putin was personally highly involved in the implementation of this ambitious restitution program. He was well placed for this because in 1996 he started his career in the Kremlin as deputy chief of the Presidential Property Management Department, a department which was also in charge of Russia's properties abroad. This function gave him excellent knowledge of the many assets in Europe and the United States that could possibly be reclaimed. When Patriarch Aleksey II visited France in 2007, he demanded that Orthodox communities in France which did not belong explicitly to other autocephalic (independent) Orthodox churches should be brought under the jurisdiction of the Moscow Patriarchate.[14] However, reclaiming Orthodox church property and parishes abroad was not always easy. While descendants of White Russians might still have sentimental links with the home country of their ancestors, this was not the case for the Orthodox faithful with other national backgrounds and certainly not for French converts, whose number was not negligible. Moreover, after *eighty* years it was often difficult to justify Moscow's claims, and the active collaboration between the Moscow Patriarchate and the KGB, personified in the figure of "agent Drozdov" (Patriarch Aleksey II himself), did not help in removing mistrust.

Russian claims on tsarist property in France led to court cases in Biarritz and Nice. In Nice in 2005, the Russian authorities "sent officers of the SVR—the external espionage service [a follow-up organization of the KGB], to try to retake the Saint Nicholas Cathedral by judicial means."[15] The Russian state won the case against the parish on January 20, 2010, and became the legal owner of the Saint Nicholas cathedral, built in 1903 on a land plot offered by tsar Nicolas II.[16] This judgment was confirmed on May 19, 2011.[17] The lawyer of the association that had run the cathedral since 1923 declared that "for the first time, a foreign state has become the owner of a place of worship in France."[18] Herein precisely lies the crux of the anomaly: in caesaropapist Russia it is not the church but the state that reclaims church property.

In Biarritz, another French holiday resort, supporters of the Moscow Patriarchate tried to have the local church, which is affiliated to the Constantinople Patriarchate, revert its allegiance to Moscow. The parish council voted against, but Moscow adepts invited a group of the "faithful" from neighboring Spain to vote in a parallel council, a procedure that was described by insiders as a putsch.[19] After two appeals, a court of cassation decided that there had been irregularities in the voting procedure and that the unification with Moscow could not proceed.[20] In Paris the Moscow Patriarchate created an association that demanded the return into Moscow's fold of the famous Orthodox Cathedral Alexander Nevski in the Rue Daru. The parish council, however, successfully resisted these claims.

Another battle took place in London, where "new" Russians (Russian immigrants who had only recently arrived in Britain) succeeded in taking over the liberal and cosmopolitan Orthodox church in Ennismore Gardens. How this happened is described as follows by one of the old parishioners: "Huge numbers [of new Russian immigrants] arrived," she said. "We were a community of white Russians, Finns, French, Italians and English converts. But the incomers had a different mentality. To many, it was just a place to meet fellow Russians. They would come in halfway through service, talking loudly at the back, and started making lunch there."[21] The priests, sent over by Moscow, started to preach a fundamentalist variety of Orthodoxy at odds with the modernism and tolerant liberalism of the parish. Basil, the local bishop, asked the Moscow Patriarchate to intervene but received no reply. When Basil thereupon tried to have his diocese transferred from the jurisdiction of the Moscow Patriarchate to the Constantinople Patriarchate, he was immediately "retired" by Moscow. Basil was accepted by Constantinople and left, taking fifteen parishes with him, including half of the clergy, and 554 of the 1,161 registered church members.[22]

The Moscow Patriarchate used heavy-handed methods not only in Western Europe but also in Ukraine. Filaret, Patriarch of the Kyiv Patriarchate, accused Moscow adepts of having "started raider attacks to take away our churches."[23] According to him, the situation became worse after 2010, when Viktor Yanukovych, who was a follower of the Moscow Patriarchate, became president. Filaret gives the example of Kamianka, a village in the Donetsk region: "Some businessmen showed up offering money to the parish and the clergy to repair the church—on condition that they switched to the Moscow Patriarchate. Moreover, they were warned that, if they didn't do so voluntarily, force would be used."[24]

MOSCOW'S NEW MESSIANISM

Moscow's goal, however, is not restricted to reclaiming cathedrals and church property and bringing Orthodox parishes abroad back into Moscow's fold. The goal of the Kremlin and the Moscow Patriarchate is much more ambitious: it is about founding a genuinely *global* church under the aegis of Moscow—where "Moscow" means both the Kremlin and the Patriarchate. Building new churches, such as a new cathedral to be built in the very heart of Paris near the Eiffel Tower, is part of this program. It is clear that building

such a global church is a highly ambitious project, implying a huge missionary and financial effort. The Kremlin and the Moscow Patriarchate, however,
with the generous help of Russian oligarchs, seem to be ready to supply the
necessary financial resources.

This new missionary zeal finds expression in Orthodox publications. The
British Orthodox archpriest Andrew Phillips, for instance, writes that "with
the fall of Communism, Western Europe would have to come out of its shell
and face the real Europe, in particular Orthodox Europe, which had more
faithful Christians in it than Western Europe had Roman Catholics. Western
Europe at last realized that it would have to give up its self-centered ethno-
centricity. It had another half—and that was far more Christian than the West
was."[25] The archpriest goes on to describe Western Europe in terms of a
pagan missionary territory.

> Perhaps in reality, Western Europe is not so much "post-Christian," as "pre-
> Christian." Is not the mission of Orthodoxy to preach the Word of God in its
> Orthodox context to the four corners of the earth before the world ends?
> Western Europe is falling to the level of animals, from which it unashamedly
> proclaims that it is descended, and is becoming obsessed with the human body,
> sports and healthcare systems, sexual, eating and drinking functions, as re-
> flected in its often bestial "art" and "culture." Orthodox are called on to preach
> the Church Truth of Orthodoxy to the new pagans. Through its own apostasy
> from the heterodox vestiges of Orthodoxy, Western Europe has now become a
> missionary territory.[26]

As concerns the chances for these missionary activities, the archpriest writes:

> Since 1989 the situation of Orthodox in Western Europe has been transformed
> from that of a tiny refugee minority which barely registered on the political
> screen, to being that of representing over 8% of the EU population. Romania,
> Bulgaria and Cyprus are now together inside the EU. There are some two
> million new Orthodox in Germany (especially from Kazakhstan), one million
> in Italy, hundreds of thousands of new Orthodox in France, the UK, Portugal
> and tens of thousands in Ireland, Belgium, Holland, Switzerland, Austria,
> Sweden, Spain and Norway. New Orthodox bishops have appeared and hun-
> dreds of new Orthodox parishes have opened all over Western Europe. . . .
> Then there are new EU member countries with their own Local Orthodox
> Churches (Poland, the Czech lands and Slovakia, and Finland), on top of
> which there are new EU member countries like Latvia and Estonia with large
> Orthodox minorities. Moreover, there is talk of Serbia, Montenegro, Macedo-
> nia, Moldova and the Ukraine one day joining the EU.[27]

The perspectives are, therefore, excellent: "Orthodox are now free to speak
as missionaries to Western Europe." In his proselytizing zeal, Father Andrew
exclaimed: "1,000 Orthodox churches need to be built throughout Western
Europe. Yes, 1,000. Every Western European town of over 100,000 should

have its own Orthodox Church, premises, paid clergy and choir."[28] The goal of this huge effort is the re-Christianization of Europe. Because, writes the priest, "the European Union has become a giant and anti-democratic atheist bloc, saturated by the intolerant tide of liberal humanism."[29]

OLIGARCHS AS CHURCH BUILDERS

This new messianism is considered by the Kremlin not a task for the church alone. It is considered a collective patriotic effort which binds together the Moscow Patriarchate, the Kremlin, national and regional politicians, the Russian diaspora abroad, and Kremlin-friendly oligarchs. The role of this last category—inside as well as outside Russia—should not be underestimated. "The business and political elite have assiduously followed instructions to fund the rebuilding of churches destroyed by the Soviets across the country," writes the *Telegraph*.[30] The correspondent may well be right to use the words "followed instructions" because this financial support is certainly not always given spontaneously. Svetlana, former president Medvedev's spouse, played an important role in promoting the elite's fund-raising. She is said to have entered the church in the 1990s, when she met Father Vladimir Volgin, a Moscow priest and remarkable figure. Volgin was known for having brought into the church Irina Abramovich, the second wife of the oligarch Roman Abramovich, the owner of Chelsea Football Club, who lives in London.[31] The relationship of Father Volgin with Abramovich's wife certainly did the church no harm. On the website of the Russian Orthodox Church in England one could read about a "rumoured offer by Roman Abramovich . . . to build a new Russian Church in London," in case the Patriarchate would lose its London cathedral to "schismatics."[32]

President Medvedev's wife Svetlana and the wife of Abramovich were only two of the high-level contacts of the church. Nikolas K. Gvosdev mentions that "one of the wealthiest businessmen in Russia, Igor Naivalt, owner of Russia's largest construction firm (the Baltic Construction Company) is renowned for donating a tithe on his profits to the Orthodox Church."[33] Another Russian oligarch known for his largess abroad is Ivan Zavvidi, chairman of the board of the Agrokom Group and a Duma member for United Russia. Zavvidi, who is of Greek origin, "not only invested in [Greek] football, but also, for instance, in the restoration of some [Orthodox] churches [in Greece]."[34] During Yeltsin's presidency, Russian companies were already beginning to sponsor church activities abroad. For instance, in Romania, "in 1999, President Emil Constantinescu participated, together with the [Romanian] Patriarch Teoctist, in the sanctification of the church built by LukOil Company in the cemetery of Petrol Workers in Ploiești."[35] Lukoil building a church in Romania? There would be considerable amazement if Shell, BP, ExxonMobil, or Total were to engage in similar activities. Russian companies, however, are different. "This important company [Lukoil]," writes Gabriel Andreescu, "symbolizes the solidarity between the Russian Orthodox Church—led by the ex-KGB officer Alexei II, spokesman of the conservative powers in Russia—and the great Russian oligarchy, which paid between 2 and 3 billion dollars for the building of the Orthodox cathedral in Moscow."[36]

A similar generosity could be observed in the United Kingdom, this time in Manchester, where "a decade ago the church used by the Russian Orthodox community there began to fall down. The local community struggled to raise cash for a new building. Then, as their website reveals, 'in late 2001, the Building Trust received a very generous donation from a well-known industrialist from Russia'. It turned out to be Oleg Deripaska, the oligarch who had given support for the restoration of Orthodox churches in Russia."[37] Deripaska, an aluminium baron who married into the Yeltsin clan and has alleged links to the Mafia,[38] is one of Russia's richest and most powerful oligarchs. He is a close friend of Putin. His generosity toward the Orthodox community in Manchester had, however, a hidden price tag, which was that the community was asked to distance itself from the liberal Metropolitan Anthony in London, with whom Moscow was at odds, and to place itself under the direct authority of the Moscow Patriarchate. The parishioners, in good faith, cooperated and only later realized that they had fallen into a trap. "We did not understand what was happening," said one later. "Too late we realised it was a more orchestrated, deliberate attack."[39] "It was the tactics of Vladimir Ilyich Lenin," said another.[40]

A GLOBAL CHURCH FOR THE GLOBAL POWER

Making the Russian Orthodox Church into a *global* church has become a new, broadly shared great national endeavor in Russia in which the Kremlin, the Foreign Ministry, the Moscow Patriarchate, and Russia's oligarchs work closely together. The complete and seamless harmony in which all these actors cooperate can only be explained by the fact that the creation of a *global* Russian Orthodox Church has become a long-term strategic project of the Kremlin. In 2004, before the merger between the ROC and the ROCOR, the *Current Digest* had already written: "The ROC, the ROCA [ROC Abroad—this is the same as ROCOR] and the Russian president are all pleased that the idea that a 'superpower' like our country should have a 'superchurch' is being advanced as the main argument in favor of reunification."[41] Jean de Boishue, an adviser to French Prime Minister François Fillon, interviewed Kirill in 2006. He writes in a report: "The Russian Orthodox Church is no longer dissimulating its plan to strengthen its ties with other

Orthodox Churches in the Western world in order to jointly work with them to fulfill a mission of a universal nature,"[42] adding, "Monsignor Cyril startled us by confiding that the Church had decided to send its prelates abroad to promote the image of a living Church throughout the Western world."[43]

It is certain that we are witnessing here a totally new phenomenon: an unprecedented missionary effort on the part of the Russian Orthodox Church, supported by the Russian state and cofinanced by Russian oligarchs. The religious leadership, the state, and the world of finance are cooperating in this unique endeavor to project Russian Orthodoxy abroad and give it a powerful global presence. Religious missionary activity as such, of course, is no new phenomenon. During the past thirty years especially we have witnessed an explosive growth of missionary movements in Asia, Africa, and Latin America. In Brazil, for instance, Pentecostals now have about 25 million members. As a result, between 1965 and 2005 the percentage of Roman Catholics in the Brazilian population has decreased from 90 percent to 67 percent.[44] But the case of the Russian Orthodox Church is different. What is new here is that a *state* has entered the global religious market. The careful preparation, the coordinated efforts of the different actors, the involvement of the Kremlin and the Ministries of Foreign Affairs and Education, not to speak of the secret services, betrays a strategic, almost military planning.

The new, global character of this Kremlin-sponsored religious expansionism found its first expression in the Russian Orthodox Youth Congress that took place in Paris from July 1 to July 8, 2011. These youth forums were formerly organized by the US-based ROCOR. They began in 1973 and had been held seventeen times in the United States, Canada, Australia, and Latin America. The 2011 Youth Congress in Paris, however, had a different character: it was the first time after the restoration of unity with ROCOR that it was organized under the aegis of the Moscow Patriarchate. According to Nina Achmatova, "With Youth Day, Paris is now candidate to become the Orthodox reference point on the Old Continent. A great cultural and spiritual centre of the Moscow Patriarchate, including a cathedral, a seminary, a library, living spaces and facilities is due to be built not far from the Eiffel Tower and Elysée Palace, in the French capital."[45] The Kremlin and the Moscow Patriarchate are, indeed, planning to make the Paris region into the central "hub" in Western Europe from where to organize the Orthodox expansion. The first new Orthodox seminary to be established in Western Europe since the demise of the Soviet Union opened its doors on November 14, 2009, in Épinay-sous-Sénart, twenty-four kilometers from the French capital.[46]

THE FORMATION OF "STREET MISSIONARIES" IN RUSSIA

To be able to launch such a huge missionary effort, it is not enough for the Kremlin and the ROC to simply supply money and take over Orthodox diaspora communities abroad. It also implies the necessity for personnel to sustain these ambitious missionary efforts. Certainly, a rising number of Russian citizens identify themselves as Orthodox. According to polls conducted by the independent Moscow-based Levada Center, in 2008 71 percent of the respondents called themselves "Orthodox." This compares with 69 percent in 2007, 60 percent in 2004, and 59 percent in 2003.[47] These figures suggest that "a revival in religious convictions has occurred among the younger generation in the region, especially in Russia, although . . . this has not, as yet, been accompanied by a rise in church attendance."[48] The reason for this low church attendance is that Orthodoxy has become for most Russians more a question of national and ethnic identity than of genuine religiosity. This is confirmed by sociological research, which observed in Russia the rise of a "pro-Orthodox consensus," making the Orthodox Church the most trusted institution in the country—above the army, the government, the parliament, and the political parties.[49] "This means that for many Russians today it is possible to be an adherent of a certain faith without being a believer. . . . In fact, many nonbelievers are 'Orthodox', and even atheists can claim the same, like Belarusian president A. Lukashenko: 'I am an Orthodox atheist.'"[50]

Estimates say that only a meager 5 percent of self-confessed believers are regular churchgoers.[51] This was the reason that in December 2009 Patriarch Kirill launched a nationwide mission campaign. The Patriarchate started to finance and organize "formation courses for mission on the streets among the young people, promoting Christian values against the 'Western philosophy' of drugs, egotism and moral relativism."[52] In May 2010 the first hundred young adults attended the course. This "army" of missionary specialists was "ready to reconnect young people to religion." The missionaries would create youth groups throughout the Russian Federation. What differentiates the new group from the Orthodox Youth, existing since 1991, is that "it is intended to promote, together with religious values, an 'anti-Western philosophy', politics and patriotism."[53] It is easy to recognize here the political agenda of the Nashi, Putin's youth movement. It was, therefore, no surprise that in June 2010, the new group of Orthodox missionaries made its first appearance at the summer camp of this pro-Kremlin movement. Boris Yakemenko, the leader of the Orthodox wing of the Nashi, was tasked with preparing them to be trained to "street missionary activity."

NOTES

1. Daniel P. Payne, "Spiritual Security, the Russian Orthodox Church, and the Russian Foreign Ministry: Collaboration or Cooptation?" *Journal of Church and State* 52, no. 4 (2010), 716.

2. Yuri Zarakhovich, "Putin's Reunited Russian Church," *Time* (May 17, 2007).

3. Nadia Kizenko, "Church Merger, Putin's Acquisition," *The Wall Street Journal* (May 25, 2007).

4. Antoine Arjakovsky, *Russie Ukraine—De la guerre à la paix?* (Paris: Parole et Silence, 2014), 227.

5. "Irina Papkova: We Should Focus on Strengthening ROCOR Internally," interview conducted by Andrei Psarev, *rocorstudies.org* (May 1, 2010).

6. "Irina Papkova: We Should Focus."

7. Suzanne Sataline, "Cold War Lingers At Russian Church in New Jersey: Orthodox Dissidents Defy New Union with Moscow, Fearing Putin's Spies," *The Wall Street Journal* (July 18, 2007).

8. Metropolitan Kirill of Smolensk and Kaliningrad, "Cooperation between the Russian Orthodox Church and Russian Diplomacy: Yesterday, Today, and Tomorrow," *International Affairs* (Moscow) 47, no. 4 (2001), 158, quoted in Daniel P. Payne, "Spiritual Security, the Russian Orthodox Church, and the Russian Foreign Ministry: Collaboration or Cooptation?" *Journal of Church and State* 52, no. 4 (2010), 718.)

9. Cf. "The Prime Minister of the Russian Federation M.M. Kasyanov Visited the Cathedral of the Dormition of the Mother of God in Budapest," Department for External Church Relations of the Moscow Patriarchate, *orthodoxeurope.org* (September 9, 2003).

10. Cf. Raffaele Lorusso, "La Chiesa russa passa a Mosca 'Accordo storico, volo da Putin,'" *La Repubblica* (April 18, 2008).

11. Aleksandr Soldatov, "Shiroko shagaet pravoslavnaya tserkov," *Novaya Gazeta* (February 19, 2010).

12. "Churches Try to Repair Russian-Polish Ties," *The New York Times* (July 17, 2012).

13. "Churches Try to Repair Russian-Polish Ties."

14. Cf. Olivier Roy, *Holy Ignorance: When Religion and Culture Part Ways* (New York and Chichester: Columbia University Press, 2010), 181. A great number of Orthodox churches are in Paris. They are divided between Russian, Armenian, Ukrainian, Coptic, Syriac, Greek, Serb, Chaldean, Romanian, and Georgian. (Cf. Roy, 19.) Each national Orthodox Church has its own Patriarch. The *primus inter pares* of the Patriarchs is the Patriarch of Constantinople.

15. Vincent Jauvert, "L'affaire de la cathédrale du Kremlin à Paris," *Nouvel Observateur* (May 28, 2010).

16. "French Court Hands Nice Cathedral to Russia," *RFE/RL* (January 20, 2010).

17. Aliette de Broqua, "La bataille de la cathédrale orthodoxe de Nice n'est pas finie," *Le Figaro* (May, 20, 2011).

18. "French Court Hands Nice Cathedral to Russia."

19. Jauvert, "L'affaire de la cathédrale du Kremlin à Paris."

20. Robert C. Blitt, "Russia's "Orthodox" Foreign Policy: The Growing Influence of the Russian Orthodox Church in Shaping Russia's Policies Abroad," *University of Pennsylvania Journal of International Law* 33, no. 2 (May 2011), 37.

21. Paul Vallely, "The Battle over Britain's Orthodox Church," *The Independent* (February 11, 2009).

22. Vallely, "The Battle over Britain's Orthodox Church."

23. Olena Chekan, "When Evil Turns to Good—Filaret, Patriarch of Kyiv and All Rus-Ukraine, Talks about Raider Attacks on Churches Belonging to the Kyiv Patriarchate and the Delusion of a 'Russian World,'" *Ukrainian Week* (March 14, 2011).

24. Chekan, "When Evil Turns to Good."

25. Archpriest Andrew Phillips, "The Future of the Orthodox Church in Western Europe," *Orthodox England on the 'net* (December 4–17, 2009), http://www.orthodoxengland.org.uk/futowe.htm.

26. Phillips, "The Future of the Orthodox Church."

27. Phillips, "The Future of the Orthodox Church."

28. Phillips, "The Future of the Orthodox Church."

29. Phillips, "The Future of the Orthodox Church."

30. Adrian Blomfield, "Orthodox Church Unholy Alliance with Putin," *The Telegraph* (February 23, 2008).

31. Paul Goble, "Russian First Lady Seen Actively Promoting Orthodox Church—Analysis," *Eurasia View* (May 9, 2011).

32. Andrew Phillips, "The Time-Bomb That Went Off: Happier Prospects after the Sourozh Schism" (June 5–18, 2006), http://www.orthodoxengland.org.uk/timebomb.htm.

33. Nikolas K. Gvosdev, "An Orthodox Look at Liberty and Economics in Russia," *Religion & Liberty* 14, no. 4 (July/August 2004).

34. Michael Thumann, "Russen gehen auf Einkaufstur in Griechenland," *Zeit Online* (November 15, 2012).

35. Gabriel Andreescu, *Right-Wing Extremism in Romania* (Cluj: Ethnocultural Diversity Resource Center, 2003), 40, http://www.edrc.ro/docs/docs/extremism_eng/RightwingExtremismInRomania.pdf.

36. Andreescu, *Right-Wing Extremism in Romania.*

37. Vallely, "The Battle over Britain's Orthodox Church."

38. In a judgment in 2008, the British High Court detailed the alleged social and business links between Deripaska and Anton Malevsky, the head of one of the most powerful Russian crime gangs. Malevsky's brother Andrei had a 10 percent stake in Deripaska's company. (Cf. Steven Swinford and Jon Ungoed-Thomas, "Peter Mandelson Oligarch Oleg Deripaska Linked to Mafia Boss," *The Sunday Times* (October 26, 2008).)

39. Vallely, "The Battle over Britain's Orthodox Church."

40. Vallely, "The Battle over Britain's Orthodox Church."

41. "The Strength and Weakness of Orthodoxy," *The Current Digest of the Post-Soviet Press* 55, no. 51 (January 21, 2004), 19–20, quoted in Daniel P. Payne, "Spiritual Security, The Russian Orthodox Church, and the Russian Foreign Ministry: Collaboration or Cooptation?" *Journal of Church and State* 52, no. 4 (2010), 716–717.

42. Jerôme Monod and Jean de Boishue, *The Russian Comeback: Chronicles of a Journey through Eastern Europe from 27 May to 9 June 2006* (Paris: Fondation pour l'Innovation Politique, July 2006), 29, http://www.fondapol.org/.

43. Monod and de Boishue, *The Russian Comeback*, 31.

44. Cf. Roy, *Holy Ignorance*, 1, 14.

45. Nina Achmatova, "First Ever Russian Orthodox Youth Day in Europe," *AsiaNews.it* (February 14, 2011).

46. "Inauguration du séminaire orthodoxe russe en France" (November 16, 2009), http://www.egliserusse.eu/Inauguration-du-seminaire-orthodoxe-russe-en-France_a886.html.

47. Quoted in Jarosław Ćwiek-Karpowicz, "Role of the Orthodox Church in Russian Foreign Policy," *Bulletin*, no. 109 (185), The Polish Institute of International Affairs (August 9, 2010), 336.

48. Pippa Norris and Ronald Inglehart, *Sacred and Secular: Religion and Politics Worldwide* (Cambridge and New York: Cambridge University Press, 2004), 115–116.

49. Kimmo Kääriäinen and Dmitrii Furman, "Orthodoxy as a Component of Russian Identity," *East-West Church & Ministry Report* 10, no. 1 (Winter 2002).

50. Kääriäinen and Furman, "Orthodoxy as a Component of Russian Identity."

51. Monod and Boishue give an estimated percentage of 3 to 4 percent (*The Russian Comeback*, 28). Their figure refers, however, to the percentage of the *whole* population and seems, therefore, to confirm the other figure cited.

52. Nina Achmatova, "A New 'Army' of Young People for the Russian Orthodox Church," *AsiaNews.it* (August 2, 2010).

53. Achmatova, "A New 'Army' of Young People."

Chapter Eleven

The Russian Orthodox Church

A Pillar of Russian Neoimperialism?

The Russian Orthodox Church is clearly used by the Kremlin as one of its most prominent *soft-power* instruments for spreading the new ideology of the Russian state. There are several reasons to be concerned. These reasons number at least *five*:

1. The Russian Orthodox Church is *not* independent.
2. The Russian Orthodox Church is *not* the universal moral standard-bearer it pretends to be.
3. The Russian Orthodox Church is a declared *adversary of freedom of religion* and supports the repression of religious and sexual minorities.
4. The Russian Orthodox Church is often an *adversary of democracy and universal human rights*.
5. The Russian Orthodox Church actively *supports Putin's neoimperialist policy* and has itself developed a religious variant of this neoimperialism.

These five features are analyzed in greater detail in the following paragraphs.

THE RUSSIAN ORTHODOX CHURCH IS NOT INDEPENDENT

The ROC often refers to its cooperation with the state by using the term *symphonia*. This "symphony" refers to an old Byzantine concept of church-state relations in which the state is concerned with worldly affairs and the church with matters divine. While the two are considered interdependent, neither is supposed to be subordinated to the other. In practice, however, in

Russia such a harmonious "symphony" has seldom existed, and Putin's reign is just another example of what some have called an "asymmetric symphonia":[1] a continuation of the subordination of the church to the state, as was the case in tsarist and Soviet times. The Russian population is not fooled by talk of independence. According to Roman Lunkin, director of the Moscow-based Institute of Religion and Law, most Russians do not consider the Russian Orthodox Church as separate and distinct from the Russian state.[2]

THE RUSSIAN ORTHODOX CHURCH IS NOT A UNIVERSAL MORAL STANDARD-BEARER

Marquis De Custine, who visited Russia in 1839, had already written about the close relationship between Orthodox priests and the state: "One sees the priests despised by the people, despite the protection of the kings, or, better, precisely because of this protection, which makes them dependent on the ruler, even in the practice of their divine mission. . . . A servile priest will never teach his disciples anything other than to bow their necks under the yoke."[3] This dependence of the church upon the state, according to him, also had an immediate impact on the *moral role* the church played in society. "I have seen in Russia a Christian Church, which nobody attacks, which everybody respects, at least on the surface: a Church for which there are no obstacles in the exercise of its moral authority, and nevertheless this Church has no authority at all, no influence on the people's hearts; it can produce only hypocrites or superstitious people."[4] Still in our day, instead of acting as an independent moral voice and standing up for the rights of innocent victims, the Russian Orthodox Church was shamefully silent when Russian troops committed appalling crimes against the civilian population in Chechnya during Putin's ten years of war in this North Caucasian republic. Michael Bourdeaux, director of the Keston Institute at Oxford University, calling Putin the "butcher of Grozny," writes that "the Moscow Patriarchate stressed the duty of all young Russian males to serve in the army—thus not falling far short of implicitly condoning genocide."[5] This support for the Kremlin's policies was also clear during the Maidan revolt in Ukraine. "On December 26, [2013,] in a text of the Holy Synod, the patriarch vigorously condemned Maidan as a movement manipulated by the West. On January 7, [2014,] on the occasion of his Christmas message, the patriarch, on the first TV channel Rossiya 1, again condemned the Euromaidan."[6] After the annexation of the Crimea and the subsequent Russian aggression against Ukraine, the Orthodox Church remained silent. On July 18, 2014, however, during a ceremony commemorating Saint Sergius of Radonezh—an important religious event attended by Putin—Patriarch Kirill abandoned his apparent "neutrality," declaring: "God grant that everyone understand that Russia is not a source of a military or any other threat to humanity," and he thanked Putin "for formulating thoughts and ideas which unite people."[7] Archpriest Vsevolod Chaplin, chairman of the ROC's Synodal Department for the Co-operation of Church and Society, was even less circumspect, asking some days before the annexation of the Crimea for "a peacekeeping mission of Russia in Ukraine," emphasizing that "the Russian people—a nation that is divided within its historical territories, has the right to unite itself in one state."[8]

THE RUSSIAN ORTHODOX CHURCH IS A DECLARED ADVERSARY OF FREEDOM OF RELIGION

The ROC is characterized by a deep-seated ideology of *illiberalism*. It reserves the right to religious freedom mainly for itself, often acting as an ardent enemy of the religious freedom of other denominations. When, in October 1990, under Gorbachev the liberal law "On Freedom of Religious Denomination" was passed—a law introducing religious freedom—this was for Russia an unprecedented historical event. It was the first time in Russia's long history that believers of all persuasions received overnight virtually complete religious freedom. Stalin's law of 1929, which had subjugated churches to the state, was abolished, as was the Council for Religious Affairs, a KGB agency which kept a critical eye on believers. But the leaders of the Russian Orthodox Church were not pleased when, following the introduction of the law, many new denominations entered the religious market in Russia and started proselytizing.[9] The Moscow Patriarchate soon mounted an offensive to amend the law with the aim of restricting the freedom of other religions, which were accused of being dangerous sects. In an interview with the German weekly *Der Spiegel*, Kirill expressed the fears that haunted the Moscow Patriarchate after the introduction of the new law on religion. "We were weakened by atheism," he said, "and then we were faced with a double burden. We were like a boxer who walks around for months with his arm in a cast and is then abruptly shoved into the ring, accompanied by shouts of encouragement. But there we encountered a well-trained opponent, in the form of a wide variety of missionaries from America and South Korea who tried to convert the Russian people to other faiths."[10]

In 1992, immediately after the demise of the Soviet Union and two years after the adoption of the liberal law on religious freedom, the ROC began to pressure the communist-dominated Duma for changes. Yeltsin, however, twice refused to sign the amended law.[11] The violent conflict in the fall of 1993, in which Yeltsin and the Parliament were in opposition, brought these attempts to change the law to a premature end. However, notwithstanding Yeltsin's opposition, the church continued its aggressive lobbying campaign. To strengthen its case against the "foreign intruders," the Patriarchate began to use the term "totalitarian sects"—a term coined in 1994 by the anti-cult crusader Aleksandr Dvorkin. To use the adjective "totalitarian" in order to obtain the repression of religious movements was, to say the least, a little strange for a church which itself had suffered the duress of persecution by a totalitarian regime. "The use of the Cold War 'totalitarian' label," writes Julie Elkner, "in order to justify what amount to totalitarian policies is one of the paradoxes of the post-Soviet Russian political scene."[12]

However, it was not only the Moscow Patriarchate that was concerned about the influx of foreign missionaries. Similar concerns were aired by the Ministry of the Interior and the FSB, accusing the missionaries of working as agents for foreign (read: American) intelligence services.[13] The combined lobbying of the Patriarchate and the intelligence services continued. In July 1997 the Duma voted with a great majority for a new law restricting religious freedom. US President Bill Clinton and the pope expressed their concern. The new law was discriminatory for "minority religions," including Protestantism and Catholicism, which had to prove that they existed "for more than fifteen years" in Russia in order to be registered. Yeltsin refused to sign and won praise from Washington.[14] However, the proponents of a restrictive law finally met with success. Yeltsin agreed to an amended version of the law, which came into force on October 1, 1997. The new law made a distinction between "traditional faiths" and "nontraditional faiths." The four "traditional faiths"—Orthodoxy, Islam, Judaism, and Buddhism—were given the status of "religious *organizations*" that had a legitimate place in Russia. This was not self-evident for the "nontraditional faiths," which were given the status of "religious *groups*."[15] The latter included the diverse Protestant denominations and even Roman Catholicism (which was not included in the "traditional faiths" group although it had been present in Russia since the seventeenth century). The result of the new law was that many Christian denominations, such as the Salvation Army, the Pentecostals, and Jehovah's Witnesses, could no longer function freely in Russia. Problems began with the mandatory registration process, a necessity for gaining legal status, without which a religious group could not hire or buy church property, open a bank account, collect gifts, pay salaries, and so on. Religious associations that had already been registered before 1997 had to reregister. In November 2001 the registration of Jehovah's Witnesses was delayed by the Moscow procurator on the grounds that the group represented a national security threat.[16] Harassment of this group did not stop there. Jehovah's Witnesses were prosecuted in 2010 on the basis of another law, the controversial anti-extremism law, adopted in 2002, for "inciting religious hatred."[17] This allegation was based on the fact that in their pamphlets the Jehovah's Witnesses claim to have the true faith—a claim which, as a matter of fact, every religion makes. According to the SOVA Center, in 2010 the ban on Jehovah's Witnesses' basic texts spurred more than fifty police detentions and searches in a three-month period alone.[18] In June 2011 the FSB and the local authorities intervened in Saint Petersburg and prevented the Jehovah's Witnesses from organizing two reunions in a sports complex.[19] On November 13, 2014, Russia's Supreme Court sustained the ruling of Samara's regional court on declaring the Jehovah's Witnesses an "extremist organization."[20] In January of the same year, the municipal court in Kurgan declared the Jehovah's Witnesses' booklets "extremist literature." The subversive pamphlets were titled "How to Achieve Happiness in Life," "What Is the People's Hope?," "How to Develop Close Relations with God?," and "What Should We Know about God and Its Sense?"[21] "We remember what happened to Jehovah's Witnesses in the Soviet era, in the 50s, when some 1,000 were exiled to Siberia. Now it seems this is all being repeated," said Grigory Martynov, a spokesman for the group, which has about 162,000 followers in Russia.[22]

The Church of Scientology, which had already been officially registered on January 25, 1994, applied eleven times for reregistration to the Moscow Justice Department, which almost every time produced new arguments for refusing registration. When finally, on April 5, 2007, the case came before the European Court of Human Rights, the court decided "that there had been a violation of Article 11 (freedom of assembly and association) of the European Convention on Human Rights read in the light of Article 9 (freedom of thought, conscience and religion)."[23] The decision of the European Court of Human Rights did not prevent the Russian authorities' continuing their harassment of the group. In 2011, four years after the decision of the European Court, the anti-extremism law was used to ban the book *What Is Scientology?* by Ron Hubbard, the founder of the movement, together with other booklets, on the grounds that "these materials contain calls for extremist activity" and that the members of the movement "are trained for the flawless execution of their functions, many of which are confined to fighting with the rest of the world."[24] The court decided that the books were to be "included in the federal list of extremist materials and forbidden to be disseminated on Russian Federation territory."[25]

Another case was that of the Salvation Army, which fought for its reregistration in the Moscow courts without success. According to a report of the Parliamentary Assembly of the Council of Europe, "One of the court judgments even found this renowned Christian religious and charitable organization, which feeds more than 7,000 homeless a month in Moscow, to be a "foreign paramilitary organization aiming at the violent overthrow of the Russian Federation."[26] The farcical and ridiculous arguments used by the courts remind one of former Soviet days which were thought to be over. The strategy of the Russian authorities, however, was clear. After having been corrected repeatedly by the European Court of Human Rights, they changed tactic and relied increasingly on the anti-extremism law to repress religious minorities.

At present, the most vital force within Russian Orthodoxy rejects the trend of developments which most of the West seems to be expecting to emerge from the rubble of the fallen Soviet system. And because the Russian Orthodox Church is the largest single religious institution in Russia, this means that the most influential force within the religious population of that country resists democracy, free market economics, and a pluralist society. Instead it favors the restoration of the geopolitical integrity of the traditional Russian empire, an authoritarian political system, and a centrally controlled economy, with the Russian church occupying a privileged position in state and society.[27]

THE RUSSIAN ORTHODOX CHURCH IS AN ADVERSARY OF DEMOCRACY AND UNIVERSAL HUMAN RIGHTS

The restriction of the religious freedom for other denominations championed by the Russian Orthodox Church meant a *double* blow for the young Russian democracy: first, because of growing legal and political repression that put an end to the seven-year period between 1990 and 1997, which had been characterized by unprecedented freedom, tolerance, and openness; and second, because this religious "rollback" also had more indirectly negative consequences for the democratic development of Russian civil society. The reason is that the evangelical, "nontraditional" faiths often act as the standard-bearers of democracy. This fact is confirmed by Roman Lunkin, director of the Moscow Institute of Religion and Law. "Protestantism," he writes, "has become a considerable social movement in Russia in the 1990s. In the post-Soviet period the leaders of different Evangelical Churches are more active in defending democratic values and human rights for the sake of the development of democratic society, than representatives of other confessions in Russia."[28]

The Russian state, by giving a privileged position to the Russian Orthodox Church and discriminating against other religions, not only violated the Constitution of the Russian Federation, which, in article 14, guarantees the separation of state and religion and, in article 28, guarantees the freedom of religion and conscience.[29] In addition, it championed precisely that religion: Orthodoxy, which was least compatible with personal freedom and a modern liberal democracy. Inna Naletova writes:

> One can assume that Orthodox beliefs may restrict the development of individualism and encourage collective values. Indeed, Orthodox concern for sacramental and collective salvation rather than with individuals' personal relations to God may create an obstacle for the development of respect for the rule of law, human rights, and individual freedoms, including freedom of speech, of the press, and of worship.[30]

In the preceding chapter we analyzed the dubious role played by the Russian Orthodox Church in international fora, such as the UN Human Rights Council, where it actively promotes policies which make the implementation of human rights dependent on so-called traditional values. This position is a logical consequence of the definition of human rights as formulated in the "Bases of the Social Concept" of the ROC, which states that "for the Christian sense of justice, the idea of human freedom and rights is bound up with the idea of service. The Christian needs rights so that in exercising them he may . . . fulfill . . . his duty . . . before other people, family, state, nation and other human communities."[31] That an individual needs rights to *fulfill his duty before the state* is a complete reversal of the sense of human rights conventions, which intend to grant the individual inalienable rights which may not be infringed upon by any state, in order to avoid a state's invoking arbitrary "duties" from the individual before the state.[32] As for the democratic credentials of the leadership of the Russian Orthodox Church, these were revealed in a 2001 survey which "found 37 percent of [Orthodox] bishops supporting the suggestion that 'democracy is not for Russia.'"[33]

THE RUSSIAN ORTHODOX CHURCH: A PILLAR OF PUTIN'S NEOIMPERIALIST POLICY

Maybe even more disconcerting is the ROC's unconditional support for Putin's aggressive neoimperialist policies in the former Soviet space. The Moscow Patriarchate not only actively supports the Kremlin's expansionist policies but also has an expansionist policy of its own which supports and complements the Kremlin's policy. The keyword here is *canonical territory*. Canonical territory is a central concept in the church organization of Eastern Christian Orthodoxy. Since the schism in 1054 between Rome and Constantinople, Orthodoxy was organized around the Ecumenical Patriarchate of Constantinople.[34] Although the Patriarch of Constantinople had less power than the pope of Rome, he was the primus inter pares among the Orthodox Patriarchs and he could—and still can—claim three rights. These are, first, the right to establish a court of final appeal for any case in the Orthodox world. Second is the right to summon the other Patriarchs and heads of autocephalous churches to a meeting. And third, he has the right to grant permission for the establishment of new autocephalous (mostly national) churches. Among the different Patriarchates the principle of *canonical territory* was upheld. This meant that one Patriarch had no right to compete or proselytize on the territory of another Patriarch. If the faithful from one Patriarchate migrated to the territory of another Patriarchate, they were no longer affiliated with the Patriarchate of origin but with the Patriarchate of the host country.[35] In a way, the organization resembled a modern business cartel, intended to prevent competition among different national Orthodox churches on the same territory. A second organizational principle was that any Orthodox faithful living in the diaspora beyond the Orthodox world (for instance, in Western Europe) fell under the jurisdiction of the Ecumenical Patriarch of Constantinople.

Both principles were challenged by the Moscow Patriarchate after the demise of the Soviet Union. When Estonia was restored its independence in 1991, the country wanted to resurrect the autonomy which the Estonian Orthodox Church had enjoyed before the Soviet occupation in 1939. In 1993, fifty-four of the eighty-three Orthodox parishes in Estonia asked to come under the jurisdiction of Constantinople under the name of the Autonomous Church of Estonia. This request was granted by Bartholomew, the Ecumenical Patriarch of Constantinople, on February 20, 1996.[36] Although a correct ecclesiological procedure was followed, the Moscow Patriarchate was furious and accused Constantinople of "invasion into the territory of another local Orthodox Church."[37] Thereupon, Moscow began to boycott the Ecumenical Patriarch and no longer took part in meetings in which Constantinople was represented.

Another case is Ukraine. Attempts by Ukraine to set up a Ukrainian Orthodox Church independent of the Moscow Patriarchate resulted in an open religious war. After Ukraine became an independent state, Moscow did not acknowledge the legitimacy of the newly established "Ukrainian Orthodox Church-Kyivan Patriarchate" (UOC-KP), which had the support of the first Ukrainian President Leonid Kravchuk. Its Patriarch, Filaret, was excommunicated and defrocked by the Moscow Patriarchate, but the Kyivan Patriarchate did not recognize Moscow's authority. At the same time, the Patriarch of Constantinople was deterred by Moscow from taking Kyiv under its jurisdiction. The struggle between the two churches reflected the ongoing political struggle in Ukraine between pro-Russian forces and the supporters of Ukrainian independence. President Kuchma (1994–2005), who in the beginning supported the Moscow Patriarchate, later took a more neutral stance. His successor, President Yushchenko (2005–2010), wanted to strengthen Ukraine's national church and actively supported the Kyivan Patriarchate.

However, things took a different turn in 2010 with the election of Viktor Yanukovych, who was a staunch supporter of the Moscow Patriarchate. Yanukovych immediately began to undermine the position of the Kyivan Patriarchate. This led the Synod of Bishops to send, in December 2010, an open letter to the president, asking him "to stop openly lobbying the UOC-MP [Moscow Patriarchate] and the practice of meeting only with the clergy and hierarchs of that church."[38] In January 2011 Patriarch Filaret sounded the alarm. He complained that "in all regions of Ukraine representatives of the government or priests of the Moscow Patriarchate hold talks with our priests. They are invited to come to the subordination of the Moscow Patriarchate for different kinds of support and help."[39] Seventy percent of the priests in the Donetsk region had allegedly already been contacted. "Illegal takeovers of our churches commenced. . . . And the government is always on the side of the Russian Church," said Patriarch Filaret.[40] According to him, "the cases are a part of one plan." In April 2011 Filaret made an appeal to the president to rethink his policies, adding, "I think that the current president will also understand that he is the Ukrainian president and not a Russian governor."[41]

One of the apples of discord was a government project to grant the Ukrainian Orthodox Church, Kyivan Patriarchate the status of a legal entity. This project was strongly opposed by the Kyivan Patriarchate because it would give the rival Moscow-affiliated church the opportunity to go to court and claim the churches and church property of the Kyivan church. (The existing situation was that not the church, but only the parishes, monasteries, and educational centers had the status of legal entity, which made attempts by the Moscow Patriarchate to claim church property in Ukraine more difficult.) Given the fact that courts in Ukraine are not independent, this would undoubtedly lead to a takeover of the Kyivan church by the Moscow Patriarchate. "Remarkable is . . . the fact," writes J. Buciora, "that the Moscow Patriarchate defines its local Church as Russian that embraces in its boundaries the other national local Churches. If the local Church of the Moscow Patriarchate is defined as Russian, then the other Orthodox Churches of other independent countries are still Russian Churches even though the local Churches find themselves in sovereign and independent countries."[42]

Another author, Yury Chornomorets, writes: "The Moscow Patriarchate cannot be at the same time a nationalist church in Russia and a universal church in Ukraine."[43] He is right. The Russian Orthodox Church cannot claim to have a universal message when it continues to define itself as a narrow, national, Russian church, and certainly not when it seamlessly identifies itself with the neoimperialist policies of the Kremlin that has never really accepted the sovereignty of the newly independent neighboring states, in particular that of Ukraine.

Patriarch Kirill visited Ukraine in 2008 and 2009. In 2010 he visited Ukraine as many as three times. Similarly, he visited Belarus and Kazakhstan. He made these visits in the framework of the Russkiy Mir (Russian World) program, considered by observers in Russia's "neighborhood" as a Kremlin-inspired neoimperialist program. The ROC, wrote J. Buciora, with its "developed theory of the 'pan-Slavic' identity, that preserves a strictly Russian national character and tradition, has as its main objective the restoration of the former 'natural' borders of the Russian state, that is the borders of the USSR."[44] In a film produced by Metropolitan Hilarion, which was broadcast on national television in 2013, one went so far as to compare the "trinity" of Russia, Belarus, and Ukraine with the Holy Trinity—granting Moscow's revisionist territorial ambitions a quasi-mystical luster.[45] The Moscow

Patriarchate's objectives, therefore, seem to coincide seamlessly with the Kremlin's neoimperialist strategy. For this reason it is, perhaps, only logical that in a list of Russia's one hundred most important political figures, published by *Nezavisimaya Gazeta* in 2010, Kirill was ranked in seventh place—just behind Putin, Medvedev, and four of their closest allies and before heavyweights such as Foreign Minister Sergey Lavrov and Aleksey Miller, the head of Gazprom.[46]

NOTES

1. Cf. John Anderson, "Putin and the Russian Orthodox Church: Asymmetric Symphonia?" *Journal of International Affairs* 61, no. 1 (Fall/Winter 2007).

2. Paul Goble, "Window on Eurasia: Russians No Longer View Orthodox Church as Separate from the State, Lunkin Says," *Window on Eurasia* (April 28, 2011).

3. Marquis Astolphe de Custine, *Lettres de Russie : La Russie en 1839*, ed. Pierre Nora (Paris: Gallimard, 1975), 360.

4. Custine, *Lettres de Russie*, 374.

5. Michael Bourdeaux, "The Complex Face of Orthodoxy," *The Christian Century* (April 4, 2001), 18.

6. Antoine Arjakovsky, *Russie Ukraine: De la guerre à la paix?* (Paris: Parole et Silence, 2014), 223.

7. Quoted by Katarzyna Jarzyńska, "Patriarch Kirill's game over Ukraine," *OSW Commentary* (August 14, 2014).

8. "Protoierey Vsevolod Chaplin rassmatrivaet missiyu Rossii na Ukraine kak mirotvorcheskuyu," *Interfax* (March 1, 2014).

9. According to Patrick Johnstone and Jason Mandryck, between 1994 and 2001 the number of nonindigenous Protestant missionaries in Russia grew from 505 to over 2,200, an increase of 336 percent. In some other post-Soviet states the percentage of increase was still greater: 1,450 percent in Lithuania, 1,267 percent in Belarus, and 865 percent in Ukraine. (Patrick Johnstone and Jason Mandryck, "Non-Indigenous Protestant Missionaries in Post-Soviet States, 1994–2001," *East-West Church & Ministry Report* 10, no. 1 (Winter 2002).)

10. "'The Bible Calls It a Sin': Interview with Russian Orthodox Metropolitan Kyrill," *Spiegel Online* (October 1, 2008).

11. Cf. Anita Deyneka, "Russia's Restrictive Law on Religion: Dead or Delayed?" *East-West Church & Ministry Report* 1, no. 4 (Fall 1993), http://www.eastwestreport.org/articles/ew01401.htm.

12. Julie Elkner, "Spiritual Security in Putin's Russia," *History and Policy* (January 2005), http://www.historyandpolicy.org/papers/policy-paper-26.html.

13. Missionaries are explicitly mentioned as a security risk in the 2000 National Security Concept, which referred to the necessity of "resistance to the negative influence of foreign religious organizations and missionaries." ("National Security Concept of the Russian Federation," 10.) In the same vein, the "Doctrine of Information Security of the Russian Federation," which expounded the National Security Concept as applied to the information sphere and which was approved by President Putin on September 9, 2000, spoke about the necessity "of counteracting the negative influence of foreign religious organizations and missionaries." ("Doktrina informatsionnoy bezopasnosti Rosssiyskoy Federatsii," Moscow (September 2000), 12, http://www.scrf.gov.ru/documents/5.html.) In the same doctrine, however, one can read that information security implies "the freedom of conscience, which includes the right to freely choose, have and spread religious and other beliefs" (11).

14. Cf. "Le veto de Boris Eltsine à une loi sur les religions satisfait Washington," *Le Monde* (July 25, 1997).

15. It is interesting that Pope Benedict XVI expressed a similar concern about the rise of the evangelical denominations. During a visit to Germany, the pope warned against the dangers "of

a new form of Christianity": the proliferation of evangelical churches in the world, showing "a missionary dynamism that is in the form it has taken a reason for concern." This "Christianity with little institutional depth, with little rational substance, and still less dogmatic coherence and little stability," obliged the "historical churches" to conduct a "common reflection on what has lasting value and on what can and must be changed." (Cf. Stéphanie Le Bars, "Benoît XVI appelle les chrétiens à une alliance contre la 'sécularisation,'" *Le Monde* (September 25–26, 2011).) The pope's concern for the position of the "historical" churches resembles the ROC's concern for the position of the "traditional" churches.

16. Cf. Inna Naletova, no title, *Perspective* 12, no. 3 (January–February 2002).

17. Alexander Verkhovsky, "Inappropriate Enforcement of Anti-extremist Legislation in Russia in 2010," *SOVA Center for Information and Analysis*, Moscow (April 11, 2011).

18. Alissa de Carbonnel, "Russia Uses Extremism Law to Target Dissenters," *Reuters* (December 16, 2010).

19. "V Sankt-Peterburge chinovniki prepyatstvuyut provedeniyu kongressov Svideteley Iegovy," *Portal Credo.ru* (June 22, 2011).

20. "Russia's Supreme Court Rules Jehovah's Witnesses from Samara Extremist Organization," *TASS* (November 13, 2014).

21. "Russia's Supreme Court Rules."

22. Alissa de Carbonnel, "Russia Uses Extremism Law to Target Dissenters."

23. European Court of Human Rights Registrar, "Chamber Judgment: Church of Scientology Moscow v. Russia" (application no. 18147/02), press release (April 5, 2007).

24. "Russian Court Bans Ron Hubbard's Books as Extremist," *ITAR-TASS* (June 30, 2011). The court ruling took place in the town of Shchyolkovo, near Moscow, on June 30, 2011.

25. "Po trebovaniyu Shchelkovskoy gorodskoy prokuratury Moskovskoy oblasti priznany ekstremistskimi knigi Rona Khabbarda," Generalnaya Prokuratura Rossiyskoy Federatsii (official website of the general procurator of the Russian Federation) (June 30, 2011), http://genproc.gov.ru/news/news-72454/?print=1.

26. Kevin McNamara, "Russia's Law on Religion," report, Committee on Legal Affairs and Human Rights, Parliamentary Assembly of the Council of Europe (March 25, 2002).

27. Paul D. Steeves, "Russian Orthodox Fascism after Glasnost," paper presented to the Conference on Faith and History, Harrisburg, Pennsylvania (October 8, 1994), http://www2.stetson.edu/~psteeves/rusorthfascism.html.

28. Roman Lunkin, "Protestantism and Human Rights in Russia: Creation of the Alternative to the Authorities," paper for the Fourth Annual Lilly Fellows National Research Conference, Samford University, Birmingham, AL (November 11–14, 2005).

29. Article 14.1 states, "The Russian Federation is a secular state. No religion may be established as a state or obligatory one." And article 14.2 states: "Religious associations shall be separated from the State and shall be equal before the law." Article 28 states, "Everyone shall be guaranteed the freedom of conscience, the freedom of religion, including the right to profess individually or together with other [*sic*] any religion or to profess no religion at all, to freely choose, possess and disseminate religious and other views and act according to them." (Constitution of the Russian Federation, available at http://www.constitution.ru/en/10003000-01.htm.)

30. Inna Naletova, "The Orthodox Church in the Mirror of Public Opinion: An Analysis of Recent Polls and Surveys," in: *Questionable Returns*, ed. Andrew Bove, IWM Junior Visiting Fellows Conferences, vol. 12 (Vienna, 2002).

31. "Bases of the Social Concept of the Russian Orthodox Church," Department for External Church Relations of the Moscow Patriarchate, Moscow (2000), 15, http://orthodoxeurope.org/print/3/14.aspx.

32. In article 29.1 of the Universal Declaration of Human Rights, the only article in which duties explicitly are mentioned, one can read that "everyone has duties to the community in which alone the free and full development of his personality is possible." Note that the duties mentioned in this article are duties to the *community* and not to the state.

33. John Anderson, "Putin and the Russian Orthodox Church: Asymmetric Symphonia?" 191.

34. The Constantinople Patriarchate is also called Istanbul Greek Orthodox Patriarchate (IGOP).

35. In Europe there are fifteen autocephalous, mostly national, churches. These include the four ancient Patriarchates of Constantinople (Istanbul), Antioch, Alexandria, and Jerusalem; four autocephalous churches headed by Patriarchs: Russia, Serbia, Romania, and Bulgaria; six countries or regions headed by (lower-placed) metropolitans or archbishops: Albania, Greece, Cyprus, the Czech Republic and Slovakia, Poland, and Sinai; and, finally, Georgia, led by a Catholicos-Patriarch. (Cf. Janice Broun, "Divisions in Eastern Orthodoxy," *East-West Church & Ministry Report* 5, no. 2 (Spring 1997).)

36. Cf. Fr. J. Buciora, "Canonical Territory of the Moscow Patriarchate: An Analysis of Contemporary Russian Orthodox Thought," *Orthodox Christian Comment*, no date, 1, http://www.orthodox-christian-comment.co.uk/canonical_territory_of_the_moscow_patriarchate.htm.

37. Asli Bilg, "Moscow and Greek Orthodox Patriarchates: Two Actors for the Leadership of World Orthodoxy in the Post Cold War Era," *Religion, State, and Society* 35, no. 4 (2007).

38. "Patriarchate of Ukrainian Orthodox Church—Kyivan Patriarchate Received Letter from the Presidential Administration," *Religious Information Service of Ukraine RISU* (February 3, 2011).

39. "Patriarch Filaret: Government Intends to Liquidate Ukrainian Orthodox Church of Kiev before June," *Ukrainians.ca* (January 31, 2011).

40. "Patriarch Filaret: Government Intends to Liquidate Ukrainian Orthodox Church."

41. "Patriarch Filaret on President Yanukovych's Church Policy," *Religious Information Service of Ukraine RISU* (April 4, 2011).

42. Buciora, "Canonical Territory of the Moscow Patriarchate," 5.

43. Yury Chornomorets, "Pochemu Moskovskiy Patriarchat neizbezhno 'poteryaet' Ukrainu?" *Chelovek i ego vera* (January 3, 2005).

44. Buciora, "Canonical Territory of the Moscow Patriarchate," 4.

45. Antoine Arjakovsky, *Russie Ukraine: De la guerre à la paix?* (Paris: Parole et Silence, 2014), 234.

46. Cf. Thomas de Waal, "Spring of Patriarchs," *The National Interest* (January 27, 2011).

III

Undermining Atlanticism: Building a "Strategic Triangle" Moscow-Berlin-Paris

Chapter Twelve

An Emerging Moscow-Berlin Axis?

The wisdom and generosity of Russian and German peoples, as well as the foresight of statesmen of the two countries, made it possible to take a determining step towards building the Big Europe. The partnership of Russia and Germany has become an example of moving towards each other and of aspiration for the future with care for the memory of the past. And today, the Russian-German cooperation plays a major positive role in international and European politics.[1]
—Vladimir Putin, August 31, 2009

INTRODUCTION: MOSCOW'S TWO "STRATEGIC TRIANGLES"

In this part we will analyze the effects of Moscow's propaganda and soft-power offensive in two European countries: Germany and France. This is an explicit choice because Germany and France occupy a special place in the Kremlin's foreign policy agenda, which consists of building "strategic triangles." This project predates Putin's rule. Samuel Huntington had, in 1999, already observed that

> gatherings occur from which the United States is conspicuously absent, ranging from the Moscow meeting of the leaders of Germany, France, and Russia (which also excluded America's closest ally, Britain) to the bilateral meetings of China and Russia and of China and India. . . . Russian Prime Minister Yevgeni Primakov has promoted Russia, China, and India as a "strategic triangle" to counterbalance the United States, and the "Primakov doctrine" reportedly enjoys substantial support across the entire Russian political spectrum.[2]

Immediately after Putin's assumption of the Russian presidency, he began to implement the "Primakov doctrine." It was a fundamental change to Moscow's foreign policy course, which, under Yeltsin, in spite of recurring ten-

179

sions, had been oriented toward integration with the West. Putin took the initiative for the organization of the BRICS, the core of which consists of Primakov's Russia-China-India triangle. Another forum was the Shanghai Cooperation Organization, a group founded by Moscow and Beijing in which India has observer status. However, Putin has also invested much time and money in building a second triangle: a Moscow-Berlin-Paris axis in Europe. This triangle had already been dreamed up by his predecessor Boris Yeltsin,[3] who had a good personal relationship with German Chancellor Helmut Kohl. However, it would become an explicit strategic goal only under Putin. In the spring of 2000, immediately after his election, Putin declared Germany to be "Russia's leading partner in Europe and the world."[4] Although he succeeded in establishing a close relationship with German Chancellor Gerhard Schröder, the real breakthrough in Russian-German relations came with the Iraq War. "In the Iraq War," writes Alexander Rahr, "Putin succeeded with the help of Germany and France in isolating America in the Security Council. Encouraged by the traditionalists in the Kremlin, he may dream of setting up in the future, together with the two most powerful states of the old continent, a regime of 'soft containment' of America."[5] By building these two triangles, Putin wanted to realize three objectives: first, to enhance Russia's global role; second, to build a countervailing coalition against the hegemonic Anglo-Saxon world (the United States, United Kingdom, Canada, Australia, and New Zealand); and third, by participating in *two* separate triangles to give Russia a central position.[6] Already in June 2003 John C. Hulsman, an American analyst, warned that

> The Continental Europe of today . . . remains divided into Gaullist and Atlanticist camps. . . . A Europe of many voices, where the nation-state is again seen as the primary unit of foreign policy decision-making, will best suit American interests well into the future. In addition, helping to retard the perpetuation of a Franco-German-Russian alliance designed to balance against the US must be seen as a primary American national interest.[7]

In 2015, twelve years later, Hans Kundnani would again point to the dangers for the West's coherence if Putin's efforts were to be crowned with success, writing that

> a post-Western Germany could take much of the rest of Europe with it, particularly those central and eastern European countries with economies that are deeply intertwined with Germany's. If the United Kingdom leaves the EU, as it is now debating, the union will be even more likely to follow German preferences, especially as they pertain to Russia and China. In that event, Europe could find itself at odds with the United States—and the West could suffer a schism from which it might never recover.[8]

It is, therefore, not surprising that Putin started the construction of his European triangle with a soft-power offensive directed toward Germany. He was able to take advantage of several favorable circumstances which made this task easier. In the first place, there was Germany's immense gratitude toward Gorbachev, who had agreed with the reunification of Germany. There was, further, the personal friendship between Putin's predecessor, President Boris Yeltsin, and the German Chancellor Helmut Kohl, followed by the even closer friendship between Putin himself and Kohl's successor, Gerhard Schröder. There was, furthermore, the specific German "disposition"—characterized by pacifism and an aversion to military adventures abroad, which was present amongst both the German people and its political class—which reassured the Russians that Germany, having become a peaceful giant, would not meddle in what the Kremlin considered its privileged affairs in Russia's Near Abroad. There was, finally, Germany's position as the most developed European export economy, which enabled it, in Russian eyes, to play an important role in the economic modernization of Russia. This economic complementarity was augmented by a psychological attraction between both countries: clearly, a Russian-German axis was in the making.

THE TESTAMENT OF PETER THE GREAT

The idea of a Russian-German axis was, in itself, not new. In the nineteenth century, for instance, a document emerged that was said to be the "Testament of Peter the Great." The document became a subject of heated discussions in European capitals and embassies. The central question was: Is the document authentic? "Peter became retrospectively implicated in Russia's territorial ambitions by the 'discovery' of the 'Testament of Peter the Great,'" writes John Sainsbury, "the first English translations of which appeared at the beginning of the Crimean War. In it, Peter appears to lay down a blueprint for Russian expansionism. (The provenance of this curious document is furiously debated.)"[9] The origin of the document was, indeed, contested. It is assumed that it was a forgery and that the British government was behind its publication. This does not make the document less interesting, because it provides a good insight into how European governments in that period regarded Russian foreign policy. Among tsar Peter's fourteen "instructions," two precepts in particular catch the eye because they still seem to be inspiring Putin's foreign policy today. These two precepts are:

- No opportunity must be lost in taking part in the affairs of Europe, especially in those of Germany, which from its vicinity, is of the most direct interest to us.

- The consorts of the Russian princes must always be chosen from among the German princesses, in order to multiply our family alliances with the Germans, and thus to unite our interests with theirs. And thus, by consolidating our influences in Germany, to cause it to spontaneously attach itself to our policy. [10]

It is striking how Putin almost literally followed the "instructions" of tsar Peter because in his foreign policy we find both

- An emphasis on the necessity of Russian-German cooperation
- The wish to bind German partners to Russia

In 1997 Zbigniew Brzezinski wrote: "Both France and Germany consider themselves entitled to represent European interests in dealings with Russia, and Germany even retains, because of its geographic location, at least theoretically, the grand option of a special bilateral accommodation with Russia." [11] Brzezinski would have been surprised how an option that he considered in 1997 only "theoretically" possible had become an existing reality a decade later. One could not only observe the emergence of a flourishing bilateral economic cooperation but also a relationship that had developed into a real entente cordiale. The relationship had even become so warm and close that some observers—inside as well as outside Germany—had started to worry. Was it true that what Brzezinski in 1997 was still calling a "theoretical" option had developed into the reality of an emerging Moscow-Berlin axis—an axis not unlike the one that existed at the time of Bismarck between imperial Germany and tsarist Russia?

At least *four factors* explain this rapprochement between the two countries:

- the explicit *political will* of politicians and political leaders on both sides;
- *the evolution of public opinion*, which modified previously existing friend-foe images;
- *the reemergence of geopolitical ideas* in both Russia and Germany which were reminiscent of the closing decades of the nineteenth century; and
- last but not least, the *economic interests* of business lobbies, which, on the Russian side, were led and shaped by the strategic and geopolitical considerations of the Kremlin.

In this chapter we analyze the first three of the above-mentioned factors—seen from the Russian side. In the next chapter we will do the same but from the German perspective. The fourth, economic, factor we will analyze in a separate chapter.

PUTIN "THE GERMAN"

It is a well-known fact that from 1985 to the end of 1990 Vladimir Putin worked as a KGB agent in Dresden in the former German Democratic Republic. Those five years were of great importance to him. Putin not only became fluent in German, but he also learned to appreciate the German way of life, which was, in the former communist GDR, more strict and regulated than in the Federal Republic. In particular, the East German preoccupation with order and discipline was completely in tune with Putin's deeper inner self.[12] His time in Dresden also brought him many important contacts: not only with agents of the Stasi—the East German sister organization to the KGB—but also with leaders of the East German political and economic establishment. Putin's (ex-) wife, Lyudmila, a former flight attendant, was also fluent in German, as are his two daughters, who later attended the German School in Moscow. When Putin became an adviser to Leningrad's Mayor Anatoly Sobchak in May 1990, he got the nickname *nemets*, which in Russian means "the German." To be called "the German" in Russia was something positive because in present-day Russia, anything German is highly valued.[13] It is no exaggeration to say that in recent years a majority of Russians have become convinced Germanophiles. Andreas Umland writes:

> The Federal Republic of Germany has become the preferred major foreign partner by almost all sections of the Russian elite. Not only have Russian Westernizers or moderate nationalists, including Vladimir Putin, singled out Germany as the country that would be most welcome as a worthy ally of Russia on the international arena, and preferred counterpart for economic and cultural cooperation. Even various ultra-nationalists, including Vladimir Zhirinovsky, Aleksandr Dugin or Gennadii Zyuganov, have admitted their admiration for Germany and interest in closer Russian-German relations.[14]

It is telling, for instance, that in the paragraph on foreign policy of the party program of Zhirinovsky's Liberal Democratic Party one can read: "The party of Zhirinovsky is in favor of peaceful cooperation in Europe, especially with Germany."[15] In a Russian opinion survey conducted by Levada in May 2007, respondents, asked to mention Russia's enemies, mentioned Estonia, Georgia, Latvia, the United States, and Lithuania. Asked to mention Russia's friends, Germany occupied third place—after Kazakhstan and Belarus but before China.[16] This Russian Germanophilia leads to several questions, such as, for instance: What are the roots of this phenomenon? How do the Germans react to Russian overtures? Is this Russian Germanophilia reciprocated by an equivalent Russophilia in Germany? And what will be the eventual consequences of this German-Russian rapprochement for the EU, NATO, and the transatlantic relationship?

THE FIVE REASONS BEHIND RUSSIA'S GERMANOPHILIA

Let us start with the first question. What are the reasons for Russian German-ophilia? There are at least five reasons: psychological, historical, cultural and philosophical, geopolitical, and economic.

The *psychological* reasons for Russian Germanophilia are rooted in the Russian people's long-standing admiration for specific character traits that are generally ascribed to Germans: their intellectual rigor, their Protestant work ethic, their punctuality, their discipline, and their trustworthiness. Most of these character traits are what the Germans call *Sekundartugende*: not real, but secondary virtues.[17] They do not necessarily make people behave more ethically but tend to create affluence, make social life more orderly, and make government action more efficient and predictable. In Russian public opinion polls, this admiration for Germans is often expressed. A sociological study published in 2004, at the end of Putin's first presidency, included two chapters on Russian-German relationships, one titled: "What Do Russians Think about Russian-German Relationships and Perspectives for Their Development," and the other, "The Image of Germany and the Germans in the Russian Consciousness."[18] In this study one could see a growing optimism in the Russian population concerning the bilateral relationship. Asked in 1996 whether they thought that the relationship with Germany would improve in the long term, 36 percent thought that this would be the case. This percentage had jumped to 55 percent by 2002.[19] This sympathy, wrote the researchers, was based partly on the fact that "the majority of the Russians do not observe in contemporary Germany any specific expansionist tendencies, which is different from, for instance, the United States."[20] The sympathy for Germany, however, was not evenly divided across the population. The younger generation and those with higher incomes or with relatives in Germany were more positive. Members of the Communist Party were more skeptical than members of centrist and right-wing parties. Other factors were at play here because this party had relatively older and less wealthy members. Asked what they considered to be the major barriers to Russian-German relationships, respondents answered that the most significant problem was the status of the Kaliningrad region. This might surprise a Western reader, but it could indicate uncertainty concerning this former German region which was annexed by Stalin after World War II. The second important problem mentioned by the respondents—and this is more in line with what one might expect—was the memory of the Second World War. A third problem that was mentioned was the unwillingness of Germany to render Russian works of art that were stolen during the war.

When asked to characterize Germany, 56 percent of the respondents mentioned "order and discipline"; 30 percent that "one can learn from them"; 22.1 percent that it is an "example of economic success"; and 20.3 percent that "they produce quality products."[21] However, this Russian admiration for German *Gründlichkeit* (thoroughness) and *Tüchtigkeit* (proficiency) was only one side of the coin.[22] When asked to attribute a list of virtues and attitudes to Germans and Russians, Russian respondents gave much higher scores to Germans not only for good manners (65.3 percent versus 17.6 percent), punctuality (88.8 percent versus 4.2 percent), accuracy (94.4 percent versus 2.5 percent), and law abidingness (79 percent versus 8.3 percent), but also for egoism (46.1 percent versus 14.4 percent) and greed (72 percent versus 5 percent). At the same time, the Russian respondents gave themselves much higher scores for virtuousness (84 percent versus 4.7 percent), hospitality (87 percent versus 8.2 percent), tolerance (80.4 percent versus 6.3 percent), courage (78.5 percent versus 5.8 percent), and spirituality (62.9 percent versus 14.4 percent).[23] Russian admiration for the positive German character traits was, therefore, qualified. It was the *secondary* virtues of the Germans which were highly valued by the Russians. They thought that they themselves did not possess these sufficiently. However, at the same time, they had a sense of superiority in the area of *primary* virtues, such as virtuousness, hospitality, and tolerance: the real virtues that count in life.

Russian Germanophilia is not a new phenomenon; in fact, it has a long history. In the eighteenth century Germany was, together with Holland, a model for the modernizing tsar Peter the Great. In his youth tsar Peter had direct personal experience of the German way of life because Germans had their own quarter in Moscow. "From the time of his youth in the German section of Moscow, Peter had viewed the West as superior in technology, organization, and cleanliness. These virtues were what Peter wanted to import to Russia."[24] Interestingly, he gave his new capital Saint Petersburg a *German* name: Sankt Peterburg (Санкт Петербург), including the German prefix, *Sankt*, instead of the Russian word *svyatoy*.[25] In 1763, tsarina Catherine the Great, herself of German origin, issued a manifesto inviting foreign settlers, especially Germans, to Russia and offering them free land and freedom from taxes, which led to an influx of farmers, the so-called Volga Germans, who settled along the Volga River. In the nineteenth century other groups of Germans followed, settling in the Black Sea region, the Crimea, and Bessarabia (present Moldova). Germans were considered the ideal immigrants by the Russians because of their highly praised "secondary virtues": they were hardworking, frugal, and efficient. But Germans were not only Russia's favorite immigrants to cultivate its new farmlands. According to Herfried Münkler,

> Since the time of Peter the Great, the tsars largely fell back on non-Russians to administer their huge empire. Germans played a prominent role in this respect: not only the Baltic German nobility, which came under tsarist rule with the

expansion of the early eighteenth century and enjoyed a number of special privileges, but also officers and administrators recruited in Germany itself. In the eighteenth and nineteenth centuries, some 18 percent of senior officials in Russia were of German origin, and by the turn of the twentieth century the proportion had probably risen even higher.[26]

It is also interesting to note that in the hundred years after 1816, no fewer than three Russian foreign ministers were of Baltic German origin.[27]

THE DOUBLE AMNESIA OR
"THE GREAT HISTORICAL PARENTHESIS"

The nineteenth century—the time of the Holy Alliance and the Concert of Europe following Napoleon's defeat—was particularly a golden age for Russian-German (Prussian) relations, and this may also be the reason that in present-day Russia, interest in this period is livelier than ever. One might ask where this interest comes from. Have Russians suddenly forgotten that in the twentieth century they fought two world wars against Germany? It may seem strange, but this is—almost—the case, because in contemporary Russia, a *double* reinterpretation of history is taking place. The first concerns the history of Russia itself, and the second concerns the history of Russian-German relations. To start with the former: Russians are constructing what I would call *the Great Historical Parenthesis*. They tend to consider the communist era (1917–1991) as a temporal deviation from the "normal" course of Russian history. A partly conscious, partly unconscious amnesia is taking place by which Russians are trying to forget[28] their communist past, wanting to reconnect with the pre-communist era of "normal Russia." This "normal Russia" was Russia as it existed before World War I. It was the Russia of the tsars: an Orthodox, capitalist, and imperialist Russia.[29]

BACK TO BISMARCK?

This process of reconnecting with the pre-communist past has led simultaneously to a reevaluation of Russian-German relations and of German history. The "Great Historical Parenthesis" suppresses not only the bad memories of the Stalinist period[30] but equally the bad memories of Nazi Germany.[31] It is a strange process, full of contradictions, because at the same time the Great Patriotic War (World War II) continues to play a key role in the national consciousness. However, Germany can be said to have profited from the fact that the Russian historical memory has put the communist period between brackets and has reconnected with the nineteenth century. The autocratic tsar Alexander III (1881–1894) in particular is enjoying immense popularity in present-day Russia, a popularity he shares with his German contemporary,

Chancellor Otto von Bismarck. Bismarck knew Russia well. Before German unification, he had already been Prussian ambassador in Saint Petersburg between 1859 and 1862. Bismarck was, if not a full-fledged friend, a close ally of Russia. He had his strategic reasons for this. Wanting to avoid the possibility of a defeated France forming an anti-German coalition with either Russia or Austria, which could lead to a war on two fronts for Germany, in 1873 Bismarck took the initiative for the *Dreikaiserbund*: the "League of the Three Emperors" that linked Germany with Russia and Austria.[32] "There is so much strength in an alliance between the two empires," writes Bismarck to Count Pyotr Shuvalov, the Russian ambassador in London, "that I get angry at the very idea that one day it could be compromised for no political reason whatsoever, only by the whim of some statesman who wants change or who finds the Frenchman more pleasant than the German."[33] "Over what could Russia and Prussia ever seriously come into conflict?" he asked. He gave himself the answer: "There exists no issue between them that would be serious enough."[34]

Bismarck was eager to maintain the coalition with Russia, even after the "League of the Three Emperors" finally collapsed.[35] It is interesting that on the Russian side, admiration for Bismarck remained intact in Soviet times. "Beginning with Lenin," writes Georgi Derluguian, "the Soviet leaders deeply envied the effectiveness of German bureaucracy, and thus their inspiration was Bismarck perhaps even more than Karl Marx."[36] During World War II, Bismarck was "rediscovered in Soviet pamphlets as a representative of a better, more moderate Germany."[37] It is, therefore, no surprise that in recent years Bismarck has become a kind of icon for Russians. He is by far their favorite German politician.[38] The Russian presidential administration is even reconstructing Bismarck's villa near Kaliningrad,[39] the former East-Prussian town of Königsberg. It is also telling that Bismarck has been employed to improve the image of Stalin. In new textbooks for teachers of history, introduced by Putin in 2007, not only is the communist dictator portrayed as "the most successful Russian ruler of the twentieth century," but he is also explicitly compared with Bismarck.[40] The first signs of the Russian drive to rebuild a Bismarckian Russia-Germany axis were already emerging in 1992–1993, immediately after the demise of the Soviet Union, when Karl-Heinz Hornhues, deputy leader of the CDU Bundestag faction, reported that Russian leaders were suggesting that Germany and Russia form a counterweight to the United States.[41] It was, in fact, the continuation of a historical line. "A number of Russian statesmen," writes Andrei Tsygankov, "beginning with foreign ministers Nikolai de Giers and Alexander Gorchakov, have historically favored a strong continental alliance with France and Germany, viewed as essential for preserving peace and continuing with modernization at home."[42]

THE EVER-PRESENT RUSSIAN APPETITE
FOR GERMAN IDEOLOGY

Apart from the aforementioned psychological and historical reasons, there exists a third reason for Russian Germanophilia, which is the enduring *cultural and philosophical* influence Germany has exerted over Russia during the past two centuries. German philosophy has found fertile soil in Russia. This is especially true for German philosophy with *historicist* undertones that could be used in a messianic (re-)interpretation of Russian history. It was no surprise, therefore, that in the nineteenth century Hegel and Marx became extremely popular in Russian intellectual circles.[43] Both offered a vision of history as a progressive, dialectic process. For Hegel it was the *Weltgeist* (the world spirit) that developed itself to higher stages of consciousness. For Marx it was the dialectic between the productive forces and the relations of production that inevitably would lead to the advent of communism. We should not forget that the Soviet Union was the inheritor and executor of a *German* philosophy: Marxism. Half of the quartet that made up the Soviet pantheon—Marx, Engels, Lenin, and Stalin (in Soviet times abbreviated to MELS)—were Germans. Ernst Cassirer has pointed to the Hegelian legacy, which led to two combating schools: the Left Hegelians, represented by Marx and Engels, and the Right Hegelians, the state-abiding nationalists who were the forerunners of Hitler's national socialists. He asks "whether the struggle of the Russians and the invading Germans in 1943 was not, at bottom, a conflict between the Left and Right wings of Hegel's school."[44] Cassirer adds: "That may seem to be an exaggerated statement of the problem but it contains a nucleus of truth."[45]

HALFORD MACKINDER'S EURASIAN HEARTLAND AND THE
MOSCOW-BERLIN AXIS

Today's post-communist Russia has abandoned Marxism. This does not mean, however, that German ideology has lost its influence on Russian politics. On the contrary: in recent years the ideological void that emerged after the collapse of communism has been filled with another German ideology: *Geopolitik*. The English word for *Geopolitik* is geopolitics. "Geopolitics" is, in itself, a neutral word. It was a new discipline, developed at the end of the nineteenth century, concerned with the analysis of how the geographic conditions of a country tended to influence its foreign policy. Because geographic conditions over time do not fundamentally change, they give rise to more or less permanent foreign policy patterns, which are relatively independent from ideological considerations. One of the leading and most influential theorists was an Englishman, Sir Halford Mackinder, who in 1904 developed the theory of the "pivot area."[46] This "pivot area," or "heartland," was, according to him, the Eurasian continent. Around this "heartland" was an inner crescent of coastal areas, which included Western Europe and South and Southeast Asia. Farther away was a periphery, an outer crescent of islands: the Americas, Japan, and Australia. According to Mackinder, the power that dominated the Eurasian heartland was able to dominate the world. It was, therefore, in the interests of the island powers to prevent the formation of a power monopoly in the heartland because this would pose an immediate threat. Mackinder adapted his theory—without, however, changing the basic concept—during his active life as a geopolitician, which spanned a period of forty years. In one of his last articles, "The Round World and the Winning of the Peace," published in *Foreign Affairs* in July 1943,[47] he stated that

> it is sufficiently accurate to say that the territory of the U.S.S.R. is equivalent to the Heartland. . . . All things considered, the conclusion is unavoidable that if the Soviet Union emerges from this war as conqueror of Germany, she must rank as the greatest land Power on the globe. Moreover, she will be the Power in the strategically strongest defensive position. The Heartland is the greatest natural fortress on earth. For the first time in history it is manned by a garrison sufficient both in number and quality.[48]

In 1943, when the German defeat became imminent, Mackinder considered the Soviet Union as the potential hegemon of the heartland. His greatest fear, which he had already articulated in his article of 1904, was a possible alliance of Russia and Germany. In 1904 he wrote: "The oversetting of the balance of power in favour of the pivot state, resulting in its expansion over the marginal lands of Euro-Asia, would permit of the use of vast continental resources for fleet-building, and the empire of the world would then be in sight. *This might happen if Germany were to ally herself with Russia.*"[49]

RUSSIA'S RECENT RECEPTION OF GERMAN *GEOPOLITIK*

Mackinder published his first article on the Eurasian heartland in 1904. This was the same year that the father of German *Geopolitik*, Friedrich Ratzel, died. Anglo-Saxon geopolitics, in both its English and American variants, was never a totally value-free science. Even if it did not directly serve the national strategic interest, it undoubtedly had implications for national policy choices. In Germany, however, things were different. German *Geopolitik* did not even try to uphold the objective of scientific value neutrality. In the 1920s and 1930s it became an outright legitimation theory and a direct ideological tool in the service of German territorial expansionism and aggressive Nazi conquest.

This tendency was, in principle, already present in the theory of Friedrich Ratzel. Ratzel developed an organic state theory. States were, according to him, living creatures that could not be restricted by frontiers: they expanded or contracted according to their organic structure. They needed *Lebensraum*, "living space." This was a fortiori the case for Germany. Because at the end of the nineteenth century the recently unified Germany was in a growth phase, it needed *Lebensraum* in Eastern Europe. It is clear that Ratzel's theory was incompatible with the principles of international law concerning the inviolability of national frontiers. Later German geopoliticians, such as Karl Haushofer and—even more so—the Nazi ideologue Carl Schmitt, adapted Ratzel's theory to the needs of Hitler's Germany. Schmitt, for instance, claimed for the German *Reich* a "spatial sovereignty" (*Raumhoheit*), which was directly inspired by Ratzel's theory of "living space." Schmitt was also very clear about the practical implications of this concept. This German spatial sovereignty, he wrote, "exceeds its national frontiers."[50]

After World War II, German *Geopolitik* was considered an integral part of the Nazi ideology and banned from German universities. It even led to a more widespread taboo on geopolitical thinking in other countries by a process of "guilt by association."[51] It is interesting to note that this taboo was very strong in the Soviet Union. According to Jean-Christophe Romer, "one can find only one single Soviet work, explicitly on geopolitics, that has been published in the Soviet Union during a period stretching from Stalin to Chernenko."[52] And this single work, he wrote, was "very critical." One reason for this absence of geopolitical thinking in the Soviet Union was ideological:

> In a word, the Soviet Union cannot tolerate geopolitics officially, because there exists a fundamental ideological incompatibility between, on the one hand, geopolitical ideas which are based on a certain geographical determinism in order to explain the evolution of the world and its power relationships, and, on the other hand, the Marxist-Leninist ideology that is characterized by a historical determinism. Without even mentioning the words used to disqualify geopolitics: "reactionary" and "anti-scientific"—just remember that Marxism-Leninism is a science! In a sense, until the end of the 1980s we find in the Soviet Union a conception concerning geopolitics that was widespread in the West and in the United States in particular, that it no longer had the right to exist because of having being "entangled" with the Third Reich. But, contrary to what happened in the West, which rehabilitates or rediscovers it at the end of the 1970s, the Soviet Union remains firm in its total condemnation of the discipline.[53]

The gradual comeback of geopolitical thinking in the United States and Western Europe at the end of the 1970s, to which Romer refers, left the Soviet Union untouched. The new emerging geopolitical thinking in the West, however, did *not* rehabilitate its German variant, *Geopolitik*, but reconnected with the Anglo-Saxon tradition and authors, such as Alfred Thayer Mahan, Halford Mackinder, and Nicholas Spykman. The reason why this revival of geopolitical thinking did not take place in the Soviet Union in the 1980s is not only because of ideological reasons—as Romer suggests. Overstretched by its imperialist adventure in Afghanistan, the Soviet Union went through a period of deep internal crisis that led to Gorbachev's perestroika. Absorbed by its huge economic and societal problems and subject to extremely strong centrifugal forces, this was for Soviet Russia certainly not the moment for imperialist geopolitical speculation.

This situation changed, however, after the sudden dissolution of the Soviet empire and the disintegration of the Soviet Union. In a period of somewhat more than three years, Russia was reduced from a huge empire to a country that found itself globally within its seventeenth-century frontiers. This was a tremendous shock for the Russian psyche. Territories that for centuries had been part of the Russian empire suddenly became foreign countries. And in these foreign countries lived sizable Russian minorities. The traumatism caused by this situation was experienced as *the Great Historical Amputation*. And this "Great Historical Amputation" provided a fertile soil for the return of geopolitical thinking in Russia in the 1990s. "Geopolitics as a theory has been almost an outcast for nearly half a century," writes Sergei Karaganov, Honorary Chairman of the Presidium of the Council on Foreign and Defense Policy. "In [the] Soviet Union it was blacklisted as bourgeois, while in the West it was blacklisted as politically incorrect."[54] "These days," he continues, "geopolitics is a catchword on everybody's tongue again, and it is quickly regaining both political correctness and legitimacy."[55]

The revival of geopolitics in Russia concerned in the first place the theories of Halford Mackinder. With his theory of the Eurasian heartland he gave Russia the special position Russians craved. He also offered theoretical support for their hope that Russia could regain its former status as a world power. However, the 1990s provided a fertile soil not only for the reception of Anglo-Saxon geopolitics but also for its other—less presentable—branch: German *Geopolitik*. This was a surprising development: for the second time in a century a *German* ideology, which was unpopular or banned in its country of origin, found refuge in Russia. The first time this concerned Marxism. The second time this concerned German *Geopolitik* because it is, indeed, the German variant of geopolitics—based on naked power politics and with grandiose territorial ambitions—which, in recent years, has become influential in Russia. This emergence of German *Geopolitik* is not accidental. It was the historic conditions of the Weimar Republic that provided the fertile soil for the rise of German *Geopolitik*. The historic situation in Russia in the 1990s was almost identical: both countries lost important territories, both passed through a protracted period of internal turmoil and deep economic crisis, both countries had authoritarian political traditions, and both countries experienced a rise of extremist political parties with nationalist and revanchist agendas.[56]

ALEKSANDR DUGIN: THE RUSSIAN APOSTLE OF *GEOPOLITIK*

Every theory needs its apostles to spread the message. In the case of Marxism, it was Lenin and the leaders of the Bolshevist Party who played a crucial role in the reception and adaptation of this originally German ideology to the Russian situation. German *Geopolitik* equally found its Russian apostles. The most well known is Aleksandr Dugin, a semimythical thinker who in the 1980s was close to conservative and even monarchist circles. After the demise of the Soviet Union, he drew closer first to Zyuganov's Communist Party and then to the even more extremist National Bolshevik Party, whose leader, Edvard Limonov, described Dugin as "the Cyril and Methodius of fascism, because he brought Faith and knowledge about it to our country from the West."[57] Dugin's influence was in the beginning restricted to nationalist movements and political parties of the extreme right, such as Vladimir Zhirinovsky's crypto-fascist Liberal-Democratic Party. But after the publication in 1997 of his book *The Foundations of Geopolitics: Russia's Geopolitical Future*, his influence became much broader. The book has been reissued four times in three years and became a best seller in academic and political circles. Dugin found many admirers, especially in the army. He was invited to lecture at the Academy of the General Staff and at the Institute for Strategic Research in Moscow, and he wrote columns in the *Krasnaya Zvezda* (the *Red Star*), the official army paper. On April 21, 2001, Dugin started his own political movement, Evraziya (Eurasia), with the help of the Kremlin pundit Gleb Pavlovsky.[58] One year later, on May 30, 2002, Dugin transformed the Evraziya movement into a political party that claimed ten thousand members and was welcomed by Aleksandr Voloshin, head of Putin's presidential administration. But after an alliance with the reactionary Rodina (Fatherland) Party, led by Dmitry Rogozin, failed, he left electoral politics definitively and, in November 2003, transformed the party into the "International Eurasian Movement."

WHAT IS "DUGINISM"?

Dugin is not an original thinker. His geopolitical ideas are a sort of a mixture of Halford Mackinder's heartland theory and Carl Schmitt's *Großraum* (large space) theory, which—again—is a variant of Ratzel's *Lebensraum* theory. He is also a great admirer of other national conservative German writers and thinkers, such as the novelist Ernst Jünger or Arthur Moeller van den Bruck, who coined the term "Third Reich." According to Marlène Laruelle,

> *Dugin attaches great value to his German heritage*, and he wishes to be viewed as a continental geopolitician on a par with Schmitt and Haushofer; Russia's centrality and continental expanse, to him, are comparable to those of Germany in the 1920s and 1930s. He thus develops his own bipolar interpretation of the world, opposing the "Heartland," which tends toward authoritarian regimes, to the "World Island," the incarnation of the democratic and commercial system. He combines the classic Eurasianist theories with this bipolar division of the world into sea-based and land-based powers. [59]

Not only is Dugin an avid reader of German *Geopolitik*, he also gives Germany a prominent place in his theories. He divides the world into four civilizational zones: the American zone, the Afro-European zone, the Asian-Pacific zone, and the Eurasian zone. Russia should seek alliances that are organized in concentric circles. In Europe, Russia should ally itself with Germany because Germany, situated in the heart of Europe, will dominate Central Europe. In Asia, Russia should ally itself with Japan; in the south, Russia should ally itself with Iran. In this Russia-Germany-Japan-Iran alliance, the principal role will be played by Russia, which occupies the central heartland. This Eurasian quartet has to take on the "thalassocracies" (sea powers), consisting of the United States, Britain, China, and Turkey. This "goal of Eurasian geopolitics—the establishment of a Moscow-Berlin-Tokyo axis"— reappears in Dugin's founding declaration of his International Eurasian Movement. [60] Although Dugin's ideas have unmistakably influenced the Russian political leadership and in particular Putin's project for a Eurasian Union, it is clear that they have not been adopted 100 percent. Putin, for instance, preferred to build a Moscow-Beijing axis instead of a Moscow-Tokyo axis. [61] However, as concerns the two other geopolitical priorities formulated by Dugin, building a Moscow-Tehran axis and a Moscow-Berlin axis, these two objectives have become central pillars of Putin's foreign policy. The influence of "Duginism" has become even more prominent during Putin's third presidency. In an article in *Izvestia* in October 2011, Putin announced the creation of "Eurasian Union" (Evraziyskiy Soyuz) as the main foreign policy goal of his new presidential term. [62]

NOTES

1. Vladimir Putin, "Pages of History: Reason for Mutual Complaints or Ground for Reconciliation and Partnership?" article for *Gazeta Wyborcza* (August 31, 2009), available at http://www.premier.gov.ru/eng/events/3514.html.
2. Samuel P. Huntington, "The Lonely Superpower," *Foreign Affairs* 78, no. 2 (March/April 1999), 44–45.

3. Cf. Charles Clover, "Dreams of the Eurasian Heartland: The Reemergence of Geopolitics," *Foreign Affairs* 78, no. 2 (March/April 1999), 11.

4. Cf. Angelo Codevilla, "Europe's Dangerous Dalliance with the Bear," *Wall Street Journal Europe* (June 7, 2001).

5. Alexander Rahr, "Will Russland die 'weiche Eindämmung' Amerikas?" *GUS-Barometer*, no. 33 (April 2003), 3.

6. However, participating in a triangle does not per se mean that one plays a central role. On the basis of an analysis of the voting behavior of the member and observer states of the SCO in the United Nations General Assembly, Flemming Hansen concludes that although a policy convergence had taken place, "Russia remains a leading outlier. The policy convergence is a Chinese-led process, and it seems safe to assume that Beijing is more satisfied with this development than is Moscow. . . . What is good for China . . . is of course not necessarily good for Russia." (Flemming Splidsboel Hansen, "China, Russia, and the Foreign Policy of the SCO," *Connections* 11, no. 2 (Spring 2012), 102.)

7. "Prepared Statement of John C. Hulsman, PhD, Research Fellow for European Affairs, The Davis Institute for International Studies, The Heritage Foundation," House Committee on International Relations, Subcommittee on Europe (June 11, 2003), http://www.house.gov/international_relations/108/huls0611.htm.

8. Hans Kundnani, "Leaving the West Behind: Germany Looks East," *Foreign Affairs* 94, no. 1 (January/February 2015), 116.

9. John Sainsbury, "Peter the Great through British Eyes: Perceptions and Representations of the Tsar since 1698," *Canadian Journal of History* (April 2003).

10. "The Testament of Peter the Great," available at http://www.nipissingu.ca/faculty/coryf/HIST2705/resources/THE%20(forged)%20TESTAMENT%20OF%20PETER%20THE%20GREAT.doc.

11. Zbigniew Brzezinski, *The Grand Chessboard: American Primacy and Its Geostrategic Imperatives* (New York: Basic Books, 1997), 42.

12. In Putin's biographical *First Person*, his wife Lyudmila made the following observations on life in the GDR: "Of course life in the GDR was very different from life in Russia. The streets were clean. They would wash the windows once a week. . . . There was one detail that surprised me. It was trivial—should I even mention it? It was the way German women would hang out their clothes. In the morning, before work, about 7:00 A.M., they would go out in the backyard. And each housewife would stretch a rope between these metal poles, and then she would hang her laundry out on the lines in very, very neat rows, with clothespins. They were all alike. The Germans were very orderly in their daily life, and their standard of living was better than ours." (Cf. Vladimir Putin, *First Person: An Astonishingly Frank Self-Portrait by Russia's President*, with Nataliya Gevorkyan, Natalya Timakova, and Andrei Kolesnikov (New York: Public Affairs, 2000), 75.)

13. Cf. Matthias Nass and Stefan Schirmer, "Sie nennen ihn den Deutschen," *Die Zeit* (May 22, 2014). Boris Reitschuster, who worked as a German journalist in Moscow for the magazine *Focus*, experienced personally this positive appreciation of Germany and Germans in present-day Russia. Ordinary Russians told him, for instance, that in the time that (the German) tsarina Catherine the Great was in charge, "there reigned more order in Russia." Equally, according to Reitschuster, "when with Putin a 'German' again occupies the Kremlin, most Russians associate it with the hope for orderliness, trustworthiness, zeal, determination, and cool pragmatism." (Cf. Boris Reitschuster, *Wladimir Putin: Wohin steuert er Russland?* (Berlin: Rowohlt, 2004), 101.)

14. Andreas Umland, "Post-Weimar Russia? There Are Sad Signs," *History News Network* (May 28, 2007), http://hnn.us/articles/38422.html.

15. *Obrashchenie Vladimira Zhirinovskogo predsedatelya Liberalno-Demokraticheskoy Partii Rossii k chlenam LDPR i sochuvstvuyushchim—Programma Liberalno-Demokraticheskoy Partii Rossii—Ustav LDPR* (Moscow, 1992), 9.

16. Andrei Zagorski, "Russian Opinion Surveys: Friends and Enemies, International Relations," in *Russian Foreign Policy: Key Regions and Issues*, ed. Robert Orttung, Jeronim Perovic, Heiko Pleines, and Hans-Henning Schröder, Forschungsstelle Osteuropa Bremen, Arbeitspapiere und Materialien No. 87 (November 2007), 11.

17. Even trustworthiness, which at first sight seems to be a primary moral virtue, may in practice be only a secondary virtue—as in the case of a criminal who is considered trustworthy by other gang members because he always shows up in time for a planned burglary.

18. M. K. Gorshkova, N. E. Tikhonovoy, and L. A. Belyayeva, *Izmenyayushchayasya Rossiya v zerkale sotsiologii* (Moscow: Letniy Sad, 2004).

19. Gorshkova, Tikhonovoy, and Belyayeva, *Izmenyayushchayasya Rossiya*, 233.

20. Gorshkova, Tikhonovoy, and Belyayeva, *Izmenyayushchayasya Rossiya*, 235.

21. Gorshkova, Tikhonovoy, and Belyayeva, *Izmenyayushchayasya Rossiya*, 248.

22. The Russian self-image of a people lacking discipline is mirrored in the way Germans view Russians. According to Gerd Ruge, "It was the nationalistic fantasies of German historians and politicians, who considered times of unrest proof of the fact that the Russians (and more generally the Slavs) as Slavs were unable to build a well-ordered state and could be governed and civilized only by strong rulers (preferably of German origin)." (Cf. Gerd Ruge, *Russland* (Munich: C. H. Beck Verlag, 2008), 110.)

23. Gorshkova, Tikhonovoy, and Belyayeva, *Izmenyayushchayasya Rossiya*, 252, table 77. The results are for the year 2002.

24. Ian Buruma and Avishai Margalit, *Occidentalism: The West in the Eyes of Its Enemies* (New York: Penguin, 2004), 86.

25. After the outbreak of World War I in August 1914, when anti-German feelings ran high, the German name of the town was Russified into Petrograd. In 1924 this name was changed into Leningrad. It is interesting that since 1991, Leningrad has regained its original *German* name.

26. Herfried Münkler, *Empires: The Logic of World Domination from Ancient Rome to the United States* (Cambridge: Polity Press, 2007), 23. Richard Pipes remarks that "the idea of office-holding as a public service was entirely alien to the Russian bureaucracy; it was something imported from the west, mainly Germany. It was Baltic Germans, who first demonstrated to the Russians that an official could use his power to serve society. The imperial government greatly valued these men and they acquired a disproportionate share of the topmost ranks." (Richard Pipes, *Russia under the Old Regime* (London and New York: Penguin, 1995), 286–287.)

27. They included Count Karl Robert Nesselrode, foreign minister from 1816 to 1856; Nikolay Von Giers, foreign minister from 1882 to 1894; and Count Vladimir Lambsdorff, foreign minister from 1900 to 1906. Karl Nesselrode was born in Lisbon, where his father was Russian ambassador. Because his mother was a Protestant, he was baptized in the British embassy and thereby became a de facto member of the Church of England. Minister Von Giers was also a Protestant. This was no impediment to the Orthodox, Slavophile tsar Alexander III's retaining him until the end of his reign. It is interesting that Hitler in *Mein Kampf* also referred to these Baltic German nobles who served the Russian state—but only to denigrate the Slavs, writing that "the organisation of a Russian state was not the result of the state political capacities of the Slavs in Russia, but more just a wonderful example of the state political activity of the Germanic element in an inferior race. . . . For centuries Russia has profited from this Germanic core of its higher leading echelons." (Adolf Hitler, *Mein Kampf* (Munich: Verlag Franz Eher Nachfolger, 1933), 742–743.)

28. This amnesia concerns especially the *negative* aspects of the communist era. Apart from this process of amnesia—which is actively promoted by a vigorous policy of suppression of the memory of these negative aspects by the Russian leadership—a parallel process of *reinterpretation* is taking place in order to save the "positive accomplishments" of the communist era.

29. Interestingly, a similar process seems to be taking place on the German side. Jacob Heilbrunn writes that "Germany is forging a new national identity that is less influenced by the Nazi past and that looks to the broader sweep of the country's place in European history dating back to the eighteenth and nineteenth centuries. Germany is increasingly looking back at its Prussian ideals, which it sees as having been betrayed, not represented by, Nazism." (Jacob Heilbrunn, "All Roads Lead to Berlin," *The National Interest* no. 122 (November/December 2012), 41.)

30. The recent rehabilitation of Stalin seems to contradict this theory. But this is only superficially so. Stalin is rehabilitated only insofar as he has continued the tsarist, imperialist

policies of "normal Russia" and created the greatest Russian empire ever. Stalinist repression and mass murders, on the contrary, almost disappear into oblivion.

31. Christopher Clark has drawn attention to the fact that even during World War II, the Russians still made a distinction between Prussia and Hitler's Nazi regime. Unlike the Western powers, for instance, they evaluated positively the assassination attempt by Prussian officers on Hitler on July 20, 1944. According to Clark, this was an expression of the specifically Russian view of Prussian history. This is because the history of the relations between both states was certainly not one of "reciprocal hate." Other examples of the "long tradition of cooperation" between the two countries that Clark mentions, are the support for the beleaguered Bolshevists in 1917–1918 and the close cooperation of the German Reichswehr and the Red Army in the Weimar period. (Cf. Christopher Clark, *Preußen—Aufstieg und Niedergang 1600–1947* (Munich: Pantheon Verlag, 2008), 765–766.)

32. The League of the Three Emperors held until 1887. It was interrupted in the period 1877–1881 due to Russian-Austrian rivalry in the Balkans.

33. In the original: "Il y a tant de force et de sécurité dans une alliance des deux empires, que je me fâche à l'idée seule qu'elle pourrait être compromise un jour sans la moindre raison politique, uniquement par la volonté de quelque homme d'état qui aime à varier ou qui trouve le Français plus aimable que l'Allemand." (Letter of Bismarck to Count Shuvalov of February 15, 1877. In Otto Fürst von Bismarck, *Gedanken und Erinnerungen*, 2. Band (Stuttgart and Berlin: J. G. Gotta'sche Buchhandlung Nachfolger, 1919), 254.)

34. Bismarck, *Gedanken und Erinnerungen*, 264.

35. When the League of Three Emperors collapsed in 1887, Bismarck continued his cooperation with Russia, signing the Reinsurance Treaty on June, 18, 1887. In this treaty, Germany promised to stay neutral in the event of Russia being attacked by Austria, and Russia promised to stay neutral should Germany be attacked by France. German Emperor Wilhelm II's refusal to renew this treaty in 1890 led to an 1892 Russian-French alliance and the development of two opposing blocks in Europe, something which Bismarck had tried to prevent.

36. Georgi Derluguian, "Introduction—Whose Truth?" in *A Small Corner of Hell—Dispatches from Chechnya*, by Anna Politkovskaya (Chicago and London: University of Chicago Press, 2003), 15.

37. Dieter Langewiesche, "Mächtiger Gegner: Der Bismarck-Mythos im Übergang vom deutschen Kaiserreich zur Weimarer Republik," *Frankfurter Allgemeine Zeitung* (May 26, 2008).

38. It is telling that the first signs of anti-German feelings in Russia appear only at the end of Bismarck's reign. The Russian Pan-Slavist Nikolay Danilevsky writes, for instance, in his pamphlet "Rossiya i Evropa" ("Russia and Europe") (1889), that "Europe does not recognize us as its equal. It considers Russia and the Slav in general as something strange and at the same time as something that simply cannot serve as material . . . which can be formed and shaped . . . as the Germans especially have done, who, despite their famous cosmopolitanism, await the salvation of the world only from a salvaging of German civilization. Europe considers therefore the Russian and the Slav not only as a strange, but also as a hostile element." (Nikolay Danilevsky, "Russland und Europa," in *Russischer Nationalismus: Die russische Idee im 19. und 20. Jahrhundert. Darstellung und Texte*, ed. Frank Golczewski and Gertrud Pickhan (Göttingen: Vandenhoeck & Ruprecht, 1998), 181.) However, it is interesting to note that this critical assessment of Germany by Russian Pan-Slavists still had *German* roots. Ian Buruma and Avishai Margalit rightly stress that "Russian Slavophilia was rooted in German romanticism, just as Russian liberalism took its cues from German liberal ideas." (Buruma and Margalit, *Occidentalism*, 77).

39. The villa, of which only four walls are left, is being rebuilt in accordance with archive documents. (Cf. "Russia Rebuilds Bismarck's Villa," *Kommersant* (February 28, 2008).

40. Undoubtedly Putin has a great personal admiration for Bismarck. In an interview with the Italian paper *Corriere della Sera* Putin mentioned Bismarck, quoting his dictum "It is not speeches, but potential, that is important." (In reality Bismarck said: "The great questions of the day will not be settled by means of speeches and majority decisions, but by iron and blood.") (Cf. Paolo Valentino, "Putin al Corriere della Sera: 'Non sono un aggressore, patto con l'Europa e parità con gli USA,'" *Corriere della Sera* (June 15, 2015).) Also Putin's idea of

introducing "patriotic" history textbooks seems to have been inspired by Bismarck. On June 20, 2007, at a conference on the reform of history textbooks organized by the Kremlin, Vladislav Surkov, deputy head of the presidential administration, recalled "the famous words of German Chancellor Otto von Bismarck, who contended it was the Prussian teacher who won the decisive battle of Sadowa during the Austro-Prussian War of 1866. Surkov maintained Russia's own future victories would be owed to the service of its teachers." ("'Sovereign Democracy' and Politicization of History: Commentators See Politics Behind Putin Comments on History," Finnish-Russian Civic Forum, (July 18, 2007), available at http://www.finrosforum.fi/?p=360.) Cf. also Leon Aron, "The Problematic Pages," in *The New Republic* (September 24, 2008); Simon Sebag Montefiore, "Putin in the Shadow of the Red Czar," *The New York Times* (August 24, 2008); Michael Knox Beran, "Bismarcks's Shadow: Freedom in Retreat," *National Review* (September 28, 2007); and Steve Chapman, "Putin and Stalin: Revising the Past," *Chicago Tribune* (September 2, 2007).

41. Cf. Marc Fisher, "Germany Says Russia Seeks a Policy Ally," *International Herald Tribune* (February 3, 1993), quoted in Kenneth N. Waltz, *Realism and International Politics* (New York and London: Routledge, 2008), 196.

42. Andrei P. Tsygankov, "Preserving Influence in a Changing World: Russia's Grand Strategy," *Problems of Post-Communism* 58, no. 1 (March–April 2011).

43. This despite the fact that both Marx and Engels were often openly anti-Russian. Friedrich Engels, for instance, does not hesitate to call them "barbarians" when, in 1849—after the revolution of 1848—Russian troops were ready to intervene in Germany: "Half a million armed and organized barbarians," he writes, "wait for the opportunity to attack Germany and to make us serfs of the Pravoslavny Tsar, the Orthodox tsar." (Friedrich Engels, "Die Russen," originally published in *Neue Rheinische Zeitung*, on April 22, 1849. Published in *Marx Engels Werke (MEW)*, Band 6, (Berlin: Dietz Verlag, 1969), 432–433.)

44. Ernst Cassirer, *The Myth of the State* (New Haven and London: Yale University Press, 1975), 249.

45. Cassirer, *The Myth of the State*, 249.

46. Halford J. Mackinder, "The Geographical Pivot of History," republished in Halford J. Mackinder, *Democratic Ideals and Reality* (Washington, DC: National Defense University Press, 1996), 175–193.

47. Halford J. Mackinder, "The Round World and the Winning of the Peace," republished in *Democratic Ideals and Reality*, 195–205.

48. Mackinder, "The Round World and the Winning of the Peace," 201.

49. Mackinder, "The Geographical Pivot of History," 191–192 (emphasis mine).

50. Carl Schmitt, *Der Nomos der Erde im Völkerrecht des Jus Publicum Europaeum* (Berlin: Duncker & Humblot, 1997), 256.

51. This is how the decline of geopolitical theory in the United States is—in part—explained by Colin S. Gray. (Cf. Colin S. Gray, *The Geopolitics of the Nuclear Era: Heartland, Rimlands, and the Technological Revolution*, Strategy Paper no. 30, National Strategy Information Center, Washington, DC (New York: Crane, Russak, 1977), 11.) Two other reasons for this decline were, according to him, "academic fashion" and changes in military—especially nuclear—technology.

52. Jean-Christophe Romer, *Géopolitique de la Russie* (Paris: Economica, 1999), 25.

53. Romer, *Géopolitique de la Russie*, 25–26.

54. Sergei Karaganov, "The Map of the World: Geopolitics Stages a Comeback," *Russia in Global Affairs* (May 19, 2013).

55. Karaganov, "The Map of the World."

56. See, for a detailed comparison of the situation in Weimar Germany and post-Soviet Russia and the many striking resemblances, my book *Putinism: The Slow Rise of a Radical Right Regime in Russia* (Basingstoke and New York: Palgrave MacMillan), 2013.

57. Quoted in Marlène Laruelle, *Russian Eurasianism: An Ideology of Empire* (Washington and Baltimore: Johns Hopkins University Press, 2008), 109.

58. Laruelle, *Russian Eurasianism*, 111–113.

59. Laruelle, *Russian Eurasianism*, 116 (emphasis mine).

60. Aleksandr Dugin, *Evraziystvo ot filosofii k politike: Doklad na Uchreditelnom sezde OPOD 'Evrazii' 21 aprelya 2001 g., Moskva* (Moscow, 2001).

61. According to Ilan Berman, "these developments are not inconsistent with Dugin's theories: Given Moscow's current difficulties with Tokyo, Dugin sees Sino-Russian alignment as a viable strategic partnership in the near term, to be replaced later by a Russo-Japanese bloc." (Cf. Ilan Berman, "Slouching toward Eurasia," *Pundicity* (September–October 2001), http://www.ilanberman.com/5947/slouching-toward-eurasia.)

62. Vladimir Putin, "Novyy integratsionnyy proekt dlya Evrazii: budushchee, kotoroe rozhdaetsya segodnya," *Izvestia* (October 3, 2011).

Chapter Thirteen

Germany's Kremlin-Friendly Political Class

Berlin is familiar to every Russian and many Russians have their own special places here. [1]
—President Dmitry Medvedev, June 2008

In the previous chapter we saw that in the Kremlin there exists an explicit political will to build a Moscow-Berlin axis. However, it is clear that the realization of such a project needs the support of the other side. The question is, therefore, whether Russian Germanophilia is met by an equivalent Russophilia on the German side. This chapter takes a closer look at the German side and shows in more detail how German politicians and political parties, as well as the German press and media and German intellectuals, react to Russian overtures.

According to a 2007 survey commissioned by the German economic magazine *Capital* and conducted among a German "elite panel" made up of six hundred leaders coming from politics, business, and the government, 67 percent of the panel thought that the relationship between Germany and Russia was "good to very good." According to the *Capital* editor,

The elite shows great tolerance towards Moscow's hard political course. More than two thirds (68 percent) of the elite agrees with Russia that democratization still needs more time. Lacking historical experience of free elections and popular sovereignty means it would be impossible to visibly speed up the process. 70 percent praise the stability of the regime. . . . In one point the elite shares the same opinion: 99 out of 100 top people think that close cooperation with Russia is an important foundation for Germany's future. [2]

What is striking here is the great tolerance towards Moscow's hard political course displayed by the German elite. One might even wonder whether this is a case of "Putinophilia" rather than Russophilia. According to Rolf Füchs, director of the Heinrich Böll Foundation, a think tank connected to the Green Party, one of the factors behind the German Russophilia is German guilt toward Russia for Germany's role in World War II. These views would especially hold sway in the Social-Democratic Party (SPD), a party with a graying membership where memories of the war, until recently, were still vivid.[3]

KREMLIN-FRIENDLY SOCIALISTS

One of the Kremlin's biggest trump cards is, indeed, the existence of a powerful pro-Russian lobby in Germany's political establishment. The most telling example is former SPD chancellor Gerhard Schröder, who was not only a political ally of Putin but also a close personal friend. The Putin and Schröder families spent their Christmas holidays together, and in August 2004 Gerhard Schröder and his wife adopted a three-year-old girl from an orphanage in Saint Petersburg, thanks, it was said, to the personal intervention of Putin. "For those interested in symbolism," writes the *New York Times* in a commentary at the time, "the adoption is yet another sign of the warming trend in Russian-German relations over the past few years. Bitter enemies in World War II, tense neighbors during the cold war, the two are in the midst of a burgeoning political and culture exchange."[4] In an article in the German paper *Welt am Sonntag* Henry Kissinger writes that Schröder had won the elections of 2002 through a "combination of pacifism, leftwing and rightwing nationalism, and an appeal to a specific German way that recalls reminiscences of Wilhelmine Germany."[5] "But when Germany insults the U.S.," writes Kissinger, " . . . and acts without consultation with the other European states in the name of a 'German Way,' it is threatened by isolation and a return to the European situation that existed prior to World War I." Kissinger concludes: "The new German way is not only a challenge to the USA, but also to Europe. . . . It allows the emergence of questions about the European leadership, *eventually in cooperation with Russia*, that point to many Prussian ideas of the 19th century."[6] A similar concern is expressed by Robert D. Kaplan, who writes: "So will a debellicized Germany partly succumb to Russian influence, leading to a somewhat Finlandized Eastern Europe and an even more hollow North Atlantic Treaty Organization? Or would Germany subtly stand up to Russia through various political and economic means, even as its society remains immersed in postheroic quasi pacifism?"[7] These were, indeed, pertinent questions.

After leaving office, Gerhard Schröder became the well-paid president of the shareholders' committee of the Nord Stream consortium that built a direct gas pipeline between Russia and Germany under the Baltic Sea. Nord Stream, of which 51 percent is owned by Gazprom, obtained a secret €1 billion German loan guarantee issued a few days before the German chancellor left office. "His close relationship with Putin triggered charges of cronyism from German politicians, as well as claims that he's sold his country out," wrote *Time Magazine* at the time. "'Gazprom is Putin and Putin is Gazprom. By taking this job, Schröder has made himself a salesman for Putin's politics,' alleged Reinhard Bütikofer, a leader of Germany's Greens."[8]

Frank-Walter Steinmeier, a socialist foreign minister and former vice chancellor, is equally known for his Kremlin-friendly behavior. He started his career in the 1990s as *chef de cabinet* of Gerhard Schröder when Schröder was prime minister of the German state of Lower Saxony. Later, when Schröder became chancellor, he followed his boss to Berlin. Being in the right place at the right time, this loyal civil servant, who had never been elected to any public office, was catapulted to the position of foreign minister and vice chancellor in the Great Coalition of SPD and CDU/CSU in 2005 thanks to the personal intervention of Gerhard Schröder. As a foreign minister Steinmeier became the most outspoken protagonist of a Russia-friendly policy in the coalition government. At the Bucharest NATO summit In April 2008, he fervently opposed granting Ukraine and Georgia NATO Membership Action Plans, telling his colleagues that a "divided" Georgia would not be fit to join because of its "frozen conflicts" in Abkhazia and South Ossetia. Condoleezza Rice retorted "that these conflicts were 'not Georgia's problem, but Russia's.'"[9] She added that if this argument had been used in 1955, Germany—at that time equally divided—would not have become a NATO member. After the Russian invasion of Georgia in August 2008, Steinmeier maintained his "even-handed" approach, refusing to distinguish between the military actions of Georgia that were conducted within its national borders and the military actions of Russia that were an invasion of a foreign, sovereign country. He also opposed putting substantial sanctions in place against Russia after those events. In 2012, when Steinmeier was leader of the opposition, he wrote an essay titled "Realism and Principled Attitudes—Foreign Policy in the Sign of New Global Balances,"[10] in which he attacked Chancellor Angela Merkel's values-based foreign policy. He declared himself to be against a policy of "moral rigorism" and against "accusations and a refusal of dialogue." Instead, he wrote, one should start a dialogue with the "emerging powers in the East" without allowing oneself to be held back by "setbacks" in the realization of democracy and human rights. After the elections of September 2013, when a new coalition government of CDU/CSU and SPD was in the making, the German weekly *Die Zeit* published an article titled

"Why He Should Not Come [Back] to the Foreign Ministry."[11] "Steinmeier," wrote the paper, "considers himself a friend of Russia," and therefore "he can be the leader of the parliamentary group, a Labor Minister or a Finance Minister. However, preferably not a Foreign Minister."[12] Criticisms like these of his Kremlin-friendly attitude did not prevent Steinmeier from be-coming—again—foreign minister in the new Great Coalition government, which was formed on December 17, 2013. During the Ukraine crisis in 2014, Steinmeier remained a steadfast supporter of "dialogue" with Moscow. In November 2014, after Putin got an icy reception at the G20 summit in Bris-bane from his Western colleagues—including Chancellor Merkel—Stein-meier went to Moscow to meet with Putin and Foreign Minister Lavrov, pleading for "moderation," risking an open rift with the chancellor.[13] Some weeks later an open letter was published in the weekly *Die Zeit*, titled "Once More War in Europe? Not in Our Name."[14] The open letter, which was signed by sixty-three public personalities, suggested that any informed jour-nalist "will understand the fear of the Russians after NATO members invited Georgia and Ukraine in 2008 to become members of the alliance. It is not about Putin. Political leaders come and go. It is about Europe." The signato-ries, who did not mention the Russian invasion of Georgia, which took place equally in 2008, and—almost reluctantly—admitted that Russia's annexation of the Crimea was "against international law," emphasized in particular "the Western expansion to the east, which was threatening for Russia." "We need a new policy of détente for Europe," they wrote. "We may not push Russia out of Europe." The reader could get the impression that, far from being the aggressor in Ukraine, Russia was the victim. It was certainly no surprise that the hard core of the signatories consisted of SPD dignitaries, led by Gerhard Schröder.[15] Another signatory of the open letter, former SPD chairman Mat-thias Platzeck, who is not only a close friend of Steinmeier but also chairman of the German-Russian Forum, was the most explicit representative of the German socialists' appeasing mood. In an interview, he said that "after the fact the annexation of the Crimea should be legalized in international law, so that it is acceptable to everyone."[16] This plea for a legal recognition of Putin's land grab led in Germany to a wave of criticism. However, this appeasing mood of the political elite found an echo in the population: in a poll conducted for the ARD TV station, 39 percent of Germans wanted the annexation of Crimea to be recognized (48 percent were opposed), and 27 percent of Germans wanted the sanctions imposed on Russia to be lifted.[17]

Neutralist and pro-Russian tendencies are, as such, not new in the SPD. In 1959 the SPD was already wanting to develop an independent "third way" between East and West when it launched its "Deutschlandplan"—a plan for a neutral, reunified Germany that tried to revive earlier proposals made by Stalin in 1952. Stalin had proposed a reunified, neutral Germany to prevent Germany's rearmament. Western analysts feared, however, that the withdrawal of Soviet troops from East Germany and of American and Allied troops from West Germany was more risky for the Western side than for the Soviets.[18] At that time Chancellor Konrad Adenauer (CDU) chose the irreversible integration of Germany into Euro-Atlantic structures—including NATO. Adenauer's reaction was equally negative when, in 1963, Foreign Minister Andrey Gromyko for the first time proposed the building of a gas pipeline between Russia and Germany.

When in 1969 the Social-Democrat Willy Brandt became chancellor and began to implement his "Ostpolitik," the first result of this "Opening to the East" was the signing of the famous "pipes in exchange for gas" contract in 1970 with the Soviet Union. In the late 1970s, 60 percent of Mannesmann's production of large-diameter pipes (for the transportation of natural gas) was exported to the Soviet Union.[19] Russian gas began to flow in 1973.[20] Brandt's Ostpolitik of "small steps" in the field of human contact and economic cooperation was intended to bring about "change through rapprochement" (*Wandel durch Annäherung*). It certainly brought a certain détente in the relationship between the two Germanies. But did it also encourage Russia towards more peaceful behavior, as the SPD claimed it did? "Presented as the route towards a future peace," Jean-Sylvestre Mongrenier rightly observes, "This first East-West pipeline did not prevent the Soviet Union from starting a new expansionist policy (Angola and Mozambique, 1975), from deploying SS-20 missiles in Europe (1977) and from invading Afghanistan (1979)."[21] The growing Russian-German interdependence in the 1970s, far from encouraging Soviet Russia toward more peaceful behavior in Europe and elsewhere, seemed rather to have the opposite effect of increasing Russian belligerence.

The pro-Russia stance of Schröder and Steinmeier could also be observed in another SPD heavyweight, former chancellor Helmut Schmidt. In a bestselling book published in 2008, titled *Ausserdienst: Eine Bilanz* (*Out of Service: An Inventory*), Schmidt writes that "also after the demise of the Soviet Union Russia under Yeltsin and Putin has remained peaceful. . . . Putin has succeeded in restoring great self-confidence to the Russian nation."[22] Schmidt continues: "Unfortunately, in the Western world, especially in the United States, they do not understand the immensely difficult internal problems with which each Russian government is confronted day after day, neither do they acknowledge the fact that since Gorbachev we deal in Moscow with friendly governments that are willing to cooperate with the West."[23] Schmidt expresses his surprise that "one hardly ever comes across Russians expressing anti-German resentment." According to him, "we have to be grateful for this." And he concludes: "For this reason alone we do not have the right to have anti-Russian feelings."[24] It is not clear whether Schmidt equates criticism of the Kremlin's repressive policies with the expression of "anti-Russian feelings." However, he shows less restraint vis-à-vis the United States, which he attacks in the same book for its supposed "excrescences of military thinking" (*Wucherungen eines militärischen Denkens*).[25]

It would be interesting to know whether, after the Russian invasion and dismemberment of Georgia, the annexation of the Crimea, and the slow-motion invasion into Eastern Ukraine, Schmidt still supports the view that Russia under Putin has remained "peaceful" (his book was published shortly after the war in the Caucasus but probably written before). Ultimately, however, even these deliberate acts of aggression might not change Helmut Schmidt's positive view of Putin. Schmidt has the reputation of being a political realist: he was in the 1970s the first European politician to ask the United States to station Pershing II missiles and cruise missiles in Europe to counter the Soviet deployment of SS-20s. One can only speculate as to why Schmidt's realism has given way to this rosy view of the Putin regime. Is it due to his advanced age (in 2008, the year in which the book was published, he celebrated his ninetieth birthday), to naïveté, or to German feelings of guilt vis-à-vis a nation that seems to have forgiven its former enemy?

An even more telling example of a pro-Kremlin bias is Erhard Eppler, Willy Brandt's minister for development cooperation (1968–1974), who warned against the "demonization" of Putin. After the Russian annexation of the Crimea he declared: "I cannot imagine that a Russian president, whatever his name, would patiently watch whilst a clearly anti-Russian government tries to push Ukraine toward NATO, [and] even less so when this government has not been elected."[26] Eppler also criticized "the West's insistence on the integrity of Ukraine's territory."[27] The guilty conscience of an old man? (Eppler joined Hitler's NSDAP in 1944 when he was seventeen). Or are Eppler's and Schmidt's rosy views the result of the permanent Russian *charm offensive* in Germany's direction? This charm offensive had already started under Gorbachev (who, with the nickname "Gorby," is still the most popular Russian politician in Germany) and continued under Yeltsin, who went to the sauna with Chancellor Helmut Kohl. Under Putin, this charm offensive has not only been put into a higher gear, but it was also given a new focus. Yeltsin's friendship with Kohl was—apart from personal affection—driven mostly by *economic* motives. In the early 1990s, Germany was the most important source of loans and foreign direct investment. The German government also paid for the housing in Russia of former Red Army personnel who left East Germany after reunification. Under Putin this economic dimension is still present, but a second, *geopolitical* dimension has been added: Germany—in Putin's eyes—has become the most important European ally in the fight against what is perceived by him as the "the Anglo-Saxon world hegemony."

MORE RUSSOPHILES:
THE GREEN PARTY AND THE LEFT PARTY

Among the German political parties, the SPD is the most important representative of the new German-Russian rapprochement. However, a pro-Russia stance is not confined to the SPD. It is equally present in the Green Party and the liberals of the FDP. An interesting case is the former German foreign minister Joschka Fischer of the Green Party. In an interview in *Der Spiegel* in 2007, he distanced himself from his former coalition partner Chancellor Gerhard Schröder. Asked what he found "most objectionable" in Schröder, he answered: "His position on Russia."[28] But in January 2009, in an op-ed in the *Guardian*, Fischer seemed to have become much more open to Russia's needs than two years earlier. Five months after the Russian invasion of Georgia, Fischer wanted to give Russia "a significantly enhanced role within NATO, including the perspective of full membership." "Why not think about transforming NATO," asked Fischer, "into a real European security system, including Russia?"[29] Why did Fischer suddenly come up with this far-reaching proposal? NATO membership for an illiberal, authoritarian country, such as Russia, with a sham rule of law, would, in the first place, be in flagrant contradiction of the preamble of the Washington Treaty, according to which membership is open to parties that are "determined to safeguard the freedom, common heritage and civilization of their peoples, founded on the principles of democracy, individual liberty and the rule of law." In the second place—and this would be even more important—Russian membership in NATO would give Russia the possibility of vetoing and blocking any NATO initiative. It would in fact emasculate and bury the organization, which is a long-time, explicit Russian foreign policy goal.

Pro-Russian attitudes are also present in Die Linke, the party of the radical left, a merger between a group of dissident social democrats and the PDS, the successor party of the SED, the East German Communist Party. The party got 8.7 percent of the vote in the parliamentary elections of 2005, 11.9 percent in 2009, and 8.6 percent in 2013. Because of its East German communist roots, Die Linke is not only the third-biggest party in the "new lands" of Eastern Germany, but it has also inherited its pro-Russian bias. According to Wolfgang Gehrcke, the foreign affairs speaker of Die Linke in the German parliament, "Germany should become in the European Union the protagonist for an improvement in relations with Russia. This is socially, economically, and strategically, in Germany's interests. A new European Ostpolitik is necessary."[30] Attacking the SPD from the left, Die Linke presents itself as the true and real friend of Russia and as the real inheritor of Willy Brandt's *Ostpolitik*.

THE PRO-RUSSIAN VOLTE-FACE OF THE
GERMAN EXTREME RIGHT

Other—more unexpected—defenders of a close German-Russian relation-ship are the German parties of the extreme right. Like Die Linke, these parties have found a fertile soil in the eastern part of Germany.[31] It is an interesting phenomenon, for instance, that these parties, which tended to be virulently anti-communist, seem to have moved to a more positive assess-ment of the former communist regime. "In the former Eastern Germany," writes Pascal Perrineau, "one of the most important parties of the German extreme right, the NPD, finds virtues in the former communist regime of the 'German Democratic Republic' and pretends that the GDR was a better Germany than the Federal Republic."[32] This positive reassessment of the GDR goes hand in hand with affection for the GDR's former "communist mother country," Russia. Since the end of communism, the extreme right German parties have embraced like-minded parties and organizations in Rus-sia, with which they not only share the same political ideas but also the same revisionist and revanchist geopolitical goals. Six weeks after the war in Geor-gia, for instance, the *National-Zeitung*, the paper of the extreme right party Deutsche Volksunion, published an interview with Vladimir Zhirinovsky, the leader of the crypto-fascist Liberal Democratic Party of Russia, with the title "Together Germany and Russia Cannot Be Blackmailed."[33] This interview starts as follows:

> Question: Is Bismarck's thesis still valid according to which ultimately be-tween Germany and Russia there exist no conflicts of interest that cannot be resolved and that both (countries) should complement each other? Zhirinov-sky: I totally agree with your genial chancellor. There do not exist any con-flicts between Germany and Russia that cannot be resolved. And only together can we uphold the status of powers that cannot be blackmailed. Therefore I would be pleased if we should take care of our rapprochement. I am in favor of the restitution of all eastern territories to Germany. German workers should be free to move anywhere in Russia. For Germany, Russian resources mean se-curity. A pact between our countries brings stability. Germany should not remain in NATO. It should not use a foreign currency. The German Mark was held in higher esteem than the euro. All foreign armies should leave Germany and Germany should regain its eastern territories.[34]

The champion of Russian chauvinist revisionism is playing the German revi-sionism card in order to create a common German-Russian front in Europe that is reminiscent of the Molotov-Ribbentrop Pact with its secret protocol to divide the countries of Central and Eastern Europe between them. However, these pro-Russia feelings of the German extreme right are less extravagant than they, at first sight, seem to be. Walter Laqueur writes that in the 1920s,

Goebbels and other Nazis were already dreaming of a Russian-German alliance against the capitalists of the "plutocratic" West but that these plans were thwarted by Hitler, who had other plans.[35]

THE PRO-RUSSIAN "NEW RIGHT"

Anti-Atlanticist, nationalist, and pro-Russian attitudes cannot only be found in the "official" political parties of the extreme right, such as the NPD, DVU, and the Republikaner. In 1996 Jacob Heilbrunn had already drawn attention, in *Foreign Affairs*, to the emergence of the so-called New Right, a more civilized form of German nationalism and anti-Atlanticism. "The German new right," writes Heilbrunn, "consists not of skinheads in jackboots but journalists, novelists, professors, and young lawyers and business executives." "Paradoxically," he continues, "the new right is made up of nationalists from both ends of the political spectrum. Nationalists on the left hope to remake the SPD; nationalists on the right, the Free Democratic Party."[36] "Hatred of the United States," he concludes, "is what binds the right nationalists and defectors from the left who make up the movement."[37]

It is no surprise that the representatives of this New Right target especially Germany's *Westbindung*, its bond with the West. In a book with the same title,[38] published shortly after Germany's reunification, many of their geopolitical arguments are to be found. The authors criticize Chancellor Konrad Adenauer for his decision to anchor Germany in the West. They openly question whether Adenauer really wanted Germany's reunification and complain that "since the 1960s it was often considered a taboo to speak of national interests and to analyze geopolitical facts as conditions for action."[39] The New Right authors say they want to "overcome taboos," and their new keywords are "nation," "neutrality," or "non-alignment" (*Blockfreiheit*)[40] and Germany's "special location" (*Sonderlage*), which would lead to "a special consciousness" (*Sonderbewußtsein*). They plead for a Germany that is neutral. Germany's neutrality is, according to them, logical because of Germany's supposed "fate to be situated in the center" (*Schicksal der Mittellage*) which makes it "a mediator between East and West."[41]

One of the authors, Rainer Zitelmann, expressed his admiration for Reich Chancellor Gustav Stresemann, who, in 1922, signed the Treaty of Rapallo with the Soviet Union, notwithstanding the fact that this treaty was considered by the Western powers as an overt anti-Western pact that was directed against the Treaty of Versailles. "For him (Stresemann) foreign policy necessity was more important than the wishes of his Western friends," writes Zitelmann. The author regrets that "the work of Stresemann afterwards had been ditched. The mistake of foreign policy after 1945 has been the belief 'that one just could forget about the geographical situation of Germany. The old task of Germany, to be a mediator between East and West, had been denied.'"[42] The message is clear: Germany should mind its own interests and no longer let its foreign policy choices be influenced by Western powers or by guilt over its past. Another author writes, "[The fact] that 'military pacts and national interests' collide in politics, is not new knowledge."[43] Members of the New Right are not only against NATO membership, they are also critical of European integration. They criticize the Treaty of Maastricht and warn about the risks of a policy "that prescribes the utopia of Germany's total integration into the West, into a European federal state."[44] The author uses here the German neologism *Totalwestintegration*. One has only to say it aloud slowly to taste the hidden allusion to something hideous and totalitarian.

Neutralism and anti-Americanism go hand in hand, but, as Jan Herman Brinks rightly remarks: "This anti-western position, which is primarily directed against the United States . . . *generally goes with a latent sympathy for Russia.*"[45] The reason for this "latent sympathy" of the New Right for Russia is the fact that the old foe, Soviet communism, no longer exists. Russia has transformed itself into a country that comes close to the ideals of the extreme right and the New Right: it is anti-Western, xenophobic, anti-American, authoritarian, and state capitalist, and it glorifies a strong state.[46]

ALTERNATIVE FÜR DEUTSCHLAND: THE NEW RUSSOPHILIA OF THE POLITICAL CENTER

Until 2013 the new German Russophilia was restricted mainly to parties of the extreme right and extreme left, as well as sections of the SPD. The German political center-right, the CDU, seemed largely to resist Moscow's siren songs, notwithstanding that some members of the CDU's conservative Bavarian sister organization, the CSU, did not hesitate to express their sympathy for the Kremlin. In March 2013, for instance, during a meeting of the foreign affairs committees of the Bundestag and the Duma, the conservative CSU MP Peter Gauweiler raised "in 'really pathetic words' the German-Russian friendship. Thereupon, deeply moved, Gehrcke took the stage: that he, as a 'German communist,' could live to see the day that he agreed with a 'German conservative.'"[47] The *Süddeutsche Zeitung* commented: "Whenever it concerns Russia strange alliances are formed in the Bundestag."[48] These are signs that the pro-Russia consensus also has a grip on the conservative fringe of the CDU/CSU. Due to the euro crisis and an increasing malaise amongst the German population concerning the role of their country as Europe's *Zahlmeister* (paymaster), there are more indications that the political center has begun to shift. On April 14, 2013, in Berlin a new party, the Alternative für Deutschland (Alternative for Germany), or AfD, was founded. It was a Eurosceptic party that wanted the crisis-ridden Eurozone countries of southern Europe—including France!—to leave the Eurozone voluntarily. This should then lead to a restoration of the German deutschmark or to the consolidation of a smaller Eurozone, consisting of Germany and some central and northern European countries, which shared Germany's competitiveness and budgetary discipline. The new party, led by Bernd Lucke, an economics professor from Hamburg, was said to be "founded by an alliance of economics professors, constitutional lawyers, and conservative commentators."[49] The party, called a *Professorenpartei* (professors' party), could not be accused of cheap populism or extreme right ideas. It attracted predominantly (male) representatives of the liberal professions and counted amongst its membership many academics. According to a secret (but leaked) paper from the SPD, the party was "a populist splinter from the CDU and FDP, [and] it confirms the trend of political erosion of black-yellow [the CDU-FDP coalition government]. Half of the national leadership of the AfD consists of former CDU-members."[50] This was true. Party leader and spokesperson Bernd Lucke, for instance, was a member of the CDU for thirty-three years and left the party only in December 2011. One of the three deputy spokespersons, Alexander Gauland, is a former CDU politician who was state secretary in the government of the Land of Hessen under Prime Minister Walter Wallmann (CDU). According to Manfred Güllner, director of the opinion polling agency Forsa, support for the party was "coming from a peculiar section of the population of which the nucleus is the radicalized middle classes."[51] Güllner used the expression "radicalized middle classes" possibly to assuage the concerns of outsiders, but unfortunately, it evoked memories of the 1930s before the advent of Hitler, when a radicalized middle class left the political center and drifted to the right. The leadership, however, tried to do its best to avoid anything that could be used by opponents to denounce the party. Therefore, the party program, voted in April 2013, was very concise.[52] It was, for instance, completely silent on foreign policy.

However, when this omission was rectified by an official paper, written by Alexander Gauland and presented to the party leadership on September 10, 2013, it included a real surprise. The last part of this paper—about a third of the text—was completely dedicated to Germany's relations with Russia. The author writes that "Russia never got over the separation from 'Holy Kiev,' the embryo of Russia. That is also difficult to imagine, because this separation can be compared only with the separation of Aachen or Cologne from Germany. The EU should, when moving closer towards these countries, act with great caution, taking into account Russia's sensitivities."[53] The author continues: "Germany and Europe have no interest in a further weakening of Russia and with it also of the whole Eurasian space. We should always manage the relationship with Russia carefully. We Germans sometimes forget that at decisive moments in German history Russia has played a positive role and has saved Prussia from defeat. That is true of 1763, 1806/07, 1813, Bismarck's unification of 1866/70 and the German reunification of 1990/91."[54] Therefore, concludes the author, "elements of Bismarck's reinsurance policy vis-à-vis Russia should be maintained."[55] Bismarck's secret reinsurance treaty of 1887 guaranteed that Russia would remain neutral in any future war between Germany and France. France, which the AfD wants removed from the Eurozone, still seems to be considered the hidden enemy. In his paper the author makes no mention of the French-German axis—the centerpiece of European integration. He also denies that his pro-Russian policy would have negative consequences for relations with Poland, which has fallen victim several times to a German-Russian rapprochement. "After the integration of Poland into the EU and NATO," he writes, "such a policy cannot be understood as anti-Polish, because both countries are too closely connected."[56] "Back to Bismarck" and to Bismarck's pro-Russia policy seems to be the new slogan of the German neonationalists from the right, the left, and the center—irrespective of their political affiliation. In Moscow, as well as in Berlin, Bismarck seems, indeed, to be the pivotal historical figure and necessary point of reference for those who want to establish a close German-Russian cooperation.

WARM FEELINGS TOWARDS RUSSIA IN THE FORMER GDR

It is telling that the importance of Bismarck for Russian-German relations was already recognized in the former GDR, where, in February 1983, the (communist) Central Institute for History in East Berlin had accorded Bismarck the title of "statesman of high rank" (*Staatsmann von hohem Rang*).[57] It is, therefore, no surprise that the former GDR still plays a central role in the new wave of sympathy toward Russia. We have to bear in mind that the reunified Germany anno 2014 with its capital in Berlin is no longer the old Federal Republic anno 1989 with its capital in the small, provincial town of Bonn in the western part of Germany. Almost simultaneously both Russia and Germany have experienced huge changes in territory and population size. These changes took them in opposite directions. While Russia experienced a painful territorial contraction, accompanied by a substantial loss of population, the territory of the reunified Germany expanded, and its population grew from about sixty to eighty million. But the twenty million East Germans who suddenly became citizens of a new, reunified Germany were—and still are—different from their West German fellow countrymen. Since 1933 they had lived *without interruption* under a totalitarian regime: first under the Nazis, then under the communists. Three generations of these new Germans had never experienced what it was like to live in a democracy with free elections, free media, an active civil society, and an independent judiciary. In itself, this lack of democratic tradition is a problem that can be overcome, as the experience in other former communist countries of Eastern Europe shows. The problem was that in the German "new lands" the jubilation of the first years quickly soured into a growing disaffection with the capitalist economy and Western democracy. In the east not only did there emerge a nostalgia (ironically called *Ostalgie*: "east-algia") for the tranquility and job security of the former GDR, but there also survived a broad popular reservoir of warm feelings towards Russia, the former Warsaw Pact ally and "socialist brother country" with which East Germany had been aligned for almost half a century. Elisabeth Noelle-Neumann wrote in 1993: "In the past decades East Germans have developed a sense of community with Eastern Europe, which will certainly have consequences in the future."[58]

She was right. It is, therefore, no coincidence that today East Germans play a prominent role in German-Russian organizations. On the board of the Deutsch-Russisches Forum (German-Russian Forum), we find, for instance, Lothar de Maizière, the first and last freely elected prime minister of the GDR, and Manfred Stolpe, who after 1990 became a minister in the cabinet of Helmut Kohl and who was minister president of the East German Land of Brandenburg. Both men have been accused of links with the Stasi, the powerful East German secret service.[59] East Germany combines both: it is the most pro-Russian part of Germany, and it is also the most fertile soil for right-wing extremism. In a survey by the Free University of Berlin conducted in 2005, one could read "that extreme right orientations can generally be found one and a half times more frequently in the East compared to the West (27 percent against 18 percent).[60] Jan Herman Brinks writes:

> The GDR always propagated fairly authoritarian standards in its methods of upbringing. Values regarded as essentially "socialist" included the old "Prussian values": order, discipline and punctuality, the sense of duty, cleanliness and physical toughness. These virtues, which were originally quite ascetic, were converted by the East German party communists into submissive attitudes, strikingly similar to the values that (intellectual) right-wing radicals had been advocating for years.[61]

It was these secondary German virtues—as we saw in the previous chapter—that evoked the admiration of ordinary Russians, and it was these same virtues that they admired in their leader: "Nemets Putin" ("Putin the German").

NOTES

1. "President of Russia Dmitry Medvedev's Speech at Meeting with German Political, Parliamentary and Civic Leaders," Berlin (June 5, 2008), text available at website of Ministry of Foreign Affairs of the Russian Federation.

2. "Deutsche Führungsspitzen auf Kuschelkurs mit Russland," *Capital* (November 19, 2007).

3. Cf. Gregory Feifer, "Too Special a Friendship: Is Germany Questioning Russia's Embrace?" *RFE/RL* (July 11, 2011).

4. Mark Landler, "Schröder's Bond with Russia: A Little Girl, Now His Own," *The New York Times* (August 18, 2004).

5. Henry Kissinger, "Deutschland droht die Isolation," *Welt am Sonntag* (October 20, 2002) (emphasis mine), http://www.welt.de/printwams/article608216/Deutschland_droht_die_Isolation.html.

6. Kissinger, "Deutschland droht die Isolation."

7. Robert D. Kaplan, "The Divided Map of Europe," *The National Interest*, no. 120 (July/August 2012), 24.

8. Adam Smith, "Gerhard Schroder's [*sic*] Next Big Job," *Time Magazine* (December 17, 2005). According to Edward Lucas, "Tom Lantos, the American congressman and Holocaust survivor . . . wanted to call Schröder a 'political prostitute,' but that the sex workers in his congressional district objected." (Cf. Edward Lucas, *The New Cold War: Putin's Russia and the Threat to the West* (New York and Houndmills: Palgrave Macmillan, 2008), 167.)

9. "With Allies Like These," *The Economist* (April 5, 2008).

10. Frank-Walter Steinmeier, "Realismus und Prinzipientreue: Außenpolitik im Zeichen neuer globalen Balancen," in *Wertewandel mitgestalten: Gut handeln in Gesellschaft und Wirtschaft*, ed. Brun-Hagen Hennerkes and Georg Augustin (Freiburg, Basel, Wien: Herder, 2012), 82–99.

11. Jörg Lau, "Warum er nicht ins Auswärtige Amt sollte," *Die Zeit* (October 3, 2013).

12. Lau, "Warum er nicht ins Auswärtige Amt sollte."

13. Nikolaus Blome, Peter Müller, Christian Neef, Ralf Neukirch, and Christoph Schult, "Am Nullpunkt," *Der Spiegel* (November 24, 2014).

14. "Wieder Krieg in Europa? Nicht in unserem Namen," *Die Zeit* (December 5, 2014), http://www.zeit.de/politik/2014-12/aufruf-russland-dialog.

15. Other names on the list include Hans-Jochen Vogel (SPD), former minister of justice; Herta Däubler-Gmelin (SPD), former minister of justice (who, in 2002, resigned after having compared US President George W. Bush to Adolf Hitler); Manfred Stolpe (SPD), former prime minister of the Land Brandenburg and federal minister of transport (in 2003 it was revealed that he had collaborated with the Stasi, the East German secret service, under the code name "IM Sekretär"); Erhard Eppler (SPD), former minister of development cooperation (who, in the 1970s, was a vocal opponent of NATO's double decision); Matthias Platzeck (SDP), former party chairman; Walther Stützle (SPD), former state secretary of defense; Lothar de Maizière (CDU), former prime minister of the German Democratic Republic (he resigned in 1991 as chairman of the CDU Brandenburg after it became known that he had worked with the Stasi under the code name "Czerni"); and Klaus Mangold, former chairman of the "East Committee" (Ostausschuss) of the German employers' organization and honorary consul of the Russian Federation in Baden-Württemberg.

16. "Platzeck fordert Anerkennung der Krim-Annexion," *Die Zeit* (November 18, 2014), http://www.zeit.de/politik/ausland/2014-11/platzeck-russland-ukraine.

17. Cf. Artur Ciechanowicz, "Russia Is Driving a Wedge into Germany," *OSW Analyses*, Warsaw (November 26, 2014).

18. Cf. Philip Windsor, *German Reunification* (London: Elek Books, 1969), 67: "And there was a risk: a reunified Germany would have been subject to Soviet influence to a far greater extent than to American influence, if the bulk of the American troops had gone home. Soviet forces could always return much more quickly than American forces."

19. Cf. "Germany: Regulatory Reform in Electricity, Gas, and Pharmacies," *OECD Country Studies 2004* (Paris: OECD, 2004), 9.

20. It is telling that East German households did not receive any gas from their Russian "brother country" until after they left the Eastern bloc and were integrated into the Federal Republic. (Cf. "Germany: Regulatory Reform," 9.)

21. Jean-Sylvestre Mongrenier, "La sécurité énergétique, nouvelle frontière de l'Union européenne," in *Tribune* (Institut Thomas More), no. 23 (January 2009), 4.

22. Helmut Schmidt, *Ausserdienst: Eine Bilanz* (Munich: Siedler, 2008), 115.

23. Schmidt, *Ausserdienst*, 117.

24. Schmidt, *Ausserdienst*, 118.

25. Schmidt, *Ausserdienst*, 211.

26. Erhard Eppler, "Putin, Mann fürs Böse," *Süddeutsche Zeitung* (March 11, 2014), http://www.sueddeutsche.de/politik/russlands-praesident-wladimir-putin-mann-fuers-boese-1.1909116-2.

27. Eppler, "Putin, Mann fürs Böse."

28. Joschka Fischer, "An Anti-American Axis? That's Nonsense," *Spiegel Online* (February 10, 2007).

29. Joschka Fischer, "Finding Russia's Place in Europe," *The Guardian* (January 11, 2009).

30. "EU-Russland-Gipfel muss Ausgangspunkt für neue europäische Ostpolitik werden," Presseerklärung *Die Linke* (November 14, 2008).

31. In the 2004 election for the regional parliament of Sachsen, the neo-fascist NPD (Nationaldemokratische Partei Deutschlands) won 9.2 percent of the votes, and in Mecklenburg-Vorpommern, 7.3 percent. Another party of the extreme right, the DVU (Deutsche Volksunion), won in 2004 6.1 percent of the votes for the parliamentary elections in Brandenburg. (Cf. Delphine Iost, "L'implantation du NPD dans les nouveaux *Länder* allemands," in *Hérodote: Revue de géographie et de géopolitique*, no. 128 (1er trimestre 2008), 87–102.) In the elections of 2009, the DVU remained stable in Brandenburg with 6.08 of the votes, but in Sachsen the NPD got only 5.6 percent.

32. Pascal Perrineau, "De quoi le populisme est le nom," in *Populismes: l'envers de la démocratie*, edited by Marie-Claude Esposito, Alain Laquièze, and Christine Manigand (Paris: Vendémiaire Éditions, 2012), 77.

33. *National-Zeitung*, Pressemitteilung (September 22, 2008).

34. "Zusammen sind Deutschland und Russland nicht erpressbar, Interview mit Dr. Wladimir Schirinowski, Vizepräsident der russischen Staatsduma," http://www.news4press.com/1/MeldungDruckansicht.asp?Mitteilungs_ID=392669. Zhirinovsky had already expressed similar ideas before in his book *Poslednyy brosok na yug* (*Last Push to the South*) (Moscow: Liberalno-Demokraticheskaya Partiya, 1993), in which he wrote that "the Germans will throw back the Poles. Poland may be built somewhere in the region Wolin, Brest" (139).

35. Walter Laqueur, *Mein 20. Jahrhundert: Stationen eines politischen Lebens* (Berlin: Propyläen, 2009), 35.

36. Jacob Heilbrunn, "Germany's New Right," *Foreign Affairs* 75, no. 6 (November/December, 1996), 81.

37. Heilbrunn, "Germany's New Right."

38. Rainer Zitelmann, Karlheinz Weismann, and Michael Grossheim, eds.,*Westbindung: Chancen und Risiken für Deutschland* (Frankfurt am Main and Berlin: Propyläen, 1993).

39. Michael Grossheim, Karlheinz Weismann, and Rainer Zitelmann, "Einleitung: Wir Deutschen und der Westen," in Zitelmann et al., *Westbindung*, 13.

40. The word "blockfrei"—free of being integrated into a military block—is often preferred over its equivalent "neutral." This is a deliberate choice. "Neutral" has a more or less negative connotation of indecisiveness and aloofness; "block free" has a positive connotation of freedom and being liberated of the pressure from awkward allies.

41. It is interesting that many arguments of the German New Right resemble that of Russian Eurasianists, such as Aleksandr Dugin, who equally claims for Russia "a position in the center" and the function of a "bridge" between Europe and Asia. Russia's "special situation" is for Dugin a reason to claim for Russia equally a special *political* status in which Western values, such as individual freedom, human rights, democracy, and the rule of law, do not apply or do not apply in the same way. This relativization of Western values can also be observed in the German "New Right."

42. Rainer Zitelmann, "Neutralitätsbestrebungen und Westorientierung," in Zitelmann et al., *Westbindung*, 176.

43. Heinz Brill, "Deutschland im geostrategischen Kraftfeld der Super- und Großmächte (1945–1990)," in Zitelmann et al., *Westbindung*, 271.

44. Grossheim, Weismann, and Zitelmann, "Einleitung: Wir Deutschen und der Westen," 15.

45. Jan Herman Brinks, "Germany's New Right," in *Nationalist Myths and the Modern Media: Cultural Identity in the Age of Globalisation*, ed. Jan Herman Brinks (London: I.B. Tauris, 2005), 129 (emphasis mine).

46. The demise of the Soviet Union made possible a convergence of the positions of the New Left and the New Right. After the end of communism, both the New Left and the New Right were united in their shared anti-Americanism.

47. Daniel Brössler, "Eigentümliche Allianzen," *Süddeutsche Zeitung* (March 14, 2013).

48. Brössler, "Eigentümliche Allianzen."

49. Quentin Peel, "Germany's Eurosceptic Party Could Yet Tip Electoral Scales," *Financial Times* (August 16, 2013).

50. Frank Wilhelmy, "Vermerk: Die Alternative für Deutschland (AfD) nach ihrem Bundesparteitag" (April 17, 2013).

51. Tony Paterson, "Rise of the Eurosceptics Casts Shadow over German Election," *The Independent* (September 5, 2013).

52. There were, however, some party activists with rather radical opinions. Roland Vaubel, for instance, an economics professor and member of the scientific advisory board of the party, published in 2007 proposals for a two-chamber system in which one chamber would be elected by those who paid most direct taxes—a proposal which would reintroduce a census (tax-based) suffrage and suspend the principle of democratic equality. (Cf. "Brüche im Establishment (II)," *German-Foreign-Policy.com* (September 12, 2013).) Another case was that of Dr. Irina Smirnova, a professor at St. Petersburg University, called by the press "a mysterious Russian woman." She was one of the ten people elected to the board of the party. Being an expert on "PR, political 'imageology,' intercultural hermeneutics, and journalism," she was responsible for the party's integration policy. Smirnova proposed compulsory education for immigrants. According to her, the number of immigrants would increase "and consequently the problems also"—apparently forgetting that she herself was an immigrant. (Cf. "Mysteriöse Russin sorgt für Wirbel bei Anti-Euro-Partei," *Focus online* (June 7, 2013); and "Rätselhafte Russin im Vorstand der Euro-Gegner AfD," *Eurasisches Magazin*, no date.)

53. "Thesen zur Außenpolitik von Dr. Alexander Gauland zur PK vom 10.09.2013," available on the website of the party, https://www.alternativefuer.de/2013/09/11/thesenpapier-aussenpolitik/ (accessed September 17, 2013).

54. "Thesen zur Außenpolitik."

55. "Thesen zur Außenpolitik."

56. "Thesen zur Außenpolitik." In September 2013 the party won 4.7 percent of the vote—a respectable result for a new party, although not enough to get over the 5 percent barrier and enter the Bundestag, the German parliament. However, the party was more successful on August 31, 2014, in Saxony, where it won 9.8 percent of the vote in regional elections, and on September 14, 2014, in Thuringia and in Brandenburg, where it got respectively 10.6 percent and 12.2 percent of the vote.

57. Cf. Günther Lachmann, "Die AfD will zurück zu Bismarcks Außenpolitik," *Die Welt* (September 10, 2013).

58. Elisabeth Noelle-Neumann, "Der Westbindung im Spiegel der Demoskopie," in Zitelmann et al., *Westbindung*, 291.

59. Lothar de Maizière joined the East German Christian Democratic Union (a bloc party, linked with the communist SED in the "National Front") in 1957. He became minister without portfolio in October 1990 in Kohl's first cabinet of a reunified Germany but had to resign in December of the same year after allegations that he had worked for the Stasi, the East German secret service. Manfred Stolpe was between 1969 and 1981 secretary of the Union of Evangelical Churches in the GDR and received in 1978 the "Medal of Merit of the GDR." Although he

denied having been an unofficial collaborator of the Stasi, he had met with agents of the Stasi and appeared in the files of the Stasi under the code name "Secretary."

60. "Projekt Gewerkschaften und Rechtsextremismus," Freie Universität Berlin, Otto-Suhr-Institut für Politikwissenschaft (2005), 434, http://www.polsoz.fuberlin.de/polwiss/forschung/oekonomie/gewerkschaftspolitik/materialien/GEWREXSCHLUSS/Kapitel_In.pdf.

61. Jan Herman Brinks, "Nationalism in German Politics as Mirrored by the Media since Reunification," report for the one-day workshop "Apocalyptic Politics, Archaic Myths and Modern Media" (London, March 28, 2006), 6, http://www.sussex.ac.uk/Units/cgjs/publications/PolicyReportBrinks.pdf. In a 2008 survey on the mutual images of Germans and Russians, one questionnaire—on the appreciation of freedom—contains a subdivision for answers from West Germans and East Germans. Questions on "freedoms that are personally very important" get the following scores:

- Free speech: West Germans 83 percent positive, East Germans 74 percent, and Russians 36 percent.
- Freedom to demonstrate: (respectively) 38 percent, 31 percent, 10 percent.
- Having a choice between different political parties: (respectively) 62 percent, 49 percent, 17 percent.

East Germans clearly lagged behind West Germans in the appreciation of liberal democratic values. However, their scores were closer to those of West Germans than those of Russians. (Cf. Prof. Dr. Renate Köcher, "Das Russlandbild der Deutschen—das Deutschlandbild der Russen—Ergebnisse repräsentativer Bevölkerungsumfragen in Deutschland und Russland," Institut für Demoskopie Allensbach, Berlin (September 18, 2008).)

Chapter Fourteen

Russian-German *"Verflechtung"*

Creating Mutual Economic Interdependence

Another important factor that explains the German Russophilia is the existence of a powerful *pro-Russian business lobby* in Germany. This business lobby is led by some of the biggest and most important German banks and companies. Both Russia and Germany view each other as mutually economically complementary nations. Russia sells Germany the energy and minerals it needs, while Germany produces the machinery and high-tech products Russia needs to modernize its antiquated industrial base. When analyzing Russian-German economic relations, we have to keep in mind, first, that before German reunification *both* Germanies, the GDR and the Federal Republic, had already been major trading partners with the Soviet Union and, second, that after the negative experience with US advice on Russia's economic transition, the Russian government preferred to emulate the German model, which provided for a larger state role in the economy. [1] On this existing basis, the German-Russian trade relationship has rapidly expanded in recent years. Exports from Germany to Russia exploded between 1995 and 2004, growing by 76 percent and making Russia the number one export growth market for Germany. [2] German exports to Russia continued to grow: they almost doubled between 2003 and 2007. [3] In 2007 Russian exports to Germany were worth €28.8 billion (of which 69 percent consisted of oil and gas), and Russia's imports from Germany were worth €28.1 billion (mostly cars, trucks, machines, and chemicals). In 2007 Russia ranked number ten on the German list of importing countries and number twelve on the list of exporting countries. [4] Due to the economic crisis, the dynamism of the economic relationship decreased somewhat in 2010, when Russia's imports stood at only €26.3 billion. The value of exports from Russia to Germany,

217

however, increased to €31.7 billion.[5] In 2011 the value of German exports to Russia further increased to €34.4 billion and imports from Russia to €40.5 billion.[6] An important feature of the blossoming economic relationship between the two countries is the large number of small and medium-sized German companies that are active on the Russian market. In November 2008, 4,600 companies were involved, of which 4,300 were small and medium-sized enterprises.[7] The total number of German companies active in Russia increased in 2012 to about six thousand.[8]

A few big companies and banks have taken the lead. Prominent are the two German energy giants, E.ON Ruhrgas and Wintershall, a subsidiary of BASF. Both companies maintain close ties with the political leadership in the Kremlin. On December 14, 2008, for example, the CEO of Wintershall, Reinier Zwitserloot, was awarded the Order of Friendship of the Russian Federation, the highest state decoration that can be awarded to a non-Russian citizen. Wintershall's competitor, E.ON Ruhrgas, which had already been involved in the "gas-for-pipes" deal that was signed in 1970 with the Soviet government, is one of Gazprom's most important Western partners. It owned 6.5 percent[9] of Gazprom and was, as such, an example of the strategy of "rapprochement through interlocking" (*Annäherung durch Verflechtung*), a strategy proposed by Foreign Minister Frank-Walter Steinmeier at the end of 2006.[10] A corollary of this economic strategy of "rapprochement through interlocking" was a second—political—doctrine of "change through rapprochement" (*Wandel durch Annäherung*). The strategy of economic interlocking was expected to have all manner of positive effects on the internal situation in Russia—leading to not only an economic but also a political modernization by strengthening Russia's young democracy and improving the human rights situation. Both doctrines, therefore, promised the Germans the best of all possible worlds: not only would they boost their exports, but at the same time they would help the Russians in bringing about a modern democratic political system in Russia.

"INTERLOCKING" RUSSIAN AND GERMAN COMPANIES: HOW IT WORKED

The first part of this strategy, the interlocking of German and Russian companies, seems to have worked out well. Since the year 2000, for instance, Dr. Burckhard Bergmann, the CEO of E.ON Ruhrgas, has had a place on the board of directors of Gazprom. In 2006 Bergmann was also appointed honorary consul of the Russian Federation in North-Rhine Westphalia, and in 2007 he was elected Director of the Year in Russia. Bergmann is deputy chairman of the East Committee of the German Employers Association BDI (Ost-Ausschuss der deutschen Wirtschaft). The chairman of this committee,

Dr. Klaus Mangold of Daimler AG, is honorary consul of the Russian Federation in Baden-Württemberg. The process of "interlocking" between the captains of German industry and the *siloviki* in the Kremlin does not stop here. E.ON Ruhrgas and Wintershall cooperate with Gazprom in the joint venture that built the Nord Stream gas pipeline. In this project Gazprom assured itself of a strategic 51 percent of the shares, which gave it the power to nominate the CEO.[11]

The CEO of Nord Stream is a German, Matthias Warnig. Warnig is the former head of Dresdner Bank in Moscow. Warnig, however, was originally neither a banker nor an energy expert. He started his career as a senior officer of the Stasi, the powerful East German secret service which, at the end of the 1980s, employed 91,000 people and had 300,000 informants and was, as such, bigger than Hitler's Gestapo (which had 40,000 employees in 1939 and during the war grew to 150,000—including informants). In a small country the Stasi organized one of the most effective and repressive police states of the Eastern bloc. Putin and Warnig both declared to have met for the first time in St. Petersburg in 1991. However, according to Irene Pietsch, a personal friend of Putin's wife Lyudmila, Putin's and Warnig's families had close relations when Putin worked in the GDR as a KGB agent in the 1980s.[12] This may have been instrumental in Warnig's promotion to CEO of Nord Stream.[13]

E.ON Ruhrgas not only has its CEO on the board of Gazprom, it is also "interlocked" with Dresdner Bank and its subsidiary Dresdner Kleinwort Wasserstein. Dr. Herbert Walter, the CEO of Dresdner Kleinwort, is a member of the supervisory board of E.ON Ruhrgas. The role played by Dresdner Kleinwort in Russia is a controversial subject. On behalf of the Russian government, Dresdner Kleinwort had valued the assets of Yukos after its CEO, Mikhail Khodorkovsky, was jailed.[14] Together with Deutsche Bank, Dresdner Kleinwort was a member of the consortium of banks that made the auction of Yukos possible. This auction was branded by international investors as an illegal asset grab. According to Pavel K. Baev,

> The dismemberment of Yukos and the appropriation of its assets by Rosneft was a very messy affair until this state-owned company received a $7.3 billion Western credit. . . . Various creditors are providing this flow of money but at the center of the "teams" Deutsche Bank, Commerzbank, Dresdner Kleinwort Wasserstein are invariably present. With tacit encouragement of the (German) government, these German giants are financing the concentration of major assets in the Russian economy under the control of Putin's "team", which is estimated to preside over a conglomerate of companies valued at $222 billion. The cordial ties between the leaders is thus not the summit of a complex structure of mature political relations, which are basically absent, but the cork in a bottle of stinky subsidies and dirty deals.[15]

In 2005, Commerzbank, one of the members of the "team," was involved in a case of alleged money laundering for Telekominvest, a Russian company created in 1994 by Leonid Reiman, Putin's telecommunications minister. Reiman amalgamated two state-owned phone companies in St. Petersburg during the time that Putin was deputy mayor.[16] According to other sources, Putin's wife Lyudmila would have been directly involved in these deals.[17]

RUSSIA'S *META*-ROBBER CAPITALISM

The impression one gets is of a close, very close—even "cozy"—relationship between a powerful part of the German business elite and the Russian business world. In itself, there is nothing wrong with close business contacts, and it is quite normal for these sometimes to develop into a genuine friendship. The problem, however, is that business contacts with Russia are, as such, seldom normal—due to the specific situation of Russia. In the 1990s Russia first went through a phase of robber capitalism, which was followed by a second and even more violent phase of *meta*-robber capitalism during Putin's presidency. In this second phase of *meta*-robber capitalism, large chunks of the economy, which had been privatized in the 1990s, were partly renationalized and brought under the control of Putin's *siloviki*. I am using here the term *meta*-robber capitalism because, unlike the oligarchs in the 1990s, the new class of *siloviki* used not only state finances for their asset grabs but also the judiciary and the repressive state organs. Legal threats, criminal investigations, "tax-measures," imprisonment, blackmail, and allegedly even death threats and assassinations were among the means used to obtain a transfer of assets or an outright expropriation. Western investment banks have, through their involvement, sometimes lent an aura of respectability to these illegal and often criminal practices. By a process of contagion, German firms also exposed themselves to the risk of being enmeshed in corrupt affairs. An example of this is Siemens, which paid bribes in Russia. Lilia Shevtsova of the Moscow Carnegie Center comments: "Some Western companies have even adopted traditional Russian business practices: A German court recently investigated the multinational conglomerate Siemens for bribery of Russian officials. In Siemens's defense, it was merely playing by the rules of the game—rules written and enforced by the authorities to maintain their opaque, corrupt system."[18]

Another problem connected with doing business in Russia—especially in this second phase of *meta*-robber capitalism—is that in the Russian context, business-to-business contacts are barely disguised business-to-government contacts. This may be less so for small and medium-sized companies, but it is always the case where large German energy firms and banks have business contacts with the Russian energy giants Gazprom and Rosneft. Both companies are used as powerful instruments in the hands of the Kremlin to further its political goals. These political goals, moreover, can conflict with the interests and goals of the government of its trading partners. The limits of the policy of economic "interlocking" became clear when Russia started to use its sovereign investment fund to buy industries in Germany. The strong Kremlin involvement in this fund led to an outcry in Germany. According to the vice-chairman of the CDU, Robert Koch, "We didn't just go through all our efforts to privatize industries like Deutsche Telekom or the Deutsche Post only so that the Russians can nationalize them."[19]

THE SHTOKMAN SYNDROME: WHY GERMANY'S ENERGY GIANTS ACT AS THE KREMLIN'S SPOKESMEN

In an interview in the German weekly *Der Stern*, Robert Amsterdam, lawyer for the imprisoned Yukos chief Mikhail Khodorkovsky, drew attention to a phenomenon which he called the "Shtokman syndrome." The syndrome is named after the Shtokman field, the world's biggest gas deposit, located in the Russian part of the Barents Sea, 550 kilometers off the coast, at a depth of about 330 meters. Amsterdam uses the "Shtokman syndrome" as an analogy to the "Stockholm syndrome," the psychological state characterizing former hostages who tend to identify with their hostage takers and even go so far as to defend them.

> Just imagine a hypothetical German energy company, Germanco, that takes the decision to invest in Russia. After a short relaxed honeymoon the Russian government aggressively and in an arbitrary way acts against Germanco or its subsidiary. Thereupon Germanco uses its great influence on the German government to obtain concessions for Russia. To be honest, a brilliant way of manipulation! Some of Germany's leading energy companies (and also financial institutions) suffer from the "Shtokman Syndrome." However badly the Russian government may treat them, they want to invest in more Russian gas projects. The negative impact on Germany's national interests is clear: the more some companies are involved in business with the Russian state, the more they act to influence German politics in line with Moscow's wishes.[20]

Maybe Robert Amsterdam's fears about a *shtokmanization* of German foreign policy are exaggerated. However, there are reasons for concern. In 2010, for instance, *Spiegelonline*, the online edition of the German weekly *Der Spiegel*, published an article on a draft report of the Future Analysis Department of the Bundeswehr Transformation Center, a think tank of the German army tasked with developing scenarios for the future. The experts, led by Lieutenant Colonel Thomas Will, analyzed the consequences of a situation of "peak oil" for Germany's foreign policy. "Peak oil" refers to a situation in which global oil reserves pass their zenith and begin gradually to decline. According to the report, there was "some probability that peak oil will occur around the year 2010 and that the impact on security is expected to be felt 15 to 30 years later."[21] This new situation would strengthen the position of the oil-exporting countries, and states dependent on oil imports would, according to the authors, be forced to "show more pragmatism toward oil-producing states in their foreign policy." The article quoted some interesting examples of this "pragmatism":

> For example: Germany would have to be more flexible in relation toward Russia's foreign policy objectives. It would also have to show more restraint in its foreign policy toward Israel, to avoid alienating Arab oil-producing nations. Unconditional support for Israel and its right to exist is currently a cornerstone of German foreign policy. The relationship with Russia, in particular, is of fundamental importance for German access to oil and gas, the study says. "For Germany, this involves a balancing act between stable and privileged relations with Russia and sensitivities of (Germany's) eastern neighbors." In other words, Germany, if it wants to guarantee its own energy security, should be accommodating in relation to Moscow's foreign policy objectives, even if it means risking damage to its relations with Poland and other Eastern European states.[22]

This report, published in 2010, seems to have lost much of its relevance—due to the shale gas revolution which, in coming years, will increasingly challenge Russia's prominent position as Germany's energy provider. However, it is telling that a think tank of the Bundeswehr was anticipating a situation in which the German government should be more accommodating in relation to Moscow's foreign policy objectives. In this case, the *shtokmanization* would no longer have been restricted to (parts of) the German business community, but it would have directly affected the policies of the government in Berlin—a situation of self-inflicted dependence which would have come close to what was called "Finlandization" during the Cold War.

Apart from the political risks, there must also be mentioned the risks for the *ethical* business climate in Germany, and—consequently—in the EU as a whole. Russia is one of the most corrupt countries in the world. According to Transparency International, in 2006 it occupied the 121st place on the Corruption Perceptions Index out of a total of 178 countries, a place it shared with Rwanda and Swaziland. Its ranking even *deteriorated* between 2006 and 2010: by 2010 it occupied 154th place.[23] In July 2008 the Munich court of first instance sentenced former Siemens director Reinhard Siekaczek to two years' imprisonment and a fine of €108,000. The writing was on the wall. Siekaczek had been charged with, between June 2002 and September 2004, forty-nine cases of channeling payments of altogether close to €50 million through an "impenetrable web of fake companies."[24] The money served to finance bribe-based transactions. The Siemens case was rather unique. This is not because paying bribes by German companies must be considered a rare phenomenon, but because

> criminal liability of companies . . . is, especially in Germany, traditionally faced with reservations of principle. It is considered incompatible with the principle that punishment presupposes guilt, but corporate entities are said to be not capable of criminal responsibility like natural persons. From this however does not follow that there is no criminal responsibility of companies. . . . German legislation refused for many years to follow the example of almost all neighbouring European countries and, in doing so, bases itself on dogmatic-theological arguments which leave it open whose interests are therewith eventually protected. [25]

THE IMPACT OF GERMANY'S PRO-RUSSIAN STANCE ON ITS RELATIONS WITH ITS WESTERN PARTNERS

The question that emerges from this is: What is the risk that Germany's policies will be influenced by the leaders of the Kremlin to such an extent that Germany may no longer be considered a reliable partner—not only for the United States, but also for its neighbors in Eastern Europe, and, more generally, for the other member states of the European Union? Four areas are of particular concern:

1. the relationship with the United States
2. the relationship with NATO
3. the relationship with the new EU member states in Central and Eastern Europe
4. the relationship with the other EU member states

AN INCREASINGLY STRAINED GERMAN-US RELATIONSHIP?

German-American relations reached a historical postwar low under Chancellor Gerhard Schröder, who not only opposed the war in Iraq but also gave an anti-American edge to the German election campaigns of 2002 and 2005. Schröder's (Social-Democratic) minister of defense, Peter Struck, even went so far as to plead for an attitude of "equidistance" between Moscow and Washington, an unprecedented novum in the postwar US-German relationship. [26] Schröder continued the "Russia first" approach of his predecessor, Helmut Kohl. Not only did he strongly personalize German-Russian relations, making these relations interest driven rather than value driven, but he also concentrated government's policy on Russia in the chancellor's office, leaving his foreign minister Joschka Fischer (Green Party) to handle relations with the other East European countries. [27] This dual approach continued under his successor, Angela Merkel, but this time the roles between the chancellor and the foreign minister were inverted. The pro-Atlantic Merkel mended fences with the United States, while Frank-Walter Steinmeier, who had become foreign minister in the Great Coalition under pressure from his former boss Gerhard Schröder, became Moscow's favorite interlocutor. Steinmeier's critical stance vis-à-vis the United States led on several occasions to head-on collisions with Condoleezza Rice and US Vice President Dick Cheney.[28] Although the election of Barack Obama led to an improvement in German-US relations, there remained a number of caveats. The improved German-US relationship was very much linked to the person of Chancellor Angela Merkel and her Christian Democratic Party. But the opposition could still tap into a strong groundswell of anti-Americanism in Germany, especially in the former GDR, a territory where—without interruption—the United States has been the "official enemy" from 1933 through 1989.[29]

GERMANY AND NATO

The weak spot where this popular anti-Americanism could erupt and have a direct impact on German politics is NATO. In the past two decades the German attitude towards NATO has undergone important changes. Germany, together with Britain, used to be one of the most trustworthy US allies in Europe. This unconditional support for NATO was in the direct interest of Germany, which was situated on the front line of the East-West conflict with 200,000 US troops stationed on its soil. After reunification Germany's role changed from being mainly a security *receiver* into that of a security *provider*. It was a role for which Germany was less prepared and which it was also less willing to play. On a number of occasions the US administration expressed its dissatisfaction with Germany's low defense expenditure and its reluctance to take on battle duties in the war in Afghanistan. With the reintegration of France into the military organization of NATO, one could witness a curious inversion of roles. France, the former enfant terrible of the alliance, was making a glorious comeback as a trustworthy US ally,[30] while Germany, the former *Musterknabe* (model boy) of NATO, had developed a tendency to openly oppose US policies.

At the Bucharest NATO summit in April 2008, Germany (together with France) opposed a US proposal to give both Ukraine and Georgia Membership Action Plans (MAPs) as a preparation for full NATO membership. This refusal had a direct negative impact on the situation in the two MAP candidate countries. According to a Russian expert, "Were the two Western European states to support NATO membership for Ukraine and Georgia, it would have taken longer for the colored revolutions to run out of steam."[31] An even more serious controversy between Germany and the United States took place prior to the NATO foreign ministers' meeting in December 2008, when US secretary of state Condoleezza Rice—knowing that the MAPs for Ukraine and Georgia had no chance of being accepted by France and Germany— announced that the United States would withdraw the MAP proposals. Germany, suspicious that Washington wanted to let Georgia enter NATO without a MAP, put pressure on the United States to reaffirm that a MAP was a *necessary* step for entry. Such direct opposition to the United States by a German government led by a Christian Democrat chancellor was unexpected and quite new. According to Mikhail Margelov, chairman of the foreign affairs committee in the Russian Federation Council (upper house), Germany was Russia's "biggest helper" in its successful attempt to block the eastward enlargement of NATO.[32] The diverging views on the necessity for NATO enlargement and a more global role for NATO did not augur well for the future of German-US and German-NATO relations. According to two US analysts, the Obama administration was "unlikely to be able to restore U.S.-German cooperation to its previous levels anytime soon. For the first time in more than a generation, seismic geopolitical shifts—a restive Russia, a stalling EU and an over-stretched America—have begun to change, perhaps fundamentally, the way America's German ally looks at itself and its role on the wider transatlantic stage."[33] George Friedman, chairman of Stratfor, provided geostrategic reasons for German reticence:

> If Germany were to join those who call for NATO expansion, the first step toward a confrontation with Russia would have been taken. The second step would be guaranteeing the security of the Baltics and Poland. America would make the speeches, and Germans would man the line. After spending most of the last century fighting or preparing to fight the Russians, the Germans looked around at the condition of their allies and opted out.[34]

Friedman, however, seemed to forget that Germany, as a member of NATO, is bound by article 5 of the Washington Treaty, and is, as such, already expected to guarantee the security of the Baltic countries and Poland—together with the other members of NATO. It cannot opt out of that obligation without leaving NATO.

GERMANY AND THE NEW EU MEMBER STATES

Any loosening of Germany's *Westbindung* and further rapprochement to Russia will lead to growing concern in the neighboring countries to the east. The populations of Poland, the Baltic states, the Czech Republic, and Slovakia all have deep-seated memories of the traumatic experiences of the 1930s. The German-Polish relationship, in particular, is still not completely normalized. While, on the one hand, the Poles still feel resentment towards Germany, there exists, on the other hand, in Germany a specific kind of xenophobia directed at Poles, for which Germans even have a special word: *Polenfeindlichkeit* (animosity to Poles). This is telling, because no such word exists to express hatred for other neighbors. Anti-Polish feelings are especially strong in the eastern part of Germany. In a study by the University of Potsdam conducted among secondary school pupils living in Brandenburg's border region with Poland, one third express negative feelings towards Poles, and 64 percent say that they feel uneasy in the presence of Poles.[35] The strained relations between Germans and Poles is explicit also in opinion polls conducted in 1996 in which Americans were twice as much prepared to defend Poland against an attack by Russia compared with Germans (Germany, 30 percent; United States, 61 percent).[36] During the Soviet occupation, the mutual animosity between Poles and (East) Germans was stimulated by Moscow in a policy of divide and rule, used to discipline the unruly Poles. Former Polish minister of foreign affairs, Stefan Meller, states that

> in the year 1956 a certain game was played out by East Germany and Moscow. . . . It was the suggestion of taking Szczecin away, returning Szczecin to Germany (to Communist Germany). Moscow had never denied this idea, Gomułka had therefore to be very decisive. That is an additional ground for suspicion, which enabled the Russians to consider the Oder-Neisse frontier as a certain guarantee for (Polish) submissiveness, and at the same time as an argument that could be utilized for great political manipulation.[37]

Anti-Polish feelings, however, were not confined to East Germany: they were equally present in West Germany. Former foreign minister Joschka Fischer, for instance, says that

> Animosity toward Poles in Germany reaches farther back than the time of Hitler's fascism. My home country, the Ruhr area, became after the foundation of the German Reich in 1871 an immigration country for Polish miners, the "Ruhr Poles." So-called Polish quarters developed; in several towns half of the inhabitants were of Polish origin. After originally being treated with tolerance, they were considered more and more as a source of danger by the authorities, [and] during World War I it ended in a ban of all Polish associations.[38]

It is not surprising, therefore, that a raw nerve was touched in Poland when Germany and Russia announced their plans for the Nord Stream gas pipeline under the Baltic Sea that would circumvent Polish territory. It was considered by the Poles as an overtly hostile project. The German-Russian rapprochement also explained the Polish and Czech willingness to install on their territory ten missile interceptors and a radar system of the American ballistic missile defense, despite Russian threats to deploy Iskander missiles in Kaliningrad. For them the American military presence on their soil meant an extra security guarantee, and they did not hide their disappointment when President Obama changed the project.

During the coalition government of the CDU/CSU with the liberal FDP that was installed in the autumn of 2009, however, things seemed to change. The FDP foreign minister, Guido Westerwelle, whose portfolio included the East European countries, seemed willing to rebalance Germany's *Ostpolitik* in favor of its direct neighbors. "Germany is now more sceptical about Russia and more focused on its neighbours," wrote *The Economist*. "One reason is business. The Czech Republic buys more German exports than Russia. Add Poland, Slovakia and Hungary, and Central Europe counts for nearly a tenth of Germany's foreign trade. Exports in the first half of 2010 were €41 billion ($56 billion), against only €11 billion to Russia; imports were €40 billion, against €15 billion from Russia (including energy)."[39] However, East Europeans would soon be in for an unpleasant surprise when, on February 9, 2011, Klaus Eberhardt, chairman of Rheinmetall—a German defense firm famous for its production of the Leopard tank—signed a contract with the Russian defense minister, Anatoly Serdyukov. Rheinmetall was to build a new-generation combat training center in Russia. Defense cooperation between the two countries was not new. Previously, in April 1993, "defense ministers Volker Ruhe and Pavel Grachev signed a defense cooperation agreement . . . providing for military cooperation between Russia and Germany."[40] The impact of this agreement, however, at that point remained limited. The combat training center, to be located at Mulino near Nizhny Novgorod, was a new departure. It would be the first high-tech facility of this kind in Russia, using the latest state-of-the-art equipment to simulate realistic battlefield conditions. The project, estimated at 280 million euros, could train thirty thousand troops a year. It would enable the Russian army to shorten and improve the training process, to evaluate more effectively the competences of individual soldiers, and to cut expenses substantially. According to Igor Korotchenko, chief editor of *Natsionalnaya Oborona* (*National Defense*), the center would give Russian forces access to best-practice German training methods.[41] Polish commentators expressed their concern. "The nature of this co-operation is not strictly commercial," writes Andrzej Wilk, a Polish security analyst, "as progress in the implementation of the project to construct the centre is made, co-operation is being intensified between the Russian armed forces and the German army (they signed a memorandum of co-operation in the training of officers and non-commissioned officers in February this year [2011])."[42] Wilk adds that "the German-Russian co-operation on the building of the combat training centre has never been an issue discussed in the press. In Germany this is a taboo subject."[43] Why this project was a taboo subject one can only guess. One of the main reasons might be to silence criticism of Germany's new NATO allies, who are directly affected by the German-Russian military honeymoon. This is also the opinion of Jakub Grygiel, who writes:

> However one looks at this, the German-built center inevitably will enhance the fighting capabilities of the Russian army, increasing the risks to neighboring countries such as Georgia and Ukraine, as well as to the most exposed eastern NATO members, notably Poland and the Baltic states. But such assessments of the security impact of a transfer of German know-how to Moscow didn't seem to play a role in Germany's decision-making process, which seemed to focus instead on the economic benefits and the potential for future deals. [44]

Rheinmetall chief Klaus Eberhardt emphasized that the training center was built "with the permission of the federal government." [45] He enthusiastically called Russia a "market of the future" and stated his intention to export complete weapon systems to Moscow. This intention did not take long to materialize. By the end of 2012, Rheinmetall armored vehicles were already being tested in Russia. [46] This newly emerging German-Russian military cooperation gives rise to a feeling of déjà vu. Between 1926 and 1932, Rheinmetall-Borsig was among the German defense companies which actively participated in a secret project for German-Soviet military cooperation that started after the signing of the Rapallo Treaty in 1922. With the help of Soviet Russia, Germany was able to circumvent the restrictions imposed on it by the Versailles Treaty, training its troops and testing its tanks (called "tractors" in official documents) near Kazan in the Soviet Union. [47] Condoleezza Rice writes:

> This marriage of convenience existed since the Treaty of Rapallo in 1922. The Germans needed a place to rearm out of the view of the signatories to the Treaty of Versailles and the Soviets needed foreign military assistance. The collaboration helped the Soviets through joint production of military equipment and through German instructors sent to the Soviet Union who taught tactics and training. The Soviets are virtually silent on how extensive the collaboration was, but its most important period seems to have been in the mid-1920s. Agreements were reached on the manufacture of German aircraft (at an annual rate of three hundred, with the Soviets receiving sixty). The plant was run by German technicians with Russian raw materials and laborers. By 1923–1924 cooperation had extended to include German technical courses for Soviet airmen and to the service of German officers on the Red Army staff. [48]

One might well wonder: Is history repeating itself today? After the annexation of the Crimea in March 2014 and the continuing Russian aggression in eastern Ukraine, the Molina project was suspended as part of the EU sanctions regime. However, this did not mean that the project was definitively off the table. Hit by the sanctions regime, the Kremlin reacted by raising the stakes—apparently with success. In March 2014 Siemens boss Joe Kaeser met with Putin in Moscow.[49] On April 14, 2014—one month after the annexation of Crimea—Rüdiger Grube, the CEO of the German railway company Deutsche Bahn, traveled to Paris to discuss with his counterpart from the Russian Railways, Vladimir Yakunin, a contract to build a high-speed railway, 800 kilometers in length, connecting Moscow with Kazan. The consortium for the contract, worth 20 billion euros, consisted of Deutsche Bahn, Siemens, Deutsche Bank, and the French railway company SNCF.[50] "Business as usual" was also the motto for the German-Russian Chamber of Foreign Trade, which, on October 6, 2014, organized a seminar in Moscow on "Practical Aspects of Doing Business in Crimea," where participants were informed on subjects such as "Legal Restructuring of Doing Business in Crimea—Paying Attention to Company Law, Labor Law, and Tax Law."[51]

IS GERMANY COOLING TOWARDS FRANCE AND THE EU?

Another equally pressing question was what the impact would be of a German-Russian rapprochement on Berlin's relationship with France. It is interesting that right from the beginning, this rapprochement was viewed positively in Paris. In an article on the "dynamic of the German-Russian relationship," published in *Le Monde* in December 2001, the paper writes: "What if Russia, thanks to Germany, comes closer to the European Union?"[52] Is it not positive, asks the paper, that Germany could serve "as a stepping stone for Russia's attachment to Europe?" However, it warns, "it is not sure . . . that the new trust accorded to Russia is completely justified."[53] Interestingly, Russia's strategy of building a strategic triangle in Europe with the aim to weaken the transatlantic relationship was viewed here from an opposite—European—perspective, namely to attach Russia to Europe. Why should Paris be opposed to that? However, soon the Franco-German relationship would be challenged by the flourishing German-Russian "rapprochement through economic interlocking."

The Franco-German friendship is the cornerstone of the European Union. Every time these two countries have worked in tandem, the European project has progressed. It is no secret, however, that the close cooperation that existed under the duos of de Gaulle-Adenauer, Giscard-Schmidt, and Mitterrand-Kohl gave way to a more distant relationship under Merkel and Sarkozy. This even led to speculations that "the Franco-German couple is on the verge of divorce."[54] This was not only a question of the "chemistry" between the two leaders, it was—even more so—an expression of underlying structural differences of interest between both countries, differences that in recent years have only grown. The French tendency to build "national champions" and to block German companies from taking over French companies—which is partly inspired by a fear of German economic hegemony—

has on some occasions led to a dangerous tit-for-tat from which, apparently, Russia is profiting.

Germany was, for instance, not satisfied with the way in which the French annexed one of Germany's industrial champions, Hoechst, to create the drug giant Sanofi-Aventis. Nor did the Germans appreciate how Sarkozy, as a finance minister, blocked Siemens from a takeover of French Alstom. Another example of mutual French-German disaffection was the refusal of France to give Siemens a direct stake in Areva, the state-controlled nuclear group, with which it was co-operating in a joint venture to build nuclear reactors. In February 2009 Siemens gave notice that it intended to sell its 34 percent holding in the joint venture. Shortly afterwards, Siemens announced that it had made an agreement with the Russian state company Rosatom to design, build, and operate nuclear power plants. This move created a serious competitor for Areva on a growing global market in which four thousand nuclear power plants are planned by 2030 with an investment volume of €1 trillion.[55] The German initiative took the French totally by surprise. The danger of cooling Franco-German relations and warming Russian-German relations for the European project was that Germany, satisfied with the existence of the EU as a market for its exports, will lose its interest in a further political integration of the EU. A Germany that is losing its interest in the EU and is on the way of becoming a reticent ally in NATO could be tempted to enter into some Rapallo-like security arrangements with Russia.[56]

The present psychological climate in Germany, especially in its eastern part, is characterized by a simultaneous presence in the population of a deep-seated anti-Americanism and an often unconditional Russophilia. Both combine to influence the way in which Germans look at security problems. Anti-Americanism and Russophilia are the two lenses through which the security environment is viewed. Clearly, if one lens is too rosy and the other too dark, this will lead to a disfigured representation of the security environment. This seems, indeed, to be the case. In Germany there exists a tendency to have too negative a view of American security proposals and too positive a view of Russian initiatives in this field. This tendency exists not only amongst the wider population but also amongst the political elite.

This mental framework is not new. In the 1970s already existed a broad peace movement in Germany that was more concerned with Western reactions to the deployment of Russian SS-20 missiles than with the origin of the threat.[57] When after German reunification the archives of the Stasi, the East German secret service, were opened, it was revealed that the Stasi had not only infiltrated the West German peace movement on a massive scale but had even formulated its slogans. The fall of the Berlin Wall and the reunification of the two Germanies led in West Germany to a wave of "Gorbymania." The Soviet leader Mikhail Gorbachev acquired the status of an idol: a mixture of peace apostle and Russian Bismarck, who personally had made the second unification of Germany possible. Suddenly one seemed to have forgotten that for more than forty years, Soviet Russia had installed an oppressive regime in the eastern part of Germany, and it seemed equally to have receded into the German subconscious that it had been the United States that, for the first time in German history, had installed a stable democracy in Germany's western part and rescued West Berlin from annexation by the communist regime.

In the past decade one has been able to observe a growing tendency in Germany to disapprove of US security initiatives and to approve of Russian initiatives in this field. An example of this was the frequently harsh criticism in Germany of the American Ballistic Missile Defense project, originally a project of ten(!) missiles to be stationed in Poland with a radar system in the Czech Republic, tasked with the interception of nuclear ballistic missiles, eventually launched by Iran. This project had nothing to do with Russia's nuclear arsenal. If it had been conceived by some Dr. Strangelove at the Pentagon (as many Germans seemed to believe) to intercept a Russian attack, one could characterize the project not only as totally idiotic but also as ineffective and a huge waste of money, this for four reasons that are obvious to any military expert—Russian experts included:[58] first, because this very modest system would be confronted by an overwhelming number of Russian missiles; second, because many alternative launch trajectories are available (the shortest way for Russia to attack the United States is not via Western Europe but via the North Pole); third, because Russia has a panoply of different launching platforms at its disposal (Russian submarines could always launch an attack from near the American coast); and fourth, because different launching methods are also available (for instance, the utilization of cruise missiles that closely follow the earth's surface and cannot be targeted by anti-ballistic missiles). The Russian propaganda offensive against the American ballistic missile system was obviously aimed at obtaining concessions in other, not directly related fields. In Germany, however, it was taken at face value. It was no surprise that Putin's friend Gerhard Schröder took the lead in the attacks. On March 11, 2007, the German weekly *Der Spiegel* published an article under the title "Schröder Lashes Out at Bush's Antimissile Defense."[59] Six months later it was former chancellor Helmut Schmidt's turn to give an interview on the same subject. The title of the interview was less aggressive, but its message was similar: "Former Chancellor Schmidt Speaks Out against the U.S. Anti-missile Defense."[60]

Helmut Schmidt also wrote an article, critical of the U.S., together with former German President Richard von Weizsäcker, former Foreign Minister Dietrich Genscher, and Egon Bahr, the architect of Willy Brandt's Ostpolitik, in the *Frankfurter Allgemeine Zeitung* on January 9, 2009, entitled "For a nuclear-arms free world."[61] In this article, the four éminences grises of German politics wrote that stability in Europe "would be threatened for the first time (since 1990) by the American desire to deploy missiles with a supporting radar system on extraterritorial bases on NATO's eastern border in Poland and the Czech Republic." Please note that this article appeared in January 2009—exactly five months after the Russian invasion and dismemberment of Georgia. To claim that stability in Europe would be threatened *for the first time* by the deployment of the BMD—a defense system not directed against Russian missiles—and to say nothing about the Russian aggression at Europe's border that took place only a few months earlier, shows a surprising blind spot on the part of the authors.

RUSSOPHILIA AND GERMANY'S LOOSENING TIES TO THE WEST

It is not only foreign observers who fear that the emergence of an informal Moscow-Berlin axis constitutes an imminent danger for European and transatlantic unity. This fear is also shared by German analysts. Jan Techau, in his position of director of the Alfred von Oppenheim-Centre for European Policy Studies at the DGAP (German Council on Foreign Relations), writes, for instance,

> In recent years, strong German relations with Russia have been a concern for Eastern European countries, the EU and the United States. . . . In Washington, Germany has recently been perceived as a Russian "force-multiplier" on issues ranging from energy policy to missile defense to Iran. . . . The issue is not the perceived closeness to Russia, which clearly has its limits. The worrisome part is Germany's loosening ties to the West. In both cornerstones of its Western orientation, NATO and the EU, Germany's distancing is perceived as a major problem. . . . The coziness with Russia is not a problem per se. But it could become a problem if the counterweight, Germany's strong Western ties, is being compromised. . . . History has taught us that there can never be a German equidistance between Russia and its Western allies. [62]

According to Beate Neuss, there exists "a moralizing, mostly idealistic and sometimes irrational view of international politics amongst sections of the (German) elite and population."[63] Unfortunately, this moralizing attitude increasingly concerns Germany's Western allies while a blind eye was turned to the ugly reality in Russia. The worrisome loosening of ties to the West, to which Jan Techau referred, seemed to become a reality on March 17, 2011, when Germany did not support the French-British resolution no. 1973 in the Security Council to authorize a no-fly zone over Libya to stop the killing of civilians by Khadafi's army, thereby taking a stance against the United States and its most important EU allies. The *Süddeutsche Zeitung* wrote: "Now Germany, under the charge of Merkel and Westerwelle, has voted against the Americans, British and French, and with the Chinese, Russians, Brazilians, and Indians—against its most important Western allies and on the side of dictators, autocrats and two far democracies. Why?"[64] Former foreign minister Joschka Fischer called it a "scandalous mistake."[65] As one might have expected, the most enthusiastic supporter of the government's policy was Die Linke, the successor organization to the former East German Communist Party and, not surprisingly, Westerwelle's pro-Russian predecessor Frank-Walter Steinmeier. A feeling of malaise, however, was palpable among Germany's Western allies. "In the Foreign Ministries everyone is wondering," wrote *Le Monde*. "For the first time in its history the Federal Republic is taking a different stance from all its traditional partners, the United States, France and the United Kingdom, and—while voting for an abstention—is adopting the same position as Russia, China, Brazil, and India." The paper sadly concluded: "The image of Germany is tarnished"[66]

Is Berlin again seeking a German *Sonderweg*: a specifically "German" path, like Russia, which seems to have already elected for such an outsider position? It is too early to judge. After the return of Putin to the Kremlin in May 2012 and the subsequent introduction in Russia of a series of repressive laws, the climate in Germany seemed to change. Andreas Schockenhoff, deputy fraction leader of the CDU-CSU fraction in the Bundestag and Germany's commissioner for the coordination of German-Russian civil society, was the coauthor of a draft resolution in the Bundestag which formulated a strong criticism of these measures. The resolution was adopted on November 9, 2012. The *Economist* wrote in a comment that "Germany is increasingly prepared to be tough with Vladimir Putin."[67] The argument of Schröder and Steinmeier that the economic modernization of Russia would also lead to a political modernization seemed to be losing its powers of persuasion. Except, of course, for seasoned Russophiles, such as the analyst Alexander Rahr, who changed his job in the DGAP, Germany's leading foreign policy think tank, for a job in the oil and gas concern Wintershall that has a direct relationship with the Kremlin. Rahr continued to believe that Germany "must not lose patience, must not lose Russia," and that *Wandel durch Handel* (change through trade) is a better approach.[68] The Bundestag resolution—dubbed by Le Monde "a real requisitory"[69]—demanded that the government insist in its consultations with Moscow on the development of democracy and the rule of law. It was significant that the fractions of the SPD and Die Linke did not support the resolution and chose to abstain. Some analysts considered this resolution as an important policy shift. Lilia Shevtsova of the Moscow office of the Carnegie Endowment, for instance, writes: "The very fact that the debate took place at all is of great significance and marks a shift in Germany's Russia policy. . . . This marks the first serious attempt to free Germany from the suffocating relationship with the Kremlin."[70] Dmitri Trenin, her director, however, who is closer to the Kremlin, expressed his concern. "The special relationship, which has already existed for several decades between

Berlin and Moscow (before, as well as, in particular, after German reunification), underwent from the German side an important erosion. If this continues, there is a danger that also from the Russian side such an erosion takes place. As a result the relationship between Russia and Germany, which is the most important foundation for the stability and cooperation in Europe, can disintegrate and the international consequences of this will be serious."[71]

Is the German government, exasperated by Putin's heavy-handed methods, returning to a values-based foreign policy? A bit, but not quite. It became clear that the power of the German Russia lobby was still intact when, in March 2013, the German government suddenly asked for EU visa liberalization for so-called service passport holders.[72] This would grant Russian government officials—including officials of the military and the secret services—EU visa freedom, but not ordinary Russians. Guido Westerwelle, the German foreign minister, said: "If the visa liberalization for service passports happens, it would be nice, welcomed progress. It is a very important topic to them. Putin brings it up all the time, so it is important for us too."[73] Why a topic, brought up all the time by Putin, should be "important for us too"—apart from pleasing the Kremlin—was not explained. The German proposal was heavily criticized. It came at a period during which the Russian government was accumulating repressive measures against the opposition, and the US Congress had just adopted the Magnitsky Act, prohibiting entrance to the United States of Russian officials who were involved in the death of the lawyer Sergey Magnitsky. "Arguably," wrote Kadri Liik, "granting visa-free travel for service passport holders was a bad policy from the beginning, as it effectively would have given the Kremlin the right to decide who got it. The EU should seek to retain that right for itself."[74]

Despite German criticism of Russia, it cannot be denied that in recent years Germany's attachment to the Western bloc has been weakened, and it is a matter for concern that Eurosceptic and pro-Russian positions are no longer confined to the fringes of the political spectrum, but—with the advent of the *Alternative für Deutschland*—have reached the democratic center. After the parliamentary elections of September 2013, the Russia-friendly SPD made a comeback, and the new coalition government of the CDU/CSU and the SPD was expected to be more Kremlin-friendly than the former government. The Foreign Office has a reputation for being "realist" in its relations with Russia. The return of Frank-Walter Steinmeier as Germany's foreign minister certainly pleased the Kremlin. Gernot Erler, the SPD deputy fraction leader, who regretted that "the West, in the Syria tragedy, attributes to Moscow the role of bad guy," immediately warned that the "Russia bashing" should stop.[75] After Russia's annexation of the Crimea in March 2014 and the Russian aggression in east Ukraine, Germany was one of the countries that were against applying harsh sanctions. Former foreign minister Joschka Fischer wrote that apparently, Moscow thinks to have a chance of influencing Europe's attitude via Berlin and a vacillating German public opinion. It was, therefore, not fortuitous that Russian president Putin, in his annexation speech on the "return" of Crimea to Russia, explicitly mentioned Germany and the positive Russian attitude toward German reunification. . . . Clearly, in Moscow one has not given up the hope that Germany's anchorage in the West . . . will not prove so stable as it was previously thought. [76]

The question formulated by Robert D. Kaplan: "Will a debellicized Germany partly succumb to Russian influence, leading to a somewhat Finlandized Eastern Europe and an even more hollow North Atlantic Treaty Organization? Or will Germany subtly stand up to Russia . . .?" [77] is, therefore, still fully on the table.

NOTES

1. Cf. Nikolas K. Gvosdev and Christopher Marsh, *Russian Foreign Policy: Interests, Vectors, and Sectors* (Los Angeles: CQ Press, 2014), 255.

2. In the same period, German exports to France, the Benelux countries, Austria, Poland, and China *decreased*. (Cf. Statistisches Bundesamt Deutschland, "Deutsche Export Performance steigt seit dem Jahre 2000 wieder an," Pressemitteilung no. 437 (October 17, 2005).)

3. *Außenhandel 2007: Rangfolge der Handelspartner im Außenhandel der Bundesrepublik Deutschland*, Statistisches Bundesamt, Wiesbaden (November 14, 2008).

4. These figures, however, should be put in perspective. Imports as well as exports between Germany and Russia in 2007 did, for instance, not even represent *half* the value of the imports and exports between Germany and the Netherlands (another gas exporter to Germany). However, Russia remains a huge *potential growth market* for Germany.

5. Data from the Statistisches Bundesamt Deutschland, Statistiken Aussenhandel 2010. In 2010 Russia still ranked number ten on the list of countries exporting to Germany, but it went down one place—ranking number thirteen—on the list of countries importing from Germany.

6. Data from the Statistisches Bundesamt Deutschland, Statistiken Aussenhandel 2011. In 2011, Russia went up two places and ranked number eleven on the list of countries importing from Germany, preceded by Poland at place number ten. It ranked number seven on the list of countries exporting to Germany.

7. Ostausschuss der Deutschen Wirtschaft, "Neue Impulse für eine Deutsch-Russische Wirtschaftspartnerschaft," Pressemitteilung 24/08, November 11, 2008, http://www.ost-ausschuss.de/pdfs/11_11_2008_pm_mittelstandskonferenz.pdf.

8. Cf. Artur Ciechanowicz, Anna Kwiatkowska-Drożdż, and Witold Rodkiewicz, "Merkel and Putin's Consultation: The Economy First of All," *Centre for Eastern Studies* (November 21, 2012).

9. This percentage has gone down to 3.5 percent since the implementation of a deal made on October 2, 2008, on the participation of the two German energy companies in gas production in the Siberian field of Yuzhno-Russkoye. E.ON Ruhrgas (as well as BASF Wintershall) acquired a 25 percent stake minus one share. In return, Gazprom received from E.ON Ruhrgas a package of its own shares that totals 3 percent.

10. Steinmeier did not want to limit this interlocking (*Verflechtung*) to economic cooperation. It should, according to him, have a spillover into the *political field*. He writes, "Therefore we, Germans, should make an effort, so that in the future also we will remain an important and indispensable partner for Russia. For this reason I choose interlocking and not only an economic one." (Frank-Walter Steinmeier, *Mein Deutschland: Wofür ich stehe* (Munich: C. Bertelsmann, 2009), 182.)

11. The two German companies each got 20 percent, and the Dutch Gasunie 9 percent. In January 2009 Gazprom's CEO, Aleksey Miller, invited the French energy company GdF Suez to become a new partner in the project. He declared: "Gazprom does however stress that it does not intend to decrease its 51-percent stake in the project. That leaves the issue to the other partners who will have to reduce their respective 20 percent and nine percent shares." Miller's generosity was deceptive. He was offering GdF Suez a cigar from his partners' cigar box. (Cf. "Nord Stream Partnership Might Expand," Investmarket (January 6, 2009), available at http://eng.investmarket.ru/NewsAM/NewsAMShow.asp?ID=514799.) On March 1, 2010, GdF Suez joined the Nord Stream consortium, acquiring a 9 percent stake (4.5 percent each from Wintershall and E.ON Ruhrgas).

12. Cf. Jürgen Roth, *Gazprom: Das unheimliche Imperium* (Frankfurt am Main: Westend Verlag, 2012), 162.

13. Cf. Edward Lucas, *The New Cold War: Putin's Russia and the Threat to the West* (New York and Houndmills: Palgrave Macmillan, 2008), 169.

14. Conal Walsh, "Gerhard and Vladimir—Is It Hot Air or Gas?" *The Observer* (December 12, 2004).

15. Pavel K. Baev, "Disentangling the Moscow-Berlin-Axis: Follow the Money." *Eurasia Daily Monitor* 2, no. 148 (August 1, 2005).

16. Carter Dougherty, "Commerzbank Linked to Russia Money-Laundering Inquiry," *International Herald Tribune* (July 26, 2005).

17. According to Vladimir Kovalev, Putin needs to clarify "the business with the company SPAG that was mentioned by German authorities in relation to cases of money laundering and in which Putin allegedly worked as a consultant, as well as the most recent development over details of the privatization of Telekominvest. . . . According to the Frankfurter Rundschau, the names of Putin's wife Lyudmila, as well as the Russian communications minister Leonid Reiman, are mentioned in connection with shady deals over the communications company with the involvement of Commerzbank. The bank is currently under scrutiny by German law enforcement agencies investigating the case of money laundering." (Cf. Vladimir Kovalev, "Putin Should Settle Doubts about His Past Conduct," *The Petersburg Times* (July 29, 2000).)

18. Lilia Shevtsova, *Lonely Power: Why Russia Has Failed to Become the West and the West Is Weary of Russia* (Washington, DC, and Moscow: Carnegie Endowment for International Peace, 2010), 111.

19. Quoted in Marshall Goldman, *Oilopoly: Putin, Power, and the Rise of the New Russia* (Oxford: Oneworld, 2008), 205.

20. Robert Amsterdam, "Die SPD lässt sich von Russland erpressen," *Der Stern* (November 20, 2007). The Shtokman field was operated by a joint venture consisting of Gazprom (51 percent), Total (25 percent), and Statoil (24 percent), which in the first decade of this century invested about 12 billion euros. The plan was to liquefy the gas and export it to the United States. However, the shale gas revolution in the United States was undermining its profitability. With the United States no longer available as a future export market, the project had to be suspended—probably for several decades. (Cf. "Gazprom May Shelve Shtokman Project as US Shale Revolution Bites," *RT* (June 3, 2013).)

21. Stefan Schultz, "'Peak Oil' and the German Government: Military Study Warns of a Potentially Drastic Oil Crisis," *Spiegelonline* (September 1, 2010).

22. Schultz, "'Peak Oil.'"

23. Cf. "Corruption Perceptions Index 2010," *Transparency International*, http://www.transparency.org/policy_research/surveys_indices/cpi/2010/results.

24. Cf. Wolfgang Hetzer, "No Punishment for Bribery? When Corruption Is Business as Usual," in *Corruption*, SIAK Scientific Series, Republic of Austria, Sicherheitsakademie of the Ministry of the Interior (Vienna: 2010), 69.

25. Hetzer, "No Punishment for Bribery?" 84.

26. Cf. Hans Stark, *La politique étrangère allemande: entre polarisation et politisation*, Note du Comité d'études des relations franco-allemandes (Cerfa), no. 60, IFRI, Paris (January 2009), 12. In fact, Struck's advocacy signaled that he wanted Germany to copy de Gaulle's policy of equidistance between the Soviet Union and the United States. But even de Gaulle's

"equidistance" between the two superpowers was never really equidistant. In fact, de Gaulle was much closer to its transatlantic ally than he was ready to admit.

27. Cf. Dr. Iris Kempe, *From a European Neighborhood Policy toward a New* Ostpolitik—*The Potential Impact of German Policy*, Policy Analysis No. 3, Center for Applied Policy Research, Munich (May 2006), 6: "German Foreign Ministers had little alternative but to cede eastern policy to the Chancellor's Office while formulating their own agenda beyond the 'Russia first' approach. For example, during his term in office, Joschka Fischer placed a strong focus on conflict management in the Balkans. Other Foreign Office policies, such as an emphasis on developing a new European neighborhood policy, have sought to take a more differentiated approach toward Eastern Europe as a means of counterbalancing the 'Russia first' strategy."

28. After the SPD lost the Bundestag elections in September 2009 and Guido Westerwelle (FDP) became the new German foreign minister, there were signs that Chancellor Merkel was taking back the Russia portfolio, leaving Westerwelle in charge of "the rest" of Eastern Europe—as was the case with Joschka Fischer under Chancellor Schröder. A sign of this was the new emphasis Westerwelle put on the relationship with Poland, which was the first country he visited in his new function, and his wish to revive the *Weimar Triangle*, the summit meetings of Germany, Poland, and France, founded in 1991. (Cf. "Le nouveau chef de la diplomatie allemande veut mettre le cap à l'Est," *Le Monde* (December 30, 2009).)

29. And even *before* 1933, if we take into account US participation in World War I and the co-responsibility of the United States for the Treaty of Versailles that was deeply resented in Germany.

30. On the rapprochement of France to NATO, cf. Marcel H. Van Herpen, "I Say NATO, You Say No NATO," *The National Interest*, no. 95 (May/June 2008). A longer version of this text is available at http://www.cicerofoundation.org/lectures/Marcel_H_Van_Herpen_SARKOZY_FRANCE_AND_NATO.pdf.

31. Andrei P. Tsygankov, "Preserving Influence in a Changing World: Russia's Grand Strategy," *Problems of Post-Communism* 58, no. 1 (March–April 2011).

32. Quoted in Owen Matthews and Stefan Theil, "The New Ostpolitik," *Newsweek International* (August 3, 2009).

33. Cf. Donald K. Bandler and A. Wess Mitchell, "Ich Bin Ein Berliner," *The National Interest online* (January 22, 2009), http://www.nationalinterest.org/Article.aspx?id=20664.

34. Cf. George Friedman, "Why Germany Is Lukewarm about Nato" (October 7, 2008), available at http://www.mercatornet.com/articles/view/why_germany_is_lukewarm_about_nato/.

35. Markus Hess, "Kurzfassung zur Studie 'Perspektiven einer Grenzregion' im Rahmen des gemeinsamen Fördervorhabens Junge Menschen in Grenzregionen der neuen Bundesländer," Institute for Applied Research on Childhood, Youth, and the Family, University of Potsdam, 2002, 15–16, available at http://www.mbjs.brandenburg.de/sixcms/media.php/bb2.a.5813.de/kurzbericht_grenze.pdf.

36. Beate Neuss, "Von Bonn nach Berlin: Gibt es einen Wandel in der außenpolitischen Kultur Deutschlands seit der Einheit?" Konrad-Adenauer-Stiftung, Auslandsbüro Tschechische Republik, Prag (April 21, 2005), 15, available at http://www.kas.de/wf/doc/kas_6366-544-1-30.pdf.

37. "Stefan Meller über die polnisch-russischen Verhältnisse," available at http://www.skubi.net/meller_de.html.

38. Joschka Fischer, "Aus Feinden wurden Nachbarn" (June 6, 2004), available at http://www.michael-cramer.eu/europa/41472.html.

39. "Frau Fix-It," *The Economist* (November 18, 2010).

40. Gvosdev and Marsh, *Russian Foreign Policy*, 255.

41. Quoted in Vladimir Socor, "Made in Germany for Russia's Army," *Eurasia Daily Monitor* 8, no. 31 (February 14, 2011).

42. Andrzej Wilk, "France and Germany Are Establishing a Closer Military Co-Operation with Russia," *Eastweek* (June 29, 2011).

43. Wilk, "France and Germany Are Establishing a Closer Military Co-Operation with Russia."

44. Jakub Grygiel, "Europe: Strategic Drifter," *The National Interest*, no. 126 (July/August 2013), 34.

45. "Rheinmetall will Waffen nach Russland liefern," *Die Welt* (October 27, 2012).

46. "Leopard-Hersteller plant Rüstungsdeals mit Russland—'Nesawissimaja Gaseta,'" *RIA Novosti* (October 30, 2012).

47. "Leichte Traktor—Grosstraktor I/II/III—Neuaufbaufahrzeug PzKpfw V/VI," www.achtungpanzer.com (accessed July 10, 2013).

48. Condoleezza Rice, "The Making of Soviet Strategy," in *Makers of Modern Strategy: From Machiavelli to the Nuclear Age*, ed. Peter Paret (Princeton, NJ: Princeton University Press, 1986), 666.

49. Cf. "How Very Understanding," *The Economist* (May 10, 2014).

50. Konrad Popławski, "Germany Trying for a Lucrative Contract in Russia," *OSW*, Analyses (April 24, 2014).

51. Cf. Veranstaltungsmanagement und Mitgliederservice Deutsch-Russische Auslandshandelskammer, http://russland.ahk.de.

52. Françoise Lazare, "La dynamique des relations germano-russes," *Le Monde* (December 7, 2001).

53. Lazare, "La dynamique des relations germano-russes."

54. Emmanuelle Belohradsky and Odile Benyahia-Kouider, "Le couple franco-allemand est au bord du divorce," *Challenges* (October 10, 2007), available at http://www.challenges.fr/magazine/0096005058/le_couple_francoallemand_est_au_bord_du_divorce.html.

55. Cf. "Siemens Plans Nuclear Cooperation with Russia," *Spiegel Online* (February 25, 2009); and Paul Betts, "Fabled Franco-German Relationship Turns Radioactive," *Financial Times* (March 5, 2009). This estimate predates the Fukushima nuclear disaster of 2011 and, therefore, needs to be revised downwards.

56. The Rapallo Treaty of 1922 between Germany and the Soviet Union led to a secret cooperation between the Reichswehr and the Red Army. General Von Seeckt, the head of the German armed forces, saw the treaty as the start of a German-Russian axis that would lead to the complete extinction of Poland. (Cf. Detlev J. K. Peukert, *The Weimar Republic: The Crisis of Classical Modernity* (New York: Hill and Wang, 1993), 59 and 203.)

57. It is telling that in 1989, Dutch defense minister Frits Bolkestein, talking about the peace movement in the Netherlands, which was as active as its counterpart in Germany, said: "At the moment Dutch opinion is, I would say, much more realistic in matters appertaining to international affairs and East-West relations than is German public opinion. In Germany, things are different." (Cf. Michael Richard Daniell Foot, *Holland at War against Hitler* (London: Routledge, 1990), 195.)

58. Bobo Lo (*Vladimir Putin and the Evolution of Russian Foreign Policy*, The Royal Institute of International Affairs (London: Blackwell, 2003) reports that "my (Russian) MFA sources consistently dismissed the possibility that American deployment of a national missile defence system could materially affect the Russia-US strategic balance" (154). Lo writes that despite Russia's vociferous opposition to American strategic missile defense plans, "there was never much credence attached to the notion that these might, in time, nullify Russian retaliatory strike capabilities"(88).

59. "Schröder geißelt Bushs Raketenabwehr," *Der Spiegel* (March 11, 2007).

60. Matthias Schepp, "Altkanzler Schmidt spricht sich gegen US-Raketenabwehr aus," *Der Spiegel* (September 25, 2007). In this same interview, Schmidt "noted that since the Soviet invasion of Afghanistan neither Gorbachev, nor Yeltsin or Putin had invaded a foreign territory. Nevertheless some Americans and also, to a certain degree, NATO, remained suspicious." One year later the Russian army would invade the sovereign state of Georgia, which was followed, in 2014, by the annexation of the Crimea and the invasion of Eastern Ukraine.

61. Helmut Schmidt, Richard von Weizsäcker, Egon Bahr, Hans-Dietrich Genscher, "Für eine atomwaffenfreie Welt," *Frankfurter Allgemeine Zeitung* (January 9, 2009).

62. Jan Techau, "Germany's Eastern Temptation," *Central Europe Digest*, Center for European Policy Analysis (September 1, 2009), available at http://www.cepa.org/ced/view.aspx?record_id=198&printview=1.

63. Beate Neuss, "Von Bonn nach Berlin," 4.

64. Daniel Brössler, "Deutschland an der Seite von Diktatoren," *Süddeutsche Zeitung* (March 19, 2011).

65. Joschka Fischer, "Deutsche Außenpolitik—Eine Farce," *Süddeutsche Zeitung* (March 22, 2011).

66. Frédéric Lemaître and Marion Van Renterghem, "Le malaise allemand," *Le Monde* (April 3–4, 2011).

67. "The Shocking Mr Schockenhoff," *The Economist* (November 10, 2012).

68. "The Shocking Mr Schockenhoff."

69. Frédéric Lemaître, "L'Allemagne s'éloigne de la Russie et se rapproche de la Pologne," *Le Monde* (November 18–19, 2012).

70. Lilia Shevtsova and David J. Kramer, "Germany and Russia: The End of Ostpolitik?" *The American Interest* (November 13, 2012).

71. Dmitri Trenin, "Germanii nuzhna novaya politika po otnosheniyu k Rossii," *Moskovskiy Tsentr Karnegi* (November 21, 2013).

72. Valentina Pop, "Germany Wants EU Visa-Free Travel for Russian Officials," *EUobserver* (March 6, 2013).

73. Quoted in Andrew Rettman, "EU and Russia in Visa Talks, despite Magnitsky 'Regret,'" *EUobserver* (March 21, 3013).

74. Kadri Liik, "Regime Change in Russia," Policy Memo, *European Council on Foreign Relations* (May, 2013), 6.

75. Gernot Erler, "Schluss mit dem Russland-Bashing," *Zeit Online* (June 9, 2013).

76. Joschka Fischer, *Scheitert Europa?* (Cologne: Kiepenheuer & Witsch, 2014).

77. Robert D. Kaplan, "The Divided Map of Europe," *The National Interest* 120 (July/August 2012), 24.

Chapter Fifteen

The Kremlin's Conquest of France

Yes, it is Europe, from the Atlantic to the Urals, it is Europe, it is the whole of Europe that will decide the fate of the world.
—Charles de Gaulle, Strasbourg, November 23, 1959

THE RUSSIAN-FRENCH FRIENDSHIP
FROM CHIRAC TO SARKOZY

Apart from Germany, there was another leading European country with which the Kremlin wanted to establish close political and personal ties: France. France was the third pole in Putin's strategic "Berlin-Moscow-Paris Triangle." In Germany, Vladimir Putin had found a soul mate in Gerhard Schröder. However, at the beginning of Putin's presidency the relationship with French President Jacques Chirac was far from cordial. When Chirac visited Putin in Moscow in July 2001, the *Nouvel Observateur* wrote: "As concerns the atmosphere between the two men . . . the relationship does not seem to be very warm."[1] But the US war in Iraq proved to be an unexpected godsend. It permitted Putin not only to strengthen his relationship with German Chancellor Gerhard Schröder but also to forge closer ties with Chirac. The three leaders, opposing the US war plans, presented themselves to the world as the "peace camp." Like Putin, Chirac declared himself to be in favor of a "multipolar world." Both men were convinced that a multipolar world, instead of bringing instability, would foster peace.[2] Chirac's emerging friendship with Putin, who at that time was conducting a war in Chechnya which led to accusations of genocide, was not, in France, appreciated by everybody. The French philosopher André Glucksmann, for instance, criticized the new French-Russian alliance directed against the United States. Glucksmann wrote that Putin's troops "bound Chechen civilians together like

241

bundles of sticks, blew them up with explosives, and threw their remains into the ditch. But despite such barbaric behavior, and despite the murder of an estimated one hundred thousand civilians during the Chechen war, for French president Chirac, 'Russia fascinates, its immense riches sharpen the appetite, its brute, disproportionate use of force inspires respect.'"[3] Indeed, to say that Russia's "brute, disproportionate use of force inspires respect" was a baffling statement for the leader of a Western, democratic country. When Chirac criticized Poland and other East European countries for supporting the United States, he told them they had "missed a good opportunity to shut up." Chirac's rude and disrespectful behavior toward these countries stood in sharp contrast with his plea to treat Moscow "with respect." Alain Besançon, a French historian, comments: "One would have wished that president Chirac should understand that the dominant sentiment of these countries vis-à-vis Russia is not *respect*, but *fear*."[4] He adds that people close to the president had said that he defended "a strategic vision." "It is now my turn to be afraid," writes Besançon. "Is the pro-Russian bias of our foreign policy (after having been pro-Soviet) so ineradicable?"[5]

However, these critics could not spoil the newly emerging French-Russian honeymoon. The cherry on top of the cake of Chirac's friendship with Putin came on September 22, 2006, when Chirac decorated the Russian leader with the Grand-Croix of the *Légion d'honneur*, the highest French state order. It was the first time this order had been granted to a citizen of the Russian Federation. The ceremony was heavily criticized by Reporters without Borders, who called the award "unworthy of France" and "an insult to those who fight for freedom of speech in Russia." Putin promptly returned the favor in 2007, when Chirac visited Moscow, granting Chirac the State Prize of the Russian Federation for Humanitarian Activities. When Putin left the presidency in May 2008, his first trip as prime minister brought him to Paris, where he met with his former colleague. Again Chirac expressed his feelings of "very deep friendship" for Putin, adding: "My esteem comes from the remarkable manner in which you led Russia. Without doubt, these 10 [*sic*] years have been great years for Russia."[6]

When Chirac left the Élysée, this was felt in the Kremlin as a genuine loss. And this was even more so because Chirac's successor, Nicolas Sarkozy, seemed intent on radically changing course. Sarkozy not only planned a rapprochement with the United States and the reintegration of France into the military organization of NATO, but he also announced a new foreign policy that, unlike that of his predecessor, would be strictly based on human rights. Sarkozy had written very clearly in this respect. Respect of human rights, he wrote, "is not a 'detail' in my eyes. It is the foundation of the very idea of international community."[7] And he added: "You cannot place our economic interests and the respect of universal values on the same level."[8] Sarkozy further wrote:

I remember how during the years of the Iron Curtain one pretended to believe that the peoples of Central and Eastern Europe did not have the same aspirations for freedom as we had. The Russians were condemned to dictatorship because, after all, they had known nothing else. It was in their mentality! I do not believe in the "cultural relativity" of human rights, freedom, democracy. I believe that it is a question of universal values and that every man aspires to them.[9]

These were beautiful words. Sarkozy also mentioned that, in his opinion, "one cannot and must not remain silent in face of the Chechen drama, the illegitimate Russian interventions in Belarus, the guilty hesitations when there was the orange revolution in Ukraine."[10] Reasons enough, therefore, for Putin to fear that the cordial French-Russian relationship, established under Chirac, would turn cold. His pessimism seemed to be confirmed when Sarkozy chose André Glucksmann as one of his close advisers. This was the French philosopher who had criticized Chirac so vehemently for neglecting the atrocities committed in the Chechen war. However, things turned out quite differently than expected. Putin would soon find out that Sarkozy was not the principled fighter for human rights and democracy he had pretended to be in his election campaign. Far from being a French Jimmy Carter-bis, he was rather a Malenkiy Shirak—a "Little Chirac." Sarkozy's conversion to the principles of *Realpolitik* started the day after his inauguration as president. However, his conversion into a full-fledged *drug Putina* ("friend of Putin") would take longer, and the occasion on which this conversion took place, was—to say the least—surprising.

SARKOZY'S PRO-PUTIN CONVERSION

Sarkozy's warm personal relationship with Putin began one year later, at a moment that seemed rather inauspicious for it: the war between Russia and Georgia in August 2008. Sarkozy, at that moment president of the European Council, acted as a mediator in the conflict. Sarkozy's mediation effort has been criticized from different sides for the amateurish way in which it was conducted.[11] Being a complete *novice* in foreign policy, he was easy prey for the shrewd, well-oiled, and extremely well-prepared Russian diplomacy machine.[12] However, one can still forgive the naïveté of an inexperienced president who had to act under great pressure at a moment while the United States, the leader of the West, preferred to stay aloof. More serious, however, was the *character flaw* the French president showed on that occasion. Because one has to query why at precisely this crucial moment, when Russian troops had, for the first time since the invasion of Afghanistan, invaded a sovereign and democratic country and prepared to dismember it, had he thought it opportune to start a close and even cozy partnership with the invading power. Unfortunately, however, this was exactly what happened. On August 12, 2008, Sarkozy flew to Moscow to negotiate with the Russian leaders—at that time called "the tandem," consisting of President Dmitry Medvedev and Prime Minister Vladimir Putin. Both men had prepared themselves very well for the arrival of the French president. They informed him about the Georgian "aggression" and the "ethnic cleansing" conducted by the Georgian army in South Ossetia. But the talks in Moscow were not only about the war and how the war could be ended. The presence of the French president within the Kremlin walls offered the Russian "tandem" a golden opportunity to talk about other things, for instance how to improve French-Russian cooperation and how to strengthen mutual business ties. Juicy contracts were suggested. The Russian charm offensive was crowned with success. On August 12, 2008, at a point when South Ossetian militias were still conducting an ethnic cleansing of Georgian villages in South Ossetia, Saul Sarkozy became Paul Sarkozy: the former critical presidential candidate, the self-proclaimed defender of human rights, definitively joined the ranks of the group of "Putin-friendly" European leaders. A sign of this was a proposal made by Sarkozy in November 2008 to "stop talking" about the US missile defense shield in Europe, which, he said, "only complicates things."[13] This unilateral French proposal for a moratorium on the ballistic missile defense project was heavily criticized by Poland and the Czech Republic, which had participated in the project. The fact that some weeks earlier Russian President Medvedev had threatened to deploy short-range Iskander missiles in Kaliningrad did not help. Sarkozy seemed to give in to Russian blackmail without taking into account the interests of its new allies in NATO. Alexandr Vondra, the deputy prime minister of the Czech Republic, wrote an op-ed in *Le Monde*, titled "A Bit of Respect, Mister President," in which he reminded the French president that not only in April 2008 all NATO members, including France, had agreed with the project, but also that "there was no agreement of the 27 [EU members] in the name of which the [French EU] Presidency could speak about this project."[14] It is no surprise that Putin, in an interview with *Le Figaro* one month after the war, had only words of praise for Sarkozy. "Nicolas Sarkozy has played an important role in the pacification process [in Georgia]," he said, adding: "our relationship has a constructive character, and, progressively, we have established an extremely friendly relationship. We more and more confide in each other."[15]

A COLD MISTRAL BLOWS OVER THE BLACK SEA

On September 19, 2008, a few days after this interview, Sarkozy sent his prime minister, François Fillon, to the Russian Black Sea resort of Sochi, where Fillon met with Putin to negotiate contracts for French firms. At that very moment, Russian troops were still in Georgia. Not only had Russia not fulfilled the "six principles" negotiated with Sarkozy to end the Georgian conflict, but some weeks before, Russia had recognized the independence of Abkhazia and South Ossetia, de facto dismembering Georgia. Fillon's business visit to Sochi was considered by the Georgian government as a stab in the back. It was also heavily criticized by Poland, Britain, the Czech Republic, and the Baltic states. But nothing could stop Sarkozy's new honeymoon with the Russian leadership. Soon a big project was on the table: the sale of two French helicopter carriers of the Mistral class to Russia. This ship is the pride of the French navy. It can carry sixteen heavy or thirty-five light helicopters, four landing craft, nine hundred soldiers, and up to seventy armored vehicles, including forty tanks. The Russian navy commander Admiral Vladimir Vysotsky would declare in September 2009 that in the war with Georgia, "such warship would take just 40 minutes to do the task that the Russian Black Sea Fleet ships did in 26 hours."[16] The deal was estimated to be worth over €1 billion and the largest Russian procurement purchase abroad to date. It would be the first sale of this kind by a NATO country to Russia. "I hope you can buy this splendid ship," said Foreign Minister Bernard Kouchner, when he visited Moscow together with Defense Minister Hervé Morin in October 2009.[17]

However, the plan met with criticism not only in France, but also in Russia itself. "The Mistral purchase will have a devastating effect on Russian shipbuilders' already difficult task of selling their ships to other countries," wrote Mikhail Barabanov, a defense expert, who argued that "it would be hard to develop a more damaging advertising campaign for Russia's defense industry. Russia's shipbuilders don't deserve this negative PR."[18] However, the proposed sale caused much greater concern among Russia's neighboring states. On November 27, 2009, Georgian foreign minister Grigol Vashadze told an audience at the French Institute for International Relations (IFRI) in Paris that he was "tremendously worried" about the purchase. "The only destination for this kind of ship," he said, "is the Black Sea."[19] On December 18, 2009, six US senators, including former presidential candidate John McCain, wrote a letter to the French ambassador in Washington, with a copy to Secretary of State Hillary Clinton, in which they expressed their concern with the proposed sale. They drew attention to the fact that Russia had suspended its participation in the CFE Treaty; did not honor its 1999 commitments to withdraw from Georgian and Moldovan territory; and was not in compliance with the Russian-Georgian cease-fire agreement negotiated by the French government. "We fear," they wrote, that "this sale sends Russia the message that France acquiesces to its increasingly bellicose and lawless behavior." The French ambassador answered in a letter of December 21, 2009, "that Russian authorities, at the highest level, have clearly rejected the irresponsible statement that you mention." This sounded almost like a joke:

the ambassador was referring to the "irresponsible statement". . . made by Admiral Vysotsky that the Mistral ship would have allowed the Russian invaders of Georgia in August 2008 to accomplish their task in forty minutes. The ambassador added: "We have been keen to consult our partners, notably Georgia, before any move." "To consult" seemed for the French government only to mean "to inform" and obviously did not include the need to listen to the other side and to take the concerns of the Georgian government seriously. Thereafter, Russian officials were prudent enough to stop talking about the Black Sea. General Vladimir Popovkin, deputy minister of defense responsible for arms procurement, declared "that we need it [the Mistral] for the defense of the Kaliningrad enclave and the Kuril islands."[20] But it was evident that the Black Sea remained the most attractive place for Moscow to deploy the Mistral. Not only would it be an important reinforcement of the Black Sea Fleet, but as a helicopter carrier, the Mistral also had the advantage that it would not qualify as an aircraft carrier, which, as such, would be banned from passing through the Bosporus Strait and the Dardanelles under a 1936 convention. The diplomatic implications of the arms deal were warmly welcomed in both countries. Philippe Migault, analyst at IRIS, a French think tank, called the Mistral contract "a huge diplomatic opportunity,"[21] which, he said, would open "a new diplomatic era in Europe." This, because "a Moscow-Berlin-Paris-Rome quartet, without London, subservient to Washington, would not only make sense, but it would permit to exercise an even greater influence internationally." In the same vein, Max Fisher wrote an article in the *Atlantic* entitled "Russia-France: The New Alliance That Could Change Europe."[22] Also, for this author, the sale of the Mistral had "a huge political significance": "After standing alone in Europe for nearly a century, Russia seems to be developing its first real European partnership in generations." Fisher added: "France may seem an unusual choice, but the interests of the two nations could intertwine with surprising elegance, and there is a long history of French-Russian involvement."[23] One got the impression of experiencing a remake of the old Franco-Russian alliance, which existed for a quarter of a century between 1892 and 1917. The Kremlin's strategy, therefore, seemed rather successful. After the German-Russian side, the Franco-Russian side of its strategic "European Triangle" began to take shape.

However, the US administration, concerned about the Mistral deal, put pressure on the French government to sell the ship without the NATO standard high-tech equipment for radar and command and control. Moscow, on the other side, insisted that the electronic equipment also be included and threatened to buy the ships elsewhere. Thereupon, Sarkozy started a charm offensive. On March 9, 2010, he invited Sergey Chemezov to the Elysée Palace and decorated him with the Légion d'honneur.[24] Chemezov was not only director of Rosoboronexport, the Russian state arms export firm, but also director-general of Rostekhnologii, a huge complex of military-industrial state companies. Chemezov's background is interesting. Having worked in the 1980s as an undercover KGB agent in Dresden in the German Democratic Republic, he told *Itogi* magazine in 2005 that in East Germany, he was Putin's neighbor.[25] However, even if a Légion d'honneur for Putin's close friend Chemezov was not bad, Putin wanted more.

Showing that he and not President Medvedev was in charge, in June 2010 Putin instructed his deputy prime minister Igor Sechin to set up a working group on French-Russian cooperation in military shipbuilding.[26] In September 2010, the Kremlin increased the pressure. Although having promised Paris that the negotiations were exclusive, Russia opened an international tender and began to contact shipyards in Spain and the Netherlands. The Russian pressure had success. The French government gave in. On November 1, 2010—just four days before the international tender expired—the Russian shipyard OSK and the French military shipyard DCNS signed an agreement to form a common consortium. According to the CEO of DCNS, Patrick Boissier, the consortium could participate in tenders for the construction of "military and civilian ships."[27] It was no surprise when this consortium won the tender. At the end of January 2011, an agreement was signed in Saint-Nazaire between the French minister of defense, Alain Juppé, and Russian deputy prime minister Igor Sechin. The agreement concerned four ships, two of which would be built in France and two in Russia. However, this was not the end of the affair. The Russian government went on to haggle. In March 2011 Moscow said it wanted to pay only 980 million euros for the two Mistrals. Paris wanted at least 1.15 billion.[28] One Mistral costs between 500 and 700 million euros. Even the pro-government paper *Le Figaro* began to express its doubts. The paper revealed how at the last moment the Russian side had manipulated the Saint-Nazaire agreement, changing the wording of an article referring to the transfer of technology. The French "contribution" to a transfer of technology was alleged to have been changed into a "guarantee." This last-minute change was signed by the French defense minister Alain Juppé.[29] Again, as in August 2008, when Sarkozy conducted negotiations with the Kremlin to end the war in Georgia, the French appeared to be poor negotiators. When, finally, a deal was made, the French government refused to make the details of the technology transfer public. However, there were few doubts that the Kremlin had obtained what it wanted. Even the pro-government paper *Le Figaro* wrote: "Today France would be prepared to sell almost all technology with which the Mistral, one of the flagships of the national navy, is equipped."[30] Some of this technology, however, belonged to NATO and was blocked. But most of it was French. The paper wrote: "According to information obtained by *Le Figaro*, Paris appears thus to have accepted handing over the command and communication systems, including their codes. One of the ultrasophisticated communication systems of the Mistral, Sinik 9, is directly derived from Sinik 8, with which the *Charles de*

Gaulle [the French aircraft carrier] is equipped. Even the director of the shipyards of Saint-Nazaire has acknowledged that there existed "a risk" in connection with the transfer of technology."[31] These doubts, however, were not enough to stop the project. In June 2011 the final agreement was signed. *Le Figaro* published a page-long article, titled "France-Russia: The New Strategic Axis,"[32] in which the sale of the Mistral was presented as "only the beginning of the story." Apparently, the Kremlin could be satisfied.

The sale of the Mistral was not only a matter of concern because of the security risks that were involved for NATO members and NATO partners neighboring Russia. It was also an important *precedent*. "The French Mistral sale," wrote Vladimir Socor, "can trigger a rush by other NATO countries to sell arms to Russia, bypassing NATO and undermining Allied plans and policies. With Mistral the precedent-setting case (if this sale is allowed), a sale-and-purchase pitch has already started."[33] He warned: "If NATO fails on this issue now, then the entire issue of arms sales to Russia will spin out of the Alliance's ability to control."[34] In the aftermath of the financial and economic crisis, security concerns seemed to have become totally subservient to purely mercantilist concerns. In 2010 French arms sales almost halved, passing from 8 billion euros in 2009 to 4.3 billion euros. This situation was, according to *Le Monde*, due to the "lack of big contracts."[35] The sale of the Mistral, undeniably a "big contract," was expected to give French arms sales a boost of 25 percent.

The sale of the Mistral, presented by Sarkozy as a great personal success and a boon for the French defense industry, became a growing embarrassment for France. The delivery of the first Mistral, the *Vladivostok*, was scheduled in September 2014. At that moment, Russia was hit by Western sanctions because of its occupation of the Crimea and its invasion of eastern Ukraine. In late June 2014 four hundred Russian sailors arrived in the French port of Saint-Nazaire to be trained on board. A first ten-day training voyage with 250 Russian sailors and 200 French specialists was made in the middle of September.[36] Despite the sanctions, President François Hollande did not cancel or suspend the delivery; he only postponed it. Among the reasons put forward was that a cancellation of the contract would not only lead to expensive penalties but also damage France's credibility as an arms supplier on the global arms market. These were shaky arguments because delivery under these circumstances would constitute a more important blow to France's reputation in Western capitals with not only moral but also direct economic consequences. Jeff Lightfoot rightly remarked that

> delivery could also undermine France's hopes of winning defense business in Europe. Ironically enough, the Polish Minister of Defense cautioned that, if France delivers the Mistrals to Russia, Poland may cut France's Thales out of a major €5.8 billion defense contract in which it is one of two finalists. That

alone should have France wondering if delivering the Mistral is really the least risky option to its defense industrial base. [37]

AN ORTHODOX CATHEDRAL IN THE HEART OF PARIS: HOUSE OF GOD OR DEN OF SPIES?

The year 2010 was a year of celebration for the growing French-Russian entente, not only because of the preparation of the Mistral deal. In that year also *une année croisée* was organized. This "crossed year" consisted of a "Year of Russia" in France and a "Year of France" in Russia. The combined events in the two countries included up to four hundred cultural manifestations, ballets, and theater performances. There was an exhibition in the Louvre and high-level visits of Medvedev and Putin to Paris. The Russians hired the prominent French PR bureau Euro-RSCG to organize the publicity. The new partners praised each other, and comparisons were made with the Franco-Russian Alliance between 1892 and 1917, of which the Alexandre III bridge, a monumental Seine bridge named after tsar Alexander III and built between 1896 and 1900, is the enduring symbol. The "Year of Russia" created the right atmosphere and the necessary goodwill for another important breakthrough for the Kremlin—this time not in the field of arms sales but in the field of religion.

Since 2008 the Kremlin has had an eye on the building of Météo France, the French Meteorological Institute, which was for sale. The building was situated in a strategic location, at the Quai Branly in the heart of Paris, not far from the Eiffel Tower. Moscow wanted to build an Orthodox cathedral on this plot of 8,400 square meters. There was only one problem: Canada and Saudi Arabia were also interested in buying the building. There followed aggressive lobbying by the Russian ambassador, Alexander Orlov, who was assisted by Vladimir Kozhin, an ex-KGB officer and the head of the Kremlin's Presidential Property Management Department, a bureaucracy which employs fifty thousand employees. Putin was deputy head of the same department when he began to work in Yeltsin's presidential administration in June 1996. The department is not only tasked with the management of state property within Russia but also with the property of the Russian Orthodox Church abroad. For the operation "Paris Cathedral," the Russians had hired another French lobbying firm: ESL & Network, which had access to the highest echelons of the French government. Moscow had made it clear that it would consider it an unfriendly act if the Kremlin were not to obtain the building. In December 2009 President Medvedev spoke with Sarkozy about the project during the climate summit in Copenhagen. Sarkozy is said to have immediately phoned his budget minister from Copenhagen. A few days later the Kremlin's chief of the Property Department, Vladimir Kozhin, was invited to the ministry. [38] The Kremlin asked for a direct sale, but Paris preferred an open tender. When, on January 28, 2010, the five envelopes were opened, the offer of the Kremlin, 70 million euros, was the highest. According to an insider, quoted in *Le Nouvel Observateur*, "[The offer] was superior to the evaluation of the Property service, which is secret."[39] The magazine asked: "Has Russia benefited from privileged information? Bercy [the French Ministry of Finance], of course, denies this."[40]

Unfortunately, the sale of the site for the new cathedral was not purely a question of religion. The site is not far from the *Palais de l'Alma*, a dependency of the presidential Elysée Palace, in which the postal service of the Elysée and sixteen apartments for the staff of the president are located. Jean-David Levitte, diplomatic adviser to Sarkozy, and General Benoît Puga, Sarkozy's private chief of staff, had apartments in the building. These men, wrote *Le Nouvel Observateur*,

> dispose of the most important secrets of the republic and are, therefore, privileged targets of foreign intelligence services, especially that of Russia. The affair worries the DCRI [French counterintelligence] even more because it has discovered a very large amount of activity by the SVR (the Russian foreign secret service) in France since the election of Nicolas Sarkozy. In its briefings it even estimates that the presence of Russian spies in Paris has never been more significant since 1985. She advises therefore against handing over such a sensitive building to a church of which one knows its links and its compromises with the KGB and of which one does not know whether it really has distanced itself from the secret services. The Quai-d'Orsay [French Ministry of Foreign Affairs] joins the reservations made by the DCRI.[41]

These reservations, however, had no impact on the final decision. On March 17, 2011, a team of architects was constituted, led by the Spaniard Manuel Nuñez Yanovsky, in association with the Russian Arch Group, to construct what was no longer being called a church but a "Russian spiritual center."[42] The building in the heart of Paris would further boost the Russian Orthodox presence in France, where, in 2009, in Épinay-sous-Sénart, the biggest Russian seminary of Western Europe, had been opened to train French-speaking priests. However, there still remained some stumbling blocks. In November 2012 Sarkozy's successor, President François Hollande, suspended the project, which Paris mayor Bertrand Delanoë had criticized for its "mediocre" architecture. Delanoë had not been the project's only critic. The French Ministry of Culture also was not happy with the baroque building with its five gilded onion towers and glass curtain roof, which did not suit its environment. The French architect Jean-Michel Wilmotte, who had participated in the contest (but was not selected), was tasked with developing a new proposal together with the architects of the original project.[43] Finally, in the summer of 2014—notwithstanding the fact that at that time economic sanctions were being imposed against Russia—the construction of the building began.

The new cathedral in Paris was part of the Kremlin's strategy to gain a hold over Orthodox church buildings in France, and—via the buildings— over Russian émigré communities. France has a large Russian immigrant population, which arrived after the October Revolution. These "White" Russians have their own churches in Biarritz, Nice, and Paris. In the 1920s these churches broke with the Kremlin-dominated Moscow Patriarchate and chose instead to belong to the Constantinople Patriarchate. Since the election of Putin, the Russian Orthodox Church has been trying to bring these parishes back into the womb of the Moscow Patriarchate. To achieve this goal, the Kremlin and the Russian Orthodox Church did not shy away from using heavy-handed methods. In December 2004 they organized in Biarritz a putsch against the local council of the Orthodox parish by letting "believers" come from neighboring Spain and organize a parallel council that voted to join the Moscow Patriarchate. However, the real council went to court and won the case. In Nice the Kremlin had more success. "In 2005 in Nice they sent officers of the SVR, the external espionage service, to try to retake the cathedral of Saint Nicolas by legal action (the Kremlin was to finally win the case in first instance in January 2010)."[44] The victory in Nice was due to the fact that in the meantime, the legal position of the Russian Orthodox Church had been strengthened. On May 17, 2007, the exiled church and the Russian Orthodox Church had been reunited. "So many churches, so many pieds-à-terre that will from now on officially expand the noble mission of infiltration that the Russian state has defined for itself," wrote Hélène Blanc and Renata Lesnik on this occasion.[45] The parish of the Orthodox cathedral Saint Alexandre Nevski in the Rue Daru in Paris, however, defended itself with success against a hostile takeover. This would have been an additional reason for the Kremlin to opt for the project of the new cathedral in the center of the French capital.

These seemingly religious struggles hide, in reality, something else: a struggle for the Kremlin's control of the Russian diaspora. The project of the cathedral in the heart of Paris was also important for another reason: it was the pièce de résistance of a combined effort of the Kremlin and the Moscow Patriarchate to make the Russian Orthodox Church into a *global* church. In this project France—and within France, the region of Paris—has been assigned the position of the West European *hub* from which to start this religious conquest. The Russian Orthodox Church (ROC) has, certainly, the same rights as other churches to proselytize. The problem, however, is that the ROC is different from other churches, especially in its close, symbiotic relationship with the Kremlin and with the Russian secret services, which is a reason for concern.

THE MESEBERG INITIATIVE: TOWARD AN EU-RUSSIA
STRATEGIC PARTNERSHIP?

During Sarkozy's presidency, the Kremlin also notched up an important *diplomatic* success in France. This was built upon an initiative taken by Sarkozy on the occasion of the celebrations in Moscow on May 9, 2010, of the sixty-fifth anniversary of the end of the Second World War. Sarkozy wanted to promote the project of a *common European space* based on an entente between France, Germany, and Russia—a project that could only please Moscow as it was an exact copy of the geopolitical "triangle" the Kremlin wanted to build in Europe. In a two-page paper, the Elysée had prepared a document in which the "common values" of Europe and Russia were stressed and the wish expressed that they should become "privileged partners." *Le Monde* wrote that "France seeks to place itself in the center of a new dialogue with Moscow on political-military questions in Europe."[46] The sale of the Mistral was considered an example of this new dialogue and partnership.

During a meeting in Castle Meseberg near Berlin on June 4–5, 2010, German Chancellor Angela Merkel and Russian President Dmitry Medvedev even went so far as to propose an "EU-Russia Political and Security Committee." This would imply that Russia not only would have regular bilateral and trilateral meetings with the two leading EU countries but would get nothing less than a seat at the EU security table. In a tripartite follow-up summit meeting on October 18–19, 2010, in the French beach resort of Deauville, which was attended by Merkel, Sarkozy, and Medvedev, further details of this plan were discussed. Sarkozy spoke of an EU-Russia economic space "with common security concepts," emphasizing eventual arms deals between Russia and the EU, a domain of direct interest to France. The meeting was unique: it was the first time since 1945 that French, German, and Russian leaders had discussed European security problems without the participation of the United States and outside the NATO framework. The Poles were upset. *Gazeta Polska*, a Polish newspaper, wrote a report on the Deauville meeting under the headline "Troika Carves Up Europe."[47] Although Paris and Berlin sought to reassure Washington that the three-way meeting "had none of the anti-American undertones of the Paris-Berlin-Moscow axis that emerged in the wake of the US-led invasion of Iraq,"[48] Americans were not amused. "Will the U.S. Lose Europe to Russia?" was the title of an article in the *New York Times*. In the article, a senior US official is quoted as saying: "Since when, I wonder, is European security no longer an issue of American concern, but something for Europe and Russia to resolve? After being at the center of European security for 70 years, it's strange to hear that it's no longer a matter of U.S. concern."[49]

Vladimir Chizov, Russian ambassador to the EU, could not hide his satisfaction. He told a reporter that Russia wanted a formalized relationship with the COPS, the EU's Committee on Foreign and Security Policy. "I don't expect to be sitting at every committee session," he declared with false modesty, "but there should be some mechanism that would enable us to take joint steps."[50] The proposed EU-Russia Security Committee would be chaired by the EU's high representative for foreign policy and Russia's foreign minister. The new forum would not only be used for consultations but also for setting ground rules for joint civilian and military crisis management operations by the EU and NATO. This would mean, writes Vladimir Socor, that

> the EU-Russia Committee would be vested with greater powers than those of the NATO-Russia Council. It would also institute an EU-Russia policy coordination mechanism, such as the EU does not have with the United States or with NATO (despite the overlap in EU-NATO membership). Thus defined, the committee could open access for Russia to the EU's own decision-making process (without any influence from the EU on Russia's decisions). It could also inspire Russian demands for access to NATO decisions through the NATO-Russia Council.[51]

The dangers of this new structure were, indeed, manifold. It would, first, give Russia access to the EU's decision-making process in security matters without giving the EU an equivalent influence on Russian decision making. Even if it was intended to do so, this was excluded given the highly secretive and authoritarian character of the Kremlin's power vertical that could more easily influence discussions in a divisive EU with twenty-seven members than the other way around. Second, it would realize the hidden aim of Medvedev's project for a Pan-European security pact, which was to drive a wedge between the United States and its European allies. After Medvedev's original project had been dismissed by the West, the EU-Russia Security Committee could therefore be considered the Russian "plan B," which would replace Medvedev's security pact.[52] Europeans, however, seemed not to be conscious of the risks of such a continental *Alleingang*. Two defense experts of the European Council on Foreign Relations, Mark Leonard and Ivan Krastev, for instance, pleaded for an enlargement of the proposed bilateral EU-Russia forum into a trilateral security forum consisting of the EU, Russia, and Turkey. "Setting up an informal trialogue," they wrote in an op-ed in the *Financial Times*, "could give new life to the old institutional order and—to paraphrase Lord Ismay—work to keep the EU united, Russia post-imperial and Turkey European."[53] Unfortunately, rather the contrary could happen. This proposal would not only sideline the United States, but—instead of keeping the EU united—the Russian presence at the European security table would offer Russia a golden opportunity to play on the many disagreements among the EU-27. It would further give Russia a unique possibility to drive a wedge between Europe and the United States. It would further by no means keep Russia post-imperial because Russia's post-imperial phase ended with the start of Putin's reign.

However, ideas of a European-Russian security alliance seemed to find more and more supporters. In France, Jean-Bernard Pinatel, a former army general, published in 2010 a book with the title *Russie, alliance vitale* (*Russia, Vital Alliance*). In this book, he writes:

> A Europe-Russia alliance would . . . be capable of challenging the influence of the emerging Chinese-American condominium and could constitute, in the medium term, a more attractive power center for Latin America, Africa, and the Middle East than China or the United States. It is the only chance of seeing this multipolar world appear in which Latin America, under the leadership of Brazil, has the vocation of becoming the fourth center. . . . France and Germany (which is the first economic partner of Russia in the European Union) must propose a vision of relations with Russia that is an alternative to the American vision. The return of France in NATO to strategic military command posts is the most efficient way to neutralize a strategy that, until now, has only been conceived and put in place to serve American interests.[54]

What Pinatel proposed was, in fact, an old foreign policy goal of Russia: to sever the security bonds between Europe and the United States. In his book Pinatel also addressed "the fear of our East European partners." They were told by him to do the same as De Gaulle did: "To reach out to the occupying forces of yesterday."[55] In the end, these ideas about a Russian seat at the EU security table did not materialize due to a lack of support from the other EU member states. However, it is telling that with its charm offensive, the Kremlin almost succeeded in reviving the anti-Iraq coalition of Russia, France, and Germany—forging a trilateral entente in security affairs that excluded the United States.

The French initiative to form a strategic triangle between Moscow, Berlin, and Paris was also nurtured by the existence of a bilateral French-Russian strategic platform, the French-Russian Cooperation Council on Security Questions (CCQS),[56] created in January 2002 on the initiative of Vladimir Putin. This council consists of the ministers of defense and foreign affairs of both countries and convenes at least once a year. Michel Barnier, Chirac's minister of foreign affairs, called "this four-person dialogue . . . quite unique. I don't think that it exists with any other country."[57] For the Kremlin this forum, which, between 2002 and 2015, was convened eleven times, is of great importance, and it is eager to enhance its themes and its participants. One of the proposals, published on the website of the French-Russian Observatory (Observatoire franco-russe), a think tank created in March 2012 by the Economic Council of the French-Russian Chamber of Commerce, was "to expand the format of the CCQS" by also inviting the two ministers of the interior.[58] Another proposal, published on this website, was to launch "a permanent dialogue on strategic stability between France and Russia, initially on the level of experts." Arnaud Dubien, the leader of the French-Russian Observatory, made himself a mouthpiece of Moscow's ambitions, pleading for a Russian seat at yet another European table: the Weimar Triangle, writing that "one of the most promising formats is that of the Weimar Triangle (France, Germany, Poland), enlarged with Russia."[59]

A GALAXY OF PRO-KREMLIN ASSOCIATIONS, COORDINATED BY THE RUSSIAN EMBASSY

The Kremlin's honeymoon with French President Nicolas Sarkozy and his prime minister, François Fillon, was supported by a broad Russian soft-power offensive which targeted French civil society and public opinion. In June 2010, during the "Russia Year in France," Putin and Fillon opened a Russian exhibition in the Paris *Grand Palais*. On that occasion Putin reminded his colleague "that one should not only look at the 'common past,' but also at the 'common future.'"[60] An important instrument of the Russian soft-power offensive was the monthly paid supplement *Russie d'Aujourd'hui*, delivered with the French paper *Le Figaro*. The Kremlin's policies were also supported by the paper *France-Soir*, owned by Alexander Pugachev, son of the Russian oligarch Sergey Pugachev. This paper, however, did not survive. Pro-Kremlin or Kremlin-sponsored organizations also played important roles. One of these organizations is the Institut de la Démocratie et de la Coopération (Institute of Democracy and Cooperation) (http://www.idc-europe.org/). This foundation, based in Moscow, Paris, and New York, organizes political debates. The institute is headed by Natalya Narochnitskaya, a former Duma member for Dmitry Rogozin's ultranationalist Rodina (Fatherland) Party. Narochnitskaya shares the paranoid worldview of the Kremlin leaders. On her website (http://www.narochnitskaia.ru/) she has written that "in all Caucasian wars there are non-Islamic instigators." One of the speakers invited to her conferences in 2011 was General Alexander Vladimirov. In 2007 this general spoke about "the inevitability of war between Russia and the United States within 10 to 15 years."[61] Another forum in France is the Cercle Aristote (http://www.cerclearistote.com), which also organizes debates and conferences in the French capital. These debates have titles, such as "The Russian Opposition and Western Manipulation" (January 10, 2012) or "Should France and Britain Quit the European Union?" (June 20, 2011). The Cercle Aristote publishes a magazine called *Perspectives Libres*. Articles in this magazine have in general a Eurosceptic tendency ("Let Us Leave Europe," "The Destruction of the Nation in Europe," "The Agony of the Euro," and so on) and praise patriotism and the national state ("Youth and Patriotism in Russia," "Patriotism in Russia—A Military Point of View"). In the magazine one can find an interview on patriotism with Boris Yakemenko, the leader of the reactionary Orthodox wing of Putin's Nashi youth movement. Recently one could observe in France a real proliferation of pro-Russian associations. In the autumn of 2011 this galaxy of initiatives was brought together in a Coordination Committee of the Forum of Russians of France (CCFRC),[62] under the aegis of the Russian embassy in Paris. This committee is headed by Dimitri de Kochko, a descendant of White Russians, whose great-grandfather was chief of Moscow's criminal police. Kochko has become one of the most aggressive defenders of Putin's regime in France. For Moscow he is the right man because the purpose of the CCFRC is not only to organize Russians living in France but also to get in touch with French citizens of Russian origin, in particular with descendants of White Russians. The Russian diaspora in France, consisting of "new" Russians and old émigré communities, is estimated at about 300,000.[63] Creating "coordination committees" under the aegis of the Russian embassy is part of a broader strategy. This practice is also evident in other countries. In Estonia, for instance, there exists a Coordination Council of Russian Compatriots. According to Estonian security services, the purpose of this council is "to organize and coordinate the Russian diaspora living in foreign countries to support the objectives and interests of Russian foreign policy under the direction of Russian departments."[64] One of the active members of the CCFRC in France is Prince Alexander Trubetskoy, a descendant of White Russians who heads the Association Dialogue Franco-Russe (www. dialoguefrancorusse.com), an official forum which brings together the political, cultural, and business elites of both countries. In 2011 Vladimir Yakunin, president of the Russian Railways, and Thierry Desmarest, honorary president of the French group Total, were co-presidents. Among its members were Sergey Mndoyants, Russian deputy minister of culture, and Anne-Marie Idrac, former president of the French railways and former state secretary for foreign trade in the second government of François Fillon. This high-level group resembles the German Ost-Ausschuss (East Committee) of the German Employers' Organization, but it has a broader scope than simply business interests.

PUTIN'S RUSSIA AND THE FRENCH FRONT NATIONAL: MUTUAL WARM FEELINGS

Another forum that must be mentioned here is the Alliance France-Europe Russie (http://www.alliance-france-europe-russie.org), a club which was headed in 2010 by Fabrice Sorlin. Sorlin is not only a former candidate of the extreme right Front National, but he was in 2010 also president of the extreme right Dies Irae group, to which are ascribed paramilitary practices and racist discourses.[65] Speakers in the seminars of the alliance include David Mascré, a member of the politburo of the Front National, and the honorary consul of Russia in Biarritz. The enthusiasm of the extreme right Front National for Russia is not new.[66] Already in 1996 the leader of the party, Jean-Marie Le Pen, came to Moscow to back the presidential bid of the extreme right nationalist candidate Vladimir Zhirinovsky, who at that time was barred from free movement within France after having spat on Jewish students in Strasbourg.[67]

In an interview in October 2011 with the Russian paper *Kommersant*, Marine Le Pen expressed her admiration for Vladimir Putin and announced that if she were to win the French presidential elections in May 2012, France would leave NATO.[68] The Front National is deeply anti-Atlantic and anti-American. "The diplomacy that Marine Le Pen dreams of is built around a Paris-Moscow axis."[69] Leaving the integrated structure of NATO and building a "trilateral alliance Paris-Berlin-Moscow" was mentioned as the first point on the list of foreign policy proposals on her 2012 election website.[70] Another sign of the warm relations between the Front National and Putin's United Russia Party was a visit in December 2012 by Marion Maréchal-Le Pen, Marine's niece, who is a member of the French parliament, to Moscow. The French daily *Le Monde* even spoke of a "mysterious visit."[71] The young MP was invited by Aleksey Pushkov, chairman of the foreign affairs committee of the Duma, a man described by *Le Monde* as "anti-American, anti-Western, he is representative of the Putinist hard-liners."[72] Marion Maréchal-Le Pen was probably invited because she is a member of the friendship group France-Europe-Russie.

After the annexation of the Crimea and the Russian intervention in Eastern Ukraine, the relationship between the Kremlin and the Front National grew even closer. On March 16, 2014, Aymeric Chauprade, Marine Le Pen's foreign affairs adviser (who was to become a member of the European Parliament in May 2014), was an observer at the fake referendum in Crimea on joining Russia. Chauprade's website, *Realpolitik.tv*, defends Moscow's geopolitical views. In 2011 Louis Aliot, vice president of the Front National and Marine Le Pen's partner, founded the Club Idées-Nation, which similarly didn't hide its sympathy for Putin. The close cooperation between the Kremlin and the Front National also led to some painful inconsistencies. The Ukrainian Svoboda Party, for instance, which, in 2014, was accused by Putin of being a fascist party, was in 2009 received by Jean-Marie Le Pen, who, on that occasion, emphasized the fact that both parties "held shared ideas."[73] Apparently the "anti-fascist" Kremlin had no problem with such inconsistencies. On November 29 and 30, 2014, Andrey Isayev, deputy chairman of the Duma, and Andrey Klimov, deputy chairman of the foreign affairs committee of the Federation Council, participated in the fifteenth congress of the Front National in Lyon.[74] A week earlier the FN admitted having received a loan of 9 million euros from the First Czech-Russian Bank (FCRB). According to Mediapart, known in France as a reliable source, the amount of the Russian loan was likely to be much higher: the 9 million was said to be the first tranche of a loan of 40 million euros.[75] This happened at the very moment that President Putin brought in a law forbidding Russian political parties to accept financial support from abroad.

However, admiration for Putin is not restricted to the Front National. It can also be found in Jean-Luc Mélenchon's Front de gauche (Left Front), amongst left-wing "sovereignists" such as Jean-Pierre Chevènement, amongst centrist politicians such as senators Yves Pozzo di Borgo (a member of his family was ambassador to the tsar) and Aymerie de Montesquiou,[76] or in the Gaullist UMP (Union for a Popular Movement, the name of which, in May 2015, was changed into *Les Républicains*), where many admire Putin's policies aimed at restoring Russian national *grandeur*—whether openly or secretly. Putin also has his admirers in academic circles, such as the well-known historian Hélène Carrère d'Encausse or the economist Jacques Sapir. French movie stars, similarly, are seduced by him. Tax fugitive Gérard Depardieu was offered Russian nationality and became a close friend of both Putin and his Chechen proxy Ramzan Kadyrov. Brigitte Bardot, the famous French star and a prominent Front National sympathizer, also did not hide her admiration for Vladimir Putin. In an interview with *Nice Matin*, when asked whom she considered the ideal president, she answered without hesitation: "Putin. I find him very good and every time I ask him for something in principle he grants it. He has done more for the protection of animals than our successive presidents."[77]

TOTAL AND IFRI

In France—as in Germany—it is the great energy firms that are the Kremlin's most powerful and active supporters. The French company Total is a prominent investor in Russian oil and gas projects and has an excellent relationship with the Kremlin. It is, therefore, not a surprise that Thierry Desmarest, honorary president of Total, is co-president of the high-level group Dialogue Franco-Russe. It is quite natural for a firm like Total to become the Kremlin's voice in France. Total's CEO, Christophe de Margerie, for instance, spoke out against sanctions against Russia over Ukraine.[78] After his death in October 2014 in a plane crash in Moscow, he was hailed by Putin as "a real friend of Russia," and a Duma member even asked that he be honored with a statue at Vnukovo Airport.[79] Total not only has a direct political influence on French government policy through its participation in high-level French-Russian forums, it also has an indirect influence on the formation of elite opinion. An example is IFRI, the biggest French think tank. Only 28 percent of IFRI's budget comes from the government. The rest is financed by private clients, mostly big business, who sponsor research projects. "On Russia," wrote *L'Express*, "the most important sponsor is Total: the oil company pays for three researchers."[80] The IFRI research projects on Russia, subsidized by Total, will certainly not be characterized by an overly critical tone, even if Thomas Gomart, IFRI's vice president for strategic development and director of IFRI's Russia/NIS Center, reassures us that "the intellectual honesty of the researchers is not affected . . . nor the objectivity of the research, but it is true that subjects that do not find funding are abandoned."[81] Despite the proclaimed intellectual honesty of IFRI's Russian projects subsidized by Total, which we do not doubt, one may, however, ask whether projects that displease the Kremlin have any chance of being initiated. IFRI researcher Tatiana Kastoueva-Jean, when asked about the sanctions against Russia after the Russian aggression in Ukraine, said: "I am being asked: 'are you for or against sanctions?' . . . In general I answer that I'm neither for, nor against, I just try to get on with my research."[82] It is telling that this IFRI researcher, confronted with unacceptable Russian behavior, refuses to take sides, seeking refuge in so-called value-free science. Another example: on October 7, 2012, on the occasion of Putin's sixtieth birthday, Thomas Gomart, who is not only director of IFRI's Russia Center but also a prominent member of Putin's Valdai Discussion Club, had the honor of being quoted in a special frame on the bottom of the home page of the Russian state news agency RIA Novosti with the text: "Vladimir Putin's main success is his ability to be elected the president of Russia for two terms; he is certainly a leader with a prominent standing in Russian history."[83] In the original article, published on the Valdai website, another Valdai expert, Alexander Rahr, who is senior adviser on Russia for Wintershall Holding, the German energy giant, wrote that "Vladimir Putin will go down in history as a leader who stabilized Russia. In a couple of decades he will probably be compared to Charles de Gaulle in France or to Konrad Adenauer in Germany. He established a functioning economic and political system in Russia. Moreover, under his presidency the Russians started to live better than all of the previous generations."[84] Putin, who had already been compared with Franklin Delano Roosevelt by Vladislav Surkov, the deputy chief of the presidential administration,[85] will certainly not be dissatisfied at being put on the same level as Konrad Adenauer or Charles De Gaulle.

One thing is clear: the Kremlin, having made a massive effort in recent years to embellish its image, has achieved undisputable successes. The question is, however, whether these successes will prove to be permanent. With the election of the socialist François Hollande in May 2012 as French president, not only did Vladimir Putin lose his favorite interlocutor in the Élysée, but also the wind began to turn. In May 2012, a few days after Hollande's election, I wrote:

> Sarkozy fell easily under the charm of the Russian leader. Although his relationship with Putin did not match the personal friendship of Putin with Gerhard Schröder or Silvio Berlusconi, he chose—like them—to let commercial interests prevail over geopolitical interests and respect for democratic standards and human rights. One can expect that Hollande, who started his presidency with the proclamation of a moral code, will not be so easily duped and will maintain a pragmatic relationship with the Kremlin, while at the same time reaching out to the democratic opposition. [86]

Nine months later this early prognosis seemed to be confirmed when French-Russian relations reached a historic low. After the farcical story of Putin, who personally granted Russian citizenship to French actor and tax exile Gérard Depardieu, *Le Monde* spoke about "a Cold War climate between Paris and Moscow." [87] Bilateral problems concerned not only conflicting positions on Iran and Syria but also "recent operations of the DCRI [French counter intelligence] to thwart intense Russian secret services activities in France. One can add to this the verification procedure, launched by Hollande's team, of all armaments sales abroad negotiated under Sarkozy's presidency, in particular the potential transfer of technology. No contract has been cancelled, but 'the Russians have felt a cold wind,' says an informed source." [88] The paper quoted an unknown official who said that "the Russians, who are resuming soviet ways . . . have, in fact, always preferred a right-wing government in France." [89] This was confirmed by Arnaud Dubien, head of the Franco-Russian Observatory, who said that the "socialists tend to show little interest in Russia and . . . hold more prejudices against Russia than the previous administration." [90]

Here also, however, the last word has not yet been heard. On February 28, 2013, when Hollande visited Putin in Moscow, both men oversaw the signing of a number of economic cooperation agreements, and the climate was visibly improving. "Hollande and Putin Warm Relations," wrote *The Moscow Times*. [91] Although Hollande took care to meet also with human rights activists and members of the opposition, the message was clear: France would opt for a pragmatic approach. In August 2013 Arnaud Dubien concluded with satisfaction that Hollande's presidency had brought no downturn in Russian-French relations, writing that initial "hesitations were settled in the fall of 2012 when President Hollande appointed Jean-Pierre Chevènement as special representative to Russia. His record is impressive— former minister of the interior, defense and higher education, at the age of 35 chosen by François Mitterrand to author the Socialist platform. He is a genuine heavyweight and one of the few Socialists who has always been keen on Russia in the belief that the partnership should be a foreign policy priority." [92]

He was right. The choice of Chevènement as France's special envoy to Russia could only please Moscow. On March 8, 2014—at the very moment that Russia had occupied the Crimea—Chevènement published an article in *Le Figaro*, titled "Without Russia Something Is Missing in Europe."[93] In this article, not only did Chevènement support the Kremlin's demand to federalize Ukraine, but he also said that "no one can contest the fact that historically [the Crimea] is Russian." He spoke out further in favor of a free trade zone from Brest (France) to Vladivostok, adding that "for 23 years Russia has been respecting the rule of law." Chevènement's article led to angry reactions. Vincent Jauvert wrote in the left-leaning *L'Obs* that "for some time his opinions seem to have been growing closer to those supported by the Kremlin than by the Quai d'Orsay [French Foreign Ministry]." Jauvert asked: "Can he remain France's special representative to Russia?"[94] A good question, indeed.

THE FUTURE OF THE "STRATEGIC TRIANGLE" AFTER UKRAINE

What will be the future of the "strategic triangle?" In 2010 the Kremlin's objective of creating a "Moscow-Berlin-Paris Triangle" seemed within reach with the Meseberg initiative. However, the Kremlin's project has been jeopardized by Moscow's aggression in Ukraine. Does this mean that Russia has abandoned its strategic goal? Not at all. One should not forget that Russian foreign policy has always been characterized by its focus on long-term goals. Another point is that the Kremlin, helped by an unprecedented propaganda offensive, was able to create in France, as well as in Germany, a large reservoir of sympathizers. These *Putinversteher* (Putin apologists), who did not hesitate to condone Russia's acts of aggression, are overrepresented in parties of the extreme right and the extreme left. However, one can also find them in moderate parties, such as the German SPD and the French UMP/Les Républicains. And it is not only politicians and intellectuals who are seduced by Moscow's siren songs. Leading entrepreneurs, too, lured by the promise of lucrative contracts, have become the Kremlin's allies. The Mistral affair is a case in point. It has become a test case and a litmus test for Hollande's presidency. If Hollande were to decide to deliver the Mistral to a government which does not respect international treaties, is invading other countries, and is committing war crimes, this will not only be a political error, it will be a grave moral mistake, undermining the very values Europe is supposed to defend. In 2015 the Kremlin will accelerate its information war in both countries when RT will start French- and German-language broadcasts. It is no coincidence that the Kremlin has chosen these two languages: France and Germany remain Moscow's main targets in its project to build a "multipolar world." This does not mean that Moscow would neglect the smaller European states. On the contrary, Moscow has been very successful in forging friendly and close relations with the governments of Orbán in Hungary, Zeman in the Czech Republic, and the new Syriza government in Greece. These small alliances are part of a bigger strategic game: distancing Europe from the United States and making Europe a close ally of Russia. In this game, building a strategic triangle of Berlin-Moscow-Paris remains Moscow's main objective.

NOTES

1. "Chirac-Poutine: oui, mais . . . ," *Nouvelobs.com* (July 3, 2001).
2. On Chirac's multipolar dreams, cf. Marcel H. Van Herpen, "France: Champion of a Multipolar World," *The National Interest Online* (May 14, 2003), available at http://nationalinterest.org/article/france-champion-of-a-multipolar-world-2345.
3. Kenneth R. Timmerman, *The French Betrayal of America* (New York: Crown Forum, 2004), 248.
4. Alain Besançon, "Jacques Chirac trop 'russophile?'" *Le Figaro* (March 2, 2004) (emphasis mine). On Chirac's remark that Europeans could show "a bit more respect" vis-à-vis Russia, *Le Monde* wrote in an editorial: "The remark is even more surprising because it was made in Budapest, the capital of a country which has not always been 'respected' by Moscow." ("Respecter la Russie," *Le Monde* (February 26, 2004).)
5. Besançon, "Jacques Chirac trop 'russophile?'"
6. "Chirac Lauds 'Great Years for Russia' under Putin," *Moscow News* (June 6, 2008).
7. Nicolas Sarkozy, *Témoignage* (Paris: XO Éditions, 2006), 264.
8. Sarkozy, *Témoignage*, 264.
9. Sarkozy, *Témoignage*, 264.
10. Sarkozy, *Témoignage*, 265.
11. For an assessment of Sarkozy's foreign policy, see Marcel H. Van Herpen, "The Foreign Policy of Nicolas Sarkozy: Not Principled, Opportunistic, and Amateurish," *Cicero Foundation Great Debate Paper*, No. 10/01, Cicero Foundation, Maastricht/Paris (February 2010), available at http://www.cicerofoundation.org/lectures/Marcel_H_Van_Herpen_FOREIGN_POLICY_SARKOZY.pdf.
12. According to *Le Monde*, American documents revealed that Sarkozy fell into a trap because the Russians made "a second ceasefire text, which was a bit different from the text authorized by the Elysée. It was only below this text that president Medvedev had put his signature. Therefore, two versions of the agreement circulated, with small differences of presentation and contents, which the Russians could take advantage of on the ground." (Natalie Nougayrède, "Washington réservé sur la médiation française en Géorgie," *Le Monde* (December 3, 2010).)
13. Valentina Pop, "Sarkozy Wants New EU-US-Russia Security Accord," *euobserver.com* (November 14, 2008).
14. Alexandr Vondra, "Un peu de respect, M. le président," *Le Monde* (November 20, 2008).
15. "Nicolas Sarkozy a joué un grand rôle de pacification," interview with Vladimir Putin by Étienne Mougeotte, *Le Figaro* (September 13, 2008).
16. "FM: Tbilisi Worried over Possible Russia-French Mistral Deal," *Civil.ge* (November 26, 2009).
17. Marie Jégo, "La vente d'un porte-hélicoptère à la Russie étudiée par l'Élysée," *Le Monde* (October 7, 2009).
18. Mikhail Barabanov, "Mesmerized by the French Navy," *The Moscow Times* (August 31, 2009).

19. "Georgia Lobbies France on Warship," *The Moscow Times* (November 26, 2009), http://www.themoscowtimes.com/sitemap/free/2009/11/article/georgia-lobbies-france-on-warship/390431.html.

20. Viktor Litovkin, "NATO derzhit 'Mistral' na privyazi," *Nezavisimaya Gazeta* (April 14, 2010).

21. Philippe Migault, "Contrat Mistral: Une formidable opportunité diplomatique," *IRIS, Observatoire Stratégique et Économique de l'Espace Post-Soviétique* (January 5, 2011).

22. Max Fisher, "Russia-France: The New Alliance That Could Change Europe," *The Atlantic* (March 2, 2010).

23. Fisher, "Russia-France: The New Alliance."

24. "Sergeyu Chemezovu vruchili vyshuyu nagradu Frantsii," *lenta.ru* (March 10, 2011).

25. "Agents in Power," *The St. Petersburg Times* (February 12, 2008).

26. "Putin Orders Sechin to Form France-RF Mil Shipbuilding Coop Group," *Itar Tass* (June 11, 2010).

27. "La France et la Russie créent un consortium de chantiers navals," *Le Monde* (November 11, 2010).

28. "Ventes de Mistral: négociations dans l'impasse entre Paris et Moscou," *Le Monde* (March 3, 2011). How hard the Kremlin was playing ball becomes clear if one takes into account that on December 30, 2010, the Russian English-language news channel RT still presented the French proposal to sell the first ship for €720 million and the second for €650 million, making the total price €1.37 billion, under the heading "France offers New Year discounts on Mistral helicopter carriers." Cf.http://rt.com/news/prime-time/mistral-helicopters-discount-france/print/.

29. Isabelle Lasserre, "Avis de gros temps sur le Mistral," *Le Figaro* (March 15, 2011).

30. Lasserre, "Avis de gros temps."

31. Lasserre, "Avis de gros temps."

32. Isabelle Lasserre, "France-Russie: le nouvel axe stratégique," *Le Figaro* (May 25, 2011).

33. Vladimir Socor, "US Embassy in Moscow Indicates Acceptance of Mistral Deal," *Eurasia Daily Monitor* 7, no. 85 (May 3, 2010).

34. Vladimir Socor, "La France d'abord: Paris First to Capitalize on Russian Military Modernization," *Eurasia Daily Monitor* 7, no. 29 (February 11, 2010).

35. "En baisse—Les ventes d'armes," *Le Monde* (March 24, 2011).

36. Cf. "Mistral-Class Ship with Russian Crew Arrives in Saint-Nazaire after Training Voyage," *TASS* (September 22, 2014), http://itar-tass.com/en/russia/750617.

37. Jeff Lightfoot, "Mistral Mysteries," *The American Interest* 10, no. 3 (January/February 2015), 45. In May 2015 it was announced that France was seeking an agreement with Russia to break the contract. Paris would offer to pay back €785 million with the possibility to look for other buyers for the ships. Russia would be asking about €1.15 billion, withholding permission for sale to third parties. "The gap," the *Economist* writes, "suggests the beginning of a hard bargaining process." ("Scrapping the Mistral Deal," *The Economist* (May 15, 2015).) On August 5, 2015, the French and Russian presidents came to a final agreement. France immediately began negotiations with Egypt, which was mentioned as a possible buyer of the Mistral.

38. "French Secret Service Fear Russian Cathedral a Spying Front," *The Telegraph* (May 28, 2010), available at http://www.telegraph.co.uk/news/worldnews/europe/france/7771858/French-secret-service-fear-Russian-cathedral-a-spying-front.html.

39. Vincent Jauvert, "Opération cathédrale," *Le Nouvel Observateur* (May 27–June 2, 2010).

40. Jauvert, "Opération cathédrale."

41. Jauvert, "Opération cathédrale."

42. Cf. "La nouvelle église orthodoxe de Paris," *Le Monde* (March 19, 2011).

43. Claire Bommelaer, "La Russie va modifier le projet de l'église orthodoxe du quai Branly," *Le Figaro* (November 21, 2012).

44. Jauvert, "Opération cathédrale."

45. Hélène Blanc and Renata Lesnik, *Les prédateurs du Kremlin 1917–2009* (Paris: Seuil, 2009), 263.

46. Cf. Natalie Nougayrède, "Paris veut sceller un accord avec Berlin et Moscou sur 'l'espace commun européen,'" *Le Monde* (May 12, 2010).

47. Quoted in Walter Laqueur, *After the Fall: The End of the European Dream and the Decline of a Continent* (New York: St. Martin's, 2011), 91.

48. Katrin Bennhold, "At Deauville, Europe Embraces Russia," *The New York Times* (October 18, 2010).)

49. John Vinocur, "Will the U.S. Lose Europe to Russia?" *The New York Times* (October 25, 2010).

50. Vinocur, "Will the U.S. Lose Europe to Russia?"

51. Vladimir Socor, "Meseberg Process: Germany Testing EU-Russia Security Cooperation Potential," *Eurasia Daily Monitor* 7, no. 191 (October 22, 2010).

52. The German weekly *Der Spiegel* shared this opinion, writing that "such a move would bring Medvedev closer to his goal of a new European security architecture." ("Sarkozy Dreams of a European Security Council," *Spiegel Online* (October 18, 2010).)

53. Ivan Krastev and Mark Leonard, "We Need New Rules for a Multipolar Europe," *Financial Times* (October 20, 2010).

54. Jean-Bernard Pinatel, *Russie, alliance vitale* (Paris: Choiseul, 2010), 122, 129.

55. Pinatel, *Russie, alliance vitale*, 129.

56. The French name is Conseil de coopération franco-russe sur les questions de sécurité.

57. Natalie Nougayrède and Laurent Zecchini, "La France et la Russie vont renforcer leurs relations militaires," *Le Monde* (January 23–24, 2005).

58. Website of *L'Observatoire franco-russe*, http://obsfr.ru/, accessed January 10, 2014.

59. Arnaud Dubien, "France-Russie: renouveau et défis d'un partenariat stratégique," *Note de l'Observatoire franco-russe*, no. 1 (October 2012), 17.

60. Igor Naumov, "Ot matreshek do Kuru," *Nezavisimaya Gazeta* (June 11, 2010).

61. Theo Sommer, "Moscow Is Elbowing into Its Place in the Sun," *The Atlantic Times* (August 2007).

62. The French name is Comité de coordination du forum des Russes de France.

63. Cf. Lorraine Millot, "Les trolls du Kremlin au service de la propagande," *Libération* (October 24, 2014), http://www.liberation.fr/monde/2014/10/24/les-trolls-du-kremlin-au-service-de-la-propagande_1129062.

64. Quoted in Massimo Calabresi, "Inside Putin's East European Spy Campaign," *Time* (May 7, 2014).

65. Caroline Monnot and Abel Mestre, *Le système Le Pen: Enquête sur les réseaux du Front National* (Paris: Éditions Impacts, 2011), 46.

66. On the attractiveness of Putin's political system to extreme right parties, see Marcel H. Van Herpen, "Putin's Authoritarian Allure," *Project Syndicate* (March 15, 2013), http://www.project-syndicate.org/commentary/putinism-as-a-model-for-western-europe-s-extreme-right-by-marcel-h--van-herpen.

67. "Zhirinovsky Bid Backed by Le Pen," *The Independent* (February 10, 1996).

68. Yelena Chernenko, "Frantsiya vydet iz NATO" (France will leave NATO), interview with Marine Le Pen, *Kommersant* (October 13, 2011).

69. Monnot and Mestre, *Le système Le Pen*, 121.

70. Website of Marine Le Pen, http://www.marinelepen2012.fr/le-projet/politique-etrangere/politique-etrangere/.

71. "Le mystérieux voyage de Marion Maréchal-Le Pen en Russie," *Le Monde* (December 15, 2012).

72. "Le mystérieux voyage de Marion Maréchal-Le Pen en Russie."

73. *Daily Motion*, http://www.dailymotion.com/video/x1j5vzu_les-neo-nazis-de-svoboda-ukraine-et-le-front-national_news.

74. Cf. Isabelle Mandraud, "Deux hauts responsables russes en 'guest stars' au congrès du FN," *Le Monde* (November 30–December 1, 2014).

75. Marine Turchi, "Le FN attend 40 millions d'euros de Russie," *Mediapart* (November 26, 2014).

76. Cf. Lorraine Millot, "Le bataillon des naïfs," *Libération* (October 24, 2014).

77. "Poutine? Brigitte Bardot le 'trouve très bien,'" *Nice Matin* (April 19, 2012).

78. Sam Schechner and James Marson, "Total SA CEO Spoke Out against Russian Sanctions over Ukraine," *The Wall Street Journal* (October 21, 2014), http://www.wsj.com/articles/total-sa-ceo-spoke-out-against-russian-sanctions-1413908105.

79. Cf. "Russian Lawmaker Suggests Building Monument to TOTAL CEO Dying in Jet Crash," *ITAR-TASS* (October 23, 2014), http://itar-tass.com/en/russia/755943.

80. Dominique Lagarde, "Des chercheurs dans le désert," *L'Express*, no. 3123 (May 11–17, 2011).

81. Lagarde, "Des chercheurs dans le désert."

82. "Le débat russe, un terrain glissant," interview with Tatiana Kastoueva-Jean by Lorraine Millot, *Libération* (October 24, 2014).

83. Thomas Gomart, Alexander Rahr, Richard Sakwa, and Timothy Colton, "Vladimir Putin Turns 60," Valdai Discussion Club (October 5, 2012). In an interview with the French paper *Le Monde*, Gomart held both Russia and the West responsible for the crisis in Ukraine. The Western powers were said to have "denied the existence of a post-Soviet space." The Europeans were to blame because "everywhere in the world they encourage regional integration processes, except in the post-Soviet space." (Gaïdz Minassian, "Occident-Russie, la paix froide?" *Le Monde* (September 30, 2014).) The reality here was, of course, that most post-Soviet states did not *want* to be reintegrated with the former center (Russia) and preferred an integration into Euro-Atlantic structures.

84. Thomas Gomart, Alexander Rahr, Richard Sakwa, Timothy Colton, "Vladimir Putin Turns 60."

85. "Vladimir Putin Is Franklin Roosevelt of Our Time," *Pravda* (February 14, 2007).

86. Marcel H. Van Herpen, "The Foreign Policy of François Hollande: U-Turn or Continuity?" *Cicero Foundation Great Debate Paper*, No. 12/03, The Cicero Foundation, Paris/Maastricht (May 2012), 9–10, available at http://www.cicerofoundation.org/lectures/Marcel_H_Van_Herpen_%20FOREIGN_%20POLICY_%20HOLLANDE.pdf.

87. Natalie Nougayrède, "Derrière la saga Depardieu, le coup de froid franco-russe," *Le Monde* (January 9, 2013).

88. Nougayrède, "Derrière la saga Depardieu."

89. Nougayrède, "Derrière la saga Depardieu."

90. Arnaud Dubien, "Socialist President in France and Future of Russian-French Relations," *Valdai Discussion Club* (May 25, 2012).

91. Nikolaus von Twickel and Irina Filatova, "Hollande and Putin Warm Relations," *The Moscow Times* (March 1, 2013).

92. Daria Khaspekova, "There Has Been No Downturn in Russian-French Relations—Interview with Arnaud Dubien," *Russian International Affairs Council* (August 16, 2013), http://russiacouncil.ru/en/inner/?id_4=2231.

93. Jean-Pierre Chevènement, "Sans la Russie, il manque quelque chose à l'Europe," *Le Figaro* (March 8, 2014).

94. Vincent Jauvert, "Chevènement peut-il encore représenter Fabius en Russie?" *L'Obs* (March 8, 2014). Chevènement was not alone in condoning the annexation. Before him, Sarkozy also expressed his understanding for the Russian land grab. (Cf. Tristan Quinault Maupoil, "Nicolas Sarkozy légitime l'annexion de la Crimée par la Russie," *Le Figaro*, (February 10, 2015).)

Chapter Sixteen

Conclusions

FROM SOFT POWER OFFENSIVE TO INFORMATION WAR

In the first decade of the twenty-first century the Kremlin, trying to enhance Russia's soft power, began a "soft-power offensive." However, this offensive soon turned out to be something quite different: the start of an all-out information war. In Ukraine this information war has become part of a *real* war. The West has not only greatly underestimated the scale of the Russian propaganda effort, it has also failed to understand its function in Russia's new, "hybrid war" in its Near Abroad. At first, Russia's efforts were not even taken seriously but were regarded with a certain skepticism, if not condescension. Western commentators pointed out that soft power—a power of spontaneous attraction—could not be enhanced by government action. However, the hybrid war in Ukraine, in which the Russian propaganda outlets played a substantial role, and maybe even a decisive role, has shown that, ultimately, building soft power abroad was not the driving factor behind the Russian efforts. The real issue at stake was a policy of reimperialization of the post-Soviet space, and the Russian propaganda machine was attributed a specific role in this strategy. This role was to impose its own interpretation of events on a Western audience and in this way to undermine popular support for Western countermeasures. Even if the Kremlin did not succeed in convincing the Western public of the solidity of its arguments, it was enough to sow seeds of doubt as to the validity of the Western arguments. In this sense the Russian propaganda offensive has been very successful, and the West is still struggling to come to terms with this new, unprecedented situation.

THE KREMLIN'S ELEVEN SUCCESSES

What, exactly, are the Kremlin's successes? At first sight, the overall results are impressive. Let us enumerate:

- The Kremlin had no difficulty in engaging Western PR and communication firms. Even prestigious companies, such as Ketchum and Kissinger Associates in the United States and Euro-RSCG in France, were ready to help the Kremlin. This included lobbying politicians and government circles.
- Russian oligarchs succeeded in buying Western papers.
- The Kremlin's official paper *Rossiyskaya Gazeta* initiated the "Russia beyond the Headlines" project—adding monthly funded supplements to leading Western newspapers.
- There were cases of alleged attempts by Russian oligarchs or firms to fund political parties in Estonia, France, and the United Kingdom. The French extreme right Front National received a loan of 9 million and possibly 40 million euros from a Russian bank.
- According to experts' reports, Russian espionage activities in Western countries are back at Cold War levels. Despite temporary drawbacks, such as the discovery and expulsion from the United States of a "sleeper" spy ring, these enhanced activities are a sign that they are paying off. Russian espionage does not confine itself to infiltrating foreign government circles and positioning "agents of influence"; it also includes military and economic espionage.
- The Russian Orthodox Church (ROC) has proved to be the Kremlin's soft-power instrument *par excellence*. With Putin's help the ROC succeeded in bringing the Orthodox Church Outside Russia (ROCOR) back into Moscow's fold, giving the Moscow Patriarchate—in close cooperation with the Kremlin—a grip on the appointment of priests in foreign countries, including the United States, the United Kingdom, and France. Priests are expected to support the conservative and often openly reactionary version of Orthodoxy propagated by the Moscow Patriarchate. The Russian Orthodox Church is also acting as the Kremlin's mouthpiece in international organizations such as the UN, UNESCO, the OSCE, and the Council of Europe, where it is attacking universal human rights in the name of "traditional values."
- Putin's *personal* "charm offensives" in leading European countries were surprisingly successful. He succeeded in developing close personal relationships with several European leaders, including German Chancellor Gerhard Schröder, German Vice-Chancellor Frank-Walter Steinmeier, Italian Prime Ministers Silvio Berlusconi and Romano Prodi, French President Nicolas Sarkozy, French Prime Minister François Fillon, and—more

recently—with British Prime Minister David Cameron. This is quite an accomplishment for this former spymaster, who boasts of being "an expert in human relations."

- The Kremlin has made huge investments in the international TV channel RT (formerly Russia Today) and in an international radio station, the Voice of Russia, which is, with Sputnik, part of the revamped news agency Rossiya Segodnya. These investments have clearly paid off. RT has found a place among the world's leading cable TV stations, such as CNN, the BBC, and Al Jazeera.
- Over the past ten years the Kremlin's Valdai Discussion Club has developed into a valuable platform for the Kremlin, enabling it not only to sound out and to influence Western elite opinion but also to build a reservoir of Kremlin-friendly Western experts and politicians.
- The Kremlin founded several important new public diplomacy agencies, such as Rossotrudnichestvo and Russkiy Mir, modeled, respectively, after USAID and the British Council. Other new initiatives in this field are the Gorchakov Foundation, the Russian International Affairs Council (RIAC), and the Institute for Democracy and Cooperation (IDC), with bureaus in New York and Paris.
- The Kremlin succeeded in building important pro-Kremlin communities in Germany and France, two leading EU countries selected by the Kremlin to become part of a strategic triangle of Moscow-Berlin-Paris, which was assigned the task of rolling back the influence of the United States and the Anglo-Saxon countries.

THE LIMITS OF RUSSIA'S SOFT POWER

Given this extensive list, Russia's propaganda offensive seems at first sight to be an unrivaled success story. However, we have to keep in mind that this offensive had two different objectives which were not completely compatible. In the first place, it was meant to enhance Russian soft power abroad. In the second place it was assigned a role in the Russian information war with the West. This second objective led to a reinterpretation of "soft power," transforming it into the Russian government's instrument in the geopolitical "hard-power" competition. In the first chapter we identified three dimensions in the Russian "soft-power offensive." These were, respectively, mimesis, invention, and rollback. Mimesis consisted of copying Western practices and agencies. Invention consisted of the introduction of new methods to enhance Russian influence abroad. Rollback consisted of the introduction of (repressive) laws aiming at restricting the activities of Western NGOs in Russia, as well as of Russian NGOs which were partially or wholly funded from abroad. Examples of mimesis are agencies of public diplomacy, such as

Rossotrudnichestvo, Russkiy Mir, and the Institute for Democracy and Cooperation. RT—Russia's international cable TV channel—also falls into this category, as does the Kremlin's international radio station, the Voice of Russia. The latter is the successor of the Soviet radio station Radio Moscow. Its new name leaves no doubt about its model: it has simply copied the name of the Voice of America.

The second pillar of Russia's "soft-power offensive" is innovation. The Kremlin invented many new ways of influencing public opinion abroad. One example is the project "Russia beyond the Headlines," which started in 2007. Monthly supplements were funded and added to leading papers worldwide, which included the *Washington Post* (United States), the *New York Times* (United States), the *Daily Telegraph* (United Kingdom), *Le Figaro* (France), *Repubblica* (Italy), *El País* (Spain), and the *Süddeutsche Zeitung* (Germany). Another innovation was to hire Western PR and communication firms to "sell" the Kremlin's policies to Western governments and Western publics. The Kremlin had no difficulty in engaging the most prestigious firms of the United States and Europe. The Valdai Discussion Club also was an important innovation. This project was quite unique in organizing face-to-face discussions between the Russian leadership and Western experts, who, not enjoying such access to the leaders of their own countries, were, therefore, pleasantly surprised. Also new was the phenomenon of Russian oligarchs buying Western papers: *France-Soir* in France, and the *London Evening Standard* and the *Independent* in Britain. Although it cannot be proved that these initiatives (especially Lebedev's in Britain) were directly inspired by the Kremlin, they fit well within the Kremlin's overall strategy. Other attempts at gaining influence abroad, such as (illegally) funding political parties, were, in themselves, not new. Party funding was an instrument already used by the Soviet Union. In Soviet times, however, the majority of the funded parties were communist parties (although sometimes also noncommunist parties could be funded, such as the party of Finnish president Urho Kekkonen). However, with the end of communism, communist parties stopped being the beneficiaries of Russian largess, and a new phenomenon could be observed: that of Kremlin-related oligarchs offering financial support to a great variety of political parties.

Attempts at gaining political influence were not confined to political parties. They included approaching directly leading political personalities. Alleged attempts at gaining influence included the French center politician and presidential candidate François Bayrou, leaders of the British Conservative Party, President Roland Paksas of Lithuania (who was impeached), the Centre Party in Estonia, and the Citizens' Rights Party of Miloš Zeman in the Czech Republic. Another instrument for gaining influence abroad was espionage. Of course, this instrument was not new. A famous historical example of this approach is Günter Guillaume, Chancellor Willy Brandt's personal secretary, who worked for the Stasi, the KGB's East German sister organization. The Kremlin is still using this instrument, but it is innovating in the ways in which it is used. The opening of the frontiers after the demise of the Soviet Union led to free travel by Russian citizens and, consequently, to a huge increase in Russians studying, living, and working abroad. This made it possible to recruit new personnel for espionage activities. Young, attractive Russian girls, working as interns, have made their appearance in international organizations and in European government circles.

The Russian Orthodox Church comes closest to what can be called genuine soft power in the definition of Joseph Nye Jr. The moral authority of this venerable religious institution with a centuries-long history is great. However, the close cooperation between the Russian Orthodox Church and the Kremlin undermines its soft-power potential—at least abroad. Using the Orthodox Church for political objectives is not new in Russia. It is a long-established practice—not only under the tsars, but even under the officially "atheist" Communist regime. Under Putin the Kremlin has shown a great creativity, not only in its relationship with the church but also in terms of the objectives of this cooperation. Putin himself was personally committed to bringing about the merger between the Russian Orthodox Church and the ROCOR, the church abroad. At the same time, the Foreign Ministry began to lay claims to church property abroad—often successfully. An example of the close cooperation between the church and the Kremlin are Patriarch Kirill's pastoral visits to Ukraine, which had a clear political impact and fit perfectly with the Kremlin's strategy of bringing Ukraine back into the Russian orbit. Through the merger with ROCOR, the ROC has achieved a much greater international presence, enabling it to go beyond the confines of Russia and the former Soviet Union and become a genuinely "global" church. This expansion of the reach of the Russian Orthodox Church must be considered a major component of the Kremlin's "soft-power offensive." The Kremlin wants to establish Russia as an independent, alternative ideological and cultural powerhouse, propagating so called traditional values, which challenge Western values, presented as "decadent," "materialistic," and "gay-friendly." In this new ideological mission, the Kremlin and the Russian Orthodox Church are working hand in hand.

HOW THE KREMLIN'S ROLLBACK STRATEGY IS BACKFIRING

The third pillar of the Kremlin's "soft-power offensive" is rollback. It is clear that such a concept is completely at odds with the original definition of soft power given by Joseph Nye Jr. However, it is a constitutive component of the Russian "soft-power" variant, developed by the Kremlin. For Joseph Nye, soft power is the power of attraction. This attraction is, as a rule, spontaneous and not manipulated. Moreover, this power of attraction is sui generis, not in competition with the soft power of third parties. The attraction of a painting by Vermeer in the Rijksmuseum of Amsterdam is not diminished by the attraction of Leonardo da Vinci's *Mona Lisa* in the Paris Louvre or Goya's *Los Fusilamientos* in the Prado of Madrid. Each of these is attractive in its own way. The Kremlin's concept of "soft power," however, is different. It is based on the supposition that soft power is a zero-sum game and that the soft power of one country diminishes the soft power of another country, and vice versa. Soft power, therefore, is modeled after hard (military) power. It is considered, while not necessarily a constitutive part of a country's hard power, then at least supportive of its hard power. For this reason, it is important not only to develop and promote one's own soft power by all possible means, but it is equally important to check—and eventually diminish—the soft power of eventual competitors.

It is here that "rollback," the third component of the Russian "soft-power offensive," finds its place. The rollback strategy can be conducted outside Russia—as in the case of the "Kremlin trolls," who are active in the social media and write pro-Russian and anti-Western comments on Western blogs and in Western papers. Rollback, however, is conducted in particular within Russia itself, where it is directed at curtailing the influence of Western NGOs as well as of Russian NGOs which are funded by Western sources. A law, adopted by both houses of parliament in the first weeks of July 2012 and signed by President Putin on July 21, 2012, forced NGOs in Russia that were receiving funding from abroad and engaging in "political activity" to register with the Justice Ministry as *inostrannyy agent* (foreign agent). Putin compared these NGOs with the biblical disciple Judas, the historical prototype of the traitor, adding that this was "not the most respected biblical figure among our people." Putin's government went even further. It wanted not only to harass critical NGOs in Russia by taking their funding away but also to criminalize their activities. This was put into effect by the adoption by the Duma, on October 23, 2012, of amendments to articles 275 and 276 of the criminal code. These amendments introduced a much broader definition of treason. Treason would no longer be limited to illegally handing over secret information to foreign governments but would, in the future, also include "providing assistance in the form of information, funds and consultation to Western and international organizations." "Western organizations" could also mean Western NGOs.

At this point, however, the contradictions inherent in the Kremlin's "soft-power" concept became crystal clear. The new repressive laws led to an outcry in Europe and the United States, and the Russian government was accused of attacking and undermining the freedom of association, a fundamental political freedom. As a result, Russia's *real* soft power, its power of attraction, was severely damaged. On March 21, 2013, two thousand offices of NGOs in Russia were searched, including the office of Amnesty International in Moscow. Some days later, on March 26, 2013, in St. Petersburg the office of the Konrad-Adenauer-Stiftung, linked with the German Christian Democratic Party, was searched. A computer was confiscated. In Moscow, on the same day representatives of the Prosecutor's Office and tax authorities visited the office of the Friedrich-Ebert-Stiftung, an agency linked with the German Social-Democratic Party. A report on these events in the German weekly *Die Zeit* were given the heading "Razzia" (roundup)—a word which in Germany evokes connotations of the Nazi past.[1] Another example of how Russia's rollback strategy backfired was on September 19, 2013, when Russian special forces arrested twenty-eight Greenpeace activists of nineteen nationalities, together with a Russian photographer and a British videographer, after boarding their ship, *Arctic Sunrise*, in international waters.[2] One day earlier, four members of the group had tried to occupy Gazprom's oil platform Prirazlomnaya in the Pechora Sea as a protest against offshore drilling in this fragile Arctic environment. Actions like these are widely accepted in Western countries, where they are considered as a legitimate (although not always lawful) action of civil society. Not so with Russia. The Kremlin considered that this was a Western "soft-power" attack, which was a part of the "hard-power" struggle between the West and Russia over the Arctic's energy resources. Rosneft head Igor Sechin accused Greenpeace of acting at the behest of foreign companies or foreign governments. "Look who is paying them for this action," he said, without providing any evidence for his allegations.[3] Ilya Ponomaryov, a Duma member who worked for Khodorkovsky's expropriated Yukos oil firm, commented: "The government rejects the idea that Greenpeace could act alone because they are all former KGB agents and look for conspiracy theories everywhere."[4] The problem, however, is that Sechin's view was widely shared by the Russian population.[5] The outcome was self-defeating. Worldwide, the Russian action led to a wave of negative publicity. The French *Le Monde* published an editorial with the title "The Knout against Greenpeace, a Russia of Another Age,"[6] and the government of the Netherlands (where the Greenpeace icebreaker was registered) filed a lawsuit in the Hamburg-based International Tribunal for the Law of the Sea.[7] This happened during the Netherlands-Russia Friendship Year, a "soft-power event" meant to improve mutual relations, with cultural events taking place in Russia and the Netherlands. In April 2013, during a visit to Amsterdam to celebrate this "Friendship Year," Putin had already been confronted by angry protesters, attacking the homophobic laws that Russia had introduced shortly before. These are clear examples of incompatible Western and Russian "soft-power" concepts. For the Kremlin, the organization of a government-sponsored cultural "Friendship Year" in the Netherlands was an excellent "soft-power" initiative. It had organized similar events together with France (in 2010 and 2012) and Germany

(2012–2013). The problem is that soft power cannot be reduced to public diplomacy or to the organization of cultural events because an important part of a country's soft power consists of its policies and its political values. "The Russian state has had little success in improving its foreign image," wrote Robert Orttung. "Russia often inflicts serious damage to itself in moves that receive wide attention in the Western media. Russia's invasion of Georgia, energy conflicts with its neighbors, high levels of corruption and human rights violations at home win considerable attention in the West. The negative consequences of such actions greatly overshadow the positive benefits Russia receives from its wide ranging PR campaigns."[8] According to a Russian expert, "Russians are always irritated that Europeans speak about so-called 'shared values.' However, even for a stupid person it is clear that we don't share these [values]."[9]

Although Western countries clearly have the lead in the world's "soft-power league," this does not mean that they can sit back and relax because, as shown by the analysis in the first chapter, soft power is a variable currency and can be subject to significant fluctuations. The PRISM scandal, for instance, which was revealed in 2013 by whistleblower Edward Snowden, is a clear example of a credibility crisis that undermined US soft power—even among its closest allies.[10] Snowden's leaks have shown, write Farrell and Finnemore, that Washington "is . . . unable to consistently abide by the values that it trumpets."[11] "Yet as the United States finds itself less able to deny the gaps between its actions and its words," they continue, "it will face increasingly difficult choices—and may ultimately be compelled to start practicing what it preaches."[12] This is a fundamental truth: the United States in particular—the world's "soft-power champion"—has to live up to its proclaimed ideals and should not deviate for too long. However, in this readjustment of its practice to its theories, the United States has an important trump card, which is its existing soft-power reservoir. Building such a soft-power reservoir is a long-term process. A country which has such a reservoir can afford temporary "dips." It can repair its mistakes and make a fresh start because of this existing reservoir of goodwill. A country which does not have such a long-established soft-power reservoir and which—like Russia—in addition has to bear the brunt of a negative historical image, will face an uphill battle. For Russia, with its legacy of the Gulag and totalitarian Stalinism, this is no easy job. However, it is not impossible to overcome a negative legacy and rebrand a country's image. Germany, which over the past sixty years has successfully built a new soft-power reservoir, is a good example. The problem in Russia's case is that the goodwill created in the Gorbachev and Yeltsin era has been depleted by Putin's *siloviki*. The results of the "soft-power offensive" initiated by Putin's government will therefore remain ephemeral as long as this offensive is not accompanied by serious reforms. The Kremlin, acting abroad as a staunch supporter of Bashar al-Assad's murderous regime in Syria and internally taking an increasingly authoritarian and repressive course, has become entangled in the contradictions of its own "soft-power" strategy. After the annexation of the Crimea and the destabilization of Ukraine, which led to Western sanctions, Russian soft power in the West has reached a nadir. Even the successes the Kremlin booked in its bilateral relations with Germany and France are far from guaranteed. The only viable strategy for Russia is, therefore, to develop a *genuine* soft-power reservoir. This implies giving up its imperialist and revisionist foreign policy, implementing enduring, deep, and comprehensive economic and political reforms, leading to an attractive, modern polity with a robust political democracy, a vibrant civil society, and an independent judiciary. It is clear that Putin's Russia has not taken this road. Instead it has, in recent years, transformed its "soft-power offensive" into an instrument of the information war which accompanies its "hybrid" wars in its Near Abroad. These hybrid wars are *real* wars with the objective of recolonizing and reimperializing the former Soviet space. This is the reason why the West cannot ignore Russia's expanding propaganda machine. It is no longer a question of Russian soft power versus Western soft power but a question of war and peace, of containing Russia's aggression and territorial revisionism: in the end, it is about safeguarding peace and security in Europe as well as in the world as a whole.

SEVEN PROPOSALS TO COUNTER THE RUSSIAN PROPAGANDA OFFENSIVE

How can the Russian propaganda offensive be countered? There are, at least, seven measures which should be considered:

1. Spend more money.
2. Create an alternative Russian-language TV station.
3. Analyze the facts.
4. Raise public awareness.
5. Tell the truth.
6. Don't be too tolerant.
7. Fight trolls.

Spend More Money

In the past ten years, Russia has constantly been augmenting the budget for its propaganda effort. During this time, Western governments have been steadily decreasing the budgets made available for public diplomacy. This has already led to warnings by leading politicians, such as Hillary Clinton. Western governments should understand that in today's new international constellation, players such as Russia and China consider public diplomacy as instruments of an undeclared information war. Therefore, the West no longer has the option to take a backseat, trusting to its supposed superior soft power to do the job. Government-supported public diplomacy was and still is an important instrument for disseminating Western values, which, we should not forget, have a universal validity and a universal attraction. This does not mean that Western public diplomacy agencies should practice active "democracy promotion" nor that they should present their democracies as models to be copied and emulated elsewhere in the world. It is enough to present their countries in an objective way, just the way they are.

Create an Alternative Russian-Language TV Station

An interesting initiative is an idea floated by Poland's former foreign minister, Radek Sikorski, of creating an EU-funded Russian-language TV station. After the downing of flight MH17 in July 2014 over Donetsk, killing 193 Dutch nationals and 105 others, the Dutch government has stepped in with a grant of €500,000 to fund a study by the Brussels-based European Endowment for Democracy (EED) to enable new actors in the Russian-language infosphere, including TV, social media, and internet portals.[13] However, such an initiative requires a long-term investment and a long-term commitment. Since it is not certain that all EU member states would support such an initiative, it could also be considered by a "coalition of the willing," consisting of a group of EU member states and the United States.

Analyze the Facts

An important feature of the Russian propaganda effort is that it contains misinformation and disinformation. Misinformation is completely false, invented information. Disinformation is a mixture of true and invented facts, or it consists of true facts that are placed in a dubious context. Misinformation, as such, is easier to debunk. The story of the "crucified child in Ukraine," for instance, which was broadcast by the Russian First TV Channel on July 12, 2014, is a clear example. The lies were so obvious that Russian journalists asked questions about it during Putin's press conference on December 18, 2014. Disinformation, on the other hand, is a more difficult matter, because it is based on real, verifiable facts. The downing of the Malaysian MH17 jet on July 17, 2014, in the Donetsk region is such a fact. Russian media immediately denied that pro-Russian militias or Russian soldiers were implicated, suggesting instead the existence of a supposed Ukrainian "plot" to shoot down a plane in which Putin was returning to Russia. On another occasion they spoke of an attack by jets of the Ukrainian airforce, although there were no Ukrainian planes flying in this zone. Both myths could soon be dispelled. The huge Russian disinformation campaign was the motivation behind

Ukrainian analysts setting up a special website (stopfake.org) to check the facts and debunk Russian propaganda. This is a model which could be emulated, for instance, by setting up an "anti-information war agency" under the aegis of the EU and/or United States

Raise Public Awareness

Debunking propaganda is important. Equally important, however, is raising public awareness according to the well-known proverb "forewarned is forearmed." This is also the case here. In education, more emphasis should be placed on analyzing how propaganda works and on finding ways to prevent people being easily taken in by it. As a rule, more educated people tend to be more skeptical. However, more educated people are more susceptible to the so-called third-person effect. This is the belief that propaganda has a greater effect on others than on oneself. This belief is, as a rule, unfounded: "We often watch the mass media while we are in a mindless state. The communications are typically just not that involving or interesting. But, ironically, that often makes them all the more persuasive. In such cases . . . we . . . do not make much of an attempt to refute the message and, as a consequence, are often persuaded."[14] Of course, raising awareness and developing critical thinking skills are long-term educational investments. They should, however, be part of the secondary education curriculum in democratic societies.[15]

Tell the Truth

Western media should resist the temptation to react to Russian propaganda by producing counterpropaganda. One of the most precious Western soft-power instruments consists of its independent and objective media. This fundamental fact was emphasized by Peter Horrocks, former executive in charge of the BBC's global news operations, who said that "the role we need to play is an even handed one. We shouldn't be pro-one side or the other, we need to provide something people can trust."[16] The Western media should, therefore, not be afraid to expose the ugly sides of the West, as were the cases, for instance, regarding Guantánamo or the Abu Ghraib prison. Conveying objective and impartial news should remain its vocation and primary obligation. The truth of independent news brought by conscientious journalists will debunk all the lies disseminated by Orwellian Ministries of Truth, however intelligent and carefully these lies may be constructed. While the Kremlin acts according to Lenin's adage, "A lie told often enough becomes the truth," the West should keep in mind the words attributed to US President Franklin Delano Roosevelt, that "repetition does not transform a lie into a truth." General David Petraeus, American former commander of the International Security Assistance Force (ISAF) in Afghanistan, wrote in his counter-insurgency guidance:

> Be first with the truth. Beat the insurgents and malignant actors to the headlines. Pre-empt rumors. Get accurate information to the chain of command, to Afghan leaders, to the people, and to the press as soon as possible. Integrity is critical to this fight. Avoid spinning, and don't try to "dress up" an ugly situation. Acknowledge setbacks and failure, including civilian casualties, and then state how we'll respond and what we've learned. [17]

Telling the truth also implies that one does not shrink from calling things by their right name instead of describing unacceptable facts in woolly language, clouding the issue—as can often be observed in the case of Russia's invasion of Ukraine. "There are few fierce and fearless journalists like Oriana Fallaci to scream uncomfortable truths at timid politicians," writes Eliot Cohen. "But we can try, beginning perhaps with Havel's inspiration, by clinging to the truth. We can call things by their names—using words like *invasion and fanaticism*, for example, and not pretending that they are something tamer and less dangerous." [18]

Don't Be Too Tolerant

With RT the Kremlin has created a mighty weapon to influence Western public opinion. The Russian cable TV channel has direct access to the homes of tens of millions of Europeans and Americans. In most hotel rooms in Europe and the United States, RT is available on cable. Moscow has exploited the many opportunities offered by our open Western society to their full potential while at the same time harassing Western news agencies and Western journalists who work in Russia. In a law adopted on September 23, 2014, Western financial participation in Russian media outlets has been reduced from 50 percent to 20 percent. The law also bans foreigners from being founders of Russian mass media companies—restrictions which also apply to residents and Russians who have other citizenships. The law, which comes into force on January 1, 2016, seems to be directed, in particular, against the liberal business paper *Vedomosti*, which is owned jointly by News Corp of America, Pearson of Britain, and Sanoma of Finland. Axel Springer, a German firm which publishes the Russian edition of *Forbes*, will also have to sell. [19] Kremlin-related oligarchs are preparing to pick up the pieces and install Kremlin-friendly editors. In this situation of an undeclared information war with the Kremlin, there is no reason for the West to grant Russian media freedom which the Russian government does not grant to Western media. Reciprocity should be a condition for the Russian media presence in the West. One should keep in mind the words of Josef Korbel, a Czech émigré and Madeleine Albright's father, who pointed out that "democratic regimes create spaces for other countries to present their case directly, even when they do not reciprocate."[20] He noted that "Soviet leaders had access to the American press while Americans enjoyed no such direct access to the Soviet population."[21] As concerns this reciprocity, not much has changed since Soviet times. There is another point: Western governments should also not accept RT diffusing explicitly biased or one-sided information. Some countries already have adopted the necessary instruments. In the United Kingdom, for instance, the Office of Communications (Ofcom), a government-approved regulatory and competition authority for the broadcasting, telecommunications, and postal industries, ensures that TV channels with a British broadcasting license provide impartial news coverage. Ofcom's code, section 5.1, demands that "news, in whatever form, must be reported with due accuracy and presented with due impartiality." Already several times RT has been found in breach of these regulations. In November 2012, a documentary about Syria, broadcast on July 12, 2012, was judged biased because an interviewee was crediting "a massacre [in the Syrian conflict] to the rebels and not the government and was not challenged in any way."[22] In November 2014, Ofcom judged four RT programs—broadcast on March 1, 3, 5, and 6, 2014, during the occupation of Crimea by unidentified militias—to be in breach of the rules of due impartiality.[23] Another case is Lithuania, where on March 21, 2014, broadcasts of Gazprom-owned NTV Mir station were banned. The reason given by the government was that the station spread lies about Lithuania's move to declare independence from the Soviet Union in early 1991.[24] On April 3, 2014, Latvia's National Electronic Mass Media Council suspended the broadcast rights of Rossiya RTR for three weeks on the grounds that the station was disseminating "war propaganda."[25] However, repressive measures should be reserved for only flagrant breaches of the code of impartiality and objectivity. Estonia, for instance, "opted to leave Russian channels on and instead to compete with a barrage of 'counter-programming' through Russian-language TV, radio, and print media."[26]

Fight Trolls

The Kremlin uses an army of trolls who flood the Internet with pro-Kremlin comment. Trolls are warriors, working for the Kremlin as paid online mercenaries: "Each troll is expected to post 50 news articles daily and maintain six Facebook and ten Twitter accounts, with 50 tweets per day."[27] Overwhelmed by these posts, which clog internet forums and make a genuine dialogue impossible, papers sometimes decide to close their comment sections. On November 18, 2014, for instance, the *Moscow Times* published the message that "due to the increasing number of users engaging in personal attacks, spams, trolling and abusive comments, we are no longer able to host our forum as a site for constructive and intelligent debate. It is with regret, therefore, that we have found ourselves forced to suspend the commenting function on our articles."[28] The question is whether this is the only solution available. It would be a shame if the Kremlin were able to undermine the unique new communication channels, created by the internet, which play an important role in modern civil society. Apart from closing forums, one could, for instance, think about setting up blacklists of trolls, who then will be automatically blocked from accessing a forum. Compiling such lists is, of course, painstaking work, and the trolls will certainly try to find ways to create new identities and circumvent the lists. This kind of work could eventually be done by the same agency set up by Western governments to debunk Kremlin propaganda.[29]

NOTES

1. "Russland lässt deutsche Stiftungen durchsuchen," *Die Zeit* (March 26, 2013).

2. "Russia 'Seizes' Greenpeace Ship after Arctic Rig Protest," *BBC* (September 23, 2013).

3. Quoted in Yekaterina Kravtsova, "Greenpeace Rebuffs Talk of Arctic Protest Conspiracy," *The Moscow Times* (November 1, 2013).

4. "Greenpeace Rebuffs Talk of Arctic Protest Conspiracy."

5. According to the *Moscow Times*, in a poll conducted by the state pollster VTsIOM, "42 percent said the Greenpeace action was plotted by foreign intelligence agencies and governments to take Russia's natural resources and territories in the Arctic." ("Russians See Greenpeace Protest as a Foreign Plot," *The Moscow Times* (October 29, 2013).)

6. "Le knout contre Greenpeace, une Russie d'un autre âge," *Le Monde* (October 10, 2013). The knout is a scourge-like multiple whip that was used in Russia for corporal punishment.

7. "Netherlands to Sue Russia over Greenpeace Ship Seizure," *RIA Novosti* (October 21, 2013).

8. Robert W. Orttung, "Russia's Use of PR as a Foreign Policy Tool," *Russian Analytical Digest*, no. 81 (16 June 2010), 9.

9. Ivan Preobrazhensky, "Evropeytsy na rayone," *Russkaya Mysl*, no. 43/11 (November 2013), 9.

10. On the PRISM scandal and US and Russian soft power, see Marcel H. Van Herpen, "The PRISM Scandal, the Kremlin, and the Eurasian Union," *Atlantic-Community.org* (July 19, 2013), www.atlantic-community.org/-/the-prism-scandal-the-kremlin-and-the-eurasian-union.

11. Henry Farrell and Martha Finnemore, "The End of Hypocrisy," *Foreign Affairs* 92, no. 6 (November/December 2013), 24.

12. "The End of Hypocrisy," 23.

13. Andrew Rettman, "EU Mulls Response to Russia's Information War," *EU Observer* (January 8, 2015), https://euobserver.com/foreign/127135. Latvia has proposed a Baltic-wide Russian-language channel. Estonia, however, preferred a national channel that will be launched in the second half of 2015. (Cf. Chris McGreal, "Vladimir Putin's 'Misinformation' Offensive Prompts US to Deploy Its Cold War Propaganda Tools," *The Guardian* (April 25, 2015).)

14. Anthony Pratkanis and Elliot Aronson, *Age of Propaganda: The Everyday Use and Abuse of Persuasion* (New York: Holt, 2002), 335.

15. According to Janis Karkliņš, director of the NATO Strategic Communications Centre of Excellence in Riga, it is necessary "to raise awareness of the methods that are used, explain what trolls are, how they operate and what their targets are. There is one very simple remedy, although it will not have an immediate effect: I strongly believe that information literacy should become a part of every school curriculum, and in their education through primary and secondary school, children need to acquire certain skills that will help them orient themselves in and

distil this deluge of information, including the disinformation that is present on the internet."
(Wojciech Przybylski, "Controlling the Trolls—A Conversation with Janis Karklinš and Paul
Rebane," *New Eastern Europe* 1, no. 15 (January–February 2015), 52.)

16. Josh Halliday, "BBC World Service Fears Losing Information War as Russia Today
Ramps Up Pressure," *The Guardian* (December 23, 2014). In a comment titled "Europravda?
Nein, danke!" (Europravda, no, thank you), the German paper *Der Tagesspiegel* was quite clear
in its rejection of setting up an EU agency tasked with "anti-Kremlin propaganda." (Nik
Afanasjew, "Europravda? Nein, danke!" *Der Tagesspiegel* (March 20, 2015).) The paper
thinks, however, that an EU-sponsored agency that translates articles from Western media into
Russian would be "a step in the right direction."

17. Quoted in Lt. Col. Aaron D. Burgstein, "You Can't Win If You Don't Play—Communication: Engage Early, Engage Often," in *Air and Space Power Journal* 5, no. 4 (4th quarter
2014), 23.

18. Eliot Cohen, "The 'Kind of Thing' Crisis," *The American Interest* 10, no. 3 (January/
February 2015), 11.

19. Cf. "Interesting News," *The Economist* (November 8, 2014).

20. Quoted in Moisés Naím, *The End of Power: From Boardrooms to Battlefields and
Churches, Why Being in Charge Isn't What It Used to Be* (New York: Basic Books, 2013), 153.

21. Naím, *The End of Power.*

22. "Ofcom Broadcast Bulletin," no. 217 (November 5, 2012), 26, http://stakeholders.
ofcom.org.uk/binaries/enforcement/broadcast-bulletins/obb217/obb217.pdf.

23. "Ofcom Broadcast Bulletin," no. 266 (November 10, 2014). In these programs one
reporter stated that an "assault on administrative buildings in Ukraine's Crimea, ordered by
Kiev, is thwarted by local self-defense forces." There were no such assaults. A Ukrainian MP
made a statement that the interim Ukrainian government "might acquire nuclear weapons and
use these against Russia." http://stakeholders.ofcom.org.uk/binaries/enforcement/broadcast-
bulletins/obb266/obb266.pdf.

24. Cf. Massimo Calabresi, "Inside Putin's East European Spy Campaign," *Time* (May 7,
2014).

25. Calebresi, "Inside Putin's East European Spy Campaign."

26. Calabresi, "Inside Putin's East European Spy Campaign."

27. Paul Roderick Gregory, "Putin's New Weapon in the Ukrainian Propaganda War: Internet Trolls," *Forbes* (September 12, 2014). Note that not only the "trolls" are warriors but *all* the
participants in Moscow's information war, a fact which is publicly acknowledged by Margarita
Simonyan, head of *RT*, who declared: "When there is no war, it seems as if it (RT) is not
needed. But damn it, when there is a war, it's (RT is) downright critical. You can't create an
army a week before the war starts." (Quoted in "Putin. War: An Independent Expert Report
Based on Materials from Boris Nemtsov" (Moscow, May 2015), 9.)

28. Note to readers in article comment section, *The Moscow Times* (November 18, 2014),
http://www.themoscowtimes.com/opinion/article/putin-s-g20-snub/511377.html.

29. It is interesting that the Kremlin already closely monitors what is happening in the world
of social media. This is done by Zvezda—Tsentr Strategicheskikh Issledovaniy i Razrabotok
(Zvezda Center for Strategic Research and Development), which monitors Twitter tweets that
have hashtags such as #Russia, #Ukraine, #Putin, and so on. (Zvezda Center, accessed January
19, 2015, http://zvezda.center/tw.php.)

Bibliography

Amis, Martin. *The Second Plane: September 11: 2001–2007*. London: Jonathan Cape, 2008.

Anderson, John. "Putin and the Russian Orthodox Church: Asymmetric Symphonia?" *Journal of International Affairs* 61, no. 1 (Fall/Winter 2007).

Andreescu, Gabriel. *Right-Wing Extremism in Romania*. Cluj: Ethnocultural Diversity Resource Center, 2003. http://www.edrc.ro/docs/docs/extremism_eng/RightwingExtremismInRomania.pdf.

Andrew, Christopher. *The Defence of the Realm: The Authorised History of MI5*. London: Penguin, 2010.

———— and Vasili Mitrokhin. *The Mitrokhin Archive: The KGB in Europe and the West*. London and New York: Penguin, 2000.

Arjakovsky, Antoine. *Russie Ukraine: De la guerre à la paix?* Paris: Parole et Silence, 2014.

Aron, Leon. "Everything You Think You Know about the Collapse of the Soviet Union Is Wrong," *Foreign Policy* (July–August, 2011).

Baev, Pavel. K. "Disentangling the Moscow-Berlin Axis: Follow the Money." *Eurasia Daily Monitor* 148, no. 2 (August 1, 2005).

Bandler, Donald K., and A. Wess Mitchell. "Ich Bin Ein Berliner." *The National Interest online*, January 22, 2009.

Barbashin, Anton, and Hannah Thoburn. "Putin's Brain—Alexander Dugin and the Philosophy behind Putin's Invasion of Crimea." *Foreign Affairs* 93, no. 2 (March/April 2014).

Beaufre, André. *Introduction à la stratégie*. With a preface by B. H. Liddell Hart. Paris: Librairie Armand Colin, 1965.

Bilg, Asli. "Moscow and Greek Orthodox Patriarchates: Two Actors for the Leadership of World Orthodoxy in the Post Cold War Era." *Religion, State, and Society* 35, no. 4 (2007).

Bismarck, Otto Fürst von. *Gedanken und Erinnerungen*. 2. Band. Stuttgart and Berlin: J.G. Gotta'sche Buchhandlung Nachfolger, 1919.

Blake, Michael. "'Traditional Values' and Human Rights: Whose Traditions? Which Rights?" Cicero Foundation Great Debate Paper No. 13/06, December 2013.

Blanc, Hélène, and Renata Lesnik. *Les prédateurs du Kremlin (1917–2009)*. Paris: Seuil, 2009.

Blitt, Robert C. "One New President, One New Patriarch, and a Generous Disregard for the Constitution: A Recipe for the Continuing Decline of Secular Russia." *Vanderbilt Journal of Transnational Law* 43 (2010).

————. "Russia's 'Orthodox' Foreign Policy: The Growing Influence of the Russian Orthodox Church in Shaping Russia's Policies Abroad." *University of Pennsylvania Journal of International Law* 33, no. 2 (May 2011).

Bourdeaux, Michael. "The Complex Face of Orthodoxy." *The Christian Century* (April 4, 2001).

Bove, Andrew, ed. *Questionable Returns*. IWM Junior Visiting Fellows Conferences, vol. 12, Vienna, 2002.

Bovt, Georgi. "Soft Power of the Russian Word." Russian International Affairs Council, October 2, 2013.

Brandt, Willy. *Begegnungen und Einsichten: Die Jahre 1960–1975*. Hamburg: Hoffmann und Campe, 1976.

Brill, Heinz. "Deutschland im geostrategischen Kraftfeld der Super- und Großmächte (1945–1990)." In *Westbindung: Chancen und Risiken für Deutschland*, edited by Rainier Zitelmann, Karlheinz Weismann, and Michael Grossheim. Frankfurt am Main and Berlin: Propyläen, 1993.

Brinks, Jan Herman. "Germany's New Right." In *Nationalist Myths and the Modern Media: Cultural Identity in the Age of Globalisation*, edited by Jan Herman Brinks. London: I.B. Tauris, 2005.

———. "Nationalism in German Politics as Mirrored by the Media since Reunification." Report for the one-day workshop "Apocalyptic Politics, Archaic Myths and Modern Media," London, March 28, 2006.

Broun, Janice. "Divisions in Eastern Orthodoxy." *East-West Church & Ministry Report* 5, no. 2 (Spring 1997).

Brovkin, Vladimir N. *Russia after Lenin: Politics, Culture, and Society, 1921–1929*. London: Routledge, 1998.

Brzezinski, Zbigniew. *The Grand Chessboard: American Primacy and Its Geostrategic Imperatives*. New York: Basic Books, 1997.

———. *Second Chance: Three Presidents and the Crisis of American Superpower*. New York: Basic Books, 2007.

———. "U.S. Fate Is in U.S. Hands." *The National Interest* 121 (September/October 2012).

Buciora, Fr. J. "Canonical Territory of the Moscow Patriarchate: An Analysis of Contemporary Russian Orthodox Thought." *Orthodox Christian Comment*, no date.

Burgstein, Lt. Col. Aaron. "You Can't Win If You Don't Play—Communication: Engage Early, Engage Often." *Air and Space Power Journal* 5, no. 4 (4th quarter 2014).

Buruma, Ian, and Avishai Margalit. *Occidentalism: The West in the Eyes of Its Enemies*. New York: Penguin, 2004.

Cassirer, Ernst. *The Myth of the State*. New Haven and London: Yale University Press, 1975.

Castoriadis, Cornelius. *Une société à la dérive: Entretiens et débats 1974–1997*. Paris: Editions du Seuil, 2005.

Churchill, Winston. *Great Contemporaries*. London: Thornton Butterworth, 1937.

Ciechanowicz, Artur, Anna Kwiatkowska-Drożdż, and Witold Rodkiewicz. "Merkel and Putin's Consultation: The Economy First of All." *Centre for Eastern Studies* (November 21, 2012).

Clark, Christopher. *Preußen: Aufstieg und Niedergang 1600–1947*. Munich: Pantheon Verlag, 2008.

Clover, Charles. "Dreams of the Eurasian Heartland: The Reemergence of Geopolitics." *Foreign Affairs* 78, no. 2 (March/April 1999).

Custine, Marquis Astolphe de. *Lettres de Russie: La Russie en 1839*. Edited by Pierre Nora. Paris: Gallimard, 1975.

Ćwiek-Karpowicz, Jarosław. "Role of the Orthodox Church in Russian Foreign Policy." *Bulletin* 109 (185), The Polish Institute of International Affairs, August 9, 2010.

Danilevsky, Nikolay. "Russland und Europa." In *Russischer Nationalismus: Die russische Idee im 19. und 20. Jahrhundert. Darstellung und Texte*, edited by Frank Golczewski and Gertrud Pickhan. Göttingen: Vandenhoeck & Ruprecht, 1998.

Darczewska, Jolanta. "The Anatomy of Russian Information Warfare—The Crimean Operation, A Case Study." *Point of View*, no. 42 (May 2014), Warsaw, Center for Eastern Studies.

Derluguian, Georgi. "Introduction—Whose Truth?" In *A Small Corner of Hell: Dispatches from Chechnya*, by Anna Politkovskaya. Chicago and London: University of Chicago Press, 2003.

De Waal, Thomas. "Spring of Patriarchs." *The National Interest*, January 27, 2011.

Deyneka, Anita. "Russia's Restrictive Law on Religion: Dead or Delayed?" *East-West Church & Ministry Report* 1, no. 4 (Fall 1993).

Dezhina, Irina. "The Russian Science as a Factor of Soft Power." *Russian International Affairs Council*. June 21, 2012.

Dolinskiy, Alexey. "How Moscow Understands Soft Power." www.russia-direct.org, June 21, 2013.

Dugin, Aleksandr. *Evraziystvo ot filosofii k politike: Doklad na Uchreditelnom sezde OPOD 'Evrazii' 21 aprelya 2001 g., Moskva*. Moscow, 2001.

———. *The Fourth Political Theory*. Moscow: Arktos Media, 2012.

———. *Konspirologiya*. Available online at http://epop.ru/sub/trash/book/konspy.html.

Engels, Friedrich. "Die Russen." In *Marx Engels Werke (MEW)*, Band 6. Berlin: Dietz Verlag, 1959.

Farrell, Henry, and Martha Finnemore. "The End of Hypocrisy." *Foreign Affairs* 92, no. 6 (November/December 2013).

Fédorovski, Vladimir. *Le roman du Kremlin*. Paris: Éditions du Rocher, 2004.

Filimonov, Georgy. "Russia's Soft Power Potential." *Russia in Global Affairs*, December 25, 2010.

Fischer, Joschka. *Scheitert Europa?* Cologne: Kiepenheuer & Witsch, 2014.

Foot, Michael Richard Daniell. *Holland at War against Hitler*. London: Routledge, 1990.

Fukuyama, Francis. *The End of History and the Last Man*. London and New York: Penguin, 1992.

Galbraith, John Kenneth. *Name-Dropping – From F.D.R. On*. Boston and New York: Houghton Mifflin Company, 1999.

Goble, Paul. "Russian First Lady Seen Actively Promoting Orthodox Church: Analysis." *Eurasia View*, May 9, 2011.

———. "Window on Eurasia: Russians No Longer View Orthodox Church as Separate from the State, Lunkin Says." *Window on Eurasia*, April 28, 2011.

Goldman, Marshall. *Oilopoly: Putin, Power, and the Rise of the New Russia*. Oxford: Oneworld, 2008.

Gorshkova, M. K., N. E. Tikhonovoy, and L. A. Belyayeva. *Izmenyayushchayasya Rossiya v zerkale sotsiologii*. Moscow: Letniy Sad, 2004.

Graham, Thomas. "Putin, the Sequel." *The American Interest* 7, no. 4 (March/April 2012).

———. "Resurgent Russia and U.S. Purposes: A Century Foundation Report." New York and Washington: Century Foundation, 2009.

Gray, Colin S. *The Geopolitics of the Nuclear Era: Heartland, Rimlands, and the Technological Revolution*. Strategy Paper no. 30, National Strategy Information Center, Washington, DC. New York: Crane, Russak, 1977.

Grigas, Agnia. "Legacies, Coercion and Soft Power: Russian Influence in the Baltic States." Briefing paper. *Chatham House*, August 2012.

Grossheim, Michael, Karlheinz Weismann, and Rainer Zitelmann, "Einleitung: Wir Deutschen und der Westen," in *Westbindung: Chancen und Risiken für Deutschland*, edited by Rainer Zitelmann, Karlheinz Weismann, and Michael Grossheim. Frankfurt am Main and Berlin: Propyläen, 1993.

Grygiel, Jakub. "Europe: Strategic Drifter." *The National Interest* 126 (July/August 2013).

Gvosdev, Nikolas K. "An Orthodox Look at Liberty and Economics in Russia." *Religion & Liberty* 14, no. 4 (July/August 2004).

——— and Christopher Marsh. *Russian Foreign Policy: Interests, Vectors, and Sectors*. Los Angeles: CQ Press, 2014.

Halper, Stefan. *The Beijing Consensus: Legitimizing Authoritarianism in Our Time*. New York: Basic Books, 2012.

Hammes, Colonel Thomas X. *The Sling and the Stone: On War in the 21st Century*. St. Paul, MN: Zenith Press, 2004.

Hansen, Flemming Splidsboel. "China, Russia, and the Foreign Policy of the SCO." *Connections* 11, no. 2 (Spring 2012).

Harding, Luke. *Mafia State: How One Reporter Became an Enemy of the Brutal New Russia*. London: Guardian Books, 2011.

Hayek, Friedrich A. "Religion and the Guardians of Tradition." In *The Fatal Conceit: The Errors of Socialism*. Vol. 1 of *The Collected Works of Friedrich August Hayek*, edited by W.W. Bartley III. London: Routledge, 1988.

Heilbrunn, Jacob. "All Roads Lead to Berlin." *The National Interest* 122 (November/December 2012).

———. "Germany's New Right." *Foreign Affairs* 75, no. 6 (November/December 1996).

Hess, Markus. "Kurzfassung zur Studie 'Perspektiven einer Grenzregion' im Rahmen des gemeinsamen Fördervorhabens Junge Menschen in Grenzregionen der neuen Bundesländer." Institute for Applied Research on Childhood, Youth, and the Family, University of Potsdam, 2002.

Hetzer, Wolfgang. "No Punishment for Bribery? When Corruption Is Business as Usual." *Corruption*, SIAK Scientific Series, Republic of Austria, Sicherheitsakademie of the Ministry of the Interior, Vienna, 2010.

Hill, Fiona, and Clifford Gaddy. "Putin and the Uses of History." *The National Interest* 117 (January/February 2012).

Hitler, Adolf. *Mein Kampf.* Munich: Verlag Franz Eher Nachfolger, 1933.

Hollingsworth, Mark, and Stewart Lansley. *Londongrad: From Russia with Cash—The Inside Story of the Oligarchs.* London: Fourth Estate, 2010.

Hulsman, John C. "Prepared Statement of John C. Hulsman, PhD, Research Fellow for European Affairs, The Davis Institute for International Studies, The Heritage Foundation," House Committee on International Relations, Subcommittee on Europe, June 11, 2003.

Huntington, Samuel P. "The Lonely Superpower." *Foreign Affairs* 78, no. 2 (March/April 1999).

Iost, Delphine. "L'implantation du NPD dans les nouveaux *Länder* allemands." *Hérodote: revue de géographie et de géopolitique*, no. 128, 1er trimestre 2008.

Ivanov, Igor. "What Diplomacy Does Russia Need in the 21st Century?" *Russia in Global Affairs*, December 29, 2011.

James, Lawrence. *Churchill and Empire: Portrait of an Imperialist.* London: Phoenix, 2013.

Johnstone, Patrick, and Jason Mandryck. "Non-Indigenous Protestant Missionaries in Post-Soviet States, 1994–2001." *East-West Church & Ministry Report* 10, no. 1 (Winter 2002).

Kääriäinen, Kimmo, and Dmitrii Furman. "Orthodoxy as a Component of Russian Identity." *East-West Church & Ministry Report* 10, no. 1 (Winter 2002).

Kaplan, Robert D. "The Divided Map of Europe." *The National Interest* 120 (July/August 2012).

Karaganov, Sergei. "The Map of the World: Geopolitics Stages a Comeback." *Russia in Global Affairs*, May 19, 2013.

Kashlev, Y. B. *Razryadka v Evrope: Ot Helsinki k Madridu.* Moscow: Politizdat, 1980.

Kempe, Iris. *From a European Neighborhood Policy toward a New Ostpolitik—The Potential Impact of German Policy.* Policy Analysis no. 3, Center for Applied Policy Research, Munich, May 2006.

Kirchick, James. "Pravda on the Potomac." *The New Republic*, February 18, 2009.

Kissinger, Henry. *On China.* London and New York: Penguin, 2011.

Kivirähk, Juhan. "How to Address the 'Humanitarian Dimension' of Russian Foreign Policy?" *Diplomaatia*, no. 90, International Centre for Defence Studies, Tallinn, February 3, 2010.

Knox, Zoe. "The Struggle for Religious Pluralism: Russian Orthodoxy and Civil Society in post-Soviet Russia." PhD diss., Centre for European Studies, Monash University, Victoria (Australia), March 2002.

Korduban, Pavel. "Russian Orthodox Patriarch Kirill Visits Ukraine." *Eurasia Daily Monitor* 6, no. 155 (August 12, 2009).

Kozovoï, Andreï. *Les services secrets Russes: Des tsars à Poutine.* Paris: Tallandier, 2010.

Krastev, Ivan, and Mark Leonard. "The Spectre of a Multipolar Europe." Policy paper, European Council on Foreign Relations. London: European Council on Foreign Relations, 2010.

Kudors, Andis. "'Russian World'—Russia's Soft Power Approach to Compatriots Policy." *Russian Analytical Digest* 81 (June 16, 2010).

Kundnani, Hans. "Leaving the West Behind: Germany Looks East." *Foreign Affairs* 94, no. 1 (January/February 2015).

Kuzio, Taras. "State-led Violence in Ukraine's 2004 Elections and Orange Revolution." *Communist and Post-Communist Studies*, no. 43, 2010.

Laqueur, Walter. *After the Fall: The End of the European Dream and the Decline of a Continent*. New York: St. Martin's, 2011.

———. *Mein 20. Jahrhundert: Stationen eines politischen Lebens*. Berlin: Propyläen, 2009.

———. *No End to War: Terrorism in the Twenty-First Century*. New York: Continuum, 2003.

Laruelle, Marlène. *Russian Eurasianism: An Ideology of Empire*. Baltimore: Johns Hopkins University Press, 2008.

Lenczowski, John. Full Spectrum Diplomacy and Grand Strategy: Reforming the Structure and Culture of U.S. Foreign Policy. Lanham, MA: Lexington Books, 2011.

Lieven, Anatol. "Lunch with Putin." *The National Interest*, September 17, 2008.

Lo, Bobo. *Vladimir Putin and the Evolution of Russian Foreign Policy*. Royal Institute of International Affairs. London: Blackwell, 2003.

Lucas, Edward. *Deception: Spies, Lies and How Russia Dupes the West*. London and Berlin: Bloomsbury, 2012.

———. *The New Cold War: Putin's Russia and the Threat to the West*. New York and Houndmills: Palgrave MacMillan, 2008.

Lukin, Alexander. "From a Post-Soviet to a Russian Foreign Policy." *Russia in Global Affairs*, no. 4 (October–December 2008).

Lukyanov, Fyodor. "Putin, Russia and the West: beyond Stereotype." *Russia in Global Affairs*, February 12, 2012.

Lunkin, Roman. "Protestantism and Human Rights in Russia: Creation of the Alternative to the Authorities." Paper for the Fourth Annual Lilly Fellows National Research Conference, Samford University, Birmingham, AL, November 11–14, 2005.

Machiavelli, Niccolò. *Il Principe e Discorsi sopra la prima deca di Tito Livio*. Milan: Feltrinelli Editore, 1971.

Mackinder, Halford J. *Democratic Ideals and Reality*. Washington, DC: National Defense University Press, 1996.

Maczka, Marcin. "The Propaganda Machine." *New Eastern Europe* 3, no. 4, New Europe, Old Europe (July–Sept. 2012).

Makarychev, Andrey. "Hard Questions about Soft Power: A Normative Outlook at Russia's Foreign Policy." Deutsche Gesellschaft für auswärtige Politik, Berlin, *DGAPanalyse kompakt* no. 10, October 2011.

Marquand, David. *The End of the West: The Once and Future Europe*. Princeton and Oxford: Princeton University Press, 2011.

McClory, Jonathan. *The New Persuaders: An International Ranking of Soft Power*. London: Institute for Government, 2010.

———. *The New Persuaders II: A 2011 Global Ranking of Soft Power*. London: Institute for Government, 2011.

McNamara, Kevin (Rapporteur). "Russia's Law on Religion." Report, Committee on Legal Affairs and Human Rights, Parliamentary Assembly of the Council of Europe, Document 9393, March 25, 2002.

Merseburger, Peter. *Willy Brandt 1913–1992: Visionär und Realist.* Berlin: Pantheon, 2013.

Ministry of Foreign Affairs of the Russian Federation. "Kontseptsiya vneshney politiki Rossiyskoy Federatsii Utverzhdena Prezidentom Rossiyskoy Federatsii V. V. Putinym 12 Fevralya 2013 g."

———. "Osnovnye napravleniya politiki Rossiyskoy Federatsii v sfere mezhdunarodnogo kulturno-gumanitarnogo sotrudnichestva." Moscow, 2010.

Minzarari, Dumitru. "Soft Power with an Iron Fist: Putin Administration to Change the Face of Russia's Foreign Policy toward Its Neighbors." *Eurasia Daily Monitor* 9, no. 163 (September 10, 2012).

Mongrenier, Jean-Sylvestre. *La Russie menace-t-elle l'Occident?* With a preface by Yves Lacoste. Paris: Choiseul, 2009.

———. "La sécurité énergétique, nouvelle frontière de l'Union européenne." *Tribune* (Institut Thomas More), no. 23 (January 2009).

Monnot, Caroline, and Abel Mestre. *Le système Le Pen: Enquête sur les réseaux du Front National*. Paris: Éditions Impacts, 2011.

Monod, Jerôme, and Jean de Boishue. *The Russian Comeback: Chronicles of a Journey through Eastern Europe from 27 May to 9 June 2006*. Paris: Fondation pour l'Innovation Politique, July 2006.

Münkler, Herfried. *Empires: The Logic of World Domination from Ancient Rome to the United States*. Cambridge: Polity Press, 2007.

Naím, Moisés. *The End of Power: From Boardrooms to Battlefields and Churches, Why Being in Charge Isn't What It Used to Be*. New York: Basic Books, 2013.

Neuss, Beate. "Von Bonn nach Berlin: Gibt es einen Wandel in der außenpolitischen Kultur Deutschlands seit der Einheit?" Konrad-Adenauer-Stiftung, Auslandsbüro Tschechische Republik, Prag, April 21, 2005.

Noelle-Neumann, Elisabeth. "Der Westbindung im Spiegel der Demoskopie." In *Westbindung: Chancen und Risiken für Deutschland*, edited by Rainier Zitelmann, Karlheinz Weismann, and Michael Grossheim. Frankfurt am Main and Berlin: Propyläen, 1993.

Norris, Pippa, and Ronald Inglehart. *Sacred and Secular: Religion and Politics Worldwide*. Cambridge and New York: Cambridge University Press, 2004.

Nye, Joseph S., Jr. *Bound to Lead: The Changing Nature of American Power*. New York: Basic Books, 1990.

———. *The Future of Power*. New York: Public Affairs, 2011.

———. *The Paradox of American Power: Why the World's Only Superpower Can't Go It Alone*. Oxford and New York: Oxford University Press, 2002.

———. *Soft Power: The Means to Success in World Politics*. New York: Public Affairs, 2004.

Orttung, Robert W. "Russia's Use of PR as a Foreign Policy Tool." *Russian Analytical Digest*, no. 81 (June 16, 2010).

Panarin, Igor. *Informatsionnaya voyna, PR i mirovaya politika*. Moscow: Goryachaya Liniya, 2014.

———. *Pervaya mirovaya informatsionnaya voyna*. Moscow: Piter, 2010.

Patriarchate of the Russian Orthodox Church. "Osnovy ucheniya Russkoy Pravoslavnoy Tserkvi o dostoynstve, svobode i pravakh cheloveka." Moscow, June 26, 2008. http://www.patriarchia.ru/db/print/428616.html.

Payne, Daniel P. "Spiritual Security, the Russian Orthodox Church, and the Russian Foreign Ministry: Collaboration or Cooptation?" *Journal of Church and State*, 52, no. 4 (2010): 52 (4).

Perrineau, Pascal. "De quoi le populisme est le nom," In *Populismes: l'envers de la démocratie*, edited by Marie-Claude Esposito, Alain Laquièze, and Christine Manigand. Paris: Vendémiaire Éditions, 2012.

Petito, Fabio, and Pavlos Hatzopoulos. *Religion in International Relations: The Return from Exile*. New York and Houndmills: Palgrave Macmillan, 2003.

Peukert, Detlev J. K. *The Weimar Republic: The Crisis of Classical Modernity*. New York: Hill and Wang, 1993.

Pilkington, Hilary, Elena Omelchenko, Moya Flynn, Uliana Bludina, and Elena Starkova. *Glyadya na Zapad: Kulturnaya Globalizatsiya i Rossiyskie Molodezhnye Kultury*. Saint Petersburg: Aleteiya, 2004.

Pinatel, Jean-Bernard. *Russie, alliance vitale*. Paris: Choiseul, 2010.

Pipes, Richard. *Russia under the Old Regime*. London and New York: Penguin, 1995.

Popescu, Nicu, and Andrew Wilson. "The Limits of Enlargement-Lite: European and Russian Power in the Troubled Neighbourhood." Policy report, European Council on Foreign Relations. London: European Council on Foreign Relations, 2009.

Pratkanis, Anthony, and Elliot Aronson. *Age of Propaganda: The Everyday Use and Abuse of Persuasion*. New York: Holt, 2002.

Preobrazhensky, Ivan. "Evropeytsy na rayone." *Russkaya Mysl*, no. 43/11 (November 2013).

Putin, Vladimir. *First Person: An Astonishingly Frank Self-Portrait by Russia's President*. With Nataliya Gevorkyan, Natalya Timakova, and Andrei Kolesnikov. New York: Public Affairs, 2000.

————. "Vladimir Putin Meets with Members of the Valdai International Discussion Club. Transcript of the Final Plenary Session," *Valdai Discussion Club*, October 25, 2014.

Reitschuster, Boris. *Wladimir Putin: Wohin steuert er Russland?* Berlin: Rowohlt, 2004.

Remnick, David. "Watching the Eclipse." *The New Yorker*, August 11, 2014.

Rice, Condoleezza. "The Making of Soviet Strategy." In *Makers of Modern Strategy: From Machiavelli to the Nuclear Age*, edited by Peter Paret. Princeton, NJ: Princeton University Press, 1986.

Romer, Jean-Christophe. *Géopolitique de la Russie*. Paris: Economica, 1999.

Roth, Jürgen. *Gazprom: Das unheimliche Imperium*. Frankfurt am Main: Westend Verlag, 2012.

Roxburgh, Angus. *The Strongman: Vladimir Putin and the Struggle for Russia*. London and New York: I.B. Tauris, 2012.

Roy, Olivier. *Holy Ignorance: When Religion and Culture Part Ways*. New York and Chichester: Columbia University Press, 2010.

Ruge, Gerd. *Russland*. Munich: C. H. Beck Verlag, 2008.

Sainsbury, John. "Peter the Great through British Eyes: Perceptions and Representations of the Tsar since 1698," *Canadian Journal of History*, April 2003.

Sarkozy, Nicolas. *Témoignage*. Paris: XO Éditions, 2006.

Schmidt, Helmut. *Ausserdienst: Eine Bilanz*. Munich: Siedler, 2008.

Schmitt, Carl. *Der Nomos der Erde im Völkerrecht des Jus Publicum Europaeum*. Berlin: Duncker & Humblot, 1997.

Sharikov, Oleg. "Russian Soft Power under Construction." *e-International Relations*, February 14, 2013.

Sherr, James. *Hard Diplomacy and Soft Coercion: Russia's Influence Abroad*. London: Chatham House, 2013.

Shevtsova, Lilia. *Lonely Power: Why Russia Has Failed to Become the West and the West Is Weary of Russia*. Washington, DC, and Moscow: Carnegie Endowment for International Peace, 2010.

———— and David J. Kramer. "Germany and Russia: The End of Ostpolitik?" *The American Interest*, November 13, 2012.

Shtepa, Pavlo. *Moscovism: Origin, Substance, Form, and Historical Continuity*. Toronto: S. Stasyshin, 1968.

Shulgan, Christopher. *The Soviet Ambassador: The Making of the Radical behind Perestroika*. Toronto, Ontario: McClelland & Stewart, 2008.

Simons, Greg. "Attempting to Re-Brand the Branded: Russia's International Image in the 21st Century." *Russian Journal of Communication* 4, no. 3/4 (Summer/Fall 2011).

Smirnov, Vadim. "Russia's 'Soft Power' in the Baltic." Russian International Affairs Council, May 4, 2012.

Socor, Vladimir. "La France d'abord: Paris First to Capitalize on Russian Military Modernization." *Eurasia Daily Monitor* 7, no. 29 (February 11, 2010).

————. "Made in Germany for Russia's Army." *Eurasia Daily Monitor* 8, no. 31 (February 14, 2011).

————. "Meseberg Process: Germany Testing EU-Russia Security Cooperation Potential." *Eurasia Daily Monitor* 7, no. 191 (October 22, 2010).

————. "US Embassy in Moscow Indicates Acceptance of Mistral Deal." *Eurasia Daily Monitor* 7, no. 85 (May 3, 2010).

Solodovnik, Svetlana. "Rossiya: ofitsialnaya tserkov vybiraet vlast." *Pro et Contra*, May–August 2013.

Stark, Hans. *La politique étrangère allemande: entre polarisation et politisation*. Note du Comité d'études des relations franco-allemandes (Cerfa), no. 60, IFRI, Paris, January 2009.

Steeves, Paul D. "Russian Orthodox Fascism after Glasnost." Paper presented to the Conference on Faith and History, Harrisburg, Pennsylvania, October 8, 1994.

Steinmeier, Frank-Walter. *Mein Deutschland: Wofür ich stehe*. Munich: C. Bertelsmann, 2009.

————. "Realismus und Prinzipientreue: Außenpolitik im Zeichen neuer globaler Balancen." In *Wertewandel mitgestalten: Gut handeln in Gesellschaft und Wirtschaft*, edited by Brun-Hagen Hennerkes and Georg Augustin. Freiburg, Basel, Wien: Herder, 2012.

Techau, Jan. "Germany's Eastern Temptation." *Central Europe Digest*, Center for European Policy Analysis, September 1, 2009.

Timmerman, Kenneth R. *The French Betrayal of America*. New York: Crown Forum, 2004.

Tsygankov, Andrei P. "Preserving Influence in a Changing World: Russia's Grand Strategy." *Problems of Post-Communism* 58, no. 1 (March–April 2011).

Umland, Andreas. "Post-Weimar Russia? There Are Sad Signs." *History News Network*, May 28, 2007.

Valdai Discussion Club. "Russia Should Not Miss Its Chance—Development Scenarios." Analytical report, November 2011.

Van Herpen, Marcel H. "The Foreign Policy of François Hollande: U-Turn or Continuity?" Cicero Foundation Great Debate Paper No. 12/03, May 2012.

———. "The Foreign Policy of Nicolas Sarkozy: Not Principled, Opportunistic, and Amateurish," Cicero Foundation Great Debate Paper No. 10/01, February 2010.

———. "France: Champion of a Multipolar World." *The National Interest Online*, May 14, 2003.

———. "I Say NATO, You Say No NATO," *The National Interest*, no. 95, May/June 2008.

———. "2012: A New Assault on Georgia? The Kavkaz-2012 Exercises and Russian War Games in the Caucasus." Cicero Foundation Great Debate Paper No. 12/04, July 2012.

———. "The PRISM Scandal, the Kremlin, and the Eurasian Union." *Atlantic-Community.org*, July 19, 2013. www.atlantic-community.org/-/the-prism-scandal-the-kremlin-and-the-eurasian-union.

———. *Putinism: The Slow Rise of a Radical Right Regime in Russia*. Basingstoke and New York: Palgrave MacMillan, 2013.

———. "Putinism's Authoritarian Allure." *Project Syndicate*, March 15, 2013.

Veblen, Thorstein. *The Theory of the Leisure Class: An Economic Study of Institutions*. With an introduction by C. Wright Mills. New York and Scarborough, Ontario: Mentor, 1953.

Verkhovsky, Alexander. "Inappropriate Enforcement of Anti-Extremist Legislation in Russia in 2010." *SOVA Center for Information and Analysis*, Moscow, April 11, 2011.

Volkoff, Vladimir. *La désinformation: arme de guerre*. Lausanne: L'Age d'Homme, 2004.

Waltz, Kenneth N. *Realism and International Politics*. New York and London: Routledge, 2008.

Weber, Max. *Wirtschaft und Gesellschaft: Grundriss der verstehenden Soziologie*. Erster Halbband, herausgegeben von Johannes Winckelmann. Cologne and Berlin: Kiepenheuer & Witsch, 1964.

Welch, David (ed.). *Nazi Propaganda: The Power and the Limitations*. London: Routledge, 2014.

Wilkinson, Cai. "Putting Traditional Values into Practice: Russia's Anti-Gay Laws." *Russian Analytical Digest* 138 (November 8, 2013).

Wilson, Jeanne L. "Soft Power: A Comparison of Discourse and Practice in Russia and China." *Social Science Research Network* (August 2012). Available at http://ssrn.com/abstract=2134457.

Windsor, Philip. *German Reunification*. London: Elek Books, 1969.

Wolton, Thierry. *Le KGB au pouvoir: Le système Poutine*. Paris: Gallimard, 2008.

———. *Le KGB en France*. Paris: France Loisirs, 1986.

Zagorski, Andrei. "Russian Opinion Surveys: Friends and Enemies, International Relations." In *Russian Foreign Policy: Key Regions and Issues*, edited by Robert Orttung, Jeronim Perovic, Heiko Pleines, and Hans-Henning Schröder. Forschungsstelle Osteuropa Bremen, Arbeitspapiere und Materialien No. 87, November 2007.

Zitelmann, Rainer. "Neutralitätsbestrebungen und Westorientierung." In *Westbindung: Chancen und Risiken für Deutschland*, edited by Rainier Zitelmann, Karlheinz Weismann, and Michael Grossheim. Frankfurt am Main and Berlin: Propyläen, 1993.

Zitelmann, Rainer, Karlheinz Weismann, and Michael Grossheim, eds. *Westbindung: Chancen und Risiken für Deutschland*. Frankfurt am Main and Berlin: Propyläen, 1993.

Index

About the Author

Marcel H. Van Herpen is director of the Cicero Foundation, a think tank based in Maastricht and Paris. He specializes in defense and security developments in Russia and the countries of the former Soviet Union. His books include *Putinism: The Slow Rise of a Radical Right Regime in Russia* and *Putin's Wars: The Rise of Russia's New Imperialism.*